Stephen Coote

Stephen Coote was educated at Magdalene College, Cambridge and at Birkbeck College, University of London. He is the author of many biographies and literary studies including *A Short History of English Literature* and lives of Byron, William Morris, Sir Walter Ralegh and is working on a biography of W. B. Yeats. He lives in Oxfordshire.

D1232966

SCEPTRE

John Keats

A Life

STEPHEN COOTE

SCEPTRE

For
Ian Dawbarn

First published in 1995 by Hodder and Stoughton
First published in paperback in 1996
by Hodder and Stoughton
A division of Hodder Headline PLC
A Sceptre Paperback

British Library Cataloguing in Publication Data

Coote, Stephen
  John Keats: A Life
  I. Title
  821.7

ISBN 0 340 62487 6

Typeset by Hewer Text Composition Services, Edinburgh
Printed and bound in Great Britain by
Cox & Wyman Ltd, Reading, Berkshire

Hodder and Stoughton
A division of Hodder Headline PLC
338 Euston Road
London NW1 3BH

Contents

List of Illustrations

Keats in 1819 by William Hilton (*National Portrait Gallery*)

George Keats (*Christopher Oxford*)
Tom Keats (*Christopher Oxford*)
Charles Cowden Clarke (*National Portrait Gallery*)
Leigh Hunt (*Richard Russell*)

Engraving of Poussin's 'The Realm of Flora' (*British Museum*)
'Apollo Inspiring the Youthful Poet', after Poussin (*British Museum*)

John Hamilton Reynolds (*National Portrait Gallery*)
Benjamin Haydon (*National Portrait Gallery*)
View of the Isle of Wight (*Keith Wynn/Photocraft (Hampstead) Ltd*)

Benjamin Bailey (*Keith Wynn/Photocraft (Hampstead) Ltd*)
James Rice (*Keith Wynn/Photocraft (Hampstead) Ltd*)
Charles Dilke (*Sir John Dilke*)
Maria Dilke (*Keith Wynn/Photocraft (Hampstead) Ltd*)

Keat's life mask by Haydon (*Christopher Oxford*)

William Hazlitt (*National Portrait Gallery*)
Edmund Kean as Richard III (*Victoria & Albert Museum*)
Keat's autograph on his volume of Shakespeare (*Keith Wynn/Photocraft (Hampstead) Ltd*)

Charles Brown (*Christopher Oxford*)

Portrait of Keats by Charles Brown, 1819 (*National Portrait Gallery*)

William Wordsworth (*Wordsworth Trust*)
John Taylor (*Keith Wynn/Photocraft (Hampstead) Ltd*)
Georgiana and George Keats in later life (*Keith Wynn/Photocraft (Hampstead) Ltd*)

Keats in 1921 by Joseph Severn (*National Portrait Gallery*)

Fanny Brawne, *c.* 1829 (*Keith Wynn/Photocraft (Hampstead) Ltd*)
Ring given by Keats to Fanny Brawne (*Keith Wynn/Photocraft (Hampstead) Ltd*)
Manuscript of 'Bright Star' (*Keith Wynn/Photocraft (Hampstead) Ltd*)

Front view of Wentworth Place (*Keith Wynn/Photocraft (Hampstead) Ltd*)
Interior of Stansted Chapel (*Stansted Park Foundation*)

Manuscript of 'Ode to a Nightingale' (*Keith Wynn/Photocraft (Hampstead) Ltd*)
Love letter to Fanny Brawne (*Keith Wynn/Photocraft (Hampstead) Ltd*)
The Massacre at Peterloo (*Keith Wynn/Photocraft (Hampstead) Ltd*)

Joseph Severn (*Keith Wynn/Photocraft (Hampstead) Ltd*)
Keats's last lodgings (*Keith Wynn/Photocraft (Hampstead) Ltd*)
The Protestant Cemetery, Rome, by Samuel Palmer (*Keith Wynn/Photocraft (Hampstead) Ltd*)

'Keats on his death bed' by Joseph Severn (*Christopher Oxford*)

PREFACE

IN THIS BIOGRAPHY I have tried to show Keats as a man formed, in his own phrase, by circumstances. Those circumstances were both public and private, personal and political, and, in their combination, they gave him the material for his art. I do not believe that Keats is best seen as a 'pure' poet – whatever that may mean – a man divorced from his time, wholly devoted to aesthetic insight and following interests separate from the life about him. My Keats is a man whose deeply spiritual and questioning mind, fired by the worlds of art and nature, tried to fashion an authentic existence in a country whose political and religious institutions appeared to offer him nothing beyond a starvation diet of repression and empty form.

In order to do this, I have aimed to show how the England in which Keats reached his brief maturity was the England of the years following Waterloo – years of financial crisis, political reaction and stiflingly authoritarian religion. Britain was a country pitifully at the mercy of the cycles of trade, heavily taxed and burdened with unemployment. It was also a country in which discontent barely had an outlet. An authoritarian government seemed unable to provide any answer to contemporary malaise beyond returning to the basics of the old regime. The majority of those the government ruled had no opportunity to replace it. In Regency England, Keats did not have a vote.

This atmosphere of political claustrophobia was deepened by the reactionary influence of contemporary Christianity. Certain that their teaching had helped save the country from the anarchy unleashed by the French Revolution, priests taught their congregations the duty of submission to the established order and to see life as a vale of tears. These ideas, the last in particular, were anathema to Keats, and his resolute refusal to adopt the Christian faith is as important to his art as his liberal politics. It forced him to confront the problem of pain and find an answer to it.

That answer lay partly in Keats's vocation as a poet. In such an atmosphere as I have been describing, Keats developed his idea of the poet as the man whose responsibility it was to soothe the cares and lift the thoughts of his fellow human beings. An ideal of poetry went hand in hand with an ideal of medicine, and both were under the influence of Apollo, the god of healing and verse. Apollo is the deity invoked in Keats's earliest poetry as well as in his last. Reinterpreted as a metaphor of contemporary man's deepest needs – his yearning for understanding, for progress, for an authentic life of the spirit – ancient mythology became, in Keats's hands, a means of touching the deepest levels of the psyche in order to imagine a world better and truer than the one around him.

Yet, for all the hope of a poem like *Hyperion*, Keats is never betrayed into simplistic optimism. *Hyperion* itself is riddled with the doubt and pain that characterise the odes. And such pain is 'never done'. In a terrible world, the spirit opens itself to art and nature. For a moment it can be ecstatic in the greatest achievements of western culture or the beauty of the natural world. It seems, briefly, that here are ways of life to oppose contemporary ills and the enduring fact of mortality. But Keats will not allow these to be more than temporary respites. The problem of pain re-emerges. Organised religion could offer Keats no adequate explanation of this, and it was only with his doctrine of life as a 'vale of Soul-making' and the world as the place where suffering qualified the soul for eternity that he could find an answer to his confusion. For Keats, pain had a purpose. It created the possibility of a spiritual life. In the end, even his gods are made for suffering as much as for joy.

For his earliest reviewers, Keats's commitment to liberal politics and classical mythology was joined to a third troubling force: his open praise of sexual pleasure. This is seen most clearly in *Endymion*, and the notorious attacks on that poem reveal the society in which they were written. As a mere apothecary, a member of the capital city's lower-middle class, Keats is shown as a dangerous young man who has learned to 'lisp sedition'. He was a figure who had dared to trespass on the Elysian fields of aristocratic culture, supposedly the exclusive preserve of an Oxbridge-educated elite. Above all, Keats was a merely smutty boy whose sexual desires, besmirching the image of 'true' masculinity and thus the idea of sexual control, were seen as no more than prurient fantasies, an exercise in what Byron called Keats's 'frigging' of his imagination. The whole purpose of the reviews was to expose Keats as a committed poet and ridicule him as a danger to the society in which he lived. Keats's contemporaries were well aware of what his literary project involved.

While the public arena is of vital importance to an understanding of

Keats's poetry, a knowledge of the private man inevitably enriches it too. The unremitting tragedies of Keats's life – the loss of his father, the death of his mother, the appalling time spent nursing his younger brother during his fatal illness, the incipient advance of Keats's own tuberculosis – all these not only help explain the poetry's preoccupation with suffering but suggest how, in his refusal to be humiliated into a mere sentimental pessimism, Keats exercised a spiritual resilience that was impressive both in its emotional power and in its qualities of intellectual self-criticism.

Yet it is the very development of these qualities which presents the biographer of Keats with his first paradox, his first problem. How often when reading Keats – how often, for example, when studying *The Fall of Hyperion* or that masterpiece which is the letter on 'the vale of Soulmaking' – is one beguiled into thinking one is involved with a powerful mind nearly twice its actual age? With what a shock come some of the revelations in the letters, the innocent exposure of the naïveties of a still inexperienced young man. I have not tried to smooth this problem over, to present a synthetic, integrated Keats, for it seems to me much more humanly compelling to present the paradoxes and the contradictions in order to offer a portrait in which Keats is sometimes as elusive as only people we know really well can be.

Many of these issues reach their climax in the affair with Fanny Brawne. No incident in Keats's life is more problematic to a biographer trying to present a rounded account of his subject's life. In the past it was sometimes possible to let Keats's love letters speak for themselves. That is no longer entirely acceptable. How strongly we want to know what Fanny thought and felt, how she reacted, the stages of her maturing from the 'Minx' of Keats's first mention of her to the woman committed to a dying man. Such information is not available. Keats took Fanny's letters to his grave and we see her almost entirely in the blaze of his emotions.

And that is the problem. Keats's love letters – by turns vivid, tender and terrible – are not the record of an affair. For all their moving intensity we get only a slight impression of two people in love. What we do see – and what a biographer is obliged to dwell on – is something lesser which, because it is raised here to its highest power, is still of the greatest human interest. What the letters show us is the almost unbearable loneliness of obsessive love.

Keats believed (and the medical practice of his day went some way to confirm this) that such obsession was fatal. Frustrated desire turned in upon itself to destroy the forces of life. His was, both literally and metaphorically, a consuming passion. It is this that in part makes the last months of Keats's life almost unbearably poignant. He believed he was being destroyed by the force of his emotions. He was convinced his vocation as a poet had been an abject failure and that he had left no lasting work behind him. In both his public and his private worlds Keats had been defeated, and now, because there seemed no explanation for this, it appeared that his spiritual life was reared on a falsehood too. The doctrine of the 'vale of Soul-making' was a fantasy. Suffering – Keats's agony during the last stages of tuberculosis – had no meaning in a gratuitous world. He came to believe that his existence was something evanescent, anonymous and eventually to be forgotten – in his own words, a life 'writ in water'.

In writing this book I have incurred many debts. The great biographies by Walter Jackson Bate and Robert Gittings have been a continuous source of information. The editions mentioned in the Bibliography have, naturally, been invaluable. Of the innumerable critical studies of Keats, I have profited most from those by John Barnard, Morris Dickstein, Robert M. Ryan and Stuart Sperry. Mrs Christina Gee gave me access to the Keats Memorial Library in Hampstead. A discussion with my friend Jo Johnson helped clarify some important points in Keats's private life. The dedication of this book records an old and greatly valued friendship.

FORMED BY CIRCUMSTANCES

> I began by seeing how man was formed
> by circumstances.
>
> (*Keats to his brother George, April 1819*)

ON SUMMER AFTERNOONS in the years before Waterloo, two young men met in the arbour of an old schoolhouse in Enfield to talk of poetry and politics. The elder of them, Charles Cowden Clarke, was the son of the headmaster and was himself a teacher. Now in his twenties, and with his hair already thinning save for the defiant quiff that sprouted from the back of his head, he was a kindly, cultured man, versatile on the piano, passionately fond of cricket and the theatre, well read in poetry and, with his loud laugh, willing to share his tastes with everyone. His companion had once been his pupil and was still in his teens. He was a lonely, vulnerable boy, who was currently apprenticed to a surgeon in Edmonton. He would walk over to his old school half a dozen times a month, always clutching his latest reading under his arm. If he was lucky, the talk would ramble on until darkness fell, then he would be invited to supper.

The young men's conversation was earnest, high-minded even, but although Clarke was still to be deferred to, his ideas being more formed, his experience wider, the boy could feel his way into his companion's mind as surely as he could identify with a bird picking about on the gravel. When Clarke talked of the latest political scandal, of Mrs Siddons' recent success on the stage or of a new volume of poetry, his friend could sense behind his words the influence of the newspaper they both read, Leigh Hunt's *Examiner*.

The *Examiner* appeared each Sunday and was a journal of sixteen double-column pages. Every week its sharp and witty articles campaigned against the abuses of the slave trade, against the wide use of the death penalty, and against the 'eternal war' with Napoleon which, it claimed, 'the country had injudiciously begun and which now she finds it necessary to protract'. War-weariness was felt everywhere. The heavy burden of taxes levied to pay continental allies, the unfair distribution of those taxes and the incompetence with which the revenues were handled, all came under the *Examiner*'s attack. So too did ministerial corruption, the extravagant follies of the royal family and the government's refusal to extend the vote to Roman Catholics. Above all, and as a remedy for these ills, Hunt's paper constantly urged that 'a reform in Parliament will purify the whole constitution.'[1]

Such ideas were agreeable to both young men, as was Hunt's habit of intermingling political comment with literary reference. Whenever he thought he could illustrate his argument by an allusion to poetry Hunt did so, and an article on the incompetence of policing in the capital was garnished with quotations from the Dogberry scenes in *Much Ado about Nothing*. While this could sometimes appear an affectation, for Hunt and his writers on the *Examiner* the act of reading had become romanticised and, in a period of deepening repression, was a gesture against the widespread fear of the reading public, a fear which made the church and state 'anxious to provide us with that sort of food for our stomachs, which they thought best'.[2]

To read widely was allegedly to escape these constraints, and among Hunt's favourite poets were the renaissance writers of Italian epic and their English follower Edmund Spenser. An enthusiasm for Spenser was something Clarke also shared and, during one of their afternoon meetings, he introduced his friend to his work. Many years later, when he recalled the scene with something of the roseate condescension of the born teacher, Clarke was careful to draw attention to the fact that his pupil 'must have given unmistakable tokens of his mental bent; otherwise, at that early stage of his career, I never could have read to him the "Epithalamion".[3] In fact, the introduction changed the boy's life. Spenser's ceremonious beauty, his exulted, stately yet delicate eroticism, his play of fancy and limpid language, made such a profound appeal that Clarke ventured to lend his friend the first volume of Spenser's epic, *The Fairie Queene*. The boy took it home that night and went through the book, Clarke later declared, 'as a young horse would through a spring meadow – ramping!' When he returned to the arbour, it was with a mind enchanted. 'He breathed in a new world and became another being.'[4]

In the course of the next few weeks, the two young men ventured deep into Spenser's work, the younger pouring out his excitement as he sat in his customary pose with one leg crossed over his knee while he soothed his instep with the palm of his hand. As they talked, his strongly cut features became alive, his chin was stuck out, the red-brown curls of his hair fell about his face, and his mouth with its delicately protruding upper lip quivered with pleasure. When they came to the twenty-third stanza of the twelfth canto of the second Book, to the passage that describes the fairy knight Guyon's approach to the Bower of Bliss, so the 'wine-like lustre' of the boy's eyes glowed and 'he *hoisted* himself up, and looked burly and dominant, as he said, "what an image that is — *'sea-shouldering whales'!*"'[5]

Later that evening, when the teenage Keats reluctantly took his hat and shook hands with Clarke, he listened in the darkness while the older man's footsteps, now loud on the gravel, now lost on the grass verge, took him back to the school.[6] Clarke himself, remembering the occasion nearly seventy years after Keats's death, realised how, during the course of that afternoon, he had been in the presence of a poet: 'a true poet, too — a poet "born, not manufactured," a poet in grain'.

John Keats was born on the last day of October 1795 and christened seven weeks later at the London church of St Botolph Without, Bishopsgate, where his mother's parents had settled. Keats's maternal grandfather, John Jennings, was a man of moderate substance who, his family said, might even have been rich were it not that he was 'extremely generous and gullible'.[7] These failings, if such they are, seem unlikely in a successful London businessman, and the records suggest that Keats's grandfather was a solid, prosperous member of his class, a man who carefully accumulated such wealth and status as he possessed. Two decades before his grandson's birth he was recorded as the leaseholder of the livery stables, the Swan & Hoop, at 24 The Pavement, Moorgate. He was by then in his middle forties and, clearly feeling the time had come to establish his personal and social position, he purchased on New Year's Day 1774 his freedom of the City of London, following this with membership of the Worshipful Company of Innholders. Two weeks later, on 15 February 1774, he married Alice Whalley, a woman whose family originally came from Colne in Lancashire.

They were a well-settled couple. The scrupulous and complex nuances of trade in eighteenth-century England confirm that the Swan and Hoop was neither a tavern nor an ale-house, but an inn. As such, it was an establishment priding itself on its status, serving wine and heavy black porter to its well-heeled customers, and functioning somewhat like a modern hotel. In addition to ostlers and stableboys, the proprietor of the Swan and Hoop would have employed maids, tapsters and chamberlains. Inns were often handsomely decorated with carpets, mirrors, clocks and pictures. They provided accommodation and offered comfortable surroundings where merchants and traders from out of town especially could meet in comfort and perhaps, after concluding their business, enjoy a variety of dinners, assemblies or even the cock-fights and boxing matches that gave pleasure to contemporary audiences.

The livery stables, with their two coachhouses, large yard and stabling for three dozen horses, were an important addition to these amenities. Many London merchants lived outside the City and, somewhat to the surprise of continental visitors, commuted to their offices and warehouses. Livery stables provided accommodation for their horses and, in an age when the possession of such things was a matter of intense pride, a place where they could leave their yellow-varnished phaetons, their demi-landaux or, if they chose to drive one, their landaulets with their hoods of greasy harness leather, disagreeable to the touch and smell, and continually needing oil and blacking.

John and Alice Jennings were determined to do well for their family. They were parents to three children who needed to be educated, and, though it is uncertain if and where Keats's mother Frances was sent to school, their sons, Midgley John and Thomas, were among the earliest pupils to attend Clarke's school in Enfield. Ominously, Thomas Jennings died of tuberculosis when he was just fourteen but, soon after his sister's marriage, Midgley John joined the navy. Here, partly through the influence of friends and partly through his own ability, he was quickly promoted. In 1796, he was commissioned as a second-lieutenant in the marines, while the following year he was listed as serving on HMS *Russell*. Later he distinguished himself in the Battle of Camperdown, and perhaps as a result of this action was promoted to first-lieutenant in 1799 and transferred to Chatham Barracks.

Keats's mother had been married for a little over a year when the poet was born and it was from his father, Thomas, that Keats inherited some of his handsome looks and short but vigorous form. Little is known for certain about Thomas Keats's origins, but it must have been in part his appearance, along with what others would remember as his unaffected manners and natural good sense, that made the handsome twenty-one-year-old attractive to Frances Jennings.

Much later, when his first biographers were searching for information, Keats's mother became the victim of gossip. It was said that in addition to her wide mouth, which she probably passed on to her son, she had 'uncommonly handsome legs' which she was apt to display on such occasions as when she went shopping at a nearby grocer's shop and lifted her skirts 'very high' while she crossed the street.[8] The grocer 'was not however fatally wounded by Cupid', despite rumours that Frances's passions were so ardent that it was dangerous to be alone with her. She was, it was said, determined to marry nonetheless, and 'it was not long before she found a husband, nor did she go far for him – a helper in her father's stables appeared sufficiently desirable in her eyes to make her forget the disparity of their circumstances, and it was not long before John Keats had the honour to be united to his master's daughter.' The fact that the informant got the name of Keats's father wrong compounds with the prurient delight and sheer snobbery of his account to suggest that this picture of an over-sexed young woman marrying beneath her is at best a distortion.

For their wedding, Thomas and Frances Keats chose the prestigious church of St George in distant Hanover Square, a choice which clearly represented some social ambition on the part of the young couple, yet the fact that no relatives on either side witnessed the occasion indicates perhaps a lack of parental approval.

During his early childhood, Keats lived with his parents at a house in Craven Street, north of the City Road. At the start of 1797 his brother George was born, followed, two years later, by a second brother, Tom. George was to affirm that her eldest son remained their mother's favourite, and two further anecdotes are preserved from this period of Keats's infancy which throw some light on his character. A certain Mrs Grafty, on being told the baby she had once known had become a poet, affirmed that instead of answering questions he would make a rhyme of the last word said to him, laughing with pleasure as he did so, a not uncommon habit, perhaps, in many infants. Rather more revealingly, a family servant later declared that when he was five Keats was found holding his mother imprisoned in the house with a drawn sword. This defiant little gesture may have been characteristic of an infant whose temper was sometimes said to be violent and ungovernable, but it also indicates the passionate and even possessive relationship that had developed between the boy and his indulgent mother, who, while she had a 'doting fondness'[9] for all her children, was said to humour every whim of her eldest especially.

Nothing is known for certain about how Keats's father earned his living at this time, although stories that he worked as an ostler at the Swan and Hoop do not seem altogether unlikely. Certainly, this would have been a practical and inexpensive way of learning the trade and becoming familiar with the tasks and customs of that enormous class of men and boys who in eighteenth-century London earned their keep by their knowledge of how to 'bed down a neat tit' and rub stirrups and sponge bridles and girths. A vast folklore of expertise existed among such people, and more gullible customers might be beguiled with tales of how a 'regular kicker' could be quietened by pouring pints of ale down its throat or how the 'veriest screw' could be made to buck up by feeding it a live eel.[10]

However this may be, Thomas Keats was now to have more serious responsibilities. At the close of April 1801, a fourth son, Edward, was born to his family. The infant survived merely seven months, but it was during this period that John Jennings, now in his sixties, began to think seriously of his retirement. The leases on his Moorgate properties were due to expire in 1805, and he faced the decision about what to do. In the event, he decided to keep a controlling interest in his inn and livery business while moving out to Enfield, where he rented two of the 'smart boxes' that had been built there by speculative builders, letting one of these while living in the other.[11] Just after the death of little Edward Keats, who was buried in Bunhill Fields on 9 December, Thomas and Frances Keats moved into the Swan and Hoop, which Thomas himself would now manage, paying a rent of £44 a year.

Whatever his status had been before, Keats's father now had a position to keep up. Early in 1803 he was admitted to the Innholders' Company, while on 3 June that year his only daughter Frances Mary was born. It was also time to think about the education of his eldest sons. His wife cherished ambitions of sending them to Harrow, then a prestigious establishment for the sons of the Middlesex commercial classes as well as the aristocracy, but in the end it was decided to place them at Clarke's, where Frances's brothers had been educated. In August 1803, and probably after a period at a local dame-school, Keats and his brother George started their formal education as boarders at Clarke's. Keats himself was then in his eighth year.

The move was a standard rite of passage for a pupil of his age and class, even if he was, save for George, the youngest boy in an establishment of between seventy and eighty youngsters. But the wrench from his home life and from his mother especially was to some degree offset by the liberal and kindly atmosphere that pervaded the school. Besides, he was not alone there. He had a younger brother for company, grandparents living in the pretty village near by, and parents who visited him regularly and were held in some esteem by the headmaster, who always spoke of Keats's father with respect 'on account of his excellent natural sense, and total freedom from vulgarity and assumption'. His son, Charles Cowden Clarke, then a boy of about sixteen, also had a clear recollection of Thomas Keats's 'lively, and energetic countenance, particularly when seated in his gig, and preparing to drive his wife home, after visiting his sons at school'.[12]

The general impression is one of prosperity, energy and security, qualities that were now to be suddenly and devastatingly destroyed. On a Sunday in mid-April 1804, having visited his boys at their school, this time without his wife and carriage, Thomas Keats went to dine near by in Southgate. He returned late and, as he was riding down the City Road, his horse slipped on the cobbles. He fell and cracked his skull. His careering, riderless mount spread the alarm and he was eventually found alive but speechless and covered in blood. Although he was taken to a surgeon, identified and carried to the Swan and Hoop, Thomas Keats died early the following morning without ever regaining consciousness.

The effect on a little boy of eight and a half, the still and chilly fact of the corpse, the pallid undertakers and nodding plumes, the red-eyed griefs and sudden solicitudes of his family, must have been one of utter confusion, of fear even beside the cold vault in the church in Coleman Street. Then, in her grief and anxiety, his mother briefly vanished. Her disappearance is witnessed by the fact that when the collector of the Poor Rate called at the Swan and Hoop he found the vague, shadowy figure of Elizabeth Keats (a sister of Thomas's perhaps) apparently in charge.

The practical and financial problems the young widow had run from were considerable.[13] Her husband had died intestate leaving an estate of a little under £2000. Not only would it take Frances time to obtain administration of this sum but, when it was available, the interest on the money would hardly have been sufficient to pay rent, rates and school fees on top of her family's living expenses. Nor could she look with any more confidence at the Swan and Hoop, since the lease on this property was due to expire in just under a year. Facing the imminent loss of her entire way of life and clearly feeling that she could not turn to her family, Frances Keats reacted wildly. When she returned, she took out in her own name a short lease on the livery stables of the Swan and Hoop (but not on the inn itself) and then, a mere two months after her husband's funeral, she remarried. Once again, she chose St George's, Hanover Square and, once again, her parents did not attend. Her new husband was one William Rawlings, a bank clerk who, on very slender grounds, called himself a livery stables keeper. When the Keats boys returned from school at midsummer 1804, they found this man installed as their new father.

Although the brothers can hardly have been aware of the details, this precarious position now became the ground for financial rancour and bitter family division. On 1 February 1805, old Mr Jennings signed a less than professionally drafted will. Then, five weeks later, the ministrations of Thomas Hammond his physician having run their course, he died and was buried in St Stephen's, Coleman Street. The complications of old Jennings' will turned the divisions in his family to outright hostility. Broadly, his intention had been to leave half his estate to his widow and so secure her an income of £200 a year. In addition, a third of his estate was left to his son, the Lieutenant, while provision was also made for annual incomes to be paid to his sister-in-law and his daughter Frances, who was to receive £50 per annum. Lastly, a mortgage due from a property in Knightsbridge was to provide £1000 in cash for the Keats children.

Errors in the drafting of the will immediately became apparent, and while a united family could have solved these problems through a mutual exercise of good will, between Frances Rawlings and her mother and brother such good will did not obtain. The widow and her son, however, were determined to act in concert. On 25 March, and without Frances's knowledge, they proved the will and then, a week later, and while still keeping the details of the inheritance secret, the Lieutenant went round to the Swan and Hoop to collect the rent from his sister. This he was perfectly entitled to do and it is also clear why he and his mother were acting as they did. Both stood to inherit from a disputable will and, in a time of deep family uncertainty, mother and son were drawn together, uniting themselves against a seemingly flighty and irresponsible woman who now appeared in a position to threaten their security. When the Lieutenant called at the Swan and Hoop to collect the rent, William Rawlings promptly presented him with a bill for 'sundry sums' claimed by Frances against her father's estate.

The Lieutenant paid these sums but was to find that this was far from being the end of the matter. The newly married couple in the Swan and Hoop, thrown together in crisis, as yet unable to obtain the monies due from Thomas Keats's estate and, in addition, facing a large rent rise on their business premises, resolved to attack. There was already bitterness, insecurity and family division. Now they determined to raise the fury Litigation. Two days after receiving payment of the 'sundry sums' they had claimed against Frances's father, they brought a hostile action in Chancery. Keats's mother was fighting her family for sums in excess of £3500 and, by 8 May, the matter was before the Master of the Rolls.

Suddenly, Frances became aware of the bitter fruits of her vindictiveness. The Master of the Rolls made an order for the production of the accounts. The entire administration of the estate was placed in the hands of Chancery and, during the long year of the law's delay, Frances Rawlings faced the expiry of the lease on the Swan and Hoop, possible eviction and the freezing of her annuity. All the capital that was immediately available to her was her first husband's inheritance, and it now became apparent that she had moved herself, her second husband and, above all, her children into a desperate corner.

Mrs Jennings, as the only competent female, took charge of the children. By midsummer 1805 she had moved into a house in Church Street, Edmonton, close to Thomas Hammond, the man who had nursed her husband through his last illness. Here the Keats children found shelter as the bitter family feud continued to play around them. While the Lieutenant was careful to see that his mother was provided with sufficient funds to support her new responsibilities, he refused to pay his sister's annuity until ordered to do so by the court. Chancery itself, meanwhile, was at last prepared to deliver its verdict. Judgement was given on 22 May 1806. The court declared Mrs Jennings the absolute owner of her stock, while the unwilled residue was to be divided between mother and son. Keats's mother's hostile action had utterly failed and now, to compound her misery, it was clear that her second marriage was failing also. While Rawlings himself continued to live for a while at the Swan and Hoop, Frances had neither home nor money, family nor children. It was rumoured that, in her desperation, she lived with another man.

Her plight was indeed pitiful, but the effect on her oldest son was traumatic. The passionate, possessive little boy had lost his father and then seen his adored mother taken, taken first by another man and then lost altogether. He had been removed from his home and watched powerlessly the destruction wrought by mistrust. Loss and insecurity seemed to characterise every relationship. What was given was snatched away, while, below appearances, flowed the constant, wordless undertow of threat, the seeming certainty of pain.

Mrs Jennings tried to make a home for Keats, his brothers and sister, at her new house in Edmonton. Here, her practical, ordinary virtues, the unselfconscious daily routine, offered the children a stability they had perhaps never fully known before. Late in her own long life, Keats's sister Fanny could still remember her grandmother baking a Lancashire cake for them all, rich and heavy with raisins and cherries. Meanwhile, as Keats himself recalled, the garden offered other pleasures: 'apple tasting – pear tasting – plum judging – apricot nibbing – peach sc[r]unching – Nectarine-sucking – and Melon carving'.[14] Beneath the remembered childhood greed and the tactile, sensuous relish lurks, perhaps, a shadow of that emotional desperation such oral delights could temporarily assuage. Certainly, there is also here the pull of the affection all the boys felt for their sister. Abandoned themselves, she was someone they could treasure, indulge and vie for. As George wrote, they were 'always devising plans to amuse you, jealous lest you should prefer either of us to the others'.[15] And, when little girls were a nuisance, there were the boyish delights of 'Goldfinches, Tomtits, Minnows, Mice, Ticklebacks, Dace, Cock salmons and the whole tribe of the Bushes and Brooks'[16] to be given temporary shelter or, despite the annoyance of the maid and his 'granny-good',[17] left to swim in the washtubs.

But, while Mrs Jennings' house was a refuge, the boisterous life of Clarke's school offered Keats the outlet he needed for the vigorous energies of a little boy now constantly 'in passions of tears or outrageous fits of laughter always in extremes'.[18] He delighted in the buffoonery and pranks of his friends. He became a renowned fighter and, amid the tribal loyalties of the lower forms, such pugnaciousness assured his popularity. Boys like handsome Edward Holmes courted his friendship by trying to win fights themselves, while Keats's own 'terrier courage' was admired by all.[19] He would fight anyone, Holmes remembered, morning, noon or night. At times, this barnstorming energy could even be turned against his brothers, and Charles Clarke recalled how George, considerably the taller and stronger, used frequently to hold him down by main force, laughing when Keats was in 'one of his moods' and endeavouring to beat him.

Such outbursts were occasionally almost ungovernable, and they suggest something more in Keats than mere animal high spirits. Tough as he was, he had been hurt, and his vulnerability made him quick to sympathise with pain in others. This response, George came to realise, was wholly spontaneous. 'John's eyes moistened, and his lip quivered,' he wrote, 'at the relation of any tale of generosity of benevolence or noble daring . . . he had no fears of self thro interference in the quarrels of others, he would at all hazzards, without calculating his power to defend, or his reward for the deed, defend the oppressed.'[20] Edward Holmes recalled that it was generally reckoned Keats would make an excellent soldier.

On one occasion, this readiness to stick up for others caused Keats to strike a master who had boxed Tom's ears. In most schools, such behaviour would have resulted in expulsion or at the very least a flogging, but Clarke's establishment was run on different lines, and its unusual ethos played an important part in the shaping of the poet.[21] The school had originally been founded in Northampton by the nonconformist minister John Collet Rylands, and its aim was to prepare boys whose parents were debarred by financial considerations or religious conviction from sending their sons to the great public schools. In the tradition of such places, the school avoided an education based almost exclusively on the classics and, instead, trained its pupils in godliness while preparing them for trade or the professions. This approach was neither narrow nor merely utilitarian. Rylands himself, although no very able businessman, was a figure of wide culture whose voice was consistently in favour of religious and civil liberty. In 1786, when the Northampton school was close to financial collapse, Rylands moved with his deputy John Clarke to Enfield, where the younger man was effectively in charge.

The building itself had been erected at the start of the century by a prosperous East India merchant and was a lavish affair of hipped roofs, coigns and classical detailing. The spacious rooms provided dormitories, while the classrooms were placed in converted outhouses. The courtyard became the playground and, in one corner of the large garden, plots were set aside for some of the boys to cultivate. Beyond the iron railings stretched the meadows of the surrounding countryside 'whence the song of the nightingales in May would reach us in the stillness of the night'.[22] In such an atmosphere, Clarke continued the kindly and enlightened traditions of his forebear, being himself a 'gentle-hearted, clear-headed, and transparently conscientious' man who had thrown up a career in the law because of his objections to capital punishment.

'Simplify and repeat, simplify and repeat' had been Rylands' motto as a teacher. As a man who knew that many of his pupils were destined for trade, Rylands had encouraged their academic performance by instituting a series of account books in which a boy's performance at each lesson was recorded as 'B' for 'bene', 'O' for 'optime' or 'X' for negligence or misbehaviour. Instead of automatic floggings, a trial by his peers was instituted for a boy who broke the rules, and it was indeed an aim of the school to encourage excellence by kindling the imagination rather than by threats. To teach the boys the motions of the planets, for example, Rylands had taken his pupils out into the playground to form a human orrorey. The twirling of a mop, he claimed, would illustrate the actions of centrifugal force. On rainy afternoons and winter evenings, the boys were encouraged to play educational games, holding up cards with the name of a city or suchlike on them. Those able to provide a range of precise details moved up the table to its head, and he who made the fewest blunders was called captain for the day. The school also encouraged a delight in nature. To the end of his life, one of Rylands' pupils remembered how the headmaster took the school out to see the departure of the swallows, and one wonders whether this continued as a practice in Enfield and what effect it might have had on the poet of the ode 'To Autumn'.

Such a benevolent, earnest if slightly eccentric atmosphere cushioned Keats from the destructive adult world of his family. Here, sickness and litigation still threatened. By the close of 1807, Lieutenant Midgley Jennings, worn down by the burden of administering the estate, applied for sick-leave. The following August, and more than three years after the case went to Chancery, he received his inheritance. But by now he was spitting blood, another victim of tuberculosis, and at the end of the year he was dead. His sister, meanwhile, was in great distress. One of the Lieutenant's last acts had been to pay her annuity, but now, in 1809, she petitioned the court for more. This was granted by the wish of all the parties, and special arrangements were made to see that it was promptly settled. Such an outcome suggests there had been some measure of reconciliation between Mrs Jennings and her one remaining child, and it is probable that Keats's mother now returned to her family, a sickly woman herself and more than ever ready to lavish on her thirteen-year-old son her dangerous gift of 'doting fondness'.

Keats did everything in his power to make sure she would never go away again, and he vowed to achieve this by excelling in the one area where success would surely guarantee her love. When he returned to school in January 1809 it was with the iron determination to carry off all the first prizes in literature 'by a considerable distance'.[23] Books and hopes of emotional security had become identified. The boy who previously had been so conspicuously unliterary now rose to study long before the first class at seven in the morning. He worked through his breaks, had to be cajoled into taking exercise and, in the evening, when supper was laid in the schoolroom, he would sit back on the bench clasping a folio volume and reaching out blindly beyond it to where his plate lay on the table. In this way, Keats began to read his way through the entirety of the school library. Volumes of abridged travel writings, the novels of Maria Edgeworth, Robertson's biography of Charles V and his histories of Scotland and America were all devoured and were to leave their traces in Keats's mature poetry. Then, when he could read no more, Keats would lie on his bed in the schoolhouse listening to the headmaster's son playing Mozart, Arne or Handel on the piano.

Keats's discrimination in music was always fine, but the literary prizes were his aim. John Clarke offered three of these each year for such voluntary work as translating from French and Latin, and it was at about this time that Keats began the enormous task of preparing a prose version of Virgil. This labour in turn led him to three works of reference that were to exercise a compulsive fascination: the *Polymetis* of Joseph Spence, Tooke's *Pantheon*, and Lemprière's *Bibliotheca Classica*, a copy of which Keats was to treasure throughout his life. This last work, Clarke noted, Keats seemed almost to learn by heart. Perhaps this was one of those fixations common in adolescence, yet from these dry pages Keats derived his first acquaintance with the figures of Endymion, Phoebe and above all Apollo, the beautiful deity of the sun who, as the god of poetry and music, medicine and prophecy, was to be central to the mature poet's concern with re-creating ancient myth out of the deepest layers of his consciousness, an endeavour which places Keats among the most profound imaginative thinkers of his age.

Both Rylands and John Clarke had a wide appreciation of literature. One of their principal concerns was to nurture 'a complete and masterly skill in the English language, in order to speak and write it with the utmost propriety, energy and beauty'.[24] Poetry, they were aware, was an important element in this and they were at pains to encourage 'the consideration of verse. – Not a skill of composing, – so much as a just taste, and a grand imagination; so as to relish a fine composition.' Nonetheless, they were equally aware that their pupils were bound for the world of work, and that industry and self-discipline were necessary qualities there. For his own industrious labours, Keats was awarded at the end of term C.H. Kaufmann's *Dictionary of Merchandise . . . for the use of Counting Houses*. The banality of the title measures the distance he would have to traverse in the course of making himself a poet.

But the mother to whom Keats proudly bore home the prize was immersed in her own problems. By the second half of 1809 Frances

Rawlings' health was deteriorating even as her legal problems multiplied. Neither the capital for her annuity nor her children's legacy had been allocated while, towards the end of the year, her sister-in-law, the Lieutenant's widow, petitioned Chancery to secure her husband's capital for her own fatherless children. Harassed by these turns of events, Mrs Rawlings became more pale, more languid and thin. When Keats returned home for the Christmas holidays it was clear that his mother had tuberculosis.

Hammond was summoned to supply what ineffective aid medicine could offer, but it was Keats himself who took on the nursing of the dying woman. It was a task into which he threw all his confused adolescent energies, all his feelings of duty as the eldest male in the family, all his desperation and the ambivalent emotion he felt towards the weak and helpless woman who lay prone on the bed. He insisted on cooking her meals. He fed her the prescribed medicines. Night after night he sat with her as her hacking cough wore her down and her sputum reddened with blood. In the quiet intervals, as she slipped away from him again, he read novels to her or merely watched by her bed as she slept.

In January, Keats was obliged to return to school, continuing with his voracious study while Chancery finally ordered that his grandfather's legacy to the children be invested in 3 per cent consols and placed in trust until the heirs reached twenty-one. The same order also set aside Mrs Rawlings' capital for her and allotted it to her children after her death. This was now imminent. Keats's mother died in March and was buried in the family vault. Keats himself gave way to 'impassioned and prolonged grief'. In a classroom hushed in sympathy, he was allowed to hide himself in the alcove of his master's desk, there to wrestle as best he could with the demons of his distress.

It was time nonetheless to make plans for his future. From the wills of his mother and grandfather Keats had an inheritance of £800, held for him in Chancery until he reached his majority. Mrs Jennings now resolved to add to this sum by leaving the greater part of her own estate to be divided between her late daughter's children. She was determined to do this in a manner which, she hoped, would avoid the expense and long-drawn-out proceedings of the court. Advised by her lawyer that this could most easily be done by setting up a trust fund, she went about finding suitable men to administer it. The first of these, John Nowland Sandell, was a wealthy Russian merchant who had once had an office near the Swan and Hoop. Although he was the senior trustee, the figure who was to have by far the greater influence on Keats's life was his fellow administrator Richard Abbey, a prosperous tea and coffee warehouseman originally from the Vale of York.

Abbey was a shrewd, hard-headed and competent northerner, much concerned with the outward appearance of respectability and inwardly nursing that nasty-mindedness with which he gossiped to Keats's biographers about the poet's mother. He had come to London on reaching his majority, set himself up in business, married an illiterate girl and become, among numerous other positions, a member of the Honourable Company of Pattern Makers, a freeman of the City of London and an intrusively querulous member of the Walthamstow Sunday School Committee. Making the simple assumption that what was old-fashioned was also to be trusted, Abbey continued to dress in the clothes familiar from fifty years before, travelling between his premises in Pancras Lane and his substantial house in Walthamstow in stockings, boots and breeches.

Such an obvious pillar of society was felt to be a desirable choice as a guardian for the Keats children, and it was now a question of finding the eldest boy a career suitable to his resources and station. At the close of the midsummer term in 1810 Keats was just over fourteen and a half, the usual age at which boys left Clarke's school if they were to embark on an apprenticeship in one of the professions. Keats, it seems, had already decided what that profession should be. The most profound and terrible experience of his young life had been nursing his dying mother, and he resolved he would now become a surgeon-apothecary, something broadly equivalent to a present-day general practitioner.[25]

If this was a natural and moving choice of vocation, it was also a practical one. There was a clear divide in the medical profession of early-nineteenth-century England between physicians on the one hand and surgeons and apothecaries on the other. The physicians were a social elite of wealthy, university-educated men, entitled to call themselves 'doctor' and to charge their patients high fees for such outmoded education and practical ability as were deemed sufficient by the London College of Physicians. This, in its turn, was an ancient and privileged corporation that tended to hold itself aloof from the teaching of clinical medicine now being pursued in the London hospitals. Keats's financial position debarred him from this group, but a career in surgery or as an apothecary was open to him after a five-year apprenticeship.

Apothecaries themselves had long since ceased to be the druggists attached to the Guild of Grocers they had been in the Middle Ages, and their Worshipful Company now helped to ensure professional standards by regulating their apprentices' education as complete general practitioners, men able to examine patients, diagnose their diseases and make up and administer medicines. In 1810, apothecaries could still practise without a licence, but young men wishing to set up as surgeons were required to sit the examination of the Royal College of Surgeons, a form of professional recognition for which the apothecaries were soon also petitioning.

Not only was the choice of either of these branches of medicine suitable for a boy in Keats's position, his guardians did not have to look far for a suitable master to whom he could be apprenticed. Thomas Hammond, the man who had attended Keats's dying mother, had recently apprenticed his own son to a colleague and was now looking for a pupil. No doubt the matter was carefully considered (Hammond was asking an apprentice's premium of £210) but, despite the poor state of the stock-market, Sandell and Abbey agreed to sell £300 worth of shares to pay for Keats's initial training. In the late summer of 1810, he moved into the room over the surgery where Hammond lodged his apprentices, and there is every reason to believe that he was offered a competent grounding in his chosen profession. Hammond had trained at Guy's, where he had so far distinguished himself as to be made a dresser to William Lucas, an eminent figure in the profession. As a respected and established local doctor, Hammond doubtless kept ahead of the developments taking place at Guy's and trained his boys sufficiently for them to reflect credit on him should they ever move on to that great hospital itself.

Keats's new duties were various and demanding. In addition to such menial tasks as sweeping up, holding Hammond's horse while his master paid his visits, stocking the medicine jars and delivering the medicines themselves, he would also have begun to learn about the making up of at least the more common drugs. In addition, he would have acquired a range of basic surgical skills from the application of leeches and tooth-pulling to setting bones and, maybe, delivering babies. A certain amount of anatomy and physiology was also necessary, gained perhaps from popular textbooks and, above all, from regular attendance on patients with Hammond himself.

Such exposure to the sick familiarised Keats with the symptoms of the common ailments that it fell to the surgeon-apothecary to treat, to predict their course and, where they existed, to know their remedies. Gradually too, in an age without anaesthetics and when the pain and terror of serious illness were exacerbated by dirt and the powerlessness of medical men themselves, he would also have been encouraged to acquire something of that fine balance between concern and distance which was an essential aspect of their approach. Above all, and in the company of Hammond especially, Keats would have become familiar with the unspectacular daily routine and discipline of one of the great caring professions. In such ways, these years at Edmonton became, as Clarke later wrote, 'the most placid period of his painful life'.[26]

Keats's visits to Clarke himself meanwhile fed his growing hunger for poetry. During the early months of his apprenticeship he continued with his translation of Virgil, surprising his friend with an iconoclastic comment on what he considered the weak structure of the Latin poem. It was probably for completing this self-imposed task that, at mid-summer 1811, Keats was 'assigned' a copy of Bonnycastle's *History of Astronomy* 'as a reward of merit'. John Clarke and his son clearly recognised a continuing sense of obligation towards the orphaned boy and responded in such ways to his need of their kindness and support. These they gave generously, and now, while Hammond trained Keats in the rudiments of medicine, Clarke gave the boy a grounding in the forms and techniques of poetry.

Clarke's tastes were those of a well-read young schoolmaster, and the major renaissance poets, their lesser contemporaries and eight-eenth-century imitators lay at the core of the reading he shared with Keats. This was a necessary, even an inevitable preparation, and was an important aspect of the informed but passionate response to tradition that is a hallmark of Keats's maturing genius. In the verse epistle he later wrote his mentor, Keats made clear that these studious hours in the arbour offered pleasure, companionship and, above all, access to the world of the imagination that was now becoming an imperative for him.

The epistle suggests that the two young men read *A Midsummer Night's Dream* together, and Edward Holmes recorded that Keats had earlier studied *Macbeth*, offering the boyish opinion that no one would dare read the play at two o'clock in the morning. Clarke also introduced Keats to Milton, to his depiction of the rout of the fallen angels as well as to that aspect of *Paradise Lost* which clearly had a far greater appeal at this time, the Milton who could create 'meek Eve's fair slenderness'.[27] Keats's engagement with Milton was to become as profound as his knowledge of Shakespeare, although it was only to mature some years later. It was from Clarke that he also learned that the epic poem was considered to be the 'king' of the genres, something 'round, vast, and spanning' like the rings of Saturn illustrated in his copy of Bonnycastle. The idea of the epic poem would always fire Keats's ambition.

On a less exalted level, and in this avid pursuit of 'all the sweets of song', the two young men read some of the didactic works of Milton's eighteenth-century followers, the odes of Gray and Collins, the sonnets of Charlotte Smith, Mary Tighe, Coleridge and Leigh Hunt, as well as 'the sharp, the rapier-pointed epigram' as practised by the satirists. The eighteenth-century followers of Spenser were also studied: the Thomson of *The Castle of Indolence*, Mark Akenside, and Beattie's *The Minstrel*, whose hero, a 'visionary boy' entranced by folklore, fancy and the works of nature, learns eventually to subdue his wandering imagination to 'the influence of the philosophic mind' and so to write a more mature and humane poetry.

Consciously or unconsciously, this pattern of development was to influence Keats's own ideas about his art, but for the moment it was the romantic epics of the renaissance, 'Tasso's page' and Spenser's, that were more immediately influential. Keats's own reported comment that in reading *The Fairie Queene* he breathed a new world and became another being contains hints of escape and literary enchantment which are suggestive for his whole career. So, too, are other aspects of his enjoyment of Spenser: the music of his language, of what Keats called 'Spenserian vowels that elope with ease', and the power of the poem's vividly fanciful imagery which forced the boy to rise excited from his chair.

Access to such poetry was not necessarily straightforward, however.[28] Most books were expensive, volumes of poetry costing anywhere between six and twelve shillings, a considerable sum for a young teacher or a surgeon's apprentice. This high price of books was partly the result of the heavy duties levied on paper, which in turn meant that print was sometimes crowded on to the page. But there were other problems too. The high rate of window tax, for example, ensured that many rooms were dark during the day, while tallow dips and firelight put a strain on eyes trying to read after the frequently long hours of work. Then, to add to these practical difficulties, there was opposition to face from the forces of philistinism and snobbery.

In a period when the first signs of industrialism had inspired the beginnings of economic science and the morality that could supposedly be derived from this, utilitarian thinkers deplored time that was spent (in their view wasted) on desultory reading. Only severely practical works such as those later issued by the Society for the Diffusion of Useful

Knowledge would be allowed by many concerned with the education of boys from Keats's background, such people fearing that to let the mind luxuriate in poetry was merely to weaken it. On this point the utilitarians were united with another powerful group: the advocates of Evangelical Christianity. Their *Christian Observer*, for example, deplored 'the continual feeding of the imagination . . . which, once deceived, becomes itself the deceiver'. It was an embarrassing paradox to such people that their encouragement of Sunday schools had opened literacy to many more of the ordinary people who, in this period of reaction, were now being deluged with dreary works of moral improvement.

In such an atmosphere as this, imaginative literature could be seen as the rightful preserve only of those who had been its traditional guardians: a leisured, patriotic and ostensibly Anglican aristocracy. These Corinthian capitals of the social order, as the great conservative Edmund Burke called them, had for centuries been regarded as the arbiters of elegance and taste in the arts. 'The coxcomb who imitates their manner', wrote Burke's friend the economist Adam Smith, 'and affects to be eminent by the superior propriety of his behaviour, is rewarded with a double share of contempt for his folly and presumption.'[29] This was a lesson Keats the surgeon's apprentice was to be made painfully aware of. In the meantime, he continued to take as his masters the poets praised by Clarke and Hunt.

The result was his first poem, an 'Imitation of Spenser', which was probably written early in 1814. *The Fairie Queene* had 'awakened his genius' and now, 'enamoured of the stanza, he attempted to imitate it'.[30] What Keats offered his reader was an image of dawn rising over the 'lawny crest' of a hill and a stream which flows into a little tree-shaded lake. This last is set in a secret place of sweetness, vivid with birds and fish. A stately swan, borrowed from Milton by way of his eighteenth-century imitators, is making its way to a beautiful island, while 'on his back a fay reclined voluptuously'.

> Ah! could I tell the wonders of an isle
> That in that fairest lake had placèd been,
> I could e'en Dido of her grief beguile;
> Or rob from aged Lear his bitter teen:
> For sure so fair a place was never seen,
> Of all that ever charmed romantic eye:
> It seemed an emerald in the silver sheen
> Of the bright waters; or as when on high,
> Through clouds of fleecy white, laughs the cerulean sky.

The poem is purely a visual tableau whose principal purpose is the enjoyment of its own highly wrought luxuriousness. Its inspiration, like its language, is wholly literary, a fantasy of pleasure and escape in a world contrived through art. These are important and suggestive features, as is the debt to such passages as Spenser's Bower of Bliss. Like any teenager, Keats was racked by fantasies of unfulfilled desire. 'When I was a Schoolboy,' he later wrote, 'I though[t] a fair Woman a pure Goddess, my mind was a soft nest in which some one of them slept though she knew it not.'[31] Lines such as Spenser's could come close to triggering physical desire, and Keats was unselfconsciously explicit about associating the imaginative pleasures of poetry with the imagined pleasures of sex. When he wanted to praise Clarke for his understanding of Spenser and his nymphs, for example, he hailed him as one who had 'Fondled the maidens with the breasts of cream'.[32] Throughout his early work, Keats's own imagined bowers of bliss – his soft nests – are a constant focus of his poetry, and these fervent, often masturbatory imaginings would propel him into public conflicts of which, for the moment, he was blithely unaware.

There were signs, too, of a more turbulent adolescence. Some time during this period (and perhaps as early as 1812) Keats quarrelled with Hammond, apparently raising his fist to his master. What they disagreed about is not known, but as a result of the confrontation Keats moved out of the room over the surgery and into lodgings he may have shared with his younger brother. Tom tried working in Abbey's office for a while but, as an intelligent boy, he clearly found the work uncongenial and left. Abbey himself meanwhile was coming to realise that the young men in his charge were far from pliable. He must also have been aware of the considerable extra expense their move had put them to, an expense exacerbated by their carelessness with money.

The relation between Keats and his brothers, nurtured at Clarke's school and in the absence of parents, was deep, affectionate and, for Keats himself, a sustaining and necessary security. But, while his personal life rested on these foundations, his response to the public world was also beginning to grow. Here, once again, Clarke's school had had its part to play. John Clarke himself was a man of liberal political views and enjoyed the friendship of several distinguished and like-minded friends in the area. His son recalled that he had taken the *Examiner* from the time it was started, 'he and I week after week revelling in the liberty-loving, liberty-advocating, liberty – eloquent articles of the young editor'.[33] Keats, when he was old enough, was also lent the newspaper, and it was his reading of the *Examiner*, apparently along with his study of Bishop Burnet's *History of My Own Times*, which 'laid the foundations of his love of civil and religious liberty'.[34] Such interests were maintained by the reading and conversation the two young men enjoyed in the arbour, but Clarke himself had a more direct contact with Leigh Hunt, who was now enjoying his period of greatest fame as a radical journalist.

The threat of an action for seditious libel had hung over the *Examiner* ever since its inception, and Hunt was now determined to place himself in a position where 'no man can accuse me of not writing a libel'.[35] The objects of his attack would be the notorious extravagance and profligacy of the Prince Regent and the defence of him offered by the Tory press. Hunt's article responded point by point to a fatuous eulogy of the Prince in the *Morning Post*. Far from being such a paragon of virtue as was claimed, the future George IV was, in Hunt's view, no more than a reprobate. There was not a person in the country who did not recognise that:

> this *Adonis in loveliness* was a corpulent gentleman of fifty! In short, that this *delightful, blissful, wise, pleasurable, honourable, virtuous, true and immortal PRINCE*, was a violator of his word, a libertine over head and ears in debt and disgrace, a despiser of domestic ties, the companion of gamblers and demireps, a man who had just closed half a century without one single claim on the gratitude of his country or the respect of posterity![36]

In a country structured by rigid hierarchies of class and held in the ever tightening grip of repression, Hunt had exposed the very apex of that society as being empty of all symbolic value and moral worth. He and his brother were at once indicted for bringing the royal family into contempt (the accuracy of their attack was no defence against their alleged intent), were tried, found guilty, sentenced to two years in prison and fined £500.

Clarke determined to do what little he could. He had earlier met Hunt at a party and, having been won over by his charm, he now arranged through his father that the prisoner be provided with a weekly basket of fresh produce grown by the boys on the plots in the school grounds. Clarke himself carried this gift to Hunt in the quaintly furnished, book-lined cell he had managed to create for himself in Hungerford Road jail. When he returned, it was with stories of the great and the good of liberal London who had also visited there: Lord Byron with his friend the fashionable poet Tom Moore, Jeremy Bentham the philosopher, the painter Benjamin Haydon, who brought along his twelve-foot canvas of *The Judgement of Solomon*, and Charles and Mary Lamb, who may have taken the critic William Hazlitt with them. There was even an anonymous letter offering financial help from a largely unknown poet called Percy Bysshe Shelley. At however remote a distance, the two young men in the arbour were now in touch with that most alluring of heroes, the writer as political prisoner.

For the moment, Clarke, who was himself only the most minor of satellites, did not feel he could introduce his friend to so exalted a circle, but the great wave of release which swept over the country with the abdication of Napoleon in 1814 touched even a teenage surgeon's apprentice. In a London ablaze with festivity and hope, the *Examiner* warned of the peril of the continent returning to the narrow ways of the *ancien régime*. Keats's sonnet 'On Peace' reflects both these moods. Clumsily translating part of the Latin inscription on Somerset House as 'With England's Happiness proclaim Europa's liberty', Keats urged that the 'sceptered tyrants' of mainland Europe should be placed under the rule of law, thereby echoing Hunt's hope that Louis XVIII would not be able 'to play the tyrant like some of his predecessors'.[37]

In England itself, however, the old regime was loudly and gaudily proclaiming its prestige. August saw the centenary of the Hanoverian accession. The royal parks were thrown open, sham castles were built, miniature ships acted out the Battle of the Nile, while, from a Temple of Peace in Green Park, water cascaded into golden basins from the jaws of lions. Half a million people thronged the London streets from Piccadilly to Vauxhall, where Keats himself, briefly catching sight of an unknown young woman, was suddenly and deeply stirred. He recorded the experience in a poem. 'Fill for me a brimming bowl' is reminiscent of Byron's 'To a Beautiful Quaker', but, if Keats's own poem is lame, the experience of seeing the girl, dressed perhaps in the fashionably clinging muslins of the day, was clearly a powerful one, the first intuition of the full force of his sex drive. Over the next four or five years, the girl's image returned to him frequently, a figment of beauty irredeemably lost, yet cruel in her power of blighting the hopes she raised, a first intimation perhaps of *la belle dame sans merci*.

For the moment, such intuitions were beyond the reach of Keats's poetry, which remained superficial and imitative. A sonnet 'To Byron' written at this time paid fashionable if stilted obeisance to the most glittering literary figure of the day, while another, 'To Chatterton', celebrated the young poet and suicide as a spirit freely hymning in the heavens while his admirers wept for him below. Even genuine personal feeling could not kindle so tentative an art. The sonnet Keats wrote at the close of 1814, and about five days after the death of his grand-mother, is again merely a pastiche covering over emotions so deep that for years he 'never told anyone, not even his brother, the occasion on which it was written'.[38]

But the time had come to tell someone he was trying to become a poet, and Keats turned naturally enough to Clarke. On 2 February 1815, Leigh Hunt was released from prison and, as Clarke was walking out to congratulate him, he was met by Keats who went with him some of the way. When they parted, Keats shyly presented his friend with a sonnet 'Written on the Day that Mr Leigh Hunt left Prison'.

> What though, for showing truth to flattered state,
>   Kind Hunt was shut in prison, yet has he,
>   In his immortal spirit, been as free
> As the sky-searching lark, and as elate.
> Minion of grandeur! Think you he did wait?
>   Think you he naught but prison walls did see,
>   Till, so unwilling, thou unturned'st the key?
> Ah, no! far happier, nobler was his fate!
> In Spenser's halls he strayed, and bowers fair,
>   Culling enchanted flowers; and he flew
> With daring Milton through the fields of air:
>   To regions of his own his genius true
> Took happy flights. Who shall his fame impair
>   When thou art dead, and all thy wretched crew?

The lines are a disciple's creed, an expression of Keats's ideas on the relation between poetry and politics. Imprisoned though Hunt has been, Keats declares, reading poetry has freed his 'immortal spirit'. In culling Spenser's 'enchanted flowers', art has triumphed over circum-stance and guaranteed fame. These were ideas Keats would hugely develop, but, as the embodiment of Keats's adolescent ideal, Hunt was the man who now gave the teenage boy the courage to declare himself a poet. He handed over his sonnet with a hesitant, self-conscious look, but 'there are some momentary glances by beloved friends', Clarke later wrote, 'that fade only with life.'[39]

APOLLO'S APPRENTICE

Apollo is the God of music and poetry . . . he . . . is also
the God of medicine.

(Lemprière's Bibliotheca Classica)

FOR ALL HIS naive enthusiasm, Keats had not yet found his way as a
poet, and his verse over the next year shows him negotiating the false
paths and emotional cul-de-sacs that lay in wait for a nineteen-year-old
apprentice in poetry. The drear February of 1815, for example, saw
him sitting beside his 'solitary hearth' and composing his first two
odes.[1] Both works are pastiche, and show Keats dealing tentatively
with ideas which, in his mature poetry, he would submit to a process of
altogether more rigorous imaginative criticism. What we see here is a
very young man beginning to discover his myths.

In the 'Ode to Apollo', the tutelary deity of some of Keats's greatest
verse is celebrated as the figure whose beauty is the inspiration of the
major poets of the European tradition from Homer, through Tasso,
Spenser and Shakespeare, to Milton. Embodied as the setting sun,
Apollo's golden rays illuminate the evening world and, when he joins
with the immortals in their song, he offers mankind a vision of
universal harmony:

> But when *Thou* joinest with the Nine,
> And all the powers of song combine,
>   We listen here on earth:
> The dying tones that fill the air
> And charm the ear of evening fair,
> From thee, great God of Bards, receive their heavenly birth.[2]

Nature and art are one, and their voice is divine. Such ideas are central
to Keats's early aspirations, to his conviction of the grandeur and power

of poetry and the sacredness of the poet's vocation. For the moment, however, his technical ability lagged far behind the fervour of his belief.

The obverse of such exaltation was a gloom that bordered on the panic of despair. Apollo fades in the darkness of night, leaving the poet to nurse his 'horrid Morbidity of Temperament'[3] and to long for the power evoked in the second of these February odes: 'To Hope'. Here, amid the bloodless personifications of the work, there can be heard, if only intermittently, a voice that is truly troubled. While much of the political concern in the poem is borrowed from the *Examiner*, Keats's reflections on his family history, and by implication on the damage done to him in childhood, suggest a deep personal crisis.

His brother George, then working at Abbey's counting house, bore witness to this, to Keats's 'nervous morbidity', his 'melancholy and complaining' and 'many a bitter fit of hypochondriasm'.[4] There seems to be more here than the depression suffered by many young men in their late teens and early twenties, the feeling of personal insignificance, frustration and lassitude. These were, no doubt, present in Keats's case, but there is also the effect that the loss of his parents, his mother especially, must have had on his passionate nature. She had left him in his childhood and reappeared at the time of his adolescence only to die. Sustained maternal affection was something he had never known and could not rely on. There were many intensely bitter and confusing moments both now and later when his mind veered off into a void and was unsupported and alone. It could supply no meaning from its own experience and was either morbidly passive or vicious to the world and itself. The 'gordian complication' of Keats's later feelings towards women surely have something of their origins here.[5]

So, too, may the intensity of Keats's belief in his vocation as a poet. His studies with Clarke had borne in on him the esteem in which poetry was held, and Keats's reading of poetry was closely connected with the most valuable friendship he had known outside the circle of his brothers. To be a poet was to transform himself into something supreme, and to do so out of his emotions, his own inherent worth. To fail here, and the disparity between his early achievements and the models he hoped to imitate must surely at times have seemed like failure, was to see his own worth devalued. Such a crisis was intensely threatening, particularly to a young man whose hold on his sense of self was so tenuous. If there was much in Keats's moods of late adolescent melodrama, there was also something serious when he told 'his Brothers & in an agony he feared he should never be a Poet, & if he was not he would destroy himself'.[6]

George, who had so often been called on to hold Keats down when his temper had got the better of him at school, knew he also had to sustain him through these moods. His natural ordinariness was among the many kindnesses Keats received during his life. If Tom was closer to him in intellect, George was the brother who could help bring Keats back to some moderate degree of contentedness. Nor, with that reticence which was so marked an aspect of Keats's emotional courage, would he inflict his moods on people beyond his immediate family. 'He avoided teazing anyone with his miseries but Tom and myself,' George recalled, 'and often asked our forgiveness; venting, and discussing them gave him relief.'[7]

So, too, did company. George found introductions easier to make than his elder brother. He had now got himself into what on the surface at least must have seemed an amiable circle of poetically inclined young people centred around the Mathew family, the children of a merchant in Goswell Street. Caroline and Ann Felton Mathew were among the leaders of this, and through them his brother introduced Keats to their cousin George Felton Mathew, to Mary Frogley, to the solicitor William Haslam and, in the spring of 1816, to the artist Joseph Severn. Here, in the 'little domestic concerts and dances' of the Mathew clique, was a degree of innocent pleasure but also a lurking danger.[8]

The poetic tastes of the group were enthusiastic but often factitious. George Felton Mathew dabbled in verse, adopting a pose of Byronic melancholy and parading himself as one thoughtful beyond his years. His poems were littered with the conventional scenery of Gothic romance, suitable properties, as he thought, to embellish life's vale of woe, and he later claimed to resent the fact that Keats appeared not to share his depths of emotion. 'He used to spend many evenings reading to me,' he recalled, 'but I never observed the tears in his eyes nor the broken voice which are indicative of extreme sensibility.'[9] In fact, in Clarke's company, Keats could be moved to tears by such passages as the departure of Posthumus from Imogen in *Cymbeline*, but in the presence of George Felton Mathew his intelligence and sense of humour usually protected him from the excesses of affectation.

He was not, however, entirely immune. The circle of young friends enjoyed the Italian romances Keats had read with Clarke, but they also relished the purely ephemeral and fashionable: William Sotheby's translation of Wieland's *Oberon* and Mrs Tighe's *Psyche*. To these they may have added the preposterous verse tales of Robert Southey and, more certainly, the lyric poems – light, bright and trite – of Tom

Moore. For a few months during the summer of 1815, Keats was inveigled into imitating these.

The imitations were prompted by the Mathews sending him a shell and a copy of Moore's *The Wreath and the Chain* from their seaside holiday at Hastings. 'To Some Ladies' thanks the Mathew girls for these gifts and, as album verse, is perhaps not wholly reprehensible. The verses in which Keats apostrophised George Felton Mathew as the 'valiant Eric', however, are a ridiculous performance, but worse were three linked sonnets to Woman written some time between March and December 1815. Here the poet claims he is fortunate to have lain 'dormant' to love when he sees Woman as 'Inconstant, childish, proud, and full of fancies'. When she is 'meek', however, he burns to put on the armour of the chivalric knight and be her 'defender'. The second sonnet claims to substitute an admiration for feminine 'mild intelligences' to a drooling over their physical charms, but the depths of banality are reserved for the third sonnet:

Ah! who can e'er forget so fair a being?
   Who can forget her half-retiring sweets?
   God! she is like a milk-white lamb that bleats
For man's protection.[10]

Although such lines point to an important difficulty even in some of Keats's mature verse and try crudely to smother what would only gradually emerge as his real difficulties with sexuality, the sentiment here is probably more silly than vicious. It is a product of that lack of experience which, in this instance, caused Keats finally to weep at his own refinement when he read the passage to Mathew.

Clearly, something was needed to jolt Keats into greater maturity, and it came from an unexpected source. Since 1812, the apothecaries had been seeking to reform their profession and, in particular, to eliminate the undesirable and unlicensed by introducing a recognised examination. After eighteen months of discussion, they joined with the College of Physicians in bringing forward a Bill which gave the Society of Apothecaries powers to examine all those new candidates who wished to practise in medicine, pharmacy, chemistry, materia medica and medical botany. The Apothecaries Act, as it came to be known, was passed in July 1815 and stipulated that, after completing a five-year apprenticeship, a candidate would have to undergo at least six months' attendance on the practice of a hospital.

Both Hammond and Keats were aware of this development and, whatever the state of the relationship between them, it was clearly Hammond who, as an ex-pupil of Guy's, recommended Keats to the United Hospitals of Guy's and St Thomas's in Southwark. On Sunday 1 October, Keats paid his preliminary fee of £1 2s, following this a day later with a further £25 4s to register himself as a surgical pupil. That he was apparently aiming to become a surgeon rather than a more lowly apothecary involved him and his guardians in considerable extra expense, and this at a time when the stock-market was at a low ebb after the panic of Napoleon's return and the Hundred Days. The money was found, however, along with fees for his lecture courses, which cost a further thirty-two guineas, and various sums for the textbooks, note-books and medical instruments that also had to be purchased.

The move from Enfield into Southwark and the life of a great hospital marked a dramatic change in Keats's life. Southwark itself, or the 'Borough' as it was known, was a rough and seething area of narrow, dirty streets overhung with half-timbered tenements, crowded with coaches that brought passengers from south-east England, and lived in by a shifting population which included many of those desperate members of the underworld who, for the moment, were not incarcerated in the area's numerous prisons. Water of incredible filthiness was pumped from the river for the use of the local inhabitants, while across the Thames itself the largest cast-iron bridge in the world was then under construction. Here too, in the early years of the previous century, Thomas Guy had founded his hospital, a gracious, classical building erected round three sides of a courtyard. Now ruled over by Benjamin Harrison, the domineering governor and treasurer, Guy's and its sister hospital St Thomas's were the institutions where, amid appalling human suffering, clinical medicine was making its greatest advances in Europe. And here Keats now came among that first group of young men studying for their licences by attending lectures and walking the wards.

Keats was clearly apprehensive about the prospect, and a sonnet from his first month of living in Southwark expresses his depression and longing for escape. The poem was Keats's most considerable achieve-ment to date, and the opening lines have considerable authenticity:

> O Solitude! if I must with thee dwell,
>   Let it not be among the jumbled heap
>   Of murky buildings; climb with me the steep –
> Nature's observatory – whence the dell,

Its flowery slopes, its river's crystal swell,
  May seem a span; let me thy vigils keep
  'Mongst boughs pavilioned, where the deer's swift leap
Startles the wild bee from the foxglove bell.[11]

Although it is not clear to whom the sonnet is addressed, its expression is far removed from the artificial fancy cultivated by Mathew and his circle, and the poem was a first sign of the rift that was soon to grow between them.

Meanwhile, Keats's student day was a long one, his working week full and demanding.[12] In addition to regularly walking the wards, he attended a full course of lectures in chemistry, anatomy, dissection and the practice of medicine 'calculated to form a complete course of medical and chirurgical instruction'. His surviving *Anatomical and Physiological Notebook* testifies to what he learned, and Keats was far from averse to scientific discipline, finding it indeed to be a stimulus to his imagination. It is also clear that he was at the outset a conscientious worker, 'indefatigable in his application to anatomy, medicine, and natural history'.[13] This attachment to medicine was something wholly sincere and something that coloured his eventual commitment to poetry. Both vocations he regarded as a dedication to relieving human suffering, and both were traditionally watched over by his personal deity Apollo, the god of all the fine arts, of medicine, music, poetry and eloquence, of which he was deemed the inventor.

While Keats's lecturers provided him with some of the terms and ideas underlying his mature achievement, the daily life of a great hospital necessarily had a profound influence too. Pain was all about him. Every day he walked the wards, in his first days as one of that crowd of pupils pushing and scrambling to get near the surgeon Astley Cooper as the great man, dressed in black with short knee-breeches and silk stockings, bounded up the ward staircase. Once among his patients, Cooper took off his hat (a novelty that was favourably remarked on) while the young men hurried forward yet again, this time to secure a good place at the bedsides. Here Cooper himself, quietly reading the name card, gained his patients' confidence with his clear, silvery voice as he gently encouraged them to answer the few but pertinent questions on which he based his diagnosis.

This was a display of high professionalism amid conditions that were often as squalid as they were barbarous. It was probably Benjamin Harrison who had issued the 'Rules and Orders' to be observed by patients in the hospital wards. These demanded that patients themselves be cleaned of vermin on admittance and then provided, at a cost of 2s 9d, with towels, a tin pot, cutlery and five sheets. Piety was enforced under the threat of a patient being discharged, and a similar punishment was also the ultimate sanction against those who refused to help with cleaning the ward and fetching coals, or who brought in alcohol, pawned the bed-linen or smoked in bed. By dint of constant cleaning and scouring, Harrison succeeded in creating habitable wards out of what had previously been an augean squalor. The quality of the ward sisters was also comparatively high. The food, however, was mean and cheap, consisting of a monotonous diet of boiled mutton and rice pudding which, as it was often prepared in the wards, mixed there with the smell of sour linseed poultices.

More gruesome still were the experiences Keats was required to undergo in the small dissecting room used by the Guy's students. Cooper pointed out in the first lecture he gave that a pupil's 'anatomical knowledge cannot be perfect unless he has frequently seen and assisted in the dissection of the human body'.[14] Since the use of corpses for this purpose was forbidden by law, Cooper himself paid the fines of the body-snatchers or 'resurrection men' he had to employ to rob graves. The bodies themselves were brought to the hospital in sacks and were invariably naked since, by a legal technicality, stealing a shroud was an offence, whereas stealing a body was merely a misdemeanour. On arrival amid the overpowering stench of the dissecting room, the body was laid on a table and became prey to the enquiring scalpels of young men occupied with 'carving limbs and bodies, in all stages of putrefaction, & of all colours; black, green, yellow, blue'.[15] Drinking and horseplay helped dim the horror or rouse the faint-hearted, while the more brazen, it was said, even cooked and ate their dinners there. Others merely amused themselves by casually slicing up the maggots that wound their way out of the corpses.

For Keats, poetry was a necessary antidote to such experiences, and his reading during this period was gradually widening his tastes. The mannered fairyland of the Mathew circle still had a strong appeal, its very artificiality providing a refuge from life in the Borough and its hospitals, but other influences were also at work, in particular the recent publications of Leigh Hunt.

During his term in prison, Hunt had read deeply in the work of his contemporaries and had significantly revised his opinion of the Lake Poets and of Wordsworth in particular. In the first version of *The Feast of the Poets*, Hunt had disparaged Wordsworth's achievement. Now, as he issued new versions of his poem, so Hunt began to see, and to encourage others to see, the importance of the revolution in English literature Wordsworth was leading. These new versions of *The Feast of the Poets*, garnished with long and elaborate footnotes, provided a map of the contemporary literary landscape Keats could not ignore. Here was a view of his older contemporaries offered by an experienced critic and presided over by Leigh Hunt's own version of Apollo, the arbiter of poetic integrity.

Many of Hunt's views were to find their place in Keats's early work and were to contribute to his mauling by the critics some years later. For example, Hunt advanced the far from original view that much of the poetry of Pope marked an emotional and, just as importantly, a technical dead end. Hunt also passed some harsh judgements on such current poets as Scott, Campbell and Rogers. He admired Crabbe and praised 'the natural fineness' of Tom Moore's versification, but Southey he excoriated as a renegade hack, while Coleridge 'is a man of great natural talents, as they who most lament his waste of them, are the readiest to acknowledge'.[16] Coleridge's notorious inability to produce during his long withdrawals into opium and despair meant, Hunt declared, that Apollo 'looks upon him as a deserter'. Praise of Byron, a praise again tempered with insight, forms the climax of the poem and offered Keats a balanced view of a poet whose meteoric literary reputation and personal notoriety could easily have caused him once again to imitate aspects of the merely fashionable. Among the most influential passages in *The Feast of the Poets*, however, were Hunt's analyses of Wordsworth.

With an insight that was far from being commonly shared, Hunt praised Wordsworth as 'the Prince of the Bards of his Time!' Nonetheless, Wordsworth had in Hunt's view faults 'to endanger those great ends of poetry, by which it should assist the uses and refresh the spirits of life'. Wordsworth had encouraged the modern reader, Hunt suggested, to be 'over contemplative' and to live 'too much apart'. Summing up his views with a sentence that is as witty as it is pert, he declared of his great contemporary: 'we will emerge oftener into his fields, sit dangling our legs over his stiles, and cultivate a due respect of his daffodils; but he, on the other hand, must grow a little better acquainted with our streets, must put up with our lawyers, and even find out a heart or so among our politicians'.

It was probably during the autumn of this year that Keats himself purchased the most recent two-volume edition of Wordsworth's poems, so beginning that profound (and profoundly ambivalent) relation to the older man's work through which he was in part to develop his own. Hunt's views and his own immaturity inevitably clouded his initial reactions, but Wordsworth's influence can be detected in the sonnet Keats had already written on the dismaying prospect of moving into the Borough. The swiftly leaping deer and the bees murmuring around the foxgloves seem to owe as much to the older poet as to observation, and their presence alarmed Mathew greatly.

Keats seemed in danger of becoming influenced by a poetry which, unlike the safely factitious fairyland of *Oberon*, was concerned with real nature and natural language. To Mathew, such novelty could only appear a false step and something would have to be done to bring Keats back to 'all the bright fictions of fanciful dreams'.[17] In the *European Magazine* for October 1816 Mathew printed the verses 'To a Poetical Friend', he had written over a year before. Here, in ridiculous, jingling quatrains, Mathew concocted an equally ridiculous tradition of verse in which Keats is the heir of a poetry that derives from the 'gay fields of Fancy', an anodyne world of knights, damsels, dungeons and dragons which harmlessly beguiles the mind after work, in Keats's case his studying to be a doctor:

> And when evening shall free thee from Nature's decays,
>   And release thee from Study's severest control,
> Oh warm thee in Fancy's enlivening rays;
>   And wash the dark spots of disease from thy soul.

> And let not the spirit of Poesy sleep;
>   Of Fairies and Genii continue to tell --
> Nor suffer the innocent deer's timid leap
>   To fright the wild bee from her flowery bell.

This poisonous little warning, drawing as it does on Keats's own lines to solitude, elicited the verse epistle 'To George Felton Mathew' in reply. Here, borrowing his form from Leigh Hunt and something of his manner from such Elizabethan writers as Michael Drayton, Keats contrasted his thraldom to his studies with the delights of 'a brotherhood in song'. He imagines himself and his friend as the Beaumont and Fletcher of the age, records his joying in 'the genius-loving heart', and then expresses his fears that love and nature will never have the opportunity of delighting him, pent up as he is in the 'dark city'.

The poem is, indeed, the pastoral vision of an essentially urban young man, a cockney ideal of a landscape populated with elfs, fairies and naiads who may just possibly be meant to suggest the actual young men and women of the Mathew circle.

Keats's relationship with the Mathews would soon evaporate, but before it did so he wrote what are probably two valentine poems. The lines 'Hadst thou lived in days of old' were almost certainly written to Mary Frogley on George's behalf and, in the manner pleasing to the group as a whole, they revel in that sentimental chatter, pseudo-literary euphemism and mannered titillation which are among the worst characteristics of this sort of verse. Equally repulsive but, from the biographical point of view, more interesting is the sonnet 'Had I a man's fair form'. Supposed by some to be spoken in the voice of a fairy, the lines reflect the disadvantage Keats thought his diminutive size (he was just over five feet tall) placed him at in women's company. Such a painfully adolescent lack of self-confidence was another cause of Keats's difficulties with women, and here, he resolves to compensate for it by the power of poetry. Although the speaker declares himself to be no knight or 'happy shepherd' of literary convention, the intoxicating 'dew' of his beloved is his by right of desire:

And when the moon her pallid face discloses,
  I'll gather some by spells, and incantation.

The language of poetry becomes the language of magic, a means of changing the world that is illusory but suggestive of threat and festering personal problems Keats could not as yet face honestly. Certainly, he was not yet ready for love.

If such attempts at Regency flirtatiousness were one aspect of Keats's activities at this period, the enjoyment of male company was another. The obverse of the sentiment recorded in the Mathew poems was the braggadocio doggerel of 'Women, Wine, and Snuff', Keats's 'beloved Trinity', praised in the lines he scribbled on a fellow student's notes. Snuff was in fact widely used by the students at Guy's in an attempt to palliate the stench of the wards, and it was here that Keats's professional training had now become more serious. At the end of his first month in the hospital he was appointed to the next vacancy for a dressership, a position he took up on 3 March 1816.

A surgeon usually had four dressers appointed under him, each young man paying fifty guineas for the privilege. As a badge of status among his fellows, a dresser was entitled to carry a 'skellet' or box containing plasters, bandages and linseed meal which he took with him when the students made their rounds of the wards. The dresser attended to wounds on such occasions, but his other duties were more onerous. One week a month, for example, he acted as a house doctor, living at his own expense in the bedroom and sitting-room provided for him and attending to out-patients who required to be bled or have a tooth pulled. It was also at his discretion that cases of strangulated hernia, retention of urine and all fractures or other accidents were admitted. He would consult with his surgeon when specific problems arose, and on him also rested the decision when and whether the surgeon should be summoned in cases of emergency.

These were considerable responsibilities but, in addition, a dresser was also required to attend his surgeon during operations. At Guy's, these took place from one o'clock onwards in either of the theatres reserved for men and women respectively. Such operations could be horrific in the extreme. Crowds of eager students were packed so tightly on the horseshoe-shaped standings round the walls that there was a constant crying of 'Heads, heads' as they craned to look down at the patient on the wooden operating table and at the surgeons working away with knives, saws and tweezers at his unanaesthetised body. This was a ghastly spectacle, and when Keats's surgeon, the infamous and stone-deaf Billy Lucas, was operating, Astley Cooper usually tried to be in attendance to attempt to limit the damage as he watched his colleague 'cutting amongst most important parts as though they were only skin, and making us all shudder from the apprehension of his opening arteries or committing some other error'.[18] When Lucas had completed his work, Keats himself was left to dress the wounds.

Camaraderie among the students served for many as a counterweight to such experiences, but, while Keats had friends among his peers, none of these relationships appears to have been either deep or lasting. Keats was not, it seems, particularly tempted by the company of those whom Astley Cooper annually warned against the lure of drinking and idleness, and, although the Borough, like many parts of Regency London, offered the opportunities of easy sex, Keats was 'never inclined to pursuits of a low or vicious – Character'.

This, at least, was the opinion of another dresser, the somewhat pious John Spurgin, who, in Keats's earliest days at the hospital, tried to recruit him to the ranks of the Swedenborgians. Keats, with the firm yet undogmatic scepticism that was becoming his natural response to formal religious notions, resisted Spurgin's overtures, despite the fact that Spurgin himself recognised in his temperament an appreciation of that animating spirit which 'can give the brightest and most lucid Flame to the Fire of Poetry . . . and wander in Paths amid the Geniuses of old which I know you so much admire'.[19] By the time he wrote to Keats, however, Spurgin had left for Cambridge, and the address on his letter shows that Keats himself was living at 28 St Thomas's Street, the lodgings he first shared, perhaps at the great man's suggestion, with one of Astley Cooper's dressers and Frederick Tyrell, who was later to publish the surgeon's lectures. By the close of 1815, both these men had left, one to practise in Brentford, the other for further studies in Edinburgh. Since the rent on the apartment was too great for Keats to bear alone, he arranged to move in with two other men in the same house: Henry Stephens and George Wilson Mackereth.

There were clearly times when Stephens in particular found Keats a difficult companion to lodge with. Keats's inner insecurity was perhaps less desolate than it had been during his time at Edmonton, but it was now combined with his demanding life as a medical student and expressed itself in different ways. 'Poetry was to his mind the zenith of all his Aspirations,' Stephens recalled, 'the only thing worthy the attention of superior minds.'[20] Such attitudes could become extremely trying. 'It may be readily imagined', Stephens continued, 'that this feeling was accompanied with a good deal of Pride and some conceit, and that amongst mere Medical students, he would walk, & talk as one of the Gods might be supposed to do, when mingling with mortals.'

This slighting affectation of superiority, the pose of a poet who had, so far as his companions could see, written little to justify it, was tinged with a certain defiant naivety. While the majority of young men at Guy's wore buttoned collars and cravats, Keats dressed *à la* Byron with his collar turned down and opened to reveal a black ribbon round his neck. He was also conspicuously condescending to the poetic efforts of others. From time to time, Keats would allow Stephens to read his verses, but when Stephens returned the compliment 'I always had the mortification of hearing them – condemned, indeed he seemed to think it presumption in me to attempt to head along the same pathway as himself, at however humble a distance.' What was particularly irksome was the adulation lavished on their elder brother by George and Tom. Their being so closely thrown together in their childhood and their habits of warm mutual support seemed too cosy and too uncritical in the harsher world of Guy's, and the fact that the Keats boys 'seemed to think their Brother John was to be exalted, & to exalt the family name' clearly rankled.

In fact, Keats's poetic path was still confused, and now there lay before him another alluring but false goal. In February 1816 Leigh Hunt published his romance *The Tale of Rimini*, a version of Dante's story of the love of Paolo and Francesca. Keats read the work with interest, and, although Hunt's poem is conventionally disparaged, it has a number of virtues that are not always allowed it. Hunt's concern with metrical invention, for example, leads to a pleasantly varied and flexible use of the heroic couplet. He also had a vivid pictorial imagination, a reasonable control of narrative and some ability to dramatise. High tragedy was beyond his range, however, and, for emotional depth, he tended to substitute a cloying prettiness. The effect on Keats was an immediate desire to imitate:

> Lo! I must tell a tale of chivalry;
> For large white plumes are dancing in mine eye.

But the fervour of this ambition defeats its fulfilment and the work remains, in Keats's title, 'A Specimen of an Induction to a Poem', a fragment of frozen gestures and action postponed.

The pressure to declare himself a poet, to have evidence and proof of his ambition, was becoming strong nonetheless, and in April Keats began sorting through what he had so far written in the hope of having something published in the *Examiner*. Wisely, he chose the sonnet to Solitude, his best poem to date, signing it 'J.K.' and despatching it to Hunt. It did not appear in the next issue but, among the editorial announcements, he read 'J.K., and other Communications, next week'. On 5 May, Keats at last became a published poet.

Encouraged by this approval, Keats returned to the idea of writing a romance. 'Calidore' is again only a fragment, but its focusing of ideas marks a considerable advance on the 'Specimen'. To be sure, imitation of Hunt's more obvious mannerisms, the occasionally precious imagery, a 'bowery shore' and a hero who climbs a flight of steps 'with hasty trip', are among the poem's blemishes, but its new-found strengths are altogether more important. Keats shows how Calidore's delight in beauty nourishes and reflects his 'healthful spirit'. The natural world, alive with 'the freaks and dartings of the black-winged swallow', the 'spiral foxgloves' and the white dove 'that on the window spreads his feathers light', are all evoked as something intimately and subjectively related to man's spiritual well-being. Nonetheless, the element of flight into an enchanted and merely uncritical world is a danger here, and such a withdrawal into the anodyne and aesthetic is the explicit subject of two sonnets Keats wrote in the June of this year: 'To one who long in city pent' and 'O! how I love, on a fair summer's eve'. Such interest as the sonnets have lies less in the works themselves than in the personal circumstances that gave rise to them and, in particular, Keats's life at Guy's.

He had arranged to take his Licentiate of the Society of Apothecaries at the close of July, but the tedium of revision, especially the requirement to get by heart long lists of drugs from the *Pharmacopoeia Londoniensis*, was oppressive. There were other problems, however, besides the chore of rote learning. Keats was beginning to have doubts about his suitability for the medical profession itself. These had not yet hardened into an outright rejection, but regular attendance at the horrors of the operating theatre and his own sense of the dangers to which patients were exposed were causing him concern. Stephens began to notice how, now that lectures were over and there was time to write sonnets 'in the happy fields', such activities were altogether more welcome than the dull pages of the *Pharmacopoeia*. Besides, the opening lines of a poem, a long, important piece on which Keats would work throughout the rest of the year, had perhaps already been suggested to him 'by a delightful summer-day, as he stood beside the gate that leads from the Battery on Hampstead Heath into a field by Caen Wood'.[21]

Against such vague if potent promise stood the altogether starker fact that more than £1500 had already been invested in Keats's medical training. The time had now come to see if that money had been well spent. On 25 July, Keats was examined by Everard Brande on his knowledge of the *Pharmacopoeia*, on pharmaceutical chemistry, materia medica and the theory and practice of medicine itself. Seven of the candidates who presented themselves that day were failed, including Keats's room-mate Mackereth. Stephens had opted for a little more time. However, Keats himself, well able to satisfy the examiners despite his private doubts, emerged from Apothecaries' Hall as one of the first of a newly qualified generation of medical men. This was, by any standards, a considerable achievement.

Keats had been accepted into a profession about which he harboured doubts about his suitability and in which he was still too young to practise. Now, in urgent need of a holiday, he felt he must also get away to test himself in his other vocation. Leaving the stifling August smells of the Borough behind him, he set off for Margate and two months devoted to an exploration of poetry. His brother Tom was probably already there, a sympathetic and intelligent companion to help balance the dangers of solitude and the over-wrought imagination. In addition, Charles Wells, a friend of Tom's, had provided the brothers with letters franked with a Member of Parliament's signature which enabled them to be posted anywhere in the country free of charge. It is from this period that the flow of Keats's correspondence begins, those letters at once intimate and literary in the warmth of which he felt he could open his heart.

Margate was a newly fashionable seaside resort busy, despite the appalling summer weather, with visitors milling along the seafront or hoping to improve their health by plunging in the water from bathing machines driven two or three hundred yards out into the waves. There was also a walk to the north of the town, and Keats clearly took advantage of this when he could. The situation delighted him. It appears he had never seen the sea before, and the best lines in an artificial sonnet he wrote for George describe its effect on him: 'Its ships, its rocks, its caves, its hopes, its fears'. The sea was to enter deeply into Keats's consciousness and reappear often in his poetry. Now, however, it was the idea of poetry itself and the vocation of the poet especially that preoccupied him. Keats began a verse epistle 'To my Brother George' in which he tried to concentrate his thoughts and make explicit his dedication.

In the epistle, Apollo becomes the image and origin of that elated delight in nature and the physical world by which the poet's imagination is kindled. This is a sudden and unpredictable benevolence known only to those who are the elected servants of the god:

> there are times, when those that love the bay,
> Fly from all sorrowing far, far away;
> A sudden glow comes on them, naught they see
> In water, earth, or air, but poesy.[22]

This is the Apollonian moment of inspiration when to the poet the earth and sky are suddenly incandescent with fancy and, since Spenser and Hunt are named as the poet's masters here, inspiration comes in the form of romance, of prancing horses and armoured knights revealed amid the glimmer of sheet lightning. The 'enchanted portals open wide' and the elect poet stares into the golden light of inspiration.

The whole passage is at once fanciful and serious, an expression of ideas clumsily touched on in the early odes of 1815 and here more fully expressed. Keats now develops his belief that the poet is a rare, shamanistic individual, a priest and doctor whose service to the god of poetry and medicine is a perilous vocation, an intimation of joy won through a delight in the things of this world. And it is to this world that the god returns his devotee. The sense of service to humanity, the devotion of the divinely inspired poet to the well-being of the world, is central to Keats's poetry and was something he was to probe and question in the greatest of his mature works. He had walked the wards at Guy's and seen human suffering, he had known it himself and was to experience it more terribly yet. But now he had to ask himself how genuinely useful to pained humanity were these visionary states. Was there real worth in his vocation? The issue is raised but any answer is postponed, and the poem closes with a self-portrait of the poet lying in the grass beside the sea, his moments of insight quietened as he reveals to his brother his delight in the natural world, a delight checked only by the red waving poppies which suddenly remind him of soldiers and the 'scarlet coats that pester human-kind'.

This last image is a startling, even a violent intrusion. The savage England in which the poem was written seems to invade the text. Economic crisis was now breeding severe unrest. The leaders of the Tory government, 'Mouldy and Co', as they were labelled by the wits of the Whig opposition, resolved to counter discontent with policies of reaction. By 1816, they were engaging *agents provocateurs* and the Tory press to fabricate rumours of sedition which they hoped would be blown to such proportions that a majority of the country would assent to policies of coercion. By the close of the year, the redcoats of Keats's poem would actually be marching across England to suppress unrest. For the liberal-minded, for the readers of the *Examiner*, the England of 1816 was all but sunk in claustrophobic hopelessness.

It is against such a background that Keats offers his self-portrait, his image of a young man lying in the grass by the sea and inspired by a world in which nature, art and the imagination – 'beauty' in Keats's talismanic word – offer a way of representing existence to people in a manner altogether more humane than their daily circumstances allowed. Poetry is a consolation for the horrors of real life. As Keats developed this idea in succeeding works, so Apollo comes to be seen as the god both of medicine and of poetry, inspiring his elect so that they can soothe the minds of troubled humanity.

★ ★ ★

George kept the poem so that a fair copy could be made and, in his reply to his brother, told him of the latest happenings among their circle in London. John Clarke had retired from the school in Enfield and his son was now living with his brother and sister-in-law in Clerkenwell, where George had been to visit them. This was welcome news and, in his present state of thinking about his vocation, it inspired Keats to consider what he owed to his schoolmaster. In his epistle to George, Keats had written about his current position. Now, in his epistle 'To Charles Cowden Clarke', he gratefully reviewed the friendship that had helped make him a poet. The poem itself is a warm and self-effacing recital of his debt, but if the work was a look back at the past it was also to have a dramatic effect on Keats's future. Clarke is pictured in the poem as an intimate of Leigh Hunt's, one privileged to accompany him on his 'sweet forest walks' and to enjoy his conversation on poetry and politics. These were delights which, Keats states, 'I have never known.' Clarke took the hint and gathered together two or three of Keats's manuscripts with the intention of taking them to Hampstead when he next went to visit Hunt at the start of October.

If Hunt was wryly amused that Clarke was a friend of the anonymous and youthful 'J.K.' whose sonnet on Solitude he had published, he was quick to realise that 'J.K.' was rapidly maturing into a poet of promise. It is probable that he now read the epistle to Clarke itself, and few men could have been other than flattered by the genuine and unselfconscious expression of debt each line proclaimed. Clarke then offered further details about Keats, his 'peculiarities of mind and manner' and, having satisfied Hunt of his worth, was invited to bring his friend to visit the Vale of Health. A delighted Keats responded by declaring that such a meeting 'will be an Era in my existence'.[23]

The weeks in Margate were now over and Keats had returned to London and the Borough, where he had to rent new lodgings. These were eventually found at 8 Dean Street, a 'beastly place' of 'dirt, turnings, and windings', as he described it to Clarke, where for the few weeks that he stayed there he lived alone. The dinginess and solitude were particularly oppressive after his time in Margate, but to offset his inevitable depression Keats had the prospect of his meeting with Hunt, for whom he was now selecting and copying out his poems. He also had the company of his brothers and Clarke himself, whom he invited to visit him, giving suitable instructions for finding his lodgings after running the gauntlet over London Bridge. He also reminded Clarke of 'something in your Portfolio which I should by rights see'. This 'something' was almost certainly a 1616 edition of George Chapman's translation of Homer which belonged to Thomas Massa Alsager, a journalist on *The Times* and a member of the Hunt circle. The volume had been lent around the friends and was currently in Clarke's hands. Wisely refusing to risk coming to the Borough with such a valuable item, Clarke invited Keats to Clerkenwell for an evening that turned out to be 'our first symposium' and an occasion neither would forget.[24]

The meeting was both a summing up and a new start. The two young men were together once more and the excitement of old poetry was once again their concern. A valuable and unfamiliar volume lay between them and, in Clarke's words: 'to work we went, turning to some of the "famousest" passages, as we had scrappily known them in Pope's version.' What had previously been enclosed in eighteenth-century couplets and a forced elegance of grammar was now transformed by the contact of ancient epic with Elizabethan amplitude:

> Then forth he came, his both knees falt'ring, both
> His strong hands hanging down, and all with froth
> His cheeks and nostrils flowing, voice and breath
> Spent to all use, and down he sank to death.
> The sea had soak'd his heart through; all his veins
> His toils had rack'd t'a labouring woman's pains.
> Dead-weary was he.

Here was a previously unknown grandeur and energy, and as Clarke read through the passage, so he was rewarded by one of Keats's 'delighted stares', that intense and physical response to poetry Keats had first shown when they read Spenser together.

Enthralled by a poetry which, in Chapman's words, 'flew about our eares, like drifts of winter's snow', Keats and Clarke stayed up reading until six in the morning. When Keats finally left for home, walking the Borough streets at dawn, Chapman's lines were still surging in his head. Borne along by their movement, exhausted but exhilarated, he eventually reached his lodgings, where he sat down to write a sonnet. Making only one slight correction, he dashed out to find a post boy and sent the manuscript to Clerkenwell where, by ten o'clock, it was on Clarke's breakfast table.

> Much have I travelled in the realms of gold,
>   And many goodly states and kingdoms seen,
>   Round many western islands have I been

Which bards in fealty to Apollo hold.
Oft of one wide expanse had I been told,
  Which deep browed Homer ruled as his Demesne:
  Yet did I never breathe its pure serene,
Till I heard Chapman speak out loud and bold:
Then felt I like some watcher of the skies
  When a new planet swims into his ken,
Or like stout Cortez when with eagle eyes
  He stared at the Pacific – and all his men
Looked at each other with a wild surmise –
  Silent, upon a peak in Darien.

All Keats's previous literary experience is summed up and gloriously extended here. The prospects opened by poetry become an empire of the mind, an imaginative freedom, an imaginative conquest. Chapman's stars and seas move around skies and promontories incandescent with Apollo's gold. The might of the god has been revealed and, in Hunt's suggestive words, the 'prematurely masculine' power of Keats's sonnet 'completely announced the new poet taking possession'.[25] In a few days' time, Keats himself would confirm this at his meeting with Hunt himself. The new era in his existence was now about to begin.

GREAT SPIRITS

Great spirits now on earth are sojourning.

(*Keats in a sonnet to Haydon*)

SOME TIME DURING the week of 13 October 1816, Keats walked up Hampstead Hill to Hunt's cottage in the Vale of Health, an elated young man still a few days short of his twenty-first birthday and chattering in his excitement. He was carrying with him the sheaf of poems he had recently copied out, and Clarke, who accompanied him, noted the intense animation of his features, that combination of ardour and physical attractiveness which, he recalled, sometimes caused people to turn their heads in the street.

As the two young men approached the Heath, 'there was the rising and accelerated step, with the gradual subsidence of all talk'[1]. Keats was about to meet the man who had been his hero since his early teens. Clarke himself knew what his friend could expect: gentle encouragement, probably, and Hunt's socially able combination of high-spirited talk and 'Spartan deference in attention'. Through these, provided he could respond in kind, Keats might begin to win himself a place in the social circles of literary London. When the introductions had been made, Hunt, susceptible to his guest's 'fine fervid countenance', was handed the sheaf of Keats's poems and settled himself to read.

While he did so, Keats was able to glance round Hunt's room and absorb its atmosphere, the bohemian clutter verging on chaos. There were books everywhere, on shelves, in piles on the floor, books spilling on to sofa tables and the seats of chairs. Where there was space, busts of poets and political heroes – Alfred, Sappho, Petrarch, Kosciusko – jostled with engravings of works by Claude, Poussin and the Italian masters: grand, quiescent worlds of Flora, Echo, Narcissus, and the father of Psyche sacrificing to Apollo. There were vases of flowers, a large piano, lockets containing the hair of friends or the illustrious dead, along with piles of manuscripts for the *Examiner* perched in such tottering disorder that, lost somewhere among them, was the fair copy of Shelley's *Hymn to Intellectual Beauty*. People, too, crowded the place: Hunt's long-suffering, slatternly wife and her children, her sister and cousins, along with a few domestic servants coming to attend to the first fire of autumn, the focus of Hunt's existence and the shrine of his household gods.

'Firesider' was a word he had himself coined to suggest that intimate but cultivated domestic world where, in the England of the years after Waterloo, he tried to protect his ideals by turning them into an idyll, an idyll of friendship and snug conviviality from which he could hope 'to promote the happiness of his kind, to minister to the more educated appreciation of order and beauty, to open more widely the door of the library, and more widely the window of the library looking out upon nature'.[2]

This was a philosophy of cheer maintained in despite of the facts. For some time after his imprisonment for libelling the Prince Regent, Hunt had been unable to attend the theatre because of the feeling of claustrophobia that engulfed him even in Byron's box at Drury Lane. This was easing now, but there were other fears to threaten him, chief among them, perhaps, the panic he felt if he was obliged to be too long in his own company. Hunt had an immense gift for friendship, and less critical admirers such as Clarke were delighted by his companionship and sat willing devotees to his sallies of wit and fancy, his puns and mimicking, his adroit conversation shot through with his broad knowledge and gift of recondite allusion. But others who were no less genuinely fond of him recognised how much of this was whistling in the dark, how much of this defiant happiness was the 'product of a painful, hypochondriac soul that struggles by dwelling on the *reverse* of its own *real* thoughts, perpetually to illumine its natural and forlorn dinginess'.[3]

Problems with money only aggravated this. Hunt had a growing family to support and his share of the £500 fine to pay off. He was often careless with what he earned and, while force of circumstance obliged him to over-work, he was quite incapable of combining calculation with application. Money was something that came and went, was spent, borrowed and later even scrounged against the hope of publishers' advances that sometimes had to be returned. A Byzantine complexity of intrigue and promises masked what was essentially a near childish naivety about money. The result was that Hunt's easily wounded feelings often turned to the sort of snarling abuse that merely alienated those with whom he dealt.

There is no doubt that Hunt could be an exasperating man. Even at his own fireside he could be pettily dictatorial, too reliant on uncritical admirers, and petulant when he felt slighted or was jostled from the centre stage by friends to whom a moment previously he had offered to devote his person and his talent. But what man ever won (and lost) such friends? At various times Hunt was the confidant of Byron and Shelley, Hazlitt and Lamb, men who admired and needed the stand he had taken, and who claimed to see the virtues in some of the poetry to which he was now increasingly devoting his time. In 1816 especially, Hunt was printing great amounts of his own work in the *Examiner* and, as so conspicuous a figure, he was moving into the position where he would become the entrepreneur to younger men of genius. Hunt's cottage in the Vale of Health during the winter of 1816 was a focus of literary endeavour rarely matched in English literary history.

All of this was in the immediate future. Now, as he put down the sheaf of poems he had been reading, he declared himself impressed 'by the exuberant specimens of genuine though young poetry that were laid before me'. He and Keats became 'intimate on the spot and', Hunt continued, 'I found the young poet's heart as warm as his imagination.'[4] Their first interview was rapidly followed by two more morning calls. Keats's poems, the sonnet on Chapman's Homer especially, were sent to such luminaries as Hazlitt and William Godwin, who read them with approval. Keats's hero had become his friend and, in Clarke's mildly over-enthusiastic phrase, he 'was suddenly made a familiar of the household'.

Such excitement greatly complicated the difficulties Keats was having with medicine. He had by now resolved against a career in surgery on purely conscientious grounds. Familiarity with the too frequent accidents in the operating theatre and an ability so to sympathise with suffering patients that he dreaded making similar mistakes himself barred him, he felt, from this career. 'My last operation', he later told a friend, 'was the opening of a man's temporal artery. I did it with the utmost nicety; but, reflecting on what passed through my mind at the time, my dexterity seemed a miracle, and I never took up the lancet again.'[5] The explanation has the flavour of real experience, but it is also clear that medicine itself could no longer hold Keats's active interest and that he felt the prospect of dogged, daily duty would damage him by its constrictions.

For the few weeks before his twenty-first birthday Keats did not have the power to make a decision to quit since technically he was still Abbey's ward. He would have to bide his time and test his resolve, but in gambling on his genius pragmatism evaporated. Keats recognised this and felt obliged to cover with a slightly defensive humour what to the merely sensible appeared youthful folly. 'The other day, for instance,' he told Clarke, 'during a lecture, there came a sunbeam into the room, and with it a whole troop of creatures floating in the ray; and I was off with them to Oberon and fairyland.'⁶ In fact, far from drifting into fantasy, Keats was now involving himself with some of the leading figures of London literary and artistic life, men who for all their heroic eccentricities would have been quick to reject a callow pretender. Far from doing this, they actively sought Keats's company.

The painter Benjamin Haydon, for example, currently taking a break in Hampstead from work on his vast canvas showing *Christ's Triumphal Entry into Jerusalem*, became a fast friend.⁷ In 1816, Haydon was close to the peak of his reputation. Now in his thirties, he was a broad-chested, short-legged man whose feet energetically stamped the ground as he walked and whose hair was cut short in front and long at the back in imitation of his adored Raphael. Haydon had vowed to make it his life's work to enhance the status of English art, and this he hoped to do by reinvigorating the traditions of history painting, the production of enormous canvases in which heroic subjects were presented in an idealised manner derived from the past masters of the European tradition. It was his involvement with the Elgin Marbles, however, that showed the force of Haydon's idealism and his depth of aesthetic appreciation.

Saved by Lord Elgin from certain ruin, these ancient masterpieces of Phideas had been stored first in Elgin's London home and then in a shed at the back of Burlington House while connoisseurs squabbled over their authenticity or merely ignored them. Haydon was the first artist to appreciate their splendours, what he saw as their matchless solution to the problem of an accurate yet idealised representation of the human body in action. He was also the first man to draw them. This he did sometimes for fourteen or fifteen hours at a time, while he held a candle aloft in the freezing damp.

Nonetheless, as the worth of the Marbles came to be more widely appreciated, Haydon himself was excluded from the committee appointed to investigate the possibility of purchasing them for the nation. Hating to be placed in any position less than eminent, Haydon published a long, passionate letter in the *Examiner* crying up the worth of the Marbles and denouncing the establishment for its pusillanimity. Satisfied with very small reason that this assault had won the day, he was now, at the time he met Keats, about to return to the unfinished *Triumphal Entry*. His own words best reveal his state of mind. 'The Academicians', he wrote,

> were silenced. In high life they dared not speak. All classes were so enthusiastic and so delighted that though I had lost seven months with weak eyes, and had only accomplished the penitent girl, the mother, the centurion, and the Samaritan woman, yet they were considered so decidedly in advance of all I had yet done, that my painting room was crowded by rank, beauty and fashion and the picture was literally taken up as an honour to the nation.[8]

It is too easy to dismiss Haydon as a tragic crank, a man forever backing into the limelight of his self-esteem. Great things were genuinely expected of him, but, if these expectations remained unfulfilled, Haydon was important to Keats in a number of less tangible ways. His hapless gigantism may now seem ridiculous, yet it offered Keats an image of the contemporary artist as a man who was not afraid to conduct his development by engaging with what were then naturally accepted as the great figures of the European canon, and to do so in a way that frankly accepted the difficulties of such a challenge. For all that Haydon was a barefaced sponger, he believed in an art produced by men who did not truckle with commercialism, and he was prepared to go hungry for his ideals. He was, besides, invariably generous to younger men he believed had real talent. He recognised such ability in Keats very early. Except for Wordsworth, he later wrote, 'Keats was the only man I ever met who seemed and looked conscious of a high calling.'[9]

His friendship with Hunt and Haydon greatly enhanced Keats's appreciation of the visual arts, and this in turn was to influence his poetry. Such a connection between poetry and painting was a long-standing convention, and the revered Latin tag *ut pictura poesis* – as is painting so is poetry – had been neatly explained a century before when Lord Shaftesbury affirmed that 'in a real history-painter, the same knowledge, the same study, and views, are required, as in a real poet.'[10] Haydon himself was a widely read man with an extensive knowledge of poetry, while he derived much of his acquaintance with earlier art from the engravings both he and Hunt collected. Hunt, in his turn, had been brought up in a visually literate family (his uncle was the painter Benjamin West) and he was a regular visitor to the print shops and galleries selling reproductions of the antique that were clustered around Marylebone Road and Golden Square.

Hunt's interest in the visual arts was inevitably a dilettante one, but much of his writing on the subject had the far from negligible aim of 'exciting a public feeling for art' in a period when access to old masters especially was not always easy. The National Gallery was established only in 1824, and the general public were obliged to rely for their acquaintance with older work on exhibitions mounted by the British Institution and on the generosity of private collectors. Hence the importance of engravings, works which now helped to expand the range of Keats's visual imagination.

The atmosphere in which this discovery took place was delightfully suggested by a passage of Hunt's journalism which portrays the 'firesider' as connoisseur. 'Here we are . . . with our fire before us, and our books on each side. What shall we do? Shall we take out a Life of somebody, or a Theocritus, or Dante, or Ariosto, or Montaigne, or Marcus Aurelius, or Horace, or Shakespeare who includes them all? Or shall we *read* an engraving from Poussin or Raphael?'[11] Such an easy breadth of culture is not insignificant, and the ready move from painting to poetry, both of them matters of 'reading' and hence of interpretation, is suggestive. Keats himself may well have heard Hunt declare that 'looking through the leaves of Spenser is like turning over a portfolio of prints from the old masters' and also been entertained by the analogies Hunt drew between stanzas of *The Fairie Queene* and the works of Titian, Correggio and Poussin.

Poussin, indeed, was an important influence, for he was the revered master of French academic classicism. This somewhat chilling phrase bore no such suggestions of austerity for the art lovers in the Vale of Health. Hazlitt openly confessed to weeping before Poussin's works in a state of 'luxurious enjoyment', and declared such pleasure to be 'the highest privilege of the mind of man'. This is revealing. Perhaps nowhere else is the ambience in which Keats was now moving more clearly expressed, its difference to the contemporary world more poignantly evident. Art is seen here – frankly enjoyed here – as an intensely emotional and sensuous pleasure which derives from its appeal to western man's greatest endeavours: his civilisation. The appreciation of art in such a view becomes a reasoned, intellectual, educated and, above all, humane activity, the highest function of the cultivated sensibility. 'Here is the mind's true home,' Hazlitt wrote. 'The contemplation of truth and beauty is the proper object for which we were created, which calls forth the most intense desires of the soul, and of which it never tires.'[12] Today, such words die on our lips. For Keats they were a pledge (in time a deeply ambivalent pledge) of human hope.

As Hazlitt himself declared, Poussin is 'the painter of ideas', and in *The Inspiration of the Poet*, combining reminiscences of Raphael with classical bas-reliefs, Poussin represents Apollo seated beneath a laurel tree. To the left stands Calliope, the Muse of Epic Poetry, while to the right stands the figure of the inspired poet. Above the poet floats a putto bearing laurel crowns, the evergreen symbol of immortal poetic achievement. To '*read*' the picture, in Hunt's phrase, is to see the divinely inspired epic poet as the servant of Apollo and the supreme fulfilment of humanity. This is also the iconography of Keats's ambition:

> Open afresh your round of starry folds,
> Ye ardent marigolds!
> Dry up the moisture from your golden lids,
> For great Apollo bids
> That in these days your praises should be sung
> On many harps, which he has lately strung . . .[13]

A new generation of poets, Keats suggests, will be inspired through nature by Apollo and will sing once again of the great primal myths of mankind. The laurel crown was the reward for such endeavours, and for Keats this now became that most potent of things, the symbol of his ambition for his own excellence. Nothing other than 'the proud laurel shall content my bier'. Unfortunately, members of the Hunt circle were in the habit of presenting actual laurel crowns to each other as little tokens of esteem, and in time a rift would open up between the high, Apollonian idealism of classical art and the pleasantries of the Hampstead literati. For the moment, however, Keats was happy to play the gallant 'To a Young Lady who sent me a Laurel Crown', writing her a complimentary sonnet.

But even now such classicism was not a vision that went uncriticised among the members of Hunt's circle. 'No man feels more acutely than myself the poetical beauties of the Pagan mythology,' wrote Haydon. 'Apollo, with his fresh cheek & God like beauty, rising like a gossamer from out a laurel grove, heated with love, after having panted on the bosom of some wandering nymph, is rich, beaming, rapturous!' Such open sexuality was a potentially dangerous matter, but this was not the substance of Haydon's objection. The delights of Apollo, he declared, 'are beauties fit for those who live in perpetual enjoyment of immortality, without a care or a grief, or a want. But what consolation to the poor, what relief to the widow & the orphan, to the sick, or the oppressed?'[14]

The objection was one whose seriousness Keats would himself face (it lies at the heart of his mature engagement with pagan mythology), but for Haydon such moral questioning derived from deep Christian conviction. To place a pagan mythology over against a faith in Christ was, he felt, to diminish the sufferings of humanity. For others, to place it over and against the established church was to challenge the structures of society and social control. Such disagreements point to the heated discussion on the nature of belief that raged through the Hampstead set in the winter of 1816, a discussion that was profoundly to influence Keats's attitude to the classical world of pagan myth, and to fuel the outrage felt by many reviewers when they found this world recreated in his poetry. Keats's dedication to Apollo was both profoundly serious and, in time, deeply challenging.

Meanwhile there were new friends to make, and it was during these early days of visiting the Vale of Health that Keats met John Hamilton Reynolds, a young man just a year older than himself to whom he was to confide some of his deepest thoughts about his art.[15] Although he was only twenty-two, Reynolds had known Hunt since the older man's time in prison and he was an intimate of Haydon's too. Far more precociously talented than Keats, he had published volumes of poetry imitative of Byron and Wordsworth, both of whom had taken a personal interest in his work. An attractive young man with strong, square-cut features, large eyes and an intelligent, slightly sardonic expression, his quick if derivative intelligence and beguilingly witty manner were allied to considerable ambition.

Reynolds had early learned the importance of playing the publicity game, printing poems and essays in journals and puffing his own work and that of friends. Having left school at fifteen, he had embarked on a strenuous course of self-education, teaching himself Greek and contributing papers to the Zetosophian Society, a group of fourteen young men 'of very considerable genius' who met, as their name suggested, to 'seek wisdom' by sharing their knowledge and company through the exchange of papers and the publication of a short-lived magazine. The Society itself had disbanded in acrimony a year before, and Reynolds was now advancing his career on his own. He had recently given up the drudgery of clerking with the Amicable Assurance Company, met the girl he later hoped to marry, and been appointed to the prestigious *Champion* to manage its theatre reviews, literary essays and poetry column. He was also one of the people to whom Hunt showed Keats's poems.

Reynolds was immediately aware of their promise and praised them warmly to Haydon. If this was a far-sighted judgement, it was based on more than youthful enthusiasm. Reynolds' opinions were those of the young avant-garde, and his essays from this productive period of his life show him to have possessed a deep and sure catholicity of taste. While he had an informed love of Chaucer, Spenser and Milton, it was Shakespeare who was for Reynolds the 'divinity of the world of imagination'.[16] Bardolatory was the common coinage of the Hunt circle, and, as the leaders of taste in every generation have to discover Shakespeare afresh, so Reynolds joined with those who now swept away an eighteenth-century quibbling over literary decorum to enjoy Shakespeare as the supreme 'anatomist of the human heart'.[17]

For Reynolds, Shakespeare's characters were real people motivated by a psychology it was the critic's duty to lay bare. Schlegel's *Lectures*, published the previous year in English translation, had helped direct this approach (Coleridge's ideas were unprinted and available to him only through hearsay), but as a critic it was Hazlitt whom Reynolds imitated with a soundness of discipleship Keats too was soon to acquire. Indeed, Keats's own development towards becoming one of the greatest readers of Shakespeare was something Reynolds watched with deepening admiration. For himself, despite the volume of his own achievements, he remained uncertain of his real worth, but he had both the discrimination and the generosity of spirit to recognise Keats's genius. 'Do *you* get Fame,' he wrote later, '– and I shall have it by being your affectionate and steady friend.'[18]

In such company, Keats's poetry could blossom along with his gift for friendship. He had come across people among whom he could mature. A sonnet from this time, written according to Clarke 'on the day after one of our visits' to Hunt, idealises this mood, contrasting the 'half leafless' chill of night-time London in early winter to Hunt's cottage 'brimful of . . . friendliness' and poetry.[19] There is a knowledge of isolation and loneliness here as Keats presents himself leaving this place of serene content and walking the five cold miles back to his lodgings. The candlelight and conversation, the Poussin prints and books of poetry are behind him. Outside such warmth, as he descends Hampstead Hill, he imagines himself as an increasingly insubstantial figure while Hunt's distant cottage becomes the symbol of those high ideals for art represented by Milton, Petrarch and, by extension, Hunt himself. The sonnet is a bid for admission into something seen as established, bountiful and true.

Amid so much stimulation, Keats's brothers remained a steadying influence, and by the middle of November all three young men were reunited in lodgings they took at 76 Cheapside. Here, Keats himself was away from the squalor of the Borough but still within easy reach of Guy's. He was also a little closer to the Vale of Health, where, when evenings ran on, a bed was made up for him on a sofa. Cheapside was convenient in other ways too. Cooked food could be ordered from the Queen's Arms eating house round the corner in Bird-in-Hand Court, while Abbey's office, where George was still employed, was also close by.

On the surface at least, this bachelor household seemed quite comfortably off. Keats himself was the beneficiary of trust funds, and the apparent availability of money could be used as a shield to protect him from the sharp spasms of insecurity, the half-suppressed memories of family trauma, that afflicted him whenever he had to face money matters squarely. This was something he usually tried to avoid, and such forced diffidence obscured from him the full details of his situation. Keats was thereby placed in a false position which, later and tragically, propelled him into a desperation about money which need never have arisen. Even now, Keats failed to get sound advice or even a proper view of the facts, which should have become clear after the delay in proving he had come of age.

At twenty-one, Keats stood to inherit the residue of the trust fund set up for him by his grandmother.[20] This had been much reduced by the expenses of his medical training but, unknown to him and, it seems, to Abbey as well, there was an additional fund of about £800 left by his grandfather and still accumulating interest in Chancery. The family solicitor failed to advise Keats of the existence of this second fund, and, when Keats himself cashed in what remained of his grandmother's money, it seemed he was living off his capital and was obliged to keep up appearances, which he gradually came to think he could not afford. For the moment, his casualness about money suggested to his friends the existence of funds, while his apparently bland acceptance of the whole position points to his reluctance to have anything to do with matters that touched the insecurities of his childhood.

This underlying struggle also contributed to the depressions that still afflicted him, moods made worse perhaps by the inertia of creative fatigue. Drained of the radiance that drew his friends to him, Keats lustrous eyes darkened as if 'consumed by some secret and fatal anguish'. He would sit brooding alone, coldly intense or lashing out at real and imagined slights until they became 'a theme for Sophocles'. The barely suppressed, irrational spite of such moods, humiliating and disfiguring although it was, was something all who knew him were aware of. That it rarely alienated them for long is a tribute to Keats's warmth on other occasions, and suggests how important the company of his brothers could be in offering that quiet affection he needed for support. Keats himself was aware of this and never mentioned it without gratitude.

Such gratitude informs the sonnet he wrote for Tom on his youngest brother's seventeenth birthday. The quiet domestic circle gathered round the fire, probably in their Cheapside lodgings, is a pledge of affection and that cultured domesticity constantly urged by Hunt as a stay against a hostile world. Tom, lost in a book, is Keats's emotional anchor as his own volatile mind searches 'around the poles' of his imagination for rhymes.[21] The concluding quatrain seems, at first, a conventional expression of the hope that such quiet occasions will be enjoyed for years to come. What was poignant was that Keats was already concerned about his brother's frail health.

Such swings of mood, along with the stimulation Keats was now deriving from his busy social life, are suggested by the fact that on the evening following the completion of the sonnet Keats attended a gathering at Haydon's. Keats had dined with the painter for the first time, along with Reynolds, at Haydon's temporary lodgings in Hampstead soon after the three met. At the beginning of November he also attended a breakfast Haydon threw in his studio at 41 Great Marlborough Street, sending a letter to Clarke in which he promised to be 'as punctual as the Bee to the Clover – Very glad I am at the thought of seeing this glorious Haydon and all his Creation.' The musical pun is a Huntism, and when Keats arrived, having spent the previous day in the countryside 'to look into some beautiful Scenery – for poetical purposes', it was in the elated knowledge that the *Examiner* had that day promised to publish his 'Chapman's Homer'.[22] Now, however, as he entered Haydon's cramped lodgings – merely a room and a boxroom, fetid with the smell of turpentine, cooking and unchanged bed-linen – he almost certainly encountered Hazlitt, who was sitting for the portrait that was to be included in the *Triumphal Entry*.

As so often, Haydon's pen was shrewder than his brush, and he wrote of Hazlitt's 'sunken & melancholy face, – a forehead lined with thought and bearing a full & strange pulsation on exciting subjects, – an eye, dashed in its light with sorrow, but kindling & *living* at intellectual moments, – and a stream of coal-black hair dropping round all'.[23] The critic himself was hunched over a bottle of Haydon's wine, while the artist, three pairs of powerfully diminishing concave spectacles perched on his head, painted with his weak eyes close to the canvas or ran forward to peer at Hazlitt and then, having checked the balance of his work in a mirror, once again climbed his steps to work.

Hazlitt meanwhile talked: talked of 'the early part of his life, acknowledged his own weaknesses and follies', and then discoursed on the inept painting and trivial, vindictive time-serving of the Royal Academicians. Their determination to vilify the old masters recently exhibited at the British Institution was at one, it seemed, with the apostasy of Wordsworth, Coleridge and Southey and, indeed, the whole larger world of reactionary politics, that world which, as Hazlitt knew, so insidiously seduced even the most upright man 'while the cause of despotism flourishes, triumphs, and is irresistible in the gross mixture, the *Belle Alliance*, of pride and ignorance'.[24]

The imaginative freedom these men felt was offered by poetry appeared infinitely precious, and when Keats again visited Haydon on 19 November the artist was clearly in great form. A previous meeting had been postponed so that Haydon could attend a performance of *Timon of Athens* at Drury Lane, but now his conversation ranged so widely over literature and the arts that, as Keats declared the following morning, it 'wrought me up'. The result was the sonnet 'Great spirits now on earth are sojourning'. Here, Wordsworth, Hunt and Haydon, along with unnamed 'other spirits' who are probably meant to suggest Reynolds, Shelley and Keats himself, are praised as the men who 'will give the World another heart'. Once more, art is seen as a way of rising above the constraints of circumstance, and Haydon responded enthusiastically, suggesting a modification to the sonnet's penultimate line and then making a promise which bowled the young man over. 'The idea of your sending it to Wordsworth', he told Haydon, 'put me out of breath – you know with what Reverence – I would send my Wellwishes to him'.

In fact, Haydon delayed sending the sonnet, but the nature of Keats's debt to Wordsworth at this time is suggested by 'I stood tip-toe', the poem whose details he had recently gone to research in the countryside. As the abandoned introduction to a retelling of the classical love story of Endymion and Cynthia, the goddess of the moon, 'I stood tip-toe' develops Keats's interest in the relation between nature, myth and art explored earlier in the epistle 'To my Brother George'. Such ideas were now given greater weight by Keats's reading of Wordsworth's *Excursion*.

This was the immense poem by which Wordsworth hoped to claim the attention of the small band of his contemporaries who read his work. The fourth Book was of particular interest to Keats since it is an account of how the spirits of the Solitary, a man disillusioned by the moral and political failure of the French Revolution, are slowly reanimated by the Wanderer, who tells him how the beauties of the natural world, nourishing the subjectivity of 'the unenlightened swains of pagan Greece', encouraged them towards an animism which saw the whole world as alive with intimations of the divine.[25] 'Fancy' figured Apollo in the sun and Cynthia in the moon.

Such passages from this now rarely studied poem suggest Wordsworth's appreciation of the solace these moments seemed to offer in a world that is 'too much with us', but they also show his recognition of the irrecoverable distance between the resources of ancient paganism and modern man. In so doing, Wordsworth pointed to a fundamental problem in the attempt to revive classical myth: the fact that the burden of contemporary life lies partly in its insistence on the pastness of the past, its irrecoverability. For Wordsworth, a revived paganism could be at best a beguiling fantasy. Keats for the moment was not sufficiently mature to appreciate the pathos of this, and 'I stood tip-toe' is in part an attempt to refute Wordsworth's position. Keats suggests that, under the tutelage of Apollo, the truly modern poet has, like his ancient forebears depicted by Wordsworth, a subjective response to nature which can indeed give him access to the timeless storehouse of myth, a storehouse whose contents can be refashioned through art to solace the sickened spirits of the time.

Like so much of Keats's earliest verse, 'I stood tip-toe' is a manifesto, a declaration of intent rather than an actual achievement. The idea that the true poet is inspired by nature to fashion beautiful and consoling stories is repeatedly insisted upon, yet the fact that there is something willed about this belief is suggested by the way in which Keats's own passages of description veer wildly between simple, effective observation and that cloying mannerism whereby natural objects become poeticised into *objets de luxe*, gee-gaws to decorate what Keats himself regrettably calls a 'tasteful nook'. This is Huntian artifice at its most artificial, and it obtrudes unpleasantly on those passages such as the description of the evening breezes healing the sick where Keats's mythopoeic imagination is altogether more assured.

If 'I stood tip-toe' suggests that Keats's involvement with myth was still immature, Hunt himself was pleased with his pupil's progress. On 1 December, the *Examiner* carried an article entitled 'Young Poets' in which he praised the three figures who, it seemed to him, 'promise a considerable addition of strength to the new school' of poetry, that school which Hunt believed would soon replace the allegedly over-contrived one of Pope with 'the same love of Nature, and of *thinking* instead of *talking*, which formerly rendered us real poets'. First came praise of Shelley (along with an excuse for mislaying his manuscript), and then qualified praise of Reynolds, whose name he got wrong. Finally, Hunt turned his attention to 'the last of these young aspirants', and the youngest of them all. 'His name is JOHN KEATS. He has not yet published anything except in a newspaper, but a set of his manuscripts was handed to us the other day, and fairly surprised us with the truth of their ambition, and ardent grappling with Nature.' The article then reprinted, along with an amendment that was later adopted, a version of the sonnet on Chapman's Homer.

The effect on Keats was decisive. He had been publicly acknowledged as a poet in the vanguard of his time and, in the words of his former room-mate Henry Stephens, 'this sealed his fate and he gave himself up more completely than before to Poetry.' His future path seemed assured, and when Hunt wrote him a sonnet in which he declared he could foresee 'a flowering laurel' on Keats's brow it seemed that his dedication to Apollo was complete.

In such a mood of exultant self-confidence, Keats felt able to face the inevitable meeting with his guardian. Although the precise date of this is not recorded, Abbey himself vividly remembered the incident many years later. He had apparently recommended that Keats set up in practice near Edmonton, 'but his Surprise was not moderate, to hear in Reply, that he did not intend to be a Surgeon'.[26] Abbey asked Keats what he proposed to do instead. He was told: 'I mean to rely on my Abilities as a Poet.' To a businessman devoid of literary tastes and a guardian who had authorised the spending of considerable quantities of his ward's money on medical training, this seemed merely absurd. Keats's answer to Abbey's protests, strong and self-confident as it is, sounds as if it may have been recalled verbatim: 'My Mind is made up, said the youngster very quietly. I know that I possess Abilities greater than most Men, and therefore I am determined to gain my Living by exercising them.' All the bewildered Abbey felt able to do when faced with such resolve was mutter 'Silly Boy' and prophesy a quick end to such a plan.

Despite this determination to pursue his vocation as a poet, Keats continued to walk the wards at Guy's for some months. He was, nonetheless, as often to be found in the company of his new friends. On 15 December, for example, he met Reynolds at Haydon's studio and invited him to a party he and his brothers were holding two days later at their lodgings. While no details are preserved of the party itself, Keats's behaviour among his friends when the conversation turned from poetry and the arts is suggested by two anecdotes recalled by Clarke.

At some time during this period, Clarke was suffering from a minor stomach ailment and turned to Keats for advice. The diagnosis delighted him. Just as in his interview with Abbey Keats had shown a characteristic quiet resolve, so now he talked:

> with a remarkable decision of opinion, describing the function and actions of the organ with the clearness and, as I presume, technical precision of an adult practitioner; casually illustrating the comment, in his characteristic way, with poetical imagery: the stomach, he said, being like a brood of callow nestlings (opening his capacious mouth) yearning and gaping for sustenance; and, indeed, he merely exemplified what should be, if possible, the 'stock in trade' of every poet, viz., to *know* all that is to be known, 'in the heaven above, or in the earth beneath, or in the waters under the earth'.[27]

Keats himself would come to recognise the importance of such knowledge in stabilising and maturing the intellect, but what Clarke's rather schoolmasterly comment tends to obscure is Keats's vivacity and spontaneity, the alert and precise workings of his imagination, and his gift for humour and friendship.

These are qualities brought out in Clarke's second anecdote, which is perhaps even more valuable since it suggests a side of Keats which can be too easily obscured by a concentration on his purely intellectual interests. Clarke tells how Keats had gone to see a bear-baiting, an occasion which sets Keats firmly in the ambience of Regency London. Such occasions (which were not prohibited by law until 1835) encouraged Keats's relish of the grotesque. He gave Clarke a description of the foolishness of one of the audience but, Clarke added, 'his concurrent personification of the baiting, with his position – his legs and arms bent and shortened till he looked like Bruin on his hind legs, dabbing his fore paws hither and thither, as the dogs snapped at him, and now and then acting the gasp of one that had been suddenly caught and hugged – his own capacious mouth adding force to the persona-tion, was a remarkable . . . display'.

This image of a young man clowning for his friends, stomping over the carpet at what may have been one of his bachelor parties, a somewhat bibulous occasion perhaps and one without the company of respectable women, is an endearing one. Reynolds was certainly becoming firmly attached to Keats and was now determined to introduce him to others of his acquaintance and to his family, who had recently moved to 19 Lamb's Conduit Street. Keats was to visit here often, encouraged by the warm reception Mrs Reynolds always extended to her son's friends.

Mrs Reynolds was herself a talkative (sometimes an over-talkative) and forceful woman, devoted to her more retiring schoolmaster husband and, above all, to her children, whom she managed as firmly as she did the rest of her household, sometimes censoring her son's letters when he was a boy and reprimanding her four daughters for affectation and silliness.[28] Beneath her occasional bossiness however lay real affection. '"Dame Reynolds" is an old fashioned creature firm in love to her family,' she wrote, and something of this love was now extended to her son's new and motherless young friend. Such a warm family atmosphere was surely welcome and was made more attractive by the presence of the Reynolds girls. Twenty-six-year-old Jane had, in addition to her lively sense of humour, 'an exquisite taste both for Music and Poetry particularly the former in which she was exceedingly skilful'. She, and the younger Charlotte, would play the piano for Keats and sing to him, while Marianne, reckoned the most beautiful of the children and a girl patient and decided in character, was the favourite of George. The girls dutifully copied some of their new friend's poems into their albums, but no introduction to the Reynolds circle would have been complete without at least hearing of their acquaintance Benjamin Bailey.

An erstwhile Zetosophian who had introduced himself to that group with an essay in Spenserian stanzas on the progress of learning, Bailey was now training at Oxford for the church. After looking elsewhere, he would soon also be undergoing a protracted courtship of Marianne Reynolds. Such activities gave Bailey a status in Lamb's Conduit Street that was perhaps beyond his deserts. John Reynolds regarded him as a martyr triumphant over adversity and a future pillar of the church, while the women of the family were happy to drag Bailey's name into the conversation whenever they could. 'If you mentioned the word Tea pot – some one of them came out with an a propos about Bailey – noble fellow – fine fellow!' At the close of 1816, Keats had yet to meet the man himself, but their acquaintance was prepared by a glowing letter sent to Oxford by Reynolds at the time of the party.

While such social occasions served their turn, intellectual debate in Hampstead was working its influence, and Keats's relationship with conventional Christianity especially was now in the process of being radically criticised. His schooling had given him a firm grounding in the basic tenets of belief and this knowledge shows itself in his familiarity with the Bible and in a letter he wrote to his sister when she was preparing for her confirmation. He was, besides, surrounded by people who had an active faith. For all his attacks on the evident weaknesses of the Anglican church, Reynolds was a believer, while Haydon was an exceptionally devout man. The *Triumphal Entry* was his most grandiloquent expression of this and, some time during December 1816, he prepared his famous life mask of Keats as a means of including his young friend among that crowd of figures who are portrayed staring at their Redeemer with wonder and devotion.

Keats's own beliefs, however, were rapidly diverging from Haydon's, and at the close of the month, three days before Christmas itself, he composed a sonnet in which his irritation with conventional faith was outspoken. The poem was written in a mere fifteen minutes (a habit picked up from the Hunt circle where such sonnet-writing competitions were rather too frequent) but its content is evidently sincere. For Keats, the melancholy tolling of the church bells rings out as a summons to gloom, to 'dreadful cares' and an endless round of sermons. Far from being a call to redemption, the bells suggest that mankind is the victim of a 'black spell', an enchantment which lures him away from the true and civilised exchange of friendship and the reading of poetry. The repetitious tolling, Keats suggests, would be like death to him did he not know that the bells are sounding for the passing of the very belief they supposedly proclaim: ''tis their sighing, wailing ere they go.' What will replace their tuneless monotony, he suggests, is the religion of poetry celebrated in his own work. The strident title of the sonnet, 'Written in Disgust of Vulgar Superstition', suggests the influence of the anti-Christian attitudes harboured by some in the Hunt circle and, in particular, the conversation of a new member who had burst suddenly and exhilaratingly into their midst: Percy Bysshe Shelley.

Keats had first encountered Shelley when the older poet had called on Hunt earlier in the month. The wealthy Horace Smith was also there, but while Keats was keen to make the acquaintance of Smith, the banker was altogether more interested in meeting the newcomer whose works he had recently read.[29] He was rewarded with the immediate friendship of an aristocratic but boyish figure, expensively dressed, gracious, scholarly and able with terrifying speed to turn his vast reading to the destruction of any position which seemed to uphold the traditional injustices of religion, politics or sexual morality. Keats, less evidently of the gentry and much less well read, was, it seems, pushed into the background. And it was from this position, on the edge, withdrawn, observing and self-protective, that he was to allow Shelley's influence to work on him. Throughout, there was public reserve and diffidence on Keats's part, but also an intense curiosity. The two poems Shelley delivered to Hunt, the new copy of the *Hymn to Intellectual Beauty* and the manuscript of *Alastor*, were naturally of the greatest interest to Keats, a revelation of Shelley's alarming intellectual power and achievement. So too was the vigorous and dangerous conversation that ensued when Shelley returned to Hunt's cottage on 16 December.

Shelley himself was now immersed in the most profound and cruel drama of his life. Before his earlier visit to Hunt he had announced himself as 'an outcast from human society', a position that events were hurrying to confirm. Unknown to him, and on the very day of his first visit, the inquest was being held on the death of his estranged wife, whose body had been found floating in the Serpentine. Her suicide, wrote Hunt, 'tore his being to pieces'. Now, in anguish, Shelley returned to London, lashing out at his sister-in-law and promising marriage to his long-term companion Mary Godwin. He was also fighting in Chancery for the custody of his children by his first marriage, who, through a legal fiction, were petitioning for the appointment of a guardian on the grounds that their father was not only immoral but an atheist.

In this maelstrom of misery, it seemed that the united forces of a corrupt society, an oppressive state and a bigoted church were joined as Shelley's enemies. Now, in the violently radical talk of this London winter, personal and national wrongs seemed to coincide, for this was a season of bitter discontent. In October, the ironworkers of Tredegar had marched on the works at Merthyr Tydfil and then, swollen to a force of 12,000, had crossed the mountains to call out the miners. There were mass meetings in Manchester, Glasgow and Paisley. Penny-a-week Hampden Clubs met across the land and, fired by Cobbett's *Political Register*, debated manhood suffrage and the possibility of annual parliaments. By the middle of November, a vast and angry crowd met in Spa Fields, London, to be told by the orator Henry Hunt that their taxes were going to pay the bastards of Tory landowners and that their petition to the Prince Regent was 'the last resort before physical force'. A second mass meeting in December ended in looting and a skirmish with the Life Guards, while Shelley himself wrote to Byron claiming that the outcome of the next Parliament would be either wholesale reform or the triumph of anarchy.

While Shelley himself loathed contemporary Christianity, he saw the historical Jesus as a radical egalitarian whose doctrines of reform were so profound that, were they put into action, 'no political or religious institution could subsist a moment'. Such was the conversation of the figure whom Keats now met at a dinner party, delicately picking at his vegetarian platter and twitting Haydon as he began in his light but sweeping voice: 'As to that detestable religion, the Christian religion . . .' The party itself was hosted by Horace Smith at his home in Knightsbridge and, along with Shelley, Haydon and Keats himself, the guests included Hunt, his wife and his sister-in-law. When Haydon saw the look of delight on Hunt's face as Shelley began talking, he realised he had been set up, but it was only after the servant had gone that some of the company began a vehement argument. Keats, Haydon noted, sat quietly on the side and listened while Shelley and Haydon argued about whether Shakespeare was a Christian or a deist and whether or not the Christian and Mosaic dispensations were inconsistent.

Haydon was deeply offended by the occasion and regarded it as the climax of his long disagreement with the Hunt circle over matters of religion. 'I have known Hunt for 10 years,' he wrote later, 'during which we have scarcely ever met without a contest about Christianity.'[30] Despite Haydon's strictures, Hunt was not a man immune to the importance of belief. His ideas evolved slowly and shiftingly, yet he never abandoned the notion that 'religion is as natural to man as the sight of the stars, and the sense of a power greater than his own.'[31] What he loathed, and what he encouraged readers of the *Examiner* to disparage, were the repressive and vindictive manifestations of contemporary Christianity.

There was much evidence for these. Abroad, the Pope had been restored, Roman Catholicism was re-established in France, the Inquisition had been reintroduced to Spain, while the rulers of Russia, Prussia and Austria had banded into a Holy Alliance as 'defenders of the Christian religion'. At home, the bishops of the

Anglican High Church party proudly proclaimed themselves leaders of the one sure institution which had held the country together in its successful fight against continental anarchy. The Low Church Evangelicals, meanwhile, interspersed their undoubted good works with a fascination for hell-fire and damnation. Hunt spoke out boldly in reply: 'Bigotry itself must be destroyed; religious dogmatism must be destroyed. Foolish and violent men must no longer be suffered to palm their bad and vindictive passions on Heaven; nor must the Divine Being be supposed capable of acting upon the most half-witted and savage principles.'[32]

Hunt's use of the phrase 'Divine Being' suggests where his own sympathies lay: with the philosophers of the Enlightenment and a deism free from narrow prescription, ritual and mortification. 'The praise which God requires from creatures no greater than ourselves, is to love one another; to delight ourselves in his works; to advance in knowledge; and to thank him, when we are moved to do so, from the bottom of our hearts.'[33] Here was a form of belief at one with Hunt's philosophy of cheer, and in his *Examiner* articles and *Foliage*, the volume of poems he was working on at this time, he looked to the past for an ideal of religion altogether more liberal and humane than that which seemed to engulf Regency England. In Haydon's words: 'Leigh Hunt says he prefers infinitely the beauties of Pagan Mythology to the gloomy repentance of the Christians.'[34] Hunt felt confident that all true poets responded at their best to his view of pagan Greece. Shakespeare, although 'not a scholar', had a just and instinctive appreciation of its merits. 'Milton, when he was young and happy, wrote Grecian Mythology in his Lycidas and Comus.'[35] Now, he claimed, the new generation of poets, led by Keats and Shelley, showed a similar appreciation of the beautiful and the good.

To support this, he could cite a long poem recently completed by Keats: *Sleep and Poetry*. Here the influence of Hunt and his circle is seen at its broadest and most beneficial. Indeed, the reverie around which the work is constructed is imagined as taking place in Hunt's library, and the 'art garniture' of the room, its books, busts and prints, help suggest the atmosphere of liberal politics and high cultural endeavour in which Keats examines his vocation. In particular, a reproduction of another picture by Poussin, *The Realm of Flora*, provides the imagery by which a very young man, excited by the vista of his own growing up, imagines for himself his own poetic role. Just as Poussin portrays the beautiful but mortal garden of earthly delights presided over by the charioteer of the sun, so Keats's poem suggests his own progress from a somewhat coy and cloying world of adolescent male sexual fantasy towards an altogether more challenging vision of Apollo himself. The god descends to earth and, for the poet, nature becomes animated with:

> Shapes of delight, of mystery, and fear,
> Passing along before a dusky space
> Made by some mighty oaks: as they would chase
> Some ever-fleeting music on they sweep.
> Lo! how they murmur, laugh, and smile, and weep –
> Some with upholden hand and mouth severe;
> Some with their faces muffled to the ear
> Between their arms; some, clear in youthful bloom,
> Go glad and smilingly athwart the gloom;
> Some looking back, and some with upward gaze;
> Yes, thousands in a thousand different ways
> Flit onward . . .[36]

Accurately reflecting what would indeed be the process of Keats's development, innocent boyish sexuality matures to a vision of human life in which the exultation of poetry is profoundly involved with the deeper mysteries of existence.

Throughout these sections of the poem, Keats uses religious imagery stripped of its Christian associations. In a world where politics had become associated with repression and traditional faith with a denial of joy, poetry is evoked as a means of purification, something 'awful, sweet, and holy' that chases 'worldliness' away and offers both an immortality of fame and a means of celebration. An image of the poet is being fashioned as the man who can assume the burden of preserving the aspirations of humanity in all their freshness. Prayers to Apollo suggest the depth of the would-be poet's devotion, yet his strenuous ambition and aching for transcendence are constantly threatened by his sense of his own youthful unworthiness and his knowledge of the evanescence of divine revelation itself.

Apollo vanishes as suddenly as he came and leaves the poet with an oppressive 'sense of real things'. The poet's imaginative excitement fades in a premonition of the mature knowledge of the odes: of the nightingale fluttering away into the next valley and the Grecian urn returning to its coldly marmorial self. And, just as there are dangers within, so there is the threat of 'schism' from without. In a passage that was to bring down the wrath of the reviewers, Keats, borrowing heavily from Hunt and Hazlitt, excoriates the Augustan school of Pope and his followers as men who have blasphemed against Apollo and the true traditions of poetry upheld by the Elizabethans and, Keats suggests, by his own better contemporaries. This is the tradition which sees poetry as the visionary and healing gift of Apollo which serves:

> To soothe the cares, and lift the thoughts of man.

Poetry has here taken on many of the functions traditionally ascribed to religion, but such a commitment could not be a neutral matter. Christianity was the legally established religion of the country, and even an implied criticism of its values was potentially subversive.[37] Myth, however, gave the Hunt circle a means of developing ideas about natural religion and arguing for a joyfully natural and non-ascetic sexual ethic to place against the constraints of conventional Christian morality. Keats would develop this in his own way.

Here, honed nightly around Hunt's fireside, was the radical edge of contemporary literary thought, and while the country at large was plunged into ever deeper repression (in January 1817 *habeas corpus* was suspended after an attack on the Prince Regent) Keats and his acquaintances were advancing ideas of beauty and truth to set against a society of almost unbearable constraint. It is against this background that Keats was now gathering his poems together for his own first volume.

A surprising degree of reticence surrounds the preparation of this book. Clarke may have introduced Keats to his publishers, Charles and James Ollier, and Hunt's article 'Young Poets' no doubt helped to whet their appetite for issuing the works of a writer who was otherwise largely unknown. Keats himself, however, maintained a remarkable silence about this crucial and exciting event in his career. Such diffidence may in part have sprung from his knowledge that of necessity this would be a slim volume. A number of sonnets, written in December, helped to bulk it out, but, with the possible exception of 'On the Grasshopper and the Cricket', none of these is a work of any great merit.

Indeed, Keats must have realised that much of the verse he was going to print was juvenilia. Shelley had gone so far as to hint at this on one of the walks he took with Keats across Hampstead Heath, when he had tried to persuade him to delay publication until he had something more substantial to offer. This advice was not taken, and it is suggestive of the self-protective attitude Keats adopted in the face of his great contemporary that he also turned down Shelley's invitation to spend the summer with him at Marlow in order 'that I might have my own unfettered scope'. This was no doubt a wise move, and suggests that Keats had a sense of the threat that would be posed to his talent were he to be recruited into this circle of extreme intellects. Nonetheless, although Shelley himself and his new wife left London at the end of February, his continuing influence over Keats was felt in two ways. Both poets, it seems, agreed to write their next works, long poems of several thousand lines, in friendly competition. It was also probably Shelley's opinion of his early work that caused Keats to add a late explanatory note to his volume: 'The Short Pieces in the middle of the Book, as well as some of the Sonnets, were written at an earlier period than the rest of the Poems.'

There was, however, one addition still to be made. The final pages of the proof were delivered to Keats during a party at his lodgings in Cornhill where he was told that if he wished to print a dedicatory poem he would have to offer it to the printer immediately. In Clarke's words, Keats 'drew to a side-table, and in the buzz of a mixed conversation . . . he composed and brought to Charles Ollier, the publisher, the Dedication Sonnet to Leigh Hunt. If the original manuscript of that poem – a legitimate sonnet, with every restriction of rhyme and metre – could now be produced, and the time recorded in which it was written, it would be pronounced an extraordinary performance: added to which the non-alteration of a single word in the poem (a circumstance that was noted at the time) claims for it a merit with a very rare parallel.'[38]

Glory and loveliness have passed away;
   For if we wander out in early morn,
   No wreathed incense do we see upborne
Into the east, to meet the smiling day:
No crowd of nymphs soft voiced and young, and gay,
   In woven baskets bringing ears of corn,
   Roses, and pinks, and violets, to adorn
The shrine of Flora in her early May.
But there are left delights as high as these,
   And I shall ever bless my destiny,
That in a time when under pleasant trees
   Pan is no longer sought, I feel a free,
A leafy luxury, seeing I could please
   With these poor offerings, a man like thee.

The sonnet suggests that what remained amid the uncertainties of the modern world was friendship, and now, on 1 March when advance copies of the *Poems* became available, bound in grey boards and priced at six shillings, Keats's first impulse was to present his book to Hunt. By coincidence, the two men met by the Hampstead Ponds and Keats was invited back to Hunt's cottage for supper. Since it was a beautiful spring evening, they went into the garden after their meal to talk and drink their wine. It was a convention in the Hunt circle to present successful poets with chaplets of laurel leaves, and a high-spirited Hunt now wove one for Keats and placed it on his brow as a symbol of his ordination as the priest of Apollo. Keats, for his part, replied by weaving for Hunt a wreath of ivy.

There followed, almost inevitably, a sonnet-writing competition. Hunt actually managed to complete two poems, but as Keats, usually so fluent, struggled to complete his own frankly derivative effort, he and Hunt were interrupted by a group of women, the sisters perhaps of Reynolds. Hunt, in an effort not to look ridiculous, snatched the crown from off his own head, while Keats obstinately kept his on as he wrote a still poorer sonnet 'To the Ladies who Saw Me Crowned'. He was trying to save face. After all, on the surface the whole incident was nothing more than a piece of harmless foolery. But Keats's temporary difficulty in producing sonnets to order is suspicious and points perhaps to a feeling that something more serious was amiss. He had just presented his first volume to his master and his master had responded in a manner that he now saw hid under its charm a deep spiritual vulgarity. Keats had been inveigled into making Apollo merely a trifle in a party game. He later recognised that he had blasphemed his deepest beliefs through triviality:

> Where – where slept thine ire,
> When like a blank idiot I put on thy wreath,
> Thy laurel, thy glory,
> The light of thy story,
> Or was I a worm – too low-creeping, for death?
> O Delphic Apollo.[39]

It is not an exaggeration to say that Keats felt all the self-disgust of a man who knows he has sinned, and the laurel-crowning episode marks the first rift in his friendship with Hunt, the first sign that he had outgrown him.

As if in expiation, Keats went the following day with Haydon to see the Elgin Marbles. Perhaps the petit-bourgeois world of Hunt would be absolved in the presence of classic grandeur. Haydon himself, still bruised from his encounter with Shelley, was conducting a campaign to woo Keats away from what he considered the dangerous inadequacies of the Hunt clique and he was determined his protégé should continue his education in solitude or in the presence of what he himself felt to be the truly great. Keats's sonnet to Haydon on the Elgin Marbles tries to suggest this feeling for 'mighty things' by contrasting an apparent inability to write justly of the Marbles with Haydon's own profound appreciation of their worth. The true subject of both sonnets thus becomes less the immediate effect of great art itself than the ardent poet's reflection on the challenge such grandeur poses him.

This was precisely the response Haydon hoped to rouse, and he had no sooner read over the copies of the two sonnets sent to him than he wrote a hurried note of congratulation: 'You filled me with fury for an hour, and with admiration for ever.' Then, feeling that even such praise as this was perhaps insufficient, Haydon tore open his letter and added a second note saying how 'deeply' he felt 'the high enthusiastic praise' with which Keats had written of the artist himself. This excited mutual regard was perfectly sincere, and it is not without significance that it was Haydon rather than Hunt who now, on 3 March, threw the party that was to launch Keats's *Poems* on the world.

The loyal Reynolds at once reviewed the volume in over-en-thusiastic terms for the *Champion*, claiming that a young genius had emerged whose ability to sing 'from the pure inspiration of nature' would cause him to eclipse all his contemporaries and 'lay his name in the lap of immortality'. Nonetheless, despite 'the cheers and fond anticipation of all his circle' (Hunt, it must be said, was too preoccupied with the suspension of *habeas corpus* to notice the work in the *Examiner* for four months), the commercial failure of Keats's first volume was almost immediately apparent. Haydon wrote to him a reassuring note about his hopes for *Sleep and Poetry*, but it was left to Clarke, writing nearly sixty years after the event, to express a just sense of dismay. 'Every one of us', he wrote, 'expected (and not unreasonably) that it would create a sensation in the literary world; for such a first production (and a considerable portion of it from a minor) has rarely occurred.' What happened was quite the reverse. 'Alas! the book might have emerged in Timbuctoo with far stronger chance of fame and approbation. It never passed a second edition; the first was but a small one, and that was never sold off. The whole community, as if by compact, seemed determined to know nothing about it.'[40]

But there was one more insult to endure. The failed book appeared exactly a year after Keats paid his fees to complete his medical training.

Perhaps in the hope of proving to Abbey that he could indeed achieve something, Keats gave his erstwhile guardian another of his presentation copies. The inevitable response was heavy-handed philistinism. 'Well John I have read your Book, & it reminds me of the Quaker's Horse which was hard to catch, & good for nothing when he was caught – So your Book is hard to understand & good for nothing when it is understood.'[41] Still proud of the joke ten years later, Abbey told it again, adding: 'Do you know . . . I don't think he ever forgave me for uttering this Opinion, which however was the Truth.' Keats himself quietly retained his dignity, merely remarking in a matter-of-fact way that his book 'was read by some dozen of my friends who lik'd it; and some dozen who I was unacquainted with who did not'.

His friends stood by him, helping by their example and in more immediate ways. On 17 March, for example, the watchful and attentive Haydon wrote in his diary that Keats 'has gone to dress wounds, after spending an evening with me spouting Shakespeare'. Keats had, of course, studied Shakespeare before, but this schoolboy acquaintance was deepened now by Haydon's repeated injunction to read his work. In a confidential letter he sent Keats, Haydon suggested what this familiarity with the great masters of the past could achieve, telling Keats how at the end of a long working day and 'filled with fury I have seen the faces of the mighty dead crowd into my room, and I have sunk down & prayed the great Spirit that I might be worthy to accompany these immortal beings in their immortal glories, and then I have seen each smile as it passed over me, and each shake his hand in awful encouragement.'[42] So frank a confession could suggest to a young writer entire vistas of new experience, and Keats himself was to acquire this sense that the company of the great dead was an almost palpable gathering, a chorus presiding over his endeavour. By the middle of March he was alluding to Shakespeare and parodying Falstaff in a letter to Reynolds, and this lighthearted familiarity is a sign of what, through the rest of the year, would deepen into a profound understanding of Shakespeare.

Reynolds also offered the practical help that came from his considerable experience of the literary world. While the Olliers were beginning to realise they had a failed volume on their hands, it was almost certainly Reynolds who now introduced Keats to his own publishers, the enterprising young firm run by John Taylor and James Hessey. Taylor in particular was an ideal choice. Older than Keats himself although still only in his middle thirties, he was a man experienced in the book trade who delighted especially in discovering new talent. Taylor was a generous-spirited and knowledgeable man who recognised that his firm was now in a position to branch out into what was then the potentially lucrative market for poetry. Undeterred by the failure of the *Poems*, and more amused by than suspicious of Keats's Byronic style of dress, he recognised in Keats the highest promise. Now, while the Olliers scratched their beards and grew increasingly angry as, they claimed, irate customers complained so vehemently about Keats's volume that they felt obliged to refund their money, Taylor began to show an interest in Keats's new ideas and projects.

Keats himself meanwhile had resolved to move with his brothers to Hampstead. There was little enough to keep them in Cheapside. George had had a disagreement with a colleague in Abbey's office, while Keats's own relations with his erstwhile guardian were permanently soured. Besides, his attendance at Guy's had ceased, and, although he kept his books and notes, it seems he did not take the trouble to collect any form of certificate showing his qualifications. Hampstead had been the focus of his life through the last few exciting months, and now he and his brothers moved into lodgings on the first floor of 1 Well Walk, the house of the local postman and his wife, who were kindly, welcoming people for all that they had noisy children and their home smelt unpleasantly of worsted stockings.

Hampstead also offered the chance of new friendships, and the more easily gregarious Reynolds introduced Keats to the inhabitants of two exquisite semi-detached Regency houses collectively called Wentworth Place. One of these belonged to Charles Brown, later to become an important friend, while the other was occupied by Charles and Maria Dilke, a hospitable couple with literary interests. Maria, indeed, was something like a sister to the Keats boys, while her rather more serious-minded husband, a civil servant in the Navy Pay Office, was the editor of a six-volume collection of *Old English Plays* which in time was to broaden Keats's taste for poetic drama. These new friendships were to ripen during the summer and autumn of 1817. Meanwhile, Hunt and his circle still provided the main focus of interest in Hampstead.

Despite the widening fracture in their relationship, Keats remained alert to what was being discussed and written in Hunt's cottage, where the mythological concerns of the previous winter were beginning to show themselves in new work. 'Mr H has got a great way into a Poem on the Nymphs and has said a number of beautiful things,' Keats wrote of Hunt's latest work, a mildly erotic little pageant which he never chose to reprint in full. *The Story of Rimini*, however, was now being revised for a second edition and, Keats and Clarke having made arrangements for the proofs, Keats himself wrote an uninspired sonnet on the work which had once so excited him. Then, on 26 March, he was invited to the Oxford Street house of Vincent Novello to hear a performance of Hunt's four-part hymn 'To the Spirit Great and Good'.[43]

The occasion gave Keats the opportunity of seeing Hunt at his most 'joco-serio-musico-pictorio-poetico'. The Novellos' *musicales* were one of Hunt's great delights, while his hosts were charming, cosmopolitan people: 'the most catholic of Catholics, for their spirit embraced the whole world'. In their sitting-room, watercolours were hung on the rose-tinted walls while prints and books were strewn across the sofa-table. Bobbing socially between Mrs Novello and her sister, 'Ave Maria' and 'Salve Regina' as he nicknamed them, beer in hand and specially purchased Parmesan on his plate, Hunt was entirely happy in his role as the tame literary lion waiting for the music to begin. This was often performed by Vincent Novello, an organist who, in the words of Charles Lamb, one of his regular if less contented guests, 'by the aid of a capital organ, himself the most finished of players, converts his drawing-room into a chapel, his week days into Sundays, and these latter into minor heavens'. It was often by the organ that Keats himself would sit, listening and withdrawn. Bach, Haydn, Mozart and Beethoven provided the regular fare, but on this occasion Hunt had written the music for his hymn to a benevolent deity, a power delighted by 'loveliness' and who should be praised:

> Not with slavery or with fears
> But with a face as towards a friend, and with thin sparkling tears.

It was against this sort of occasion, the pursuit of the pretty rather than the beautiful, that Haydon had warned Keats, and in Hunt's case both the artistic and financial foundations of such pleasures were sunk in sand. Hunt was undergoing one of his periodical financial crises. He was over £1000 in debt and, by the beginning of April, the idea of decamping to the Shelleys in Marlow seemed increasingly attractive. By 6 April, a Sunday and thus a time when debtors had legal immunity, he had decided to flee. Keats, as a young friend and neighbour, was called in to assist 'in all the chaos of packed trunks, lumber, litter, dust, dirty dry fingers &c'.[44] Print by print, shelf of books by shelf of books, bust by plaster bust, the little temple of the muses Keats had so ardently sought was being dismantled. All that was left were the stains on the walls and a bundle of papers Keats himself stuffed into a spare trunk.

Depressed and embittered by these events, Keats took a walk with Haydon through the Kilburn meadows, venting his anger to the country air. He had seen Hunt's dream of art turned to so much detritus, and in one of his rarely recorded moments of savagery he burst out: 'What a pity there is not a human dust hole.' He feared some sort of contamination and his own ambition fought back. 'Byron, Scott, Southey, & Shelley think they are to lead the age, but . . .' The last words of the sentence have since been removed from the record, but it is easy enough to guess their import. 'This was said', Haydon wrote, 'with all the consciousness of Genius; his face reddened.'[45]

It was imperative to get away, to consolidate and go beyond all the experience so recently acquired. April came and Keats's plans crystallised. His new friends the Dilkes were fond of the Isle of Wight and so he decided to go there. Keats began to gather together what he needed: paper and pens, a duodecimo Shakespeare in seven volumes, some prints, a Haydon drawing and a warm woollen scarf. Underlying all this was a promise. 'We have agreed', wrote Taylor, 'for the next Edit. of Keats's Poems and are to have the refusal of his future Works. I cannot fail to think he will become a great Poet.'[46] A belief in Keats's own ambitions was shared by others. The pettiness of the past few weeks evaporated in a new ambition and a new project. He would write the mythological romance of a mortal shepherd falling in love with the moon first essayed and then abandoned with 'I stood tip-toe'. Now, as his coach rolled on its way to Southampton, he was resolved. 'I put on no Laurels till I shall have finished Endymion.'

A Test of Invention

a long Poem is a test of Invention which I take
to be the Polar Star of Poetry.

(*Keats to Bailey, 8 October 1817*)

FOR THE FIRST stages of his journey Keats rode on top of the coach then, as the spring frosts began to bite, he paid extra for a seat inside. By dawn, he was speeding towards the borders of Sussex and Hampshire and was caught with sudden surprise by the beauty of the landscape: open downland dotted with thick woods, hedgerows of elm and ash, furze and well-tended fields. By breakfast-time he had reached Southampton; at the inn, overcome by a wave of loneliness, he reached in his case for his volumes of Shakespeare and leafed through *The Tempest*. Later, he discovered that the Isle of Wight ferry did not leave until three in the afternoon and, as he wandered through the unknown town, noting its two or three churches and 'respectable old Gate with two Lions to guard it', he began to think of the friends he had left in London. George, Haydon and Reynolds shuffled through his mind by turns and, as he ended his letter to his brother, he confessed to feeling 'rather muzzy'. He was tired from the journey and a little homesick.

Having crossed to Cowes, he went to Newport, where he took a room for the night, and the following morning he set off to explore Shanklin. The spring beauty of the landscape delighted him. Woods and meadows sloped down to the Chine, a cleft filled with bushes and carpeted with primroses that stretched to the margins of the sea. Such an abundance of flowers was exhilarating, but Shanklin itself proved too expensive and Keats returned to Newport. From here he could see the south coast of England, the whole northern part of the Isle of Wight itself, and Carisbrook Castle with its ivy-covered walls and ancient colony of jackdaws. With memories of *The Tempest* still beating in his head, it seemed amid the woods, primroses and 'quick freshes' that he was on Prospero's island itself. Shakespeare, indeed, was haunting him, memories of *The Tempest* and *A Midsummer Night's Dream* mingling with the insistent repetition of a line from *Lear.* 'Do you not hear the sea?'

He found lodgings with a Mrs Cook, and even here, it seemed, Shakespeare dictated his choice. There was a print of the poet hanging in the corridor and Keats begged his landlady to be allowed to hang it in his room, where he had already unpacked his books and pinned up the other pictures he had brought. But he was still feeling 'narvus'. For the first time in his adult life he was on his own and away from London. 'Tell George and Tom to write,' he begged in a letter to Reynolds. Then an idea struck him: 'I'll tell you what – On the 23rd was Shakespeare born – now If I should receive a Letter from you and another from my Brothers on that day 'twould be a parlous good thing.' He himself was discovering new beauties in Shakespeare all the time and could admit now to his craving for poetry and the absolute demand this made on him. 'I find that I cannot exist without poetry – without eternal poetry – half the day will not do – the whole of it – I began with a little, but habit has made me a Leviathan.'[1] As he walked or rested, lines of Shakespeare continued to rise in his mind. 'Do you not hear the sea?' He set himself to writing a sonnet in an attempt to allay the strain:

> Oh ye! who have your eye-balls vexed and tired,
>   Feast them upon the wideness of the Sea –
>   Oh ye! whose ears are dinned with uproar rude,
>   Or fed too much with cloying melody –
>   Sit ye near some old cavern's mouth and brood,
> Until ye start, as if the sea-nymphs quired.[2]

The exercise 'did me some good. I slept the better last night for it.'

But so far he had managed to do nothing to *Endymion*. It is likely that some of the opening lines had already been drafted, possibly as long ago as the winter evenings spent in his Cheapside lodgings. Stephens, the friend from his student days, later recalled, perhaps rather fancifully, an occasion when they were together, Stephens reading and Keats writing.[3] After a while Keats looked up and recited the first line of his new composition:

> A thing of beauty is a constant joy.

Asked what he thought, Stephens supposedly replied that 'it has the true ring, but is wanting in some way'. Keats immediately rephrased the line:

A thing of beauty is a joy for ever.

Stephens approved and, in the following passage, Keats began to develop the significance of the idea.

The imagining of beauty is seen now as mankind's truest spiritual activity, his one pledge of unfettered abundance and joy. Beauty is made into a universal, something transcendent in which the limitations of the day-to-day world can apparently be overcome. A sense of freedom and even a quiet religious awe flow through the famous passage as Keats suggests how the harmonious mind, turning with fresh wonder both to see and make the world of beauty in which it lives, delights in its own activity. Shunning the England of Castlereagh and the struggle for power, Keats suggests that man's truth lies in the shared insights of his subjectivity rather than the common miseries of his history. Truth is the joyful perception of what the senses can relish and the imagination enter into:

Such the sun, the moon,
Trees old, and young, sprouting a shady boon
For simple sheep; and such are daffodils
With the green world they live in; and clear rills
That for themselves a cooling covert make
'Gainst the hot season . . .[4]

Such things are 'A flowery band to bind us to the earth'.

Their opposite is personal 'despondency' and the gloom inflicted on England by 'the inhuman dearth' of men of quality in government. The effect of this state of affairs was bitterly apparent to Keats even on the Isle of Wight. In his first hours there, as he travelled from Cowes to Newport, he 'saw some extensive Barracks which disgusted me extremely with Government for placing such a Nest of Debauchery in so beautiful a place – I asked a man on the Coach about this – and he said that the people had been spoiled'. That this was a young and still immature poet's anger is suggested by Keats's feeling obliged to confess, 'I did not feel very sorry at the idea of the Women being a little profligate.' Nonetheless, the seriousness of the situation was brought home to him in his lodgings that night. 'In the room where I slept at

Newport I found this on the Window "O Isle spoilt by the Mil*a*tary!"'
It was to counter the desperation of such a graffito that he would write
his poem. 'I shall', he promised Reynolds, 'forthwith begin my
Endymion.'[5]

The opening lines of the narrative offer an Arcadian vision of the
natural world: an imagined region for the lover of poetry to wander in,
and a place that can soothe his cares and lift his thoughts by offering an
alternative to the anxiety-riven actualities of Regency England. Here,
on the side of Latmos, there is neither power struggle nor social
division, neither standing army nor life-denying church. What the
greater part of mankind enjoys is a spontaneously imaginative and
spiritually satisfying sense of oneness with nature and community with
his kind.

It is to this place of delight that Keats's procession of worshippers
draw the 'fair-wrought car' of their handsome ruler in order to
celebrate what was for Keats the essence of the Greek spirit: 'the
Religion of the Beautiful, the Religion of Joy, as he used to call it'. It
is a dream of wholesome, natural delight, of abundance and community, that reaches its climax in the 'Hymn to Pan' which the
shepherds now chant. It is possible that the performance of Hunt's
little cantata inspired this passage, but the difference in quality is
absolute. Keats's lines are one of his great early achievements and a
forerunner of the major odes. His is a poem in which the quick sense
of the working of nature as something independent of man and yet
part with him of a wider cosmos is both powerful and original. The
apprehension of nature animate with spiritual life belongs to all the
worshippers, and, far from being crowded in a dismal church and
bound by dogma, their congregated spirits rise in a life-enhancing
affirmation of the ultimately mysterious bond between this world and
the next:

> 'Be still the unimaginable lodge
> For solitary thinkings; such as dodge
> Conception to the very bourne of heaven,
> Then leave the naked brain; be still the leaven,
> That spreading in this dull and clodded earth
> Gives it a touch ethereal – a new birth;
> Be still a symbol of immensity;
> A firmament reflected in the sea;
> An element filling the space between,
> An unknown – but no more! we humbly screen

With uplift hands our foreheads, lowly bending,
And giving out a shout most heaven rending,
Conjure thee to receive our humble paean,
Upon thy mount Lycean!'[6]

Then, their act of worship being over, the people fall to dancing, music, poetry and sports. Again, although culling 'Time's sweet first fruits', such activities are not a merely heedless round of pleasures. All their pastimes feed the imagination, enriching it by contact with the world of myth. Apollo presides over their entertainments, deepening their awareness of human life and its attendant pain. The death of Hyacinthus is mentioned and, in lines now often praised for their disconcerting objectivity, the slaughter of Niobe too. *Et in Arcadia ego* – 'I, even I am in Arcadia,' as Poussin's shepherds realise as they trace the lettering on a tomb and as Keats's figures also know as they sit in a philosophic circle imagining an afterlife in which they will be happily reunited with their loved ones. There is pain on Latmos and death and mystery as well, yet for all save one figure there is a sense of natural unity with the order of things. Only the hero of the poem, Endymion himself, appears alienated from this world, a youth set apart by inward, cankering sorrow.

The reposed energy of his opening lines was the product of extreme anxiety on Keats's part and an effort which left him crushed and confused. He had been working at the pitch of intensity for eight hours a day, and now his fatigue verged on panic. As he wrote in a letter to Hunt: 'I went to the Isle of Wight – thought so much about Poetry so long together that I could not get to sleep at night – and, moreover, I know not how it was, I could not get wholesome food – By this means in a Week or so I became not over capable in my upper Stories, and set off pell mell for Margate, at least 150 Miles – because forsooth I fancied that I should like my old Lodging here.'[7] In Margate, he would be joined by Tom.

This desperate dash along the southern coastline (the kindly Mrs Cook's Shakespeare print stuffed as a gift in his case) speaks tellingly of Keats's state of mind, and the days spent in jolting travel made him realise 'I was too much in Solitude, and consequently was obliged to be in continual burning of thought as an only recourse.' Such over-excitement was characteristic, and while friends later believed these experiences 'helped to wear him out', even now George was so concerned that he went to talk to Haydon. The artist wrote Keats a letter that was a model of generous support, at once admonishing, kind and the fruit of genuine experience. Keats was not to give way to his forebodings, Haydon declared. 'Every man of great views, is at times thus tormented.' He urged Keats to trust in God and his own elasticity of spirit. 'My dear Keats go on, dont despair, collect incidents, study characters, read Shakespeare and trust in Providence.'[8]

He was not, however, to trust in Hunt, and the danger Haydon believed Keats ran by this association is suggested by the depth of the painter's contempt:

> Beware for God's sake of the delusions and sophistications that is ripping up the talent and respectability of our Friend – he will go out of the World the victim of his own weakness and the dupe of his own self delusions – with the contempt of his enemies and the sorrow of his Friends – the cause he undertook to support, injured by his own neglect of character – his family disordered, his children neglected, himself, petted and his prospects ruined![9]

Part of this is a response to the atheistical influence of Shelley, to whose house at Marlow Keats had directed his own letter to Hunt. He later confessed to scarcely knowing what he said in this, but in fact the crowded sequence reflects the vertiginous excitement of his mind, hurrying as it does between the polite despatch of details concerning the proofs of *Rimini*, the chaotic state of the papers Hunt left when he hurried from his cottage, and earnest talk about two articles in the *Examiner*, both of which had had a strong effect on Keats.

The first was a piece by Hunt himself which Keats described as a 'Battering Ram against Christianity'. The background was an unsuccessful attempt to indict a Unitarian minister in Liverpool for blasphemy, a favourite charge of the political right because, if proven, it would allow them to display the comprehensive nature of the political theology by which they hoped to unite the country. Hunt himself defined blasphemy not in these political terms but as the attribution to the Supreme Being of qualities that must be odious to all decent people. Included among these charges was the belief in eternal punishment so luridly relished by Tertullian, which Hunt then contrasted to the tolerant charity of Erasmus and Philip Sidney.

Such thoughts led to a discussion of what Keats himself characterised as 'the dreadful Petzelians and their expiation by Blood'.[10] News had come to Hunt of this Austrian sect who practised human sacrifice in an attempt to atone for the sins of their elders. The parallel implied by Hunt between such macabre rites and the sacrifice that lay at the heart of Christianity was also clear to Keats: 'And do Christians shudder at the same thing in a Newspaper which they attribute to their God in its most aggravated form?' The doctrine of the atonement (the idea of a religion based on sacrifice) was as abhorrent to Keats as it was to Hunt, who now proceeded to draw further parallels between his own ideal of paganism and his revulsion at Christian bigotry: 'They dealt in loves and luxuries, in what resulted from the first laws of nature, and tended to keep humanity alive: – the latter have dealt in angry debates, in intolerance, in gloomy denouncements, in persecutions, in excommunications, in wars and massacres, in what perplexes, outrages, and destroys humanity.' In the tense political atmosphere of 1817, an atmosphere already hinted at in Keats's epistle to George, any attack on Christianity could be viewed by conservatives as an attempt at subversion, and the fervour with which Keats was now elaborating a description of an ideal society based not on the tenets of established religion but on a revived paganism should be seen as a deliberate attempt to engage with the very basis of the world in which he lived. In such a climate as this, a thing of beauty could not be politically neutral.

Other poets, of course, had capitulated, none more infamously than Southey, the Poet Laureate. The second *Examiner* article that so impressed Keats was Hazlitt's outspoken attack on his opinions. While Keats detected lapses of taste in this piece, Southey himself had recently inveighed against both Hazlitt and Hunt as men who 'live by culumny and sedition; they are libellers and liars by trade.'[11] Hazlitt's reply, passionate, eloquent and bitter, was a masterpiece of style in the service of morality, and Keats rightly praised it as 'a Whale's back in the Sea of Prose'. Southey himself, however, was riding high in the government's esteem and had secretly expressed the hope that the political writers on the *Examiner* would be arrested and transported. With the suspension of *habeas corpus*, 'every one who rose in a meeting, or sat down at his desk, to attack the measures of his majesty's ministers, now knew that he did so with a halter about his neck.'[12] Openly to be associated with Hunt and his newspaper was increasingly dangerous.

For all his allegiance, it was the pursuit of poetry and the fashioning of an alternative world of the imagination that was Keats's abiding preoccupation, drawing from him fresh confessions both of his ambition and of his modesty. He wrote to Hunt on these matters, but it was to Haydon that he opened his heart. His reply to the painter's encouragement was warm and seriously felt. 'I am sure that you do love me as your own Brother – I have seen it in your continual anxiety for me.' He now frankly recognised Hunt as a pretender to poetry – for Keats the greatest sin 'after the 7 deadly' – and to Haydon he felt he could speak unaffectedly of his own high calling and their shared recognition 'of the turmoil and anxiety' this entailed.

But there were more immediate problems too, some of which Keats was only partly aware of. The business affairs George had entered into on quitting Abbey's office had not prospered, despite his borrowing from Keats's own newly realised capital. George had also written to the Olliers in strident terms about their marketing of his brother's book. The reply was coldly venomous. They told of customers' complaints and stock unsold. While Taylor and Hessey eventually took over some of the bound copies, unbound sets were discounted at a penny-halfpenny a copy for remaindering at 1s 6d. 'We regret', the Olliers declared, 'that your brother ever requested us to publish his book.'[13]

Keats would have to look for comfort elsewhere. 'I never quite despair,' he wrote to Haydon, 'and I read Shakespeare,' whom he now imagined as his 'good Genius' presiding over his work. The intense strain he was under was beginning to show nonetheless. He began scribbling quotations and misquotations beside the critical comments of Dr Johnson printed in his edition of Shakespeare, hoping thereby to deflate the commentator by citing the poet. It was a rather sorry business and was further evidence of his fatigue. It seemed to him that despite all his hard work the 'Cliff of Poesy' still towered above him. 'Perhaps I may have done a good deal for the time but it appears such a Pin's point to me.' Money problems only made this worse. For a while they even stopped him writing, and it seemed that the promise made in the opening lines of his poem that his work would be finished by the autumn would have to be revoked. Keats had been obliged to ask his publishers for a loan, and in the letter he wrote thanking them he offered a picture of his harassed state. He had been working daily at his poem for a month and was so over-wrought he was obliged to stop. He was feeling the guilt of enforced lassitude, the need to go on and the failure to do so.

Such depression and anxiety debilitated him. He felt he was experiencing 'all the effects of a Mental Debauch', and in his rest-lessness he hoped yet another change of place might help him get away from his current state of mind: 'This Evening I go to Canterrbury – having got tired of Margate – I was not in my right head when I came.' Perhaps another 'Presidor' could be conjured to his aid: 'At Canty. I hope the Remembrance of Chaucer will set me forward like a Billiard-Ball.' Meanwhile, would Taylor and Hessey send him 'any little intelligence in the literarry or friendly way when you have time to scribble'.[14]

The sheer scale of Keats's self-imposed task oppressed him, as did the anxiety he felt about his development. Frustrated ambition jibbed at his exhausted powers. Before he had fully begun work he had written to George a paragraph which, since he later copied it out for Bailey, was clearly a sort of credo.[15] *Endymion* would be the work in which he would pass beyond the incomplete experiments and sonnet-writing competitions that had made up so much of his early work. 'Did our great Poets ever write short Pieces? I mean in the shape of Tales.' The influence of Haydon can be felt here along with the need to show that he was outgrowing Hunt, who had asked why a modern poet should 'endeavour after a long Poem' at all. But there was more to his aspiration than the pressure of the example set by men he knew. Keats had to discover the reach of his own ability, however immature its expression might for the moment be.

Aspects of this task were clear to him. *Endymion* 'will be a test, a trial of my Powers of Imagination and chiefly of my invention which is a rare thing indeed'. Invention, the fecundity of his own mind, was what he was placing on trial. It was a gift that could not be gained by effort. It was innate, the sign of the true poet and of the tradition to which Keats wished to belong. The greatest figures of the renaissance had had it, but 'this same invention seems i[n]deed of late Years to have been forgotten as a Poetical excellence'. It was, Keats believed, something readers craved for. 'Do not the Lovers of Poetry like to have a little Region to wander in where they may pick and choose, and in which the images are so numerous that many are forgotten and found new in a second Reading?'

Plenitude itself, Keats suggests, is something pleasurable, something which stands against the hurry of the modern world. 'Besides', he wrote (and the repetition of the idea suggests his earnestness), 'a long poem is a test of Invention which I take to be the Polar Star of Poetry, as Fancy is the Sails, and Imagination the Rudder.' He was well aware of what this meant for his own project. In telling of the love between Endymion and the moon, 'I must make 4000 Lines of one bare circumstance and fill them with Poetry.' This was a great challenge, and even if it were to be satisfactorily completed 'it will take me but a dozen paces towards the Temple of Fame.' Keats was facing nothing less than the labour of creating himself as a major poet, and he was to do so by writing a work he would have eventually to better and transcend.

Keats's subject would be his figure of the shepherd prince alienated from an ideal society by the burden of his visionary consciousness. By the time the festivities for Pan have come to their close, Endymion has been stultified by his anguish. His sister Peona leads him away from his people to a little boat in which she takes him to an island. Here, isolation and renovating sleep prepare Endymion's spirits for that act of confession during which he will admit to his love for the moon and begin to analyse his predicament. The outward form of the narrative becomes the vehicle for an inner quest. The progress away from the social and political worlds towards an intense subjectivity is clear.

But this was not achieved without great difficulty. The first 300 lines of this section were drafted in early May and revised when the poem was prepared for publication. 'Before I began,' Keats wrote, 'I had no inward feel of being able to finish; and as I proceeded my steps were all uncertain.' It was the more obvious signs of this uncertainty he had to eliminate, and what he chose to cut were those passages in which his Huntian mannerisms were most marked. It is likely that he had fallen back on these while attempting to draft something more complex, the truths, in fact, that Peona tries to coax from her brother.

These concern that visionary power of the poet whereby his delight in the physical world is transformed through his imagination into an intimation of eternal truth and beauty, those 'essences' as Keats called them whose power over the inner self gives them an aura of the divine. In other words, the poem affirms that the most profound reaches of human life lie in subjective experience and a vision of the sexual, psychological and spiritual wholeness symbolised by the union of the male and mortal Endymion to the eternal goddess of the moon. As Keats had already suggested in the *Poems*, it is through the creation of such myths that the poet can give coherence to the longings of mankind and present these to his audience through his art.

This was a process of discovery whose daring, in these difficult early months of 1817, cost Keats every ounce of his energy and sent him in its intense strain on his erratic journeys across southern England. That at many points his poem failed, that *Endymion* is severely damaged by *longueurs*, confusions and lapses into vulgarity, scarcely dims the nature of his endeavour. Here was a very great and original imagination trying to find its bearings. And it is the parallel endeavour of Endymion himself to make some sense of his intuitions that forms the substance of the first Book of Keats's poem.

The prince's visions have come to him in an opiated dream. Led on to enjoy a beautiful sunset (the last moments of a radiant Apollo shining over Latmos), there suddenly appeared before Endymion a magic bed of dittany and poppies, flowers sacred to Apollo's sister the moon. After he has fallen into a drugged and visionary sleep, a beautiful moon appeared to him riding the sky. Eventually she retreated into her 'dark and vapoury tent' but, as with heightened imagination the prince stared up yet again, so his visionary moon was metamorphosed into 'a bright something', a woman who is for Endymion the 'completed form of all completeness'. This incarnation of feminine beauty then descended to enjoy his caresses and give the prince intimations of a life more ardent than that he has previously known.

Poetic vision, sexual passion and ideal beauty are one. Just as in contemporary accounts of the origins of Greek myth those people who were most fully alive to the natural world created, 'by the power of fancy, a human form and a human voice in those scenes, which to a man of literal understanding may appear dead and lifeless',[16] so Endymion's imagination transfigures nature and allows him to contemplate immortal truth and beauty. And this, as Hazlitt declared, is the proper purpose of our existence: 'Here is the mind's true home.'[17] Mortals yearn towards the immortal, but as yet Endymion does not appreciate that these 'essences' also long for the earth and their incarnation in the human mind. For the moment his own mind can only aspire heavenwards and then return to earth broken and incomplete. Such a partial vision is dangerous, and Endymion's disillusioned spirit projects its own sickness on the world around him. Latmos becomes a wasteland where:

> all the pleasant hues
> Of heaven and earth had faded: deepest shades
> Were deepest dungeons; heaths and sunny glades
> Were full of pestilent light; our taintless rills
> Seemed sooty, and o'er – spread with upturned gills
> Of dying fish . . .[18]

This cruel division between ardour and anguish is the origin of Endymion's abject confusion.

Peona gently tries to lead him back to a less fervid existence, a life in which an altogether milder sense of the visionary is balanced by 'high-fronted honour' and a commitment to the social and public worlds. Endymion's reply is one of the most discussed passages in the poem. He has, he says, longed to slake his 'thirst for the world's praise', but his visionary life is altogether more intense and imperious in its demands. The pursuit of true happiness, he insists, lies not in fulfilling outward ambition but in striving after a 'fellowship with essence', in a yearning after the beautiful and the true. The fulfilment of this state will be an annihilation of the ego to which a delight in nature and art can point the way.

There are, however, other experiences which are altogether more 'self-destroying' than nature art.[19] Chief among these are friendship and love. Compared to the pursuit of love especially, all the endeavours of history and politics, all the striving of the public world of men, are nothing. Endymion suggests that the awakening of the imagination to beauty through sensual love is a spiritual imperative so powerful that it may even be the motor power of the whole universe. The most profound human truth lies not in the worldly pursuit of power but in the cultivation of the subjective and the spiritual, in an eager openness to a life of sensations in which the body and soul may become one in joy while the imagination points to a happiness which, after our deaths, will be repeated in eternity in a 'finer tone'.

This speech of Endymion's was a passage of the utmost importance to Keats. 'My having written that Argument will perhaps be of the greatest Service to me of anything I ever did,' he wrote to Taylor. And, indeed, it gathers to itself the early form of some of Keats's most fundamental impulses: his intense love of the natural world especially and that surrender of the ego in a loving union with the ideal of beauty through which the imagination glimpses truth. He was concerned that Taylor, as a 'consequitive man', might find the passage mere words. In a letter written to Bailey some months later, however, Keats was able to express his feelings more openly. 'I am certain of nothing but of the holiness of the Heart's affections and the truth of Imagination,' he wrote. 'What the imagination seizes as Beauty must be truth – whether it existed before or not – for I have the same Idea of all our Passions as of Love they are all in their sublime, creative of essential Beauty.'[20] This passage is rightly famous, and yet it is entirely in keeping with the timbre of Keats's imagination that such ideas did not harden from speculation into dogma. As he wrote of the original passage in *Endymion*, they were 'a regular stepping of the Imagination towards *a* Truth', a truth that would in time be severely tested.

The closing paragraphs of the first Book do not sustain this level of invention. Endymion recounts two more appearances of his beloved but they add little to the poem beyond their length. They are filler designed to round the Book up to near the required thousand lines. Endymion himself meanwhile merely offers an unconvincing promise to give up his quest and surrenders in his bafflement to 'demurest meditation'. Peona leads him away and then herself disappears until the close of the work. Such weaknesses reveal the dangers inherent in Keats's trusting to invention alone, and similar failures would dog the rest of the work. Now, however, tired after the great advance he had made in the earlier lines, Keats decided he was in need of a holiday. While Tom returned to Hampstead, Keats went off to the little coastal village of Bo Peep near Hastings and an unexpected light adventure.

The woman, Mrs Isabella Jones, was an attractive, lively person with a penchant for literary men. There is no record of a Mr Jones, and Mrs Jones herself seems to have been attached in some way to an elderly Irishman, Donat O'Callaghan. Keats believed she was about his own age, and he clearly found her greater worldly experience intriguing. Perhaps she was charmed by this and saw no harm in letting him get to the state where he 'had warmed with her . . . and kissed her'. He may also have written for her his tepid lyric, 'You say you love'. Isabella Jones was to reappear in his life, but there was little more to their relationship than light-hearted mutual fascination, and by 10 June Keats was back in Hampstead.[21] From there he wrote to his publishers asking to borrow a further £30, then, for nearly three months, his letters virtually stop. His vivid self-portrayal is silent.

Others were more vocal. Despite poor sales, the *Poems* were beginning to be reviewed. An anonymous mention in the *Monthly Magazine* had praised the book's contents for their 'sweetness and beauty', but in May the *European Magazine* launched a ferocious attack on a work which now threatened to 'contaminate our purity, inoculate us with degeneracy and corruption, and overthrow among us the dominion of domestic peace and public liberty'. The author of this abuse signed himself 'G.F.M.', but such near-anonymity hid nothing. Amid the desperate state of British public life, with *habeas corpus* suspended and working people desperate for food, George Felton Mathew was bidding for his place as a spokesman of the moral majority.[22] Naturally, he was piqued that Keats had deserted his circle, but, while Mathew's criticism is worthless in itself, the prejudices that motivate it are altogether more interesting.

Wading into his attack, he disparaged Keats's 'petty arguments', 'the puerility of his sentiments' and the 'unseemly hyperbole' evidenced by the sonnet on Chapman's Homer. He reserved his special venom, however, for 'Calidore', a poem not merely weak but dangerous. 'This fragment is as pretty and as innocent as childishness can make it, save that it savours too much, – as indeed do all these poems, – of the foppery and affectation of Leigh Hunt!' And that was the point. If Keats had remained in Mathew's circle he would have written 'spirited and powerful' works – at this point the 'milk-white lamb' of the sonnet 'To Woman' is trotted out for special commendation – rather than surrendering to that self-indulgent luxuriousness of the imagination and Huntian perversion of political principle which, Mathew warned, 'may in time become the ruin of a people'. It was thus an erstwhile friend who first sounded what were to become the familiar arguments of contemporary criticism of Keats: he was self-indulgent, immature and politically corrupt, a decadent adolescent who was the disciple of Hunt.

Mathew's exposition of these grotesque ideas was motivated by more than personal pique. It reflects what, in 1817, was the nationwide paranoia afflicting conservative opinion. The state, it seemed, was about to collapse, and such perverted talent as Keats revealed could only hasten its moral decline. In their desperate concern, the government instituted a period of 'Alarm'. The Hampden Clubs, fractured and impotent from internal dissent and with their members left desperate for bread, were the particular objects of fear. While government spies in the Midlands and the North fomented mutual suspicion, Secret Committees reported to both Houses of Parliament on the supposed activities of the Hampden Clubs themselves. 'It seems', they declared, 'to be part of the system adopted by these societies, to prepare the minds of the people for the destruction of the present frame of society, by undermining not only their habits of decent and regular subordination, but all the principles of morals and religion.'

It was easy to suggest that the *Examiner* and its readers were devoted to the same cause, and to the grandees of the old regime a return to basics seemed ever more urgent. Their suspension of *habeas corpus* and the passing of the Seditious Meetings Act meant the possible arbitrary suppression of any view critical of the extreme right. A mood of the deepest gloom smothered the hopes of everyone else. 'It seemed as if the sun of freedom were gone down, and a rayless expansion of oppression had finally closed over us.' For Keats, secreted in Hampstead, a man without a vote, a parliamentary party or a conventional religion, the only possibility was ever more resolutely to turn his back on the hopelessness of the public world:

> Hence, pageant history! hence, gilded cheat!
> Swart planet in the universe of deeds!

The introduction to the second Book of *Endymion* proclaims the primacy of the private, the subjective and the erotic.

These are presented through a series of mythological tableaux vivants. At the opening of the Book, Endymion has renounced the stoic vow made to his sister and, in a scene that is clearly intended to be read on an esoteric rather than a literal level, is seen chasing a butterfly, an image of Psyche or the soul. Told that he must pass the 'scanty bar' of normal human consciousness, he invokes the moon and then, in answer to a mysterious summons, descends underground to explore the 'silent mysteries of earth'. Here, amid darkness, confusion and solitude, he must begin learning to sympathise with human love and pain as well as coming to understand how the poetic imagination perceives the relationship between the mortal and the divine.

The process begins with his encountering Venus and Adonis in a passage typical of the working of the poem as a whole. The recumbent figure of Adonis himself is derived from Poussin's *Echo and Narcissus*, and this lengthy and even prolix passage of description is meant to provide both a rich example of invention to beguile 'lovers of Poetry' as well as a vivid recreation of timeless Greek myth. And in myth lies insight. Endymion now learns not only of the thwarted love of Venus for this mortal youth but also, as the goddess herself descends to the slumbering young man, how his temporary resurrection from the underworld is associated with the abundance of summer. 'Once more sweet life begin!' The union of the mortal with the immortal is shown as sexually joyous, an enhancement of the imagination and, as Endymion himself had suspected in the first Book, something intimately connected with the fecundity of the earth. It is for poets to perceive such truths and express them through myth. Now, as Endymion's reward for his growing insight, Venus promises him that, after all his wanderings, 'one day thou wilt be blest.'

Endymion's vision of his own goddess follows, a vision more intense and rewarding than those previously granted since, if it suggests the problems placed in the way of their union, it also asserts the identity of this image of womanly perfection with the moon herself. Above all, it expresses the passion she herself feels. The world of eternity is indeed in love with mortal man. But Endymion's response suggests how unstable was Keats's imagined union of earthly and divine, sexual and spiritual:

> 'Enchantress! tell me by this soft embrace,
> By the most soft completion of thy face,
> Those lips, O slippery blisses, twinkling eyes
> And by these tenderest, milky sovereignties –
> These tenderest – and by the nectar-wine,
> The passion –'[23]

This is really little more than male adolescent fantasy, a wholly inexperienced indulgence of the bowers and masturbatory dreams of Keats's earliest work, and it was to bring down the wrath of the reviewers. Keats himself soon became aware of such weaknesses. As he declared in his Preface to the published poem: 'The imagination of a boy is healthy, and mature imagination of a man is healthy; but there is a space of life between, in which the soul is in a ferment, the character undecided, the way of life uncertain, the ambition thick-sighted; thence proceeds mawkishness.' For all its insight, *Endymion* becomes a self-confessed adolescent work. It belongs to the 'space of life between', and the growing poet becomes altogether more interesting than his work.

For example, while Endymion's intense subjective response to the natural world is suggested by the final episode of Book Two, the passage is mirrored by the recollections of friends who observed a similar capacity in Keats himself. Haydon noted it, as did the painter Joseph Severn. Amiably chatty, girlishly pretty and young for his age, Severn would call at Hampstead to accompany Keats on long walks over Highgate Hill and into Middlesex Forest. Not being very well educated, he hung on Keats's every word. He wanted to be a painter of literary and historical subjects, and he found a 'new world' was opened up to him by Keats's 'taste in the arts, his knowledge of history, and his most fascinating power in the communication of these'. Severn watched his friend with almost lover-like fascination and expanded in his intensity of being. Keats seemed to notice everything: 'even the features and gestures of passing tramps, the colour of one woman's hair, the smile on one child's face, the furtive animalism below the deceptive humanity in many of the vagrants, even the hats, clothes, shoes, wherever these conveyed the remotest hint as to the real self of the wearer'.[24]

But this imaginative curiosity was extinguished as suddenly as the brilliance with which it burned. Keats would 'become taciturn, not because he was tired, nor even because his mind was suddenly wrought to some bewitching vision, but from a profound disquiet which he could not or would not explain'. The burden of pain clung as cruelly to him as to his own Endymion and was only with difficulty 'scared away by slow returning pleasure'. As Severn again noted: 'the only thing that would bring Keats out of one of his fits of seeming gloomful reverie . . . was the motion "of the inland sea" he loved so well, particularly the violent passage of wind across a great field of barley.' These were moments when the natural world corresponded to his inner need. 'He would stand, leaning forward, listening intently, watching with a bright serene look in his eyes and sometimes with a slight smile, the tumultuous passage of the wind across the grain. The sea, or thought-compelling images of the sea, always seemed to restore him to a happy calm.'

There is in this almost mystical depth of concentration a sense of that freedom and fecundity Keats also brought to his writing. He would regularly compose between thirty and forty lines a day, but would sit down to write only when his head was full of ideas. These, he told his friends, crowded through his mind, and he was 'generally more troubled by redundancy than by a poverty of images'. Invention did indeed seem to come to him with spontaneous potency, and it was a maxim he repeated in a letter to his publishers that 'if Poetry comes not as naturally as the Leaves to a tree it had better not come at all.'[25] The sonnet-writing competitions he had indulged with Hunt suggest this facility, as do the light revisions he usually felt it sufficient to make to much of his early work. The fact that *Endymion* itself was quite extensively pruned by him, however, suggests the uncertainty Keats felt about the poem (in the end he came to realise it could not be substantially improved), since his usual practice was far otherwise. 'My judgement (he says), is as active when I am actually writing as my imagination. In fact all my faculties are strongly excited, and in their full play – And shall I afterwards when my imagination is idle, and the heat in which I wrote, has gone off, sit down coldly to criticise when in possession of only one faculty, what I have written, when almost inspired?'[26]

Hunt, when he came to write his *Examiner* review of the *Poems* during June and July, dwelt at length on the faults encouraged by such a procedure. Keats, he declared, had 'a tendency to notice everything too indiscriminately'. By 'thus giving way to every idea that came across him' he risked, Hunt suggested, that lack of proportion seen so absurdly in the work of Erasmus Darwin. This was a particularly cruel comparison since Keats had developed a strong dislike of Darwin's work after an initial teenage fascination with it. Altogether more damaging, however, was Hunt's attempt to place the *Poems* within the ideals of what he was continuing to claim as his own school. Rehashing his notes from *The Feast of the Poets*, Hunt joined Keats's work, immature and faulted although he considered much of it to be, to that of those young writers he hoped would replace the Augustan traditions of Pope with a literature altogether more imaginative and profound.

In the climate of 1817, this was an increasingly dangerous thing to do. Mathew had singled out the lines from *Sleep and Poetry* which proclaimed Keats's 'enmity to the French school, and to the Augustan age of England', disparaging them for their apparent contempt for order, reason and discipline. Hunt, by contrast, gave the passage his special commendation, and to receive this sort of notice in the *Examiner* was to court the fury of the Tory press. Keats was well aware of this. He had largely outgrown Hunt as a poetic master and now he was obliged to see him as a dangerous ally. It was only after some delay that he found the resolve to visit Hunt after his return from the Shelleys' at Marlow, dressing himself for the occasion with defensive smartness 'in some sort of naval costume'. Hunt managed to win him round (he was, after all, experienced at this sort of thing) and, as Keats himself was obliged to confess, 'his make-ups are very good'. But, for all this, Hunt was a man Keats could never wholly again revere as a poet, despite his continuing to be influenced by him as a critic and, above all, as a political mentor.

In the meantime, he continued to see John Hamilton Reynolds, who was himself swept up in the angry cross-currents of political and literary journalism. Reynolds had probably returned to London at about the same time as Keats himself after a trip to Paris, where he consulted with the nominal editor of the *Champion* about its political allegiance. Having veered between the reactionary and the liberal over the last year, the columns of the *Champion* would by and large now be 'consecrated to the interests of freedom and humanity'. Reassured by this, Reynolds continued to work on the staff of the magazine and even succeeded in securing Hazlitt as a contributor. His health was never good, however, and it was perhaps because of this that he let pass a disparaging reference to Keats's work published in the *Champion* for 3 August. Two weeks later, the anonymous correspondent had his reply.

Reynolds printed Keats's sonnet 'On the Sea' and then noted characteristically: 'it is quite sufficient, we think, to justify all the praise we have given him, – and to prove . . . his superiority over any other poetical writer in the *Champion*. – J. H. R. would be the first to acknowledge this himself.'

Such praise was the more generous since Reynolds had recently completed his own finest poem, the Wordsworthian meditation *Devon*. But it was Keats's maturing genius that chiefly attracted Reynolds. Idyllic summer days were spent wandering over Hampstead Heath discussing *Endymion* (Reynolds had been deeply impressed by the 'Hymn to Pan') and reading from Keats's newly acquired facsimile edition of Shakespeare. Even here Reynolds felt surpassed, for it was surely to Keats he was referring when he praised a friend 'who *reads* Shakespeare, – and *really* to read Shakespeare, is "to be one man picked out of ten thousand"'.[27] It was becoming clear, however, that if Reynolds himself was to marry he would have to earn a more substantial living than that he made from his writing, and a mutual friend, the incurably ill James Rice, was trying to persuade him to enter the law. This he would eventually do, and the great promise that so attracted Keats would be dissipated.

But highly as Keats respected Reynolds as a fellow craftsman he was still searching, albeit unconsciously, for a man of greater intellectual weight. During the second half of 1817, this role seemed to be filled by a frequent visitor to the Reynolds household, the much praised Benjamin Bailey. The two men had met briefly after the publication of the *Poems*, and their fascination was mutual. 'I was delighted with the naturalness and simplicity of his character,' Bailey wrote later, 'and was at once drawn to him by his winning and indeed affectionate manner towards those with whom he was himself pleased.'[28] Bailey himself had recently been rejected by the woman with whom he was in love, and Keats's sympathetic company was welcome. Others of Keats's friends were, besides, out of town, while Tom and George had gone at Keats's expense on what proved to be a costly trip to France. In these circumstances, the friendship between Keats and Bailey flourished.

Bailey himself had a considerable facility for light verse, although, as he admitted, none for serious poetry. But he was well read in literature, and he had an impressive understanding of Dante, Milton and Wordsworth, as well as of the philosophy and theology that formed the core of his studies at Oxford, where he was a mature student of twenty-five. Now, at the end of the summer, and feeling the need to return early to his college, he caught the coach to Oxford on the morning of 3 September, taking Keats with him. Keats was to remain in the city for nearly five formative weeks while he worked on the third Book of *Endymion*.

The *Defiance* dropped the two men outside the Mitre and they made their way down the High to Bailey's rooms at Magdalen Hall. Autumnal Oxford delighted Keats. As he wrote to the Reynolds girls: 'here am I among Colleges, Halls Stalls plenty of Trees thank God – plenty of Water thank heaven – plenty of Books thank the Muses.' He also wrote to his sister Fanny, now fourteen and at boarding school in Walthamstow. Abbey disapproved of Keats seeing her, and this gratuitously cruel gesture rankled. Bailey recalled that Keats often spoke of his sister 'with great delicacy and tenderness of affection', and a letter was the one certain way of communicating with her. 'This Oxford I have no doubt is the finest City in the world,' he wrote, '–it is full of old Gothic buildings – Spires – towers – Quadrangles – Cloisters Groves & is surrounded with more Clear streams than ever I saw together.' A light-hearted parody of Wordsworth written at the time again suggests his fascination with the university: its architecture, scholars with mortarboards, religious services and gluttonous high tables.

But these ancient customary things could not shut out the modern world, and through that summer leading articles in the *Examiner* offered a picture of a nation suffering at the hands of a vindictive government. The iniquities of the spy system disturbed the lives of many, as they were intended to. The second suspension of *habeas corpus* sent 'an awful groan, from one corner of Great Britain to the other'.[29] State trials multiplied, collapsed, and invited ridicule and opprobrium in equal measure. 'It is as ordinary now-a-days to see witnesses tampered with, and judges inclined to fix all the odium of a trial on the prisoner, as it is extraordinary to see a judge or indeed any lawyer giving proofs of his zeal for the Constitution.' Throughout the second half of the year, the proceedings that led up to the trial of William Hone for blasphemy made abundantly clear the depths of arbitrary power the government would plumb in their effort to preserve a grotesque status quo. Week after week, the *Examiner* poured scorn on the corruption it exposed, castigated government ministers and lamented 'the extraordinary, degrading, and slavish situation in which they have placed us'.

At the opening of the third Book of *Endymion*, Keats makes clear that this is the background against which he too was writing. The lines are often disparaged, but they are the clearest indication of the near schizophrenic situation in which Keats was placed. Like everyone else, he knew that Hone had parodied the forms of the Anglican service to deride the government, and now he himself turned to biblical parody for the same end. Just as Samson had sent foxes with lighted torches into the fields of the Philistines to fire their corn, so Keats suggests the foxes of the present ministry were destroying the liberties and 'gold and ripe-eared hopes' of the people. The 'baaing vanities' of Castlereagh and his kind, men swollen with self-conceit, luridly swaggering in 'empurpled vests' while cannon, trumpets and guns uttered their endless cacophony, were creating about them a new Babylon, a glorification of the abuse of power.

It was vital to turn elsewhere, to bind up the wounded spirit with 'ethereal things', to seek the consolations of myth and nature, and sense the serene delicacy of a world transfigured by the imagination. In one of the finest passages in the poem, Keats contrasted the agony of contemporary politics to the beauty of the moonlit natural world:

> O Moon! the oldest shades 'mong oldest trees
> Feel palpitations when thou lookest in:
> O Moon! old boughs lisp forth a holier din
> The while they feel thine airy fellowship
> Thou dost bless everywhere, with silver lip
> Kissing dead things to life. The sleeping kine,
> Couched in thy brightness, dream of fields divine:
> Innumerable mountains rise, and rise,
> Ambitious for the hallowing of thine eyes;
> And yet thy benediction passeth not
> One obscure hiding-place, one little spot
> Where pleasure may be sent. The nested wren
> Has thy fair face within its tranquil ken,
> And from beneath a sheltering ivy leaf
> Takes glimpses of thee; thou art a relief
> To the poor patient oyster, where it sleeps
> Within its pearly house. The mighty deeps,
> The monstrous sea is thine – the myriad sea!
> O Moon! far-spooming Ocean bows to thee,
> And Tellus feels his forehead's cumbrous load.[30]

Benevolent nature – the moon rising over air, earth and sea, which are the three regions of Keats's poem – feeds the spirit with quietude.

Imagination and beauty seem to provide a ready and permanent form of that solace which the world of politics denied.

The third Book of *Endymion* was largely written during Keats's stay in Oxford. This was an idyllic period in many ways, and Bailey remembered it with great affection. 'He wrote, and I read,' Bailey recalled,

> sometimes at the same table, and sometimes at separate desks and tables, from breakfast to the time of our going out for exercise, – generally two or three o'clock. He sat down to his task, – which was about 50 lines a day, – with his paper before him, and wrote with as much regularity, and apparently with as much ease, as he wrote his letters . . . Sometimes he fell short of his allotted task, – but not often: and he would make it up another day. But he never forced himself. When he had finished his writing for the day, he usually read it over to me; and he read or wrote letters until we went out for a walk. This was our habit day by day. The rough manuscript was written off daily, and with few erasures.[31]

This was a very concentrated effort indeed. Occasionally Keats suffered the 'utter incapacity' of fatigue, but the notes on his draft and letters to friends jubilantly recall his progress. And, as Bailey suggests, Oxford offered its civilised distractions. 'For the last five or six days,' Keats wrote to Reynolds on 21 September, 'we have had regularly a Boat on the Isis, and explored all the streams about, which are more in number than your eye lashes. We sometimes skim into a Bed of rushes, and there become naturalised riverfolks, – there is one particularly nice nest which we have christened "Reynolds's Cove", in which we have read Wordsworth and talked as may be.'

Such reading and conversation were of the utmost importance, and to Bailey there fell the privilege of encouraging Keats towards a greater maturity. He recognised that his friend's reading had not been systematic, and during Keats's stay in Oxford they studied *Troilus and Cressida* together, *Paradise Lost* and a little Dante in translation. Above all, they read Wordsworth, who at this time Keats most valued 'in particular passages'. They read the Lucy poems, relishing the simplicity of their 'most perfect pathos', but it was Bailey's principal intention to reveal Wordsworth to Keats as 'the great imaginative and philosophic Christian Poet, which he really is'. To this end they looked again at *The Excursion* (Keats suggesting an alteration to Wordsworth's description of Apollo with which Bailey agreed), while the notes the assiduous Bailey made on their conversation suggest that the greatest effect Wordsworth was to have on Keats at this time was through his profound sense of spiritual questioning, his awareness of confusion and misgiving, and of what, in *Tintern Abbey*, Wordsworth called 'the burthen of the mystery'.

Bailey was thus helping to draw Keats towards an altogether more mature and puzzled knowledge of the world than the cocksure views he had sometimes indulged under the influence of Hunt. Conversation turned frequently to religion. Bailey was a sincere believer and was giving himself a sound preparation for his vocation in the church. Inevitably, he tried to influence Keats in the direction of his own faith. They read passages of the Bible, while the conversations on their punting expeditions were, as Bailey recalled, 'earnest'.

The basis of his own faith Bailey would outline in a pamphlet published later that year:

> If we believe the first pages of our Bible, that man fell by the greatest *evil* spirit, it is impossible in the nature of things, if a particular scheme of redemption be appointed, like the Christian, that he can rise again to his first state of perfection, but by the mediation of the highest *good* spirit. This is God. Good and evil we have seen materially and morally divide the world. The last in its deepest dye can only be effaced by the first.[32]

Bailey's faith was a solution to the problem of evil, and it was this concept he tried to implant in Keats's mind as their conversations led to a deepening of Keats's always questioning sense of moral purpose. Bailey was pleased by the result. 'He promised me,' he wrote, 'and I believe he kept his promise, that he would never scoff at religion.'[33]

It was partly the presence of Bailey himself that was so persuasive an influence. Both his friend's religious tact and his sincerity were of a high order, and, if Keats felt unable to follow him in his faith, there is no question that Bailey influenced him by his example. He represented a way of being a man that stirred Keats's imagination and respect. As he was to write at the beginning of the following year, 'that sort of probity & disinterestedness which such men as Bailey possess, does hold & grasp the tip-top of any spiritual honours, that can be paid to anything in this world.'[34] Such praise was sincere, but it is not only the feelings expressed that are so revealing, the vocabulary too is important. 'Disinterestedness' was a word Keats had recently acquired (perhaps through Bailey) from the work of the critic who was to influence him more profoundly than any other: William Hazlitt.

The subtitle of Hazlitt's *On the Principles of Human Action*, his first published work, had proclaimed the author's concern with 'the Natural Disinterestedness of the Human Mind'. Keats owned a copy of this book, and the growth of his ideas from now on continuously reveals the imprint of Hazlitt's, especially the older man's belief in the power of imaginative sympathy to enter into the identity of the life around it and so be inspired by something other than self-interest and self-love. 'I can go out of myself entirely,' Hazlitt wrote, 'and enter into the minds and feelings of others.' For Hazlitt, this was a personal contribution to an important problem in contemporary philosophy; for Keats, it was an idea wholly congenial to his own temperament: to the altruism that underlay his commitment first to medicine and then to poetry, to his political liberalism, and to a mind that experienced those moments of intense participation in the life of nature Severn had observed. Very soon, as Keats turned to Hazlitt's critical writings and to his discussion of Shakespeare particularly, he was to see such disinterestedness, the great writer's refusal to be preoccupied with self-expression and his own personality, as an essential quality of literary genius.

Keats was maturing with extraordinary speed, but if these weeks in Oxford had given his imagination a far richer and deeper image of his future than any he had previously been able to guess at, it was inevitable he would look back on the self he was outgrowing with disillusion and even distaste. He was, besides, very tired. By 26 September the thousand lines of the third Book of his poem had been written, but when he came to look over them he was disappointed. He wrote confessing as much to Haydon. 'My Ideas with respect to it I assure you are very low – and I would write the subject thoroughly again. but I am tired of it and think the time would be better spent in writing a new Romance which I have in my eye for next summer – Rome was not built in a Day. and all the good I expect from my employment this summer is the fruit of Experience which I hope to gather in my next Poem.'[35]

He had been unable to make a start on Book Four, and Bailey suggested they take a break and go to Stratford-upon-Avon for a few days. Here they did the expected things: visiting Shakespeare's birthplace, adding their names to the walls already black with signatures, and going to the church, where Keats was struck 'with the simple statue' of the poet. The whole visit indeed was staid, autumnal, pleasurable, and Bailey recalled that Keats's enjoyment of Stratford 'was of that genuine, quiet kind which was a part of his gentle nature; deeply feeling what he truly enjoyed, but saying little'. Then, on the following Sunday, with the Michaelmas term about to begin, Keats took the coach back to London, a young man changed by what he would later call the 'awakening of the thinking principle'.

All the same, he was not in the best of spirits. The weaknesses of his poem preyed on his mind and he faced the prospect of having to write another thousand lines of a work he was rapidly growing out of. He had, besides, caught some sort of infection, which he was trying to cure by taking small quantities of mercury. The notion advanced by some biographers that he had contracted a venereal disease is at best not proven. Mercury was prescribed in the treatment of tonsillitis and Keats was to show himself highly susceptible to sore throats. More importantly, there is little to suggest (and much in his poems to deny) that he was fully sexually experienced. Nonetheless, as a trained medical man Keats knew that taking mercury threatened a patient's resistance to illness generally and was even held to be an exciting cause in the development of tuberculosis. Exposure to cold and damp was reckoned particularly dangerous under such circumstances, and Keats stayed indoors during a spell of wretched weather in the middle of October. Not only did this give him the opportunity of continuing with *Endymion*, it also protected him from the disagreeable atmosphere that had settled over his London friends.

Hunt was being particularly difficult. While Keats was in Oxford Reynolds had written to tell him of a meeting with Hunt at the theatre. Reynolds had commented on how well Keats was proceeding with *Endymion* and said that he was clearly going to complete his 4000 lines. Hunt, preening himself with a little literary man's superciliousness, at once responded that if it had not been for him the poem would have run to 7000 lines. Although he did not mention it at the time, Keats was infuriated by this, Hunt's proprietorial attitude mingling perhaps with his own discontent at the poem's evident *longueurs*. For Reynolds too this was a turning point in his relationship with Hunt, whose limitations were now becoming ever clearer to him. Clarke was later to suggest that it was Reynolds who turned Keats away from Hunt, and it is likely that he did have some part to play in this. Others, however, were also trying to wean him from what they regarded as a dangerous influence.

Haydon, for example, had warned Keats not to show *Endymion* to Hunt since he would be bound to claim half the merit of the work for himself. But, if this was shrewd, it was also biased. The mutual delight the two men had in aggravating each other took a new turn when financial necessities obliged Haydon to move from Great Marlborough Street to rooms close to Hunt in Lisson Grove. Here, when Keats visited on 6 October, he found everyone at loggerheads. This was particularly disagreeable since he had hoped to escape for a few hours from his own cramped lodgings and the noise and smell of his landlord's children. But the atmosphere in Haydon's studio was far from calming. The *Triumphal Entry* was at a standstill and Hunt took the opportunity to strut up and down 'criticising every head most unmercifully'. At the same time he was trying to show off to Shelley, who was also there, harassed and distracted but at least with his own long poem *Laon and Cythna* finished, by extolling the delights of free love. Haydon, whose powerful sex drive was kept under control only by an exaggerated sense of guilt, was currently trying to suppress his desire for his new maid and was clearly on edge. Keats eventually left with relief. 'I am quite disgusted with literary Men,' he wrote to Bailey, 'and will never know another except Wordsworth.'

But it was not that easy to escape. If Hunt was irksome, Haydon could also be a trying friend. He had written to Keats during his stay in Oxford asking him to find out about the circumstances of a painter called Cripps, whom he had offered to teach for free provided the young man could support himself. In fact, Cripps was poor. Keats and Bailey made efforts to help him, but now Haydon appeared in danger of reneging on his promise. Such matters were an aggravating waste of time, and Keats's letter to Bailey of 8 October, in which he copied out the credo previously written to George, strongly asserts his wish to be independent. It was to protect this independence that he had refused Shelley's invitation to spend the summer in Marlow with him and Hunt, but it now seemed Hunt would commandeer his work anyway. 'I shall have the reputation of Hunt's elevé,' he lamented, adding: 'His corrections and amputations will by the knowing ones be trased in the Poem.'

Meanwhile, kept indoors by his illness, he continued with the work, although at a slower pace than he had enjoyed in Oxford. He sent Bailey the opening lines of Book Four – an invocation to the muse of English poetry that closes with a recognition of his own modest place at the end of this great tradition – and then, on the last day of October, he posted to Jane Reynolds a transcript of some stanzas from the 'Ode to Sorrow' sung by a newly introduced character, the Indian Maid:

To Sorrow,
I bade good-morrow,

And thought to leave her far away behind.
   But cheerly, cheerly,
   She loves me dearly;
She is so constant to me, and so kind:
   I would deceive her
   And so leave her,
But ah! she is so constant and so kind.[36]

The ode is one of the most effective passages in the Book, a rich mythological tableau partly inspired by Titian's *Bacchus and Ariadne*, which had recently been on public view. The Indian Maid herself is the lovely personification of the sorrows of the world with whom Endymion suddenly and unconvincingly falls in love. At the close of the poem, she is revealed as an avatar of the goddess of the moon, thereby suggesting in her union with Endymion that the world of the ideal is embodied in the real and that for the poet fulfilment lies in seeing there is no divorce between them.

Keats's letters to Bailey from the weeks of late October and early November tell a different tale. While he congratulated his friend on what seemed to be an offer of a curacy, his own feelings were often pained and bitter. 'In this world there is no quiet nothing but teasing and snubbing and vexation.' His friends were quarrelling, Tom's health was clearly worsening, and he felt generally oppressed. Then, suddenly, the scale of that oppression became apparent. The Bishop of Lincoln refused Bailey the curacy. To Keats, this seemed an outrageous attack on a good man, an exercise by the establishment in arbitrary power. 'The Stations and Grandeurs of the World have taken it into their heads that they cannot commit themselves towards an inferior in rank – but is not the impertinence from one above to one below more wretchedly mean than from the low to the high?' Then, having drawn a line across the page, Keats began to discuss his own problems with the establishment and, in particular, a new organ of the Tory press: *Blackwood's Edinburgh Magazine*.

The magazine had had a shaky start, and, when its proprietor reorganised it with the help of the brutal John Wilson and John Gibson Lockhart, he was resolved to exploit the political and social tensions in the country in order to boost *Blackwood's* place in the circulation war. One means of doing this was to launch an all-out attack on Leigh Hunt and his followers, and to do so under a viciously clever slogan. In the October issue of *Blackwood's*, and with an epigraph that paired Hunt's name with Keats's and printed both in capitals, the magazine launched the first of a series of articles 'On the Cockney School of Poetry'. The nastiness of this title lay in the fact that the contemporary use of the word 'cockney' was more pointed than it has since become. 'Cockney' referred not only to a native Londoner, it implied puerility, affectation and effeminacy. It suggested, in other words, everything that was marginal to an ideal of the patrician and the masculine. The *Blackwood's* reviewer 'Z' made this position breathtakingly clear: 'All the great poets of our country have been men of some rank in society, and there is no vulgarity in any of their writings; but Mr Hunt cannot utter a dedication, or even a note, without betraying the *Shibboleth* of low birth and low habits.'[37] The class structures of the old regime leap into life and, with them, a host of associated prejudices.

The reviewer claimed that Hunt (and, by extension, Keats) was ignorant of the great European tradition of classical and renaissance poetry, while his religion was a watered-down version of the blasphemies of those Frenchmen who wrote the *Encyclopédie* and so hastened the catastrophe of the Revolution. Hunt himself was a despiser of monarchical authority, while his patriotism was, not surprisingly, 'a crude, vague, ineffectual, and sour Jacobinism'. A man so completely devoid of acceptable manliness could only be described through what were intended to be vicariously lurid similes. Emasculated and living on the lowest reaches of middle-class society, Hunt and the poets of the Cockney School could excite in 'the mind of a man of fashion' the sort of disgust he must feel at a party thrown by 'a little mincing boarding-school mistress' where 'everything is pretence, affectation, finery and gaudiness' and where the guests are attorneys' apprentices, music teachers, clerks, 'faded fan-twinkling spinsters, prurient vulgar misses from school, and enormous citizens' wives'. Members of the Cockney School belong, in other words, to the socially and sexually marginal, to the genteel and the pretentious.

This, by the curious logic of prejudice, makes them dangerous, nowhere more so than on questions of sexual passion, where their own manifest deprivation condemns them to prurience, a prurience which corrupts the decencies of adult married love. Hunt, the reviewer suggests, was temperamentally committed to a tale such as *Rimini*. 'For him there is no charm in simple seduction; and he gloats over it only when accompanied with adultery and incest.' Byron, being 'one of the most nobly born of English Patricians, and one of the first geniuses the world ever produced', could, of course, write tales of incest in perfect tragic taste. Hunt and his 'younger and less important auxiliaries, the Keatses, the Shelleys', however, can only spread moral depravity: 'and we confess, that we think that poet deserving of chastisement, who pollutes his talents in a manner that is likely to corrupt milliners and apprentice-boys.'

It now seemed merely a question of time before 'Z' turned his attention to Keats himself and the insistent adolescent sexuality of the *Poems* and *Endymion*. Keats himself had hopes of the article's 'non appearance' since an advertisement had been placed in the *Examiner* challenging 'Z' to show his hand. He tried to play the matter down – 'I dont mind the thing much' – but he knew his honour was at stake and 'if he should go to such lengths with me as he has done with Hunt I mu[s]t infallibly call him to account – if he be a human being and appears in Squares and Theatres where we might possibly meet – I dont relish his abuse.'

With this threat hanging over his head, and with his worries about Tom, his disillusion with his literary and artistic friends, the continuing pressure of his social life and the numerous 'little two penny errands' he was running in the attempt to raise money for Cripps, progress with *Endymion* became difficult. Once again, Keats would have to escape and find the solitude in which he could write. He chose the Fox and Hounds, a coaching inn at Burford Bridge under Box Hill, where he arrived on 22 November. Before he could fully settle to work, he wrote letters to Bailey and Reynolds, and it is in these rather than the last sections of his poem that the greater interest lies.

The deepening of Keats's thought and the influence of Hazlitt especially are clear in his new largeness of response. For instance, the difficulties Haydon was making over the Cripps business had been irksome both to Keats and to his correspondents, but now, instead of the explosion of anger triggered by Bailey's treatment at the hands of the Bishop of Lincoln, Keats was altogether more self-effacing. 'Why don't you, as I do, look unconcerned at what may be called more particularly Heart-vexations?' he counselled Reynolds. To Bailey he wrote in a more confessional mode: 'I scarcely remember counting upon any Happiness – I look not for it if it be not in the present hour – nothing startles me beyond the Moment.' Then, in a beautiful sentence which exactly captures his capacity for sympathetic identification with the world, Keats wrote: 'the setting sun will always set me to rights – or if a Sparrow come before my Window I take part in its existence and pick about the Gravel.'[38]

It is such a submission of the ego that characterises the discussion of genius in this great letter, and Keats's reading of Hazlitt now began to combine with memories of his chemistry lectures to produce a startling image in which to express his ideas. He needed to convey his belief that the truly talented change the world not through the power of their characters but by the altogether more mysterious influence of their impersonality. Like catalysts, they precipitate change while remaining themselves unchanged. 'Men of Genius', he declared, 'are great as certain ethereal Chemicals operating on the Mass of neutral intellect – [but] they have not any individuality, and determined Character.' They are not men who come to the truth through 'consequitive reasoning', but by the submission of their intellect to intuition, to the organic processes of nature and the 'Life of Sensations' or vivid concrete experience.

It was on this basis that the imagination could ascend through friendship and love to eternal truth. As Keats reminded Bailey: 'you may know my favourite Speculation from my first Book.' Bailey himself, however, had expressed reservations about 'the authenticity of the Imagination'. These were doubts that Keats himself was later to be affected by, but for the moment he was radiantly confident. Drawing an image from Milton, he assured Bailey: 'the Imagination may be compared to Adam's dream – he woke and found it truth.' Then, excited by his own confidence, he went on to tell Bailey of another 'favourite Speculation'. The life of sensations in this world, he declared, was but a premonition of the full happiness we will know in eternity: 'We shall enjoy ourselves here after by having what we called happiness on Earth repeated in a finer tone.'

Such confidence, so innocent and free from guile, has the touching pathos of youthful certainty. But for the moment, as he set himself to finish *Endymion*, Keats's letters stopped. More than ever he was resolved to complete this period, to put it behind him if only by sheer dogged labour. Shut away in his hotel room, he wrote at an alarming rate, averaging eighty to eighty-five lines a day. Haste and fatigue show themselves in the many clumsinesses of the draft, the slack writing, and even in the apathetic exhaustion of his hero as he is hurried towards his unconvincing apotheosis. Finally, by 28 November, the work was finished, the 'test of invention' was complete.

And almost at once a new period began. Keats had earlier imagined he would bring *Endymion* to its close among the 'sober gold' and harvests of autumn, but it was fatigue amid the winter gloom that showed him the way forward.

In drear-nighted December,
    Too happy, happy tree,
Thy branches ne'er remember
    Their green felicity:
  The north cannot undo them,
  With sleety whistle through them,
  Nor frozen thawings glue them
    From budding at the prime.[39]

Nature, he had argued through the past two years, salved man's wounds by offering permanent access to eternal truths. She spoke the same language as man's unconscious mind and responded to the needs of his imagination by allowing herself to be peopled with the figures of myth. She could be turned to for a beauty that salvaged the spirit in a world otherwise wrecked by men. Despite the horrors of Regency politics, the moon shone down in her benevolence and Endymion was 'ensky'd'. Now, with heart-rending clarity, Keats could see only nature's insentience, her freedom from memory, desire and pain:

In drear-nighted December,
    Too happy, happy brook,
Thy bubblings ne'er remember
    Apollo's summer look;
  But with a sweet forgetting,
  They stay their crystal fretting,
  Never, never petting
    About the frozen time.

Mankind can share no such insouciance as the tree and the stream enjoy:

Ah! would 'twere so with many
    A gentle girl and boy!
But were there ever any
    Writhed not of passed joy?
  The feel of not to feel it,
  When there is none to heal it,
  Nor numbed sense to steel it,
    Was never said in rhyme.

Longing for joy, stretching out to imagined, permanent worlds of truth and beauty, man is forever thwarted by the burden of his consciousness and obliged to return to his aching heart. Such a discovery leads to the great works of Keats's maturity, and now, in the dark days of 1817 and with 'Apollo's summer look' obscured, Keats was at last beginning to find his true self and the anguished core of his art.

Uncertainties, Mysteries, Doubts

I mean *Negative Capability*, that is when a man is capable of being in uncertainties, Mysteries, doubts, without any irritable reaching after fact & reason.

(Keats to his brothers, 21 December 1817)

A WEEK AFTER completing *Endymion*, Keats returned to London burdened with his new anxieties and unable to write. Snow was falling and a thick yellow fog hovered above it, dirtying everything and requiring lamps and candles to be lit even at midday. Keats's brothers were planning to escape to the cleaner air of Teignmouth for the sake of Tom's health, and Keats himself would soon be on his own. To compensate for the arduous days he had spent finishing his poem and for the yet more arduous doubts that engulfed him after its conclusion, he threw himself into a round of literary meetings and parties. In this period of uncertainty, the record of his conviviality becomes frenetic.

Wordsworth was in town, and Keats was more than ever keen to see him. He had at some time sent the older man a copy of the *Poems* inscribed with 'the Author's sincere Reverence', but the fact that many pages in the volume remained uncut tells its own story. Wordsworth himself meanwhile was facing a series of personal and professional crises, and the aloof, imperiously egotistical traits in his personality came out so strongly as to force some of his followers to question their admiration. As a young man on the fringes of this company, Keats observed the presence of his living idol with a combination of questioning respect and a healthy sense of humour. But over the following months, as the contrary currents of opinion among the older generation swept about him, Keats felt obliged constantly to reform his view of the man he nonetheless recognised as the greatest poet of the age. In so doing, he would also begin to shape more thoroughly his understanding of modern poetry and the direction of his own art.

He was given his first chance of doing so when Haydon engineered a meeting. Wordsworth had been sitting to Haydon for his portrait as the great modern Christian poet in the *Triumphal Entry*, filling the studio with his voice as he recited from Milton and his own *Excursion*. An encouraged Haydon wrote a note to Tom Monkhouse (a cousin of Wordsworth's wife) asking if Keats might be introduced to the great man at his brother's house in Lambeth. Monkhouse replied that the meeting could more conveniently be held at his own home in Cavendish Square, and here Haydon escorted Keats, who showed, the painter recalled, 'the greatest, the purest, the most unalloyed pleasure at the prospect'.[1]

The immediate cause of Wordsworth's coming to London was the hope of settling various problems that had arisen on the death of his brother and which posed a risk to Wordsworth's slender financial security.[2] Although sustained by his love for his wife, whom he recognised as the bedrock of his private life, the health and future of his children concerned him, and years of hardship had been only partly relieved by his accepting a minor government post as Distributor of Stamps for his region of the Lake District. This office produced rather less than Wordsworth hoped, but for some it triggered the suspicion that he had become merely a hired hand of the Tories. Such a slur was one of several dangers now threatening his overwhelming professional preoccupation, which was to establish his poetic eminence and thereby increase his earnings. To do this, Wordsworth needed to refute the hostile criticisms that still issued from Jeffrey of the *Edinburgh Review* and the deeply loathed figure of Hazlitt.

Hazlitt, while recognising the merits of Wordsworth, had disparaged *The Excursion* in a review which highlighted its dramatic weakness, its failure to capture what for Hazlitt himself were the primary qualities of the variety and objectivity of 'real life'. He also underlined Wordsworth's unwillingness to deal adequately with the French Revolution. Above all, however, the egocentricity of the work was the very opposite of disinterested, and Wordsworth himself the reverse of Hazlitt's ideal of the artist. 'It is as if there were nothing but himself and the universe,' he wrote. 'He lives in the busy solitude of his own heart; in the deep silence of thought.' Such an attack was to influence Keats profoundly as, partly in response to *The Excursion*, he began to work out his own ideas on the nature of the poet.

It was into this gigantic, difficult presence that Haydon now ushered him, but the record of what followed has almost certainly been distorted by the years of rancorous bitterness that were eventually to lead to Haydon's suicide. Indeed, it is even possible that Haydon confused memories of two separate occasions before adding his commentary. Written nearly thirty years after the events it supposedly recounts, his memoir suggests that Wordsworth politely asked Keats what he was currently writing. Before Keats himself had a chance of answering, Haydon himself jumped in. '*I* said he had just finished an exquisite ode to Pan – and as he [Wordsworth] had not a copy I begged Keats to repeat it – which he did in his usual half chant (most touchingly) walking up and down the room.' The image is a delightful one and Haydon acknowledged its charm. 'When he had done I felt really, as if I had heard a young Apollo.'

Haydon's description of what happened next is disputable. He alleged that Wordsworth 'drily' said that the ode was 'a Very pretty piece of Paganism', and then added that Keats felt what he supposed was the implied criticism in the remark 'deeply'. Haydon then claimed that, as a result of this, Keats 'never forgave him'. Nothing in Keats's letters or his maturing view of Wordsworth indicates that this was so, and there is evidence to suggest that Wordsworth's customary use of the word 'pretty' was not derogatory. Indeed, while it is obvious that Haydon wished to present an image of youthful genius crushed by pompous and unfeeling middle age, the evidence suggests that Keats was more amused than hurt by such attitudes.

Clarke for instance recalls an anecdote probably told him by Keats which suggests that Keats himself was well able to laugh behind his hand at the weaknesses of a man he fundamentally revered. 'During that same interview,' Clarke wrote, 'someone having observed that the next Waverley novel was to be "Rob Roy", Wordsworth took down his volume of Ballads, and read to the company "Rob Roy's Grave"; then, returning it to the shelf, observed, "I do not know what more Mr Scott can have to say upon the subject."'[3] The phrase captures the man at his most unbendingly pompous, and it is not difficult to hear the shared youthful laughter with which this anecdote might first have been told. For all this, however, Keats continued to regard Wordsworth's literary achievement highly even while his responses to him as both a poet and a man were to develop and become more mature and more questioning.

George and Tom left for Teignmouth on 13 December, but although Keats was now on his own there were many people for him to see and much for him to do. Around this time he was becoming initiated into a 'sort of a Club every Saturday evening' to which he had been introduced by Reynolds's friend James Rice, a man whose judgement Keats was to come increasingly to respect.[4] All the members of the club were young and male, many of them from the business classes centred around Piccadilly. Their interests were less intellectual than convivial, their conversation being much concerned with alcohol and girls. The raciness of the group appealed to Keats, but if this rooted him firmly in a young man's Regency London there was a slight, quizzical sense of distance when he wrote about the company to his brothers. Fladgate, Martin, Rodwell and the delightfully named Squib become, by an almost inevitable metamorphosis, Hal's good lads of Eastcheap. 'They call good Wine a pretty tipple, and call getting a Child knocking out an apple, stopping at a Tavern they call hanging out. Where do you sup? is where do you hang out?'

This was a sufficiently agreeable way of passing a Saturday evening, a recreation from the more challenging concerns that were pressing on Keats and causing him to examine both his society and his art. Writing to his brothers on 21 December, for instance, Keats mentioned the trial of William Hone. This last gripped the nation, and the *Examiner* eagerly reported its progress. For the three days of his examination, Hone spoke in his own defence for a total of twenty-one hours. At issue was not merely a question of blasphemy. By their attempt to defend their religion in the courts, the grandees of the old regime were patently trying to protect the mystique of their privileges. For liberal-thinking people, for the crowds who lined the chilly streets and the one in twenty who actually gained admission to the court, the trial posed the question whether the full, oppressive weight of the establishment could be resisted by a jury. Almost alone, these men seemed able to speak for a people whose petitions had been rebuffed, who were largely denied parliamentary representation, and who were without rights of public assembly. The trial of a man arrested under the suspension of *habeas corpus* dramatically focused the degree of repression inflicted by those in power.

Hone's eventual release was a liberal triumph celebrated in Keats's unsuccessful sonnet 'Nebuchadnezzar's Dream' and, more certainly, in a letter to his brothers. 'Hone, the publisher's trial, you must find very amusing; and, as Englishmen, very encouraging – his *Not Guilty* is a thing, which not to have been, would have dulled still more Liberty's Emblazoning.' Here was a public victory over the constraints of the times, but Keats's letter is an altogether more comprehensive and personal attempt to establish what he was coming to see as the poet's necessary openness to all experience.

On the Sunday after his brothers' departure he dined with Haydon, from whom he had a standing invitation. The Cripps business was coming back to life, Haydon being once more prepared to take the young man on provided an adequate sum for his support could be raised. To this end, Keats began to solicit contributions from the more wealthy among his acquaintance, and some time during the middle of the week he exchanged the boisterous Saturday-night camaraderie of the Rice set for the silk and mahogany of Horace Smith's house in Knightsbridge.[5] Smith's two brothers, his friend Thomas Hill, along with a fashionable magazine editor and the somewhat obtuse John Kingston, Deputy Comptroller of the Stamp Office, were also there.

Empty mannerism replaced racy slang, and each man was a mirror before whom the others performed. As he had been with Shelley, Keats was a little uneasy in such company. Despite his fascination with other people's lives, he could not enter into the existence of these people. 'They only served to convince me how superior humour is to wit in respect of enjoyment – These men say things which make one start, without making one feel, they are all alike; their manners are alike; they all know fashionables; they have a mannerism in their very eating & drinking, in their mere handling of a Decanter.' Their lives seemed glassy and on the surface, inviolable to an appreciation of the worlds of the imagination and the arts. Conversation eventually turned to the theatre. 'They talked of Kean & his low company – Would I were with that company instead of yours, said I to myself!'

Edmund Kean and, indeed, the drama in general were becoming increasingly important to Keats at this time, partly because of the influence of two of his Hampstead friends: Dilke and Charles Brown. Dilke's interest in plays was scholarly, Brown's more practical, and while Dilke had become an established friend, studying *Paradise Lost* with Keats, it was only recently that the poet's friendship with Brown had begun to ripen, Brown himself having spent much of the summer in his native Scotland. There had been a mutual attraction from the start. 'It was on the Hampstead road we were introduced to each other,' Brown recalled, and 'in that interview of a minute I inwardly desired his acquaintanceship, if not his friendship.'[6] Brown, who was himself a vigorous and physical man, clearly felt drawn to similar qualities in Keats, and his description of the poet is an important corrective to more sentimentalising portraits. The author of *Endymion* 'was small in stature, well proportioned, compact in form, and, though thin, rather muscular; – one of the many who prove that manliness is distinct from height and bulk'.

Brown's relationship with Keats was to deepen in important ways as the various sides of his own complex personality unfolded themselves. He was more than eight years older than Keats, a man by turns open and canny, bookish and exuberant, qualities which at times tended to belie the tenderness of which he was capable and which allowed him to cherish what he knew to be a uniquely precious friendship. His wider experience, too, made him appreciative of what his intuitions told him. Brown had, among other things, been an unsuccessful Russia merchant, a period of his life which provided him with material for an unpublished novel and his comic opera *Narensky, or The Road to Yaroslaf*. This undistinguished piece had been produced at Drury Lane at the start of 1814 and earned Brown £300 and a silver ticket guaranteeing him free entry to the theatre for life. Now, on 15 December, Keats himself went to Drury Lane to see Kean in *Richard III*.

This was one of the actor's finest roles, offering as it did great scope for the revolutionary attention to intense detail by which Kean transformed the London stage. Hazlitt had greeted his Shylock as the 'first gleam of genius breaking athwart the gloom', and in a matter of three years Kean replaced the decorous formality of Kemble's style with an enthusiasm for his own unpatrician vehemence. As famous off-stage for his brandy drinking and loud-mouthed republicanism among low-living friends – the very characteristics which Horace Smith and his cronies had professed to disparage – Kean's style of acting rapidly gathered political associations. The management of the Drury Lane theatre was Whig in its sympathies, while what Hazlitt praised as Kean's 'gusto', his exhilarating inversion of the formal aesthetic supported by the old regime, was romantic, revolutionary and, above all, spontaneous. 'Kean delivers himself up to the instant feeling,' wrote Keats, 'without a shadow of thought about anything else.'[7]

The opportunity to express this view had been given by Reynolds, who, convinced that the *Champion* could not provide the money needed if he were to settle down and marry, had resolved to follow Rice's example and enter the law. Rice himself showed that a man could lead a cultivated life while working as a solicitor; he had, besides, paid Reynolds' fee of £110 for articles in the office of Francis Fladgate and promised to take Reynolds into partnership on the death of his own father. By 3 November, Reynolds was studying the law and slowly relinquishing his post as theatrical reviewer on the *Champion*. His kindness to Keats continued nonetheless. When the first *Blackwood's* article on the Cockney Poets came out, he exercised his skill in literary diplomacy in the hope of limiting the damage. In this he was not successful, but now, in December, he began a light revision of *Endymion*, hoping to help his friend before disappearing to visit his girl in Exeter.

Perhaps as an exchange of favours, Keats undertook to write a review of Kean's performance as Luke Traffic in *Riches*. The play was an unremarkable adaptation, and the atmosphere in which Keats was writing demanded he concentrate on the full, liberating force of Kean's genius in the major Shakespearian roles, for here was the display of a truly great art to set against the constrictions of contemporary England. This was his real subject, and Keats's review reflects a nationwide feeling of impotence and enforced pettiness. The first sentence sets the tone. '"In our unimaginative days" – *Habeas Corpus'd* as we are, out of all wonder, uncertainty and fear; – in these fireside, delicate, gilded days, – these days of sickly safety and comfort, we feel very grateful to Mr Kean for giving us some excitement by his old passion in one of the old plays.' As the review develops, so it becomes a broad plea for imaginative freedom and an amplitude which is unknown, Keats suggests, in Regency England, with its repressive politics and over-ornamented and domesticated art.

Kean, by contrast, stands unique as 'a relict of romance'. He is distinguished by his dramatic power, by his ability to draw from poetry 'pleasures both sensual and spiritual', and by the depth of his feeling. He has, Keats suggests, a Wordsworthian authority of emotion and an intense immediacy. The influence of Hazlitt is particularly clear as Keats declares 'there is an indescribable gusto in his voice, by which we feel the utterer is thinking of the past and the future, while speaking of the instant.' Kean had, in other words, those qualities which in his essay 'On Gusto' Hazlitt had defined as the great artist's ability so to penetrate the 'power or passion defining any object' that he can render it back in all its living actuality. Eventually, this becomes identified with Shakespearian intensity and a Shakespearian ability to enter imagin-atively into endless, strongly contrasted variety. By the close of the review, this force becomes the one quality to set against a Regency England in servitude to its denial of imaginative freedom. 'Kean! Kean! have . . . a pity for us in these cold and enfeebling times! Cheer us a little in the failure of our days! for romance lives but in books. The goblin is driven from the heath, and the rainbow is robbed of its mystery!'

What the failure of such an ideal meant was apparent to Keats a couple of days later when he went to see Benjamin West's enormous canvas *Death on a Pale Horse*. The picture was a popular sensation, some even hailing it as a triumph comparable to Waterloo. Others were less enthusiastic. Hazlitt, with that depth and exactitude which made him so unerring a judge, derided the lurid central figure, saying: 'he has not the calm, still, majestic form of Death, killing by a look – withering by a touch. His presence does not make the still air cold.'[8] Keats's comment reflects this view and develops his own thoughts about what is sterile in the merely melodramatic. 'It is a wonderful picture when West's age is considered,' he wrote,

> but there is nothing to be intense upon; no woman one feels mad to kiss, no face swelling into reality. the excellence of every Art is its intensity, capable of making all disagreeables evaporate, from their being in close relationship with Beauty & Truth. Examine "King Lear", & you will find this exemplified throughout; but in this picture we have unpleasantness without any momentous depth of speculation excited, in which to bury its repulsiveness.[9]

The maturity and depth of aesthetic experience this comment draws on are remarkable and point to the direction in which Keats's own art was to mature. The failure of West's painting, it is suggested, lies in its melodramatic straining after effect, its inability to achieve that genuine and unselfconscious 'intensity' which for contemporary scientists and writers alike was the measure of life and art. The picture was effectively dead, and Keats's recoil from such lapel-grabbing sensationalism as West strained after indicates what was now becoming for him the supreme importance of the artist's imagination as a faculty able to identify the fundamental passion in his subject and to do this so completely that the merely contingent is burned away. What the true artist – a Shakespeare or a Kean – gives his audience are clarity, fullness and, above all, an 'intensity' of expression which are felt at the deepest level to be both emotionally true and aesthetically harmonious. This is so even of the dreadful areas of experience charted in *King Lear*. As always, Shakespeare, especially the Shakespeare revealed to him by Hazlitt, remains Keats's measure of the highest achievement, and from Hazlitt's *Characters of Shakespeare's Plays* he now took the idea that 'the greatest strength of genius is shown in describing the strongest passions.'

Keats had been greatly stimulated over recent days, and somehow this range of new impressions had to be brought together, its personal application discovered. This happened, quite by chance, during a walk with Dilke that probably took place as the two men were returning to Hampstead after seeing the Boxing Day pantomime at Drury Lane.

Dilke himself was a man of set ideas, orderly, methodical and energetic. Perhaps it was the pull of opposites that attracted Keats to him, along with his kindness and unpredictable bursts of humour. Keats was fascinated by the way such moments seemed to throw Dilke's dominant characteristics into relief, for essentially he was a figure who believed in intellectual control. Keats himself described him as the sort of man 'who cannot feel he has a personal identity unless he has made up his Mind about everything'. Conversation with Dilke tended to become a 'disquisition' and now, as this was proceeding at one level:

> several things dovetailed in my mind, & at once it struck me, what quality went to form a Man of Achievement especially in literature & which Shakespeare possessed so enormously – I mean *Negative Capability*, that is when a man is capable of being in uncertainties, Mysteries, doubts, without any irritable reaching after fact & reason.[10]

This famous passage draws on Keats's own temperament, on impressions and ideas derived from those about him, and is above all a plea for that receptivity and openness which the words themselves exemplify. There is much here of Hazlitt's ideal of disinterestedness and of that spontaneous intensity Keats so relished in the acting of Kean. Astley Cooper's disparagement of sweeping theory may also have played its part (the timbre of a great intellect lingers in other minds long after the immediate occasion has passed), while the choice of the word 'negative' almost certainly derives from Keats's chemistry lectures, where negativity implied not a rejection, a minus or an absence, but rather a sympathetic receptive intensity. Just as, for Bailey, Keats had compared the actions of great minds to catalysts, so, for his brothers, he could imply that the 'negative capability' of the true poet was like an electrical negative: passive but, in its receptive power, quite the equal of the positive current.

Critical theory, acting, science and precept all have their part to play. So too may religion. Keats might have learned from Bailey that the influential Bishop Butler held that a man may have religious belief even though his mind remained 'in great doubts and uncertainties about both its evidence and nature'.[11] But what is so remarkable about the passage is not just the range on which it draws but its perfect adjustment to Keats's own character and that spontaneous, empathic force which from childhood had gone out from itself to the world of men and nature, the mind that read a life in the details of a beggar's dress or swam in exalted selflessness as the wind turned the corn to waves.

Freedom from the fixed, the rigid and the dogmatic was the moral element in this and is again clear in the passage itself. Like all of Keats's rapidly maturing views, this is a 'speculation', a provisional truth, tentative yet inspiring, an aspect of what he had already described to Bailey as his desire 'for a Life of Sensations rather than of Thoughts'. As Keats wrote elsewhere: 'almost any Man may like the Spider spin from his own inwards his own airy Citadel – the points of leaves and twigs on which the Spider begins her work are few and she fills the Air with a beautiful circuiting.'[12] It is these qualities of improvisation, of perceiving through images and of arriving at perceptions which coax the mind open rather than nailing it to the fine point of a logical conclusion, that breathe through the letters from now on as they become increasingly serious.

And even here the focus is on mental struggle, on 'uncertainties, Mysteries, doubts'. When Keats had written to Bailey from Burford Bridge, such things had been swept aside with youthful confidence. Now, in London and in 'drear-nighted December', Keats was on the edge of problems about the nature of consciousness that would deepen to a crisis during the following year. The rapturous marriage of the mind with the natural and spiritual worlds imagined in *Endymion* had fractured, and the pain in that poem, the hero's struggling in 'dull mortality's harsh net', was becoming altogether more urgent than a too easy insistence on a timeless union with beauty and truth.

Revealed to his hero in dreams, perhaps such a union was itself a dream, a fiction of the poet's contriving. Was *Endymion* anything more than what, in the borrowed Shakespearian motto, Keats calls 'the stretched metre of an antique song'? Man's more usual state is pain, the writhing of the unreconciled mind, and not moon-kissed self-annihilation in physical and ethereal ecstasy. In the lyric he had composed after completing *Endymion*, Keats had expressed his shocked and pained awareness of the gulf between insentient nature and suffering man. The crisis had provoked a longing for escape, for annihilation even, and 'the feel of not to feel it'. What the ideal of 'negative capability' offered was a means of facing the problem squarely: an unforced openness to the full range of experience, to pain as well as pleasure. This was an openness from which he might yet emerge as a great poet.

Company was a necessary anodyne to such reflection, and Keats's conviviality continued unabated. On 28 December he attended Haydon's 'immortal dinner', an occasion which, as the painter declared, was 'worthy of the Elizabethan age'.[13] Firelight played over the *Triumphal Entry* and its congregated heads of Voltaire, Newton and Hazlitt, as well as the portraits of Keats and Wordsworth, who themselves sat around the table below with Monkhouse, Lamb and Haydon. Homer, Virgil and Shakespeare supplied the topics of conversation, with Wordsworth 'repeating Milton with an intonation like the funeral bell of Saint Pauls and the music of Handel mingled'.

Lamb, meanwhile, was drinking and, his intuition being released with his inhibition, he began a humorous attack on Wordsworth for slighting Voltaire. While the others rallied to Wordsworth's support, Lamb raised his glass to 'the Messiah of the French nation' and then, swaying before the great canvas, picked on the figure of Newton. Why had Haydon included him, 'a Fellow who believed nothing unless it was as clear as the three sides of a triangle'? The sentiment chimed with that expressed by Keats in his *Champion* review, and the two men now agreed that Newton had destroyed all the poetry of the rainbow by reducing it to a prism. The company rose to drink 'Newton's health, and confusion to mathematics' before listening to a recital from *Endymion*.

Joseph Ritchie, a young surgeon introduced by Haydon as 'a gentleman going to Africa' in order to find a new route to the Niger ('Which is the young gentleman we are going to lose?' Lamb cried out prophetically), took greatly to Keats at this meeting and later praised him as the man likely 'to be the great poetical luminary of the age to come'. Keats, who knew that Ritchie was a good friend of Tom's, asked the explorer to take a copy of *Endymion* with him on his travels and fling it into the middle of the Sahara. The company then moved out for tea into another room where a portentous guest was waiting in silence. ('I had an instinct', Lamb said later, 'that he was the head of an office. I hate all such people.') The man had called on Haydon that morning, begging him to 'procure him the happiness of an introduction' to Wordsworth. Although Haydon had 'thought it a liberty', he had complied, and he now introduced him to the poet as John Kingston, forgetting to add that he was also Deputy Comptroller of Stamps and thus Wordsworth's superior.

The two men had corresponded but never met. 'After a while the comptroller looked down, looked up and said to Wordsworth, "Don't you think, sir, Milton was a great genius?"' Haydon recalled the embarrassment caused by so crass a question. 'Keats looked at me, Wordsworth looked at the comptroller, Lamb who was dozing by the fire turned round and said, "Pray, sir, did you say Milton was a great genius?" "No, sir; I asked Mr Wordsworth if he were not." "Oh," said Lamb, "then you are a silly fellow." "Charles! my dear Charles!" said Wordsworth; but Lamb, perfectly innocent of the confusion he had created, was off again by the fire.'

There was, in Haydon's phrase, 'an awful pause'. Then Kingston began again. '"Don't you think Newton was a great genius?"' The embarrassment was now intense. A look of questioning dismay crossed Wordsworth's face, Ritchie laughed, and, while Keats hid his face among Haydon's books,

> Lamb got up, and taking a candle, said, 'Sir, will you allow me to look at your phrenological development?' He then turned his back on the poor man, and at every question of the comptroller he chaunted –

> 'Diddle, diddle dumpling, my son John
> Went to bed with his breeches on.'

Kingston, realising that Wordsworth did not know who he was,

> said in a spasmodic and half-chuckling anticipation of assured victory, 'I have the honour of some correspondence with you, Mr Wordsworth.' 'With me, sir?' said Wordsworth. 'Not that I remember.' 'Don't you, sir? I am a comptroller of stamps.' There was a dead silence; the comptroller evidently thinking that was enough. While we were waiting for Wordsworth's reply, Lamb sung out:

> 'Hey diddle diddle,
> The cat and the fiddle.'

> 'My dear Charles,' said Wordsworth.

> 'Diddle, diddle dumpling, my son John.'

There was now only one thing to be done. 'Keats and I hurried Lamb into the painting-room, shut the door and gave way to inextinguishable laughter.' Then came the difficult task of placating 'the man in office', something only gradually achieved while the uproarious Lamb was 'struggling in the painting-room and calling out at intervals, "Who is that fellow? Allow me to see his organs once more."'

Kingston had won his little victory and, in time, 'being a good-natured man, we all parted in good humour, and no ill-effects followed.' Certainly, Kingston was sufficiently mollified to extend an invitation to Wordsworth and Keats to dine with him the following Saturday, but Keats later excused himself, not liking the thought of another evening of brittle and affected chit-chat. Having seen Wordsworth in unbuttoned mood, however, he was more than ever keen to deepen his acquaintance with him. The two men met by chance on

Hampstead Heath during the foggy last day of 1817. Then, on 3 January, Keats called on Wordsworth at Mortimer Street before the older poet went to dine with Kingston.

Keats was kept waiting for a time, and when Wordsworth did appear he was dressed in a frilled shirt, stiff collar, knee-breeches and silk stockings. Keats was clearly distressed by the sight of the greatest poet of the age wearing such conspicuously conservative livery and afterwards referred to it 'with something of anger'. Before he went off to a meeting of Rice's club he was introduced to Wordsworth's wife along with Coleridge's beloved Sarah Hutchinson, and he accepted an invitation to dine with them the following Monday.

The company of his Saturday-night friends allowed Keats temporarily to forget the distaste inspired by the formally dressed Wordsworth. They were all meeting up for a dance and their host, the tiny, lisping George Reddell, had provided far too much wine. Some eight dozen bottles were stacked on the back stairs. Like everyone else, Keats 'drank deep' and then he won half a guinea at the card table before the evening really got going. Recalling the occasion in a superbly racy letter to his brothers, Keats wrote:

> there was a younger Brother of the Squibs made him self very conspicuous after the Ladies had retired from the supper table by giving Mater Omnium – Mr Redhall said he did not understand anything but plain english – where at Rice egged the young fool on to say the Word plainly out. After which there was an enquirey about the derivation of the word C—t when while two parsons and Grammarians were settling together and settling the matter Wm Squibs interrupting them said a very good thing – 'Gentlemen says he I have always understood it to be a Root and not a Derivative.' On proceeding to the Pot in the Cupboard it soon became full on which the Court door was opened Frank Floodgate bawls out, Hoollo! here's an opposition pot – Ay, says Rice in one you have a Yard for your pot, and in the other a pot for your Yard –[14]

The flavour of Regency bachelor life is brilliantly caught here, but the very liveliness suggests how Keats was still more comfortable in male company than with women. So far, he was still sheltering from problems he did not dare fully face: his hostility to and fear of women, to which he could not as yet confess.

Perhaps Keats was still a little hung over the following day when he had two companions over to Well Walk: Severn and his old friend the Byronically handsome and mischievous Wells, who, long before, had provided the franked letters Keats had sent from Margate. Clearly this was another rather bibulous occasion since from four to ten all the men indulged a favourite pastime, imitating musical instruments and playing one of their concerts in which Keats himself often appeared as the bassoon. That evening he probably walked back to Wells's house and spent the night there, writing to his brothers the following morning before going to the Wordsworths' for dinner.

This was not an altogether easy occasion. In addition to his intense irritation with Coleridge for drawing attention to his earlier and more radical career in the *Biographia Literaria*, Monkhouse had told Wordsworth that the great Whig lawyer Henry Brougham was planning to contest Westmorland in the forthcoming general election. The seat was in all but name the hereditary possession of Wordsworth's patron Lord Lonsdale, and the 'ridiculous business' of Brougham's challenge would soon open up a vein of political obsession in Wordsworth that Keats himself observed with dismay. Meanwhile, over the dinner table in Mortimer Street, there was a dispute on some point. When Keats tried to have his say, the older man's 'fireside Divan' rallied expertly to his protection, Mrs Wordsworth gently putting her hand on Keats's arm and saying, 'Mr Wordsworth is never interrupted.'[15] The gesture personified a household, and clearly they all regarded 'little Keats' as still something of a boy. Now, while Wordsworth prepared himself to fight for the Tory cause, Sarah Hutchinson turned with bemused curiosity to *Endymion* and wondered that 'anybody should take such subjects now-a-days'.

This was the last recorded occasion on which Keats saw Wordsworth, but his silence about the evening was caused by more than mild disillusion. That morning he had been to Bedford Row to consult with Solomon Sawrey about Tom's health. Evidently the surgeon tried to calm Keats's concern in a steadfast, professional manner. 'He did not seem to be at all out at any thing I said and the enquiries I made with regard to your spitting of Blood: and moreover desired me to ask you to send him a correct account of all your sensations and symptoms concerning the Palpitation and the spitting and the Cough – if you have any.'[16] Clearly, Keats's hectic party-going covered more than creative anxiety and fatigue. Dreadful memories were stirred as it became evident that the family disease was stalking them once again and that Tom might have contracted tuberculosis.

Keats would have to face this crisis, to live once again with misery and encroaching death. Meanwhile, the 'racketing' continued for another week. He went with Wells to a seedy playhouse near Drury Lane, escaped after the first Act and used Brown's silver ticket to catch 'a Spice' of Kean's Richard III at the greater theatre. Returning to Wells, he was taken backstage during the interval and observed the actors and actresses swearing and quarrelling with each other before they appeared on stage for the farce. This was supposed to be followed by a comic opera but, the curtain failing to rise after a third reprise of the overture, actors and audience retired to a public house, giving themselves up to uninhibited chatter that was altogether more to Keats's taste.

In addition, there were two dances to attend and the business of Cripps to see to. Haydon, however, was being refractory. Mrs Leigh Hunt's slow returning of some of his cutlery led to one explosion, while the failure of Reynolds to attend the 'immortal dinner' led to a harsh exchange of letters and the breakdown of the friendship. 'Men must bear with each other' was Keats's comment as he tried unsuccessfully to reconcile them all, but Reynolds especially was under considerable strain. He had just lost a great friend, the decision to abandon the full-time pursuit of literature for the law was painful, and he began to cling to Keats with a possessiveness that would in turn encourage some of Keats's own most intimate confessions about the practice of his art.

The Reynoldses themselves were moving to a schoolhouse provided for their father by the officials of Christ's Hospital. Meanwhile, the older girls were still unmarried and were actively looking for husbands. Bailey was wooing Marianne 'with the Bible and Jeremy Taylor under his arm', but Keats thought the women of the family harboured a silent disapproval of George, who was soon to come into his inheritance and had been openly courting Georgiana Wylie, a pleasantly warmhearted, shy and original girl whom Keats had earlier praised in a sonnet. That George was approaching his majority and would soon be thinking of marriage, along with the fact that he had been unable to find paid work for many months, meant that he was having to give some hard thought to his future. The full burden of nursing Tom in distant Teignmouth was becoming a burden to him.

Keats himself had suggested he would go down to Devon and play his part, but he was still in London when, on 6 January, he began revising *Endymion*. The Christmas period had given him some excuse for postponing this, but now he was obliged to face what was inevitably a reluctant task. As he read over the work, even some of his favourite passages sounded 'vapid', but, since he was anxious to have it printed so 'that I may forget it and proceed', he tried to keep to a tight timetable, often making the numerous but mostly incidental changes to the first Book while at the Dilkes', where he found he could 'chat and proceed at the same time'.

But this apparently casual remark belies the real nature of his creative anxiety. Obliged to concentrate on a work he had grown out of, the weaknesses of *Endymion* were patent to him. No amount of tinkering could substantially improve what he recognised was 'a feverish attempt, rather than a deed accomplished', a work in which 'the foundations are too sandy.'[17] With typical candour, Keats was to write in his Preface to the poem that it was his wish 'this youngster should die away'. Nonetheless, his attitude was altogether more practical and more interesting than a lofty dismissal based on embarrassment. He recognised that by this leap 'headlong into the Sea' he had learned more effectively about 'the Soundings, the quicksands, & the rocks' than if he had 'trembled over every page' in the hope of writing 'a perfect piece' or merely 'stayed upon the green shore, and piped a silly pipe, and took tea & comfortable advice'. Above all, he had come to the mature recognition that 'the Genius of Poetry must work out its own salvation in a man: It cannot be matured by law & precept, but by sensation & watchfulness – That which is creative must create itself.'[18] The wisdom of this last phrase could be a motto for all he would go on to write.

The greater part of the revisions to Book One were complete by 19 January, and either on the previous day or on a second visit on Wednesday the 21st, Keats showed the fair copy to Hunt. The reading was not a particularly happy occasion. Keats had had 'several hints', perhaps from the rather touchy Reynolds, that both Hunt and Shelley were in a fault-finding mood, and now, looking at the work with the eye of an experienced editor and journalist, Hunt 'made ten objections to it in the mere skimming over'. In particular, he found the conversations between the hero and his sister 'unnatural & too high-flown'. Such treatment was hurtful, but just as typical of Hunt's behaviour was another incident that took place on the Wednesday visit. Hunt had recently acquired an authenticated lock of Milton's hair, and this he now put in Keats's hand, telling him whose it was and suggesting he write a poem on the subject across the blank page of a notebook in which he was drafting some of his own work.

Keats's initial response was stilted, and the expected facility was no doubt irksome to him. The pressure of the anxieties expressed in 'In drear-nighted December' meant he had written no poetry since that lyric, with the probable exception of 'Nebuchadnezzar's Dream' and, more certainly, a pallidly amusing sonnet 'To Mrs Reynolds's Cat'. The Huntian world of poetry competitions and laurel crowns continued its trivial round nonetheless, and the contrast to Miltonic endeavour could hardly have been more extreme. Courtesy obliged Keats to write something, and the opening lines of his ode pay conventional obeisance to Milton's achievement as they move towards an inevitable contrast between Keats himself and the older poet. Then comes a sudden focusing of attention, and it is significant that Keats put aside Hunt's notebook at this point and asked for a fresh sheet of paper. His own immaturity now becomes his subject and, with it, a new ideal for poetry, one of greatness slowly achieved through discipline and endeavour:

> When every childish fashion
>> Has vanished from my rhyme,
>> Will I, grey-gone in passion,
>> Leave to an after-time
>> Hymning and harmony
> Of thee, and of thy works, and of thy life;
> But vain is now the burning and the strife,
> Pangs are in vain, until I grow high-rife
>> With old Philosophy,
> And mad with glimpses of futurity![19]

The Miltonic ideal of passion allied to intellectual grandeur, of understanding won from thought as much as from feeling, is set up as the answer to the problems that had been apparent since the completion of *Endymion*. Where once Keats had written fifty or more lines a day, now 'For many years my offerings must be hushed.' This was far more than a rejection of facility. So much of *Endymion* had been an effort to create 'a thing of beauty' in defiance of a worldly misery that was acknowledged but not fully accepted. Keats's rejection in that poem of history and contemporary life, his hero's inwardness and passivity, his adolescent eroticism and longing for annihilation in ecstasy, were based on the belief that art could offer solace 'for ever' and that mankind could live in a serene if mysterious unity with nature. Such beliefs were now fractured. The pain in *Endymion*, the pain which the poem itself had failed satisfactorily to answer, had to be faced. 'An exquisite sense of the luxurious' was no longer enough. Something altogether more strenuous was required.

What this meant for Keats's artistic development was becoming clear. It implied the rejection of romance for tragedy, his leaving the world of *Endymion* for the world of *King Lear*. This was the issue he addressed the following day in a sonnet written 'On Sitting Down to Read *King Lear* Again'. The work records a moment of the utmost solemnity.

Instead of the 'golden-tongued' melody of romance by which he had been so long beguiled, Keats opens himself to something altogether more painful, to what in an early draft he called:

> the fierce dispute
> Betwixt hell torment and impassioned clay.

Keats now begins to face squarely what he was coming to accept as the terrible state of man raised out of the dust to become a living soul in a world bent on making him suffer and die. There is no longer any wish to escape, no desire for 'the feel of not to feel it'. The dreadful dialectic of pain and consciousness moves to the centre of his mind. It will remain there. Now, in this moment of self-dedication, he saw the experience in terms of a purgatorial fire from whose flames he can hope to emerge recreated, a phoenix 'to fly at my desire'. What he will aim at henceforth will not be the 'barren dream' of romance but a tragic ideal of art grounded on the acceptance of suffering. He will dedicate himself to epic and so endeavour to become 'a miserable and mighty Poet of the human Heart'. In so doing, he will also reaffirm his service to Apollo.

Hints of this were already clear. There had been some discussion between Haydon and Taylor about whether the artist would prepare a frontispiece for *Endymion*. Haydon was reluctant to undertake this because of pressure of work but said he would comply if Keats insisted. Keats did not, and suggested instead they all wait for his next work, his proposed epic on *Hyperion*, in which, as he had promised in the earlier poem, he would sing of Apollo, the 'lute-voic'd brother' of the moon goddess, whose challenge to the older Olympians would be the subject of the poem. Keats was certain this work would mark an enormous advance on what he had so far achieved, and he wrote: 'in Endymion I think you may have many bits of the deep and sentimental cast – the nature of *Hyperion* will lead me to treat it in a more naked and greecian Manner – and the march of passion and endeavour will be undeviating.'[20] This, as Keats well knew, was an approach that would appeal to Haydon, who had already done so much to urge him in the direction of the heroic. Keats was grateful for this and, as he wrote to the painter, 'I am convinced that there are three things to rejoice at in this Age – The Excursion Your Pictures, and Hazlitt's Depth of Taste.'

It was the last of these that was now to have the greatest effect on Keats. He discovered that Hazlitt had recently begun a course of Tuesday lectures at the Surrey Institution in the Borough across

Blackfriars Bridge. He had missed the first of them, 'On Poetry in General', and arrived for the second just as everyone was coming out. On 27 January, however, Keats heard Hazlitt lecture 'On Shakespeare and Milton'. The stage-fright and incompetent delivery that had marred the earlier lectures had now been overcome, and Hazlitt was in command of a lively and enthusiastic audience swept up by the force of his intellectual passion and the supple muscularity of his prose. The growing reputation of the series meant that the elegant, pillared circle of the lecture theatre was crowded, and when Hazlitt began to speak of Shakespeare, varying his delivery with 'certain slight inflections of his very calm and gentlemanly voice', it must have seemed to Keats as if he were hearing a matured version of his own best intuitions.[21]

With his Shakespeare, Hazlitt offered a portrait of the consummate poet:

> He was just like any other man, but that he was like all other men. He was the least of an egoist it was possible to be. He was nothing in himself; but he was all that others were, or that they could become. He not only had in himself the germs of every faculty and feeling, but he could follow them by anticipation, intuitively, into all their conceivable ramifications, through every change of fortune, or conflict of passion, or turn of thought.[22]

Shakespeare personified disinterestedness in the highest degree, while Milton was the embodiment of the ideal Keats had set for himself in the poem written at Hunt's a few days before. Milton, Hazlitt declared, 'did not write from casual impulse, but after a severe examination of his own strength, and with a resolution to leave nothing undone which it was in his power to do'. Keats had vowed to submit himself to the excellence of both these poets, an excellence which Hazlitt had laid bare with gusto.

His lecture also revealed, however, an altogether more subtle understanding of literary history than Keats had so far achieved, and this in turn led Hazlitt into a questioning relationship with his contemporaries that was to challenge Keats profoundly. 'Those arts, which depend on individual genius and incommunicable power, have always leaped at once from infancy to manhood,' he declared, 'from the first rude dawn of invention to their meridian height and dazzling lustre, and have in general declined ever after.' Applied to the history of his own literature, the result for Hazlitt was starkly clear. 'The four greatest names in English poetry, are almost the first four we come to – Chaucer, Spenser, Shakespeare and Milton.' Writers coming after them were, Hazlitt argued, condemned to a more limited range, to the cultivation of artifice and to an ever-widening gulf between their own concerns and the earlier attainment of amplitude and disinterestedness. Such writers' subject could only be themselves.

This was a topic to which Hazlitt kept returning and, inevitably, it involved a consideration of Wordsworth. Throughout the series of lectures, Hazlitt's ambivalent opinion of his great contemporary is evident. He could be warm in his praise, declaring Wordsworth 'the most original poet now living', of whose work 'it is not possible to speak in too high praise'. But the central problem remained: 'The great fault of the modern school of poetry is, that it is an experiment to reduce poetry to a mere effusion of natural sensibility; or what is worse, to divest it of both imaginary splendour and human passion.'[23] Once again the claim that modern egotism had replaced renaissance objectivity and amplitude was hammered home.

This was a shrewd criticism, and the manner of Hazlitt's severity delighted his audience, one of them recalling that 'momentary upward look full of malice French and not quite free from malice English by which he contrives to turn the grandest compliment into the bitterest sarcasm'.[24] Perhaps it was with such a look that Hazlitt now delivered his assault on Wordsworth. Then, having censured the egotism of modern writers, he turned back to his subject only to give teeth to a renewed attack. 'Milton and Shakespeare did not so understand poetry,' he declared. 'They gave a more liberal interpretation both to nature and art. They did not do all they could to get rid of the one and the other, to fill up the dreary void with the Moods of their own Minds.'[25] This last phrase, as many in the audience knew, referred to the title Wordsworth had given one section of his poems of 1807. In the context of the lecture, Hazlitt condemns the work as the nadir of modern egotistical poetry.

The hour of the lecture had given Keats a great deal to puzzle over. Two of his heroes had been praised in the very terms in which he himself tried to think of them. The attack on Wordsworth, however, had both passion and substance. More than that, it pointed to a problem Keats had never seen so carefully formulated before. From the days of his reading with Clarke in the arbour of his old school in Enfield, Keats had studied the poets of the past as if there were no historical divide between their aims and achievements and those of his contemporaries. Now he was encouraged to see that on the one hand there was a fullness and disinterestedness in the work of the great figures of the renaissance, while, on the other, in the poetry of those living there was a narrowed and egocentric complexity. What, then, was the worth of modern poetry, and what did it mean for a modern poet such as Keats himself to strive in an epic on Apollo and the ancient gods to emulate a *Paradise Lost* or a *King Lear*?

Keats tried to share these problems not with Hazlitt himself (he was never close to the older man) but with John Hamilton Reynolds, who was now ill with rheumatic fever. He had 'all kinds of distressing symptoms', and Keats's letters to him are an expression of his poetic concerns offered as a generous gift of friendship, an attempt 'to lift a little time from your shoulders'. The first of them, written on 31 January, contains no less than three poems, and their extreme contrasts illustrate the diverse range of Keats's preoccupations during these winter weeks. A light-hearted, bawdy lyric 'on the mystery of the maidenhead', derives from the slang of Rice's Saturday-night coterie. It is the least satisfying of the pieces, for Keats never managed to transfer to his poetry the idiomatic raciness evident in many of his letters. But the way a carefree improvisation could suddenly merge into profundity is clear from the next work.

The close of January had at last brought 'a sun-shiny day' able to kindle the mind with thoughts of 'the glory and grace of Apollo'. Keats's second poem begins as a rather heavy-handed parody of 'L'Allegro' but rapidly refines itself into something touched with a sense of real exaltation. The lines seem to recall moments in his poetry as remote as his Margate epistle to George and appear to suggest something of the mythological euphoria found in 'I stood tip-toe'. But the blithe assumption that the poet's mind spirals upwards to kindly and ethereal verities was under strain, and what Keats finds now is not coherence but fear, the experience of 'continually falling ten thousand fathoms deep and being blown up again without wings'. The gulf between the earthbound intellect and an exaltant imagination terribly without its bearings witnesses to the ruthlessness of Apollo's power and prompts a feeling akin to madness:

> God of Song
> Thou bearest me along
> Through sights I scarce can bear
> O let me, let me share
> With the hot lyre and thee,
> The staid Philosophy.
> Temper my lonely hours,
> And let me see thy bowers
> More unalarmed! —[26]

This type of experience, the panic-inducing freedom of the mind from the constraints of the understanding, haunts much of the poetry that was to follow, as does Keats's ardent belief that knowledge and experience would restore his spiritual balance.

So too might a more conscious exercise of his art, and the letter to Reynolds closes with one of Keats's finest sonnets:

> When I have fears that I might cease to be
>   Before my pen has gleaned my teeming brain,
> Before high-pilèd books, in charactery,
>   Hold like rich garners the full-ripened grain;
> When I behold, upon the night's starred face,
>   Huge cloudy symbols of a high romance,
> And think that I may never live to trace
>   Their shadows, with the magic hand of chance;
> And when I feel, fair creature of an hour!
>   That I shall never look upon thee more,
> Never have relish in the faery power
>   Of unreflecting love! – then on the shore
> Of the wide world I stand alone, and think
> Till love and fame to nothingness do sink.

Nothing could be more unexpected than this masterpiece tagged on to the letter almost like a postscript, but Reynolds in particular would have appreciated what Keats had achieved here. In the copy of Shakespeare the two men shared, Sonnet 64 was heavily marked, and Keats's own poem is a variation on Shakespeare's theme of time the destroyer. It is a nearly perfect formal exercise that stands well beside its original. It also illustrates those 'Axioms' about the nature of poetry itself which Keats sent his publisher at the end of the following month.[27] He becomes his own best commentator.

There is, first of all, the sense of common truth that underlies Keats's sonnet, a refusal of the quixotically original and egocentric. 'I think', Keats wrote to Taylor, 'Poetry should surprise by a fine excess and not by Singularity – it should strike the Reader as a wording of his own highest thoughts, and appear almost a Remembrance.' It should also be rich, and the imagery and argument of the sonnet corresponds closely to Keats's ideal. 'Touches of Beauty should never be half way therby making the reader breathless instead of content: the rise, the progress, and the setting of imagery should like the Sun come natural too him – shine over him and set soberly although in magnificence leaving him in the Luxury of twilight.' This was the most demanding of ideals – 'it is easier to think what Poetry should be than to write it' – but, for all that the constant exercise of craftsmanship was essential, it could be no substitute for unsolicited inspiration. 'If Poetry comes not as naturally as the Leaves to a tree it had better not come at all.'

Reynolds had also been writing sonnets, taking Robin Hood as his subject. These are works of minor, escapist nostalgia and Keats divined that such an evasion of the contemporary world was dangerously sentimental and ultimately impossible. His poem 'To J.H.R. In answer to his Robin Hood Sonnets' suggests that this is so even while admitting to the charm of Reynolds' idea, but the refusal of the merely escapist suggests Keats's innate toughness of mind and his commitment to an altogether more honest engagement with the contemporary world.

The problem of how to write an authentic modern poetry remained nonetheless, and Keats's letter to Reynolds of 3 February shows how shaken he had been by Hazlitt's lectures and how, for all the strength of his own self-questioning, he could still be overborne by a more mature intellect.[28] Wordsworth was once again his subject. Less than a month before, *The Excursion* had been one of the three things of the age to rejoice at. Now, 'for the sake of a few fine imaginative or domestic passages, are we to be bullied into a certain Philosophy engendered in the whims of an Egoist?' This was a question that preoccupied Reynolds, too. He had published an essay 'On Egotism in Literature' back in 1816 and argued that Wordsworth's extreme self-absorption was justified by the power of his poetry. Now he was less certain and was prepared to listen sympathetically to Keats's views, which were, after all, a vehement rephrasing of those of their joint master, Hazlitt.

Keats's irritation was palpable. 'I will have no more of Wordsworth or Hunt in particular,' and as he warmed to his theme, Keats's concern recreated Hazlitt's ideas with startlingly acute imagery. Egotism becomes a form of petty tyranny, restrictive and domineering.

Each of the moderns like an Elector of Hanover governs his petty state, & knows how many straws are swept daily from the Causeways in all his dominions & has a continual itching that all the Housewives should have their coppers well scoured: the antients were Emperors of vast Provinces, they had only heard of the remote ones and scarcely cared to visit them.

The amplitude and objectivity of the renaissance seemed altogether truer. 'Let us have the old poets.' The ideal was not fretful self-concern but something altogether more transparent and magnificent. 'Poetry should be great and unobtrusive, a thing which enters into one's soul, and does not startle or amaze it with itself, but with its subject.' It should be, in other words, like nature herself. The sentence that follows expresses this idea with a marvellous and original understanding of the chaste and unobtrusive power Keats was seeking. 'How beautiful are the retired flowers! How would they lose their beauty if they were to throng into the highway crying out, "admire me I am a violet! – dote on me I am a primrose!"'

It is this love of the quiet processes of the natural world that streams through the beautiful letter Keats wrote to Reynolds on 19 February.[29] Inspired by that mood of creative indolence in which he was coming to understand his intellect reshaped itself, this great passage of Keats's prose perfectly recreates the unforced workings of a mind at once active and delighted, weaving 'a tapestry empyrean – full of symbols for his spiritual eye, of softness for his spiritual touch, of space for his wandering of distinctness for his Luxury'. Nor is the end of this process solitude and egotism. 'Minds would leave each other in contrary directions, traverse each other in Numberless points, and all [for 'at'] last greet each other at the Journeys end.'

By being at one with the true processes of nature, man might achieve creaturely community, a chaste, generous and noble democracy of being. 'Man should not dispute or assert but whisper results to his neighbour and thus by every germ of Spirit sucking the sap from mould ethereal every human might become great, and Humanity instead of being a wide heath of Furze and Briars with here and there a remote Oak or Pine, would become a grand democracy of Forest Trees.' We should be as the violets and primroses really are. 'Let us not therefore go hurrying about and collecting honey bee-like, buzzing here and there impatiently from a knowledge of what is to be aimed at; but let us open our leaves like a flower and be passive and receptive – budding patiently under the eye of Apollo.'

In this mood, poetry can come, and Keats wrote out for Reynolds his new blank-verse sonnet:

O thou whose face hath felt the Winter's wind
    Whose eye has seen the snow-clouds hung in mist,
    And the black elm tops, 'mong the freezing stars,
    To thee the spring will be a harvest-time.
O thou, whose only book has been the light
    Of supreme darkness which thou feddest on
    Night after night when Phoebus was away,
To thee the Spring shall be a triple morn.

O fret not after knowledge – I have none,
  And yet my song comes native with the warmth.
O fret not after knowledge – I have none,
  And yet the Evening listens. He who saddens
At the thought of idleness cannot be idle,
And he's awake who thinks himself asleep.

Keats suggests exactly the degree of desolation he had felt through the doubting weeks of a London winter 'when Phoebus was away', doing so in a manner which avoids the vices he had been inveighing against and which draws effortlessly on the natural world. Depleted nature and the suffering mind are as one in the chilly image of 'the black elm-tops 'mong the freezing stars'. And, because they are portrayed as being at one, the inevitable return of spring can be thought of as a renovation of the mind. No forcing of the intellect can achieve this, and the song of the thrush teaches a patient passivity.

It seems for a moment as if the terrible knowledge of 'In drear-nighted December' has been overcome, but, as the element of fancy in the letter rises, so such thought reveals itself as a fantasy. 'I am sensible all this is mere sophistication.' What Keats says may be close to the truth – certainly to the mind's longing for unity with the earth on which it lives – but 'I will not deceive myself.' Man cannot enjoy a timeless identity with nature. The thought of the suffering Reynolds leading, as he himself wrote, 'a life of pain, sleeplessness & bleeding', returns to conclude the letter, and, with it, comes the poet–doctor's hope that he can at least alleviate suffering for a few moments. The awareness of divided consciousness and pain has not been stilled. Rather does the letter, rising up to the serenity imagined in the sonnet, return very gently to suffering. This is the pattern seen again in the great odes of the following year.

Other poems also came in this period of fertile improvisation. A second but lesser Shakespearian sonnet, 'Time's sea hath been five years at its slow ebb', referred to the unknown girl glimpsed at the centenary celebrations at Vauxhall who had also been invoked at the close of 'When I have fears'. A visit in early February to the Mermaid Tavern inspired the lines to the Elizabethan poets who were believed to have drunk there. A meeting with Hunt and Shelley involved the inevitable sonnet-writing competition in which the subject was the Nile, while a discussion with Reynolds about Spenser occasioned yet another sonnet, 'Spenser, a jealous honourer of thine'. Reynolds had apparently suggested Keats write something in the mode of the Elizabethan poet (perhaps his intention had been to cheer Keats by leading him to indulge the escapism of romance), but Keats was again too honest to believe such feigned inspiration would relieve his concerns.

Romance nonetheless remained a preoccupation. The process of revising *Endymion* was continuing, and this day-by-day concentration on an immature work remained the ground-bass to all Keats's current reflections. Hazlitt again helped teach him how to look at his own work. The revision he made to his hero's speech on the rising degrees of self-annihilating ecstasy in Book One, what Keats himself now called the 'Pleasure Thermometer' passage, sought that dramatic objectivity Hazlitt so prized. The lines were, Keats wrote, 'my first step towards the chief Attempt in the Drama – the playing of different Natures with Joy and Sorrow'.[30]

Conflict and consciousness would now have to be the focus of any narrative he might compose. His earlier understanding of romance would have to be entirely transformed and, once again, the cue came from Hazlitt. With great perception, Hazlitt had drawn attention in his lectures to Dryden's admirable versions of medieval works and then suggested that 'a modern translation of some of the serious tales in Boccaccio and Chaucer . . . could not fail to succeed in the present day'.[31] He particularly recommended the Italian poet's story of the love of Isabella and Lorenzo, which was an old favourite, and the idea began to root itself in Keats's mind. Just as the Elizabethan playwrights had taken such *novelle* and dramatised them, so Keats could take an existing story and refashion it, bringing out the contemporary implications of an already existing work rather than relying on the subjective invention attempted in *Endymion*. Such a procedure might avoid the ephemeral and egotistical, and, as Keats and Reynolds discussed the idea, so they agreed on a joint volume.

Meanwhile, the third Book of *Endymion* was being revised and proofs of the earlier sections coming in. There was another hilarious evening with Haydon when a stuff-shirted 'noodle' involved in the Cripps project was deliberately embarrassed by a 'concert'. In addition, Keats also made an important new friendship with Taylor and Hessey's lawyer, Richard Woodhouse. Precise, intelligent and literary, Woodhouse soon became a fast friend, Keats relishing not just his tact and humour but the logical, analytic cast of his mind. In time, Keats would discuss with Woodhouse his poetic plans along with his ideas about poetry itself. Woodhouse for his part was deeply taken by Keats's personality. He was now reading parts of *Endymion* and had also got hold of the *Poems*. Confident that Keats would eventually take his place at the head of his peers, Woodhouse began his scrupulous efforts to collect and annotate every scrap of Keats's poetry. Above all, he discussed the theme of *Hyperion* with him and, in a sonnet to Apollo, pronounced Keats the god's 'last born', his favoured child.

But family events were now catching up with Keats. On 21 February, a letter for George arrived from Georgiana Wylie, who was clearly expecting his imminent return from Devon. Keats knew nothing of this, but a week or so later, and around the time of his twenty-first birthday, George suddenly turned up. The pressure of his concerns had convinced him Tom was sufficiently well to be left on his own and, in the effort to take control of his own life, George now wanted to realise his inheritance from his grandmother. He, too, was unaware that there was a second legacy in Chancery but, unlike his elder brother, he had not touched his grandmother's money and the post-war boom of 1818 meant his shares were worth over a third more than Keats's had been when he cashed them. All this was disconcerting, but, when a letter from Tom arrived claiming he was well enough to come home, Keats felt obliged to act.

He knew it was highly inadvisable for Tom to return to London, and he probably suspected he was homesick. There was nothing for it but to go down to Devon himself. George would have to take Book Three of *Endymion* to Taylor and Hessey, Clarke could be called on to correct the proofs as they came in, while at some time Keats himself would have to compose the Preface his publishers had requested. The evening after Hazlitt's last lecture, Keats caught the 7.30 coach to Exeter, clearly agitated and perhaps annoyed. The London winter of doubts and uncertainties was behind him, but his time in Devonshire would show that his concerns were far from allayed.

Getting Wisdom

I mean to follow Solomon's directions of 'get Wisdom —
get understanding'.

(Keats to his publisher, 24 April 1818)

THE COACH TO Exeter drove through one of the worst storms of recent years, and for the twenty-seven hours of the journey Keats rode on the outside, lashed by wind and rain, but without 'being blown over and blown under', and avoiding too the falling trees which elsewhere in England killed some of those unfortunate enough to be out. He arrived at Exeter sodden and exhausted, only to face another fifteen-mile journey to Teignmouth, where for six days torrential rain set in. This was to continue with barely an intermission for the whole of his stay, the dreary accompaniment to an altogether more profound malaise.

Keats had not seen Tom for three months, and the pallor of his face was a painful symptom of his decline. Obliged to be constantly in his brother's company while at their lodgings on the Strand, Keats could not evade the harrowing signs of tuberculosis: the coughing that came especially on rising and going to bed, the languor alternating with feverish excitement, and the occasional expectoration of a transparent ropy fluid resembling spit. Gradually, this fluid would become speckled with opaque, ash-coloured matter and perhaps even flecked with blood. Always there would be trouble with breathing — sometimes quickness, sometimes oppression — while, especially in the evening, a hectic fever flushed the otherwise pale and flabby skin. As Keats's medical experience made him aware, many consumptive patients tried to hide such symptoms from their doctors, perhaps in the attempt to hide them from themselves.[1] Through every minute of these closely confined days, Keats would have to exercise extreme tact with a volatile and frightened boy. Such constant watchfulness added to the strain.

Gradually, this proximity brought the brothers closer than perhaps they had ever been, and at some time during these weeks Tom confessed something he had previously hidden. Since they had first been to Margate together, he had been receiving love-letters supposedly from a woman with the unlikely name of Amena Bellefilia. These were always enclosed in correspondence from Wells. Although Tom had never seen her, the writer herself claimed to be familiar with him and, in curious, mock-Elizabethan English, made advances while alleging she had to fight off the attentions of Wells himself. It was perhaps in the hope of finding her that Tom had gone with George to France, for he had convinced himself that he was deeply in love.

To the medical mind of the nineteenth century, such frustrated passion could be seen as more than adolescent heartache.[2] The hapless lover and the helpless consumptive were both victims of a poison in the blood and revealed the same symptoms. Both lived in a state of heightened emotion and, it was believed, a state of heightened sexual excitement as well. The glow of an ardent but slighted youth was akin to the hectic flush of the victim of tuberculosis. In both, the energies of life were recklessly used up, leaving the sufferer pallid and weak. The forces that should have gone out to the world turned back on themselves to destroy their origin. The lover and the consumptive both suffered from burning and panting, a quickened pulse – all the symptoms, in fact, of life morbidly transformed by its own intensity. On levels both literal and metaphorical, young men like Tom were victims of a consuming passion, people whose wasting lives dreadfully confirmed the equation between desire and death. From now on, such imagery, made horribly real during these rain-sodden weeks in Devonshire, would move to the core of Keats's poetry and lodge itself destructively amid his own sexual imaginings.

Still healthy himself, he tried to fight such impressions. His letters fulminate against sickness, weakness, depression. Their tone of humorous exaggeration only just makes civil what was obviously at times a chaotic anger. The saturated landscape exasperated him especially. Devon was 'a splashy, rainy, misty, snowy, foggy, haily, floody, muddy, slipshod county'.[3] Day after day the rain kept him indoors and as the drops beat against the window, 'they give me the same sensation as a quart of cold water offered to revive a half-drowned devil'. It was 'as if the roots of the Earth were rotten cold and drench'd'. By night he lay in bed listening to the rain beating on the roof, while by day his mind began to project its own discomfort on the world about him, distorting it into a surreal hell of uncontrolled illusion. 'Such a quelling Power have these thoughts over me', he wrote to Bailey, 'that I fancy the very Air of a deteriorating quality – I fancy the flowers, all precocious, have an Acrasian spell about them – I feel able to beat off the devonshire waves like soap froth.'

At one with the abominable weather was 'the degenerated race about me'. The local people were, in Keats's jaundiced opinion, feeble creatures, 'dwindled englishmen'. There are flashes of strident chauvinism in the letter. 'Had England been a large devonshire we should not have won the Battle of Waterloo.' As it was, the government had not thought it worthwhile recruiting such spavined examples of manhood, Keats alleged. 'Were I a Corsair I'd make a descent on the South Coast of Devon, if I did not run the chance of having Cowardice imputed to me: as for the Men they'd run away into the methodist meeting houses, and the Women would be glad of it.'

In his intense state, the horror and depression he felt at Tom's weakness seemed personified everywhere. Even Reynolds, still prostrated with rheumatic fever, was part of what appeared a conspiracy of sickness. Keats would not be trapped by it.

> I intend to cut all sick people if they do not make up their minds to cut sickness – a fellow to whom I have a complete aversion, and who strange to say is harboured and countenanced in several houses where I visit – he is sitting now quite impudent between me and Tom – He insults me at poor Jem Rice's – and you have seated him before now between us at the theatre – where I thought he had look'd with a longing eye at poor Kean. I shall say, once and for all, to my friends generally and severally, cut that fellow, or I cut you.[4]

At the centre of all this was Tom, that image of wasting humanity. How could his state be encompassed by the imagination? Keats's letter to Bailey of 13 March contains a Shakespearian sonnet on mortality: 'Four seasons fill the measure of the year'. Taken out of context, the poem is a rather ordinary comparison of man's life to the cycle of the seasons. It describes the passage from 'lusty Spring', through the dreaming, ruminating high summer of manhood, and on to autumn when man is content to look 'on mists in idleness'. Finally, in the clinching couplet:

> He has his Winter too of pale misfeature,
> Or else he would forego his mortal nature.

Life can conventionally be imagined as the steady, slow round of the seasons and the poet can even admit the truth that humankind's winter will not be followed by renovating spring. The reality of Tom dying in his teens, however, the fact that Keats's sombre analogy was hideously inappropriate to this case, could easily make such commonplace comfort look complacent.

Throughout these weeks, Keats watched the progress of his brother's illness and verged with its symptoms between optimism and despair. The likelihood of Tom's death had to be recognised, and in the face of such an outrage Keats could not accept the consolations of Christianity ponderously rehearsed in a sermon Bailey had recently written on the death of Princess Charlotte. 'You know my ideas about Religion,' Keats wrote to him, and he was more than ever determined to preserve his openness of mind.[5] 'I do not think myself more in the right than other people, and that nothing in this world is proveable.' In the face of such feelings, even the most cherished beliefs were suspect: 'I am sometimes so very sceptical as to think Poetry itself a mere Jack a lanthen to amuse whoever may chance to be struck with its brilliance.' Poetry could be seen as no more than a particularly attractive example of human inventiveness rather than an eternal truth. Like 'every mental pursuit' in a world where the mind could only speculate, poetry 'takes its reality and worth from the ardour of the pursuer – being in itself a nothing'.

In fact, Keats did not quite believe this. Among the 'Ethereal things' that kindle the imagination and can be counted real are not just the permanent forms of nature – the sun, the moon and the stars – but the eternal achievements of great art and, in particular, 'passages of Shakespeare'. In descending order below these were 'things semi-real such as Love, the Clouds &c which require a greeting of the Spirit to make them wholly exist – and Nothings which are made Great and dignified by an ardent pursuit'. In the end, it is the activity of the mind reaching out to the world that fascinates Keats rather than the craving for certainty. But 'my dear fellow', he concluded to Bailey, 'I must once for all tell you I have not one Idea of the truth of any of my speculations – I shall never be a Reasoner because I care not to be in the right, when retired from bickering and in a proper philosophical temper.' Besides, there was an altogether more brutal daily reality to cope with. Tom 'has just this moment had a spitting of blood poor fellow'.

Amid all this, there were occasional periods of relief when the rain let up and Keats could get out to saunter in the countryside, feast off cream and barley-bread, and glimpse the furze prickles catching at the girls' dresses. His mind relaxed in carefree fantasies of sex and began improvising doggerel or, in his own more suggestive pun, 'bitcherel'. He watched the young women gathering in the village streets at the close of the day, one or more of whom perhaps inspired the light and charming 'Where are ye going, you Devon maid'. A visit to Dawlish Fair prompted another lyric on a probably imaginary sexual encounter. A letter to Rice written in this mood ended with a bravura display of the sexual innuendo enjoyed by their Saturday-night set in London.

In Teignmouth, meanwhile, George and Tom had carried on a light-hearted flirtation with Marian and Sarah Jeffrey, the daughters of a warm-hearted mother who had helped find Tom a local doctor with a special interest in tuberculosis. George was keen the girls should also get to know his elder brother. 'How do you like John?' he wrote teasingly. 'Is he not very original? he does not look by any means so handsome as four months ago, but is he not handsome?'[6] Marian probably thought so. It was rumoured she fell in love with Keats and she wrote poems faintly imitating his manner which she later published.

But walks into town were not always pleasant. Keats was insulted by some man at the theatre and felt mildly resentful because he had not called him to account. From time to time he probably also went to the local library, where he could read the *Examiner*, but again this afforded scant relief. The editorials were much occupied with the passing of the Indemnity Bill, which guaranteed protection to magistrates, spies and others from the consequences of actions arising from the suspension of *habeas corpus*. The tentacles of oppression reached out, it seemed, even to a small seaside town and only worsened Keats's sense of entrapment. 'Who would live in the region of Mists, Game Laws, indemnity Bills &c. when there is such a place as Italy,' he opined to Reynolds.

It is probable that there was also a more covert pain to face in these walks into the town. The letters between George and Keats were necessarily much concerned with the state of Tom's health and, so that the invalid's mind should not be excited by their contents, George apparently addressed his correspondence care of the Teignmouth post office. He seems to have written fairly often, but only a letter of 18 March survives, clearly a reply to an emotive description of Tom's health sent by Keats. George expresses his genuine shock at the change (he really had convinced himself his younger brother was well enough to be left on his own) but there was also a firm but tacit insistence that he could himself no longer shoulder the burden of nursing Tom. That would have to be Keats's responsibility: 'I hope and trust that your *kind* superintendance will prevent any violent bleeding in future, and consequently that this alarm may prove in the end advantageous; Tom must never again presume on his strength, at all events untill he has *completely* recover'd.'[7] Everything, it seemed, conspired to fetter Keats in a terrible closeness to suffering, and one sentence in a letter to Bailey expresses all he felt about this rain-sodden, harrowing exile: 'O Devonshire, last night I thought the Moon had dwindled in heaven.'[8]

Keats's imagination was projecting its distress on to nature, forcing him to live in a world of nightmare. Surrounded by invalids, it seemed he too was diseased. For the past few weeks his letters to Reynolds particularly had, for all their veering ideas and emotions, sought an ideal of poetry that was calm, objective and beyond fretting egotism, those moods of the writers' own minds that seemed to characterise modern poetry. Now he was beginning to recognise how forceful such moods could be, how distressing and serious they were.

On the evening of 25 March, Keats sat down to compose a verse epistle to Reynolds in which he discussed this problem. The work is the longest and most interesting of his improvisations from this period. Starting with humorous grotesque, Keats goes on to evoke the calm beauty to be found in nature and art, Apollonian worlds unclouded by the dark shadows of self-consciousness. The imagination should rest content here, but it will not. It insists on going beyond its 'proper bound' and is shocked by its own discoveries:

> I was at home
> And should have been most happy – but I saw
> Too far into the sea, where every maw
> The greater on the less feeds evermore. –
> But I saw too distinct into the core
> Of an eternal fierce destruction,
> And so from happiness I was far gone.
> Still am I sick of it; and though, today,
> I've gathered young spring-leaves, and flowers gay
> Of periwinkle and wild strawberry,
> Still do I that most fierce destruction see –
> The shark at savage prey, the hawk at pounce,
> The gentle robin, like a pard or ounce,
> Ravening a worm.[9]

The mind in such moods 'spoils the singing of the nightingale'.

It also distorts the appreciation of art. The central paragraphs of the poem discuss Claude's *The Enchanted Castle*. This serene work is a canvas in which Claude, putting aside his biblical concerns and interest in Virgilian Rome, turned instead to a vision of nature suffused with a mysterious, Ovidian sense of metamorphosis. To Keats in his present mood this refined but haunting view of nature was riddled with insecurity. Claude's mountains and streams seemed to pulse with febrile emotion. The castle itself, in the original canvas a curiously satisfying amalgam of styles, deconstructs into its various and now sinister elements which are seen as infested with the supernatural, the evil and the mad. Even the pastoral figure of the herdsman is stricken with fear. The intensity of the imagination cannot make such 'disagreeables' evaporate. Rather does it give them a hallucinatory vividness. The mind sees a terrible violence which it cannot understand. Caught between a longing for the sublime and the hell of brute creation, the imagination stumbles about in a 'purgatory blind'. This chasm between the world of art and a heightened sense of the pain of mundane existence was now becoming the focus of Keats's endeavour.

The shorter poems of the next few months return again and again to the constantly changing and distorting lens of the imagination and its visions of sudden insecurity. Keats was increasingly inhabiting a self-made world of lurking threat where he could at any time be ambushed by his sense of panic. He sought urgently for ways to resolve these problems or at least to stave them off. He treasured an ideal of philosophy, of the mature and achieved wisdom he had evoked in the ode on a lock of Milton's hair, but he knew this could not be had for the asking, and his very longing pointed to his immaturity. Along with philosophy, knowledge too might balance the mind. He was reading deeply and widely. Hazlitt's lectures had sent him to the great eighteenth-century sceptics, to Voltaire and Gibbon. Now he was reading Milton again. But while the vast sweep of *Paradise Lost*, the capaciousness of Milton's mind, could serve as an ideal, the very scale of his achievement was oppressive. Milton's 'gormandising' intelligence seemed to have swallowed what Keats with bitter playfulness saw as the finite quantity of intellect in the world. The result was the mental and moral starvation of the moderns, whether in literature or, as a reference to Castlereagh makes clear, in politics.

The progressive diminution of the arts since the time of Milton, a theme which had been so prominent in Hazlitt's lectures, returned to frustrate Keats's pursuit of wider experience, yet he was compelled to make the effort, despite occasional fantasies of easy attainment. 'What a happy thing it would be', he wrote to Rice, if we could settle our thoughts, make our minds up on any matter in five Minutes and remain content – that is to build a sort of mental Cottage of feelings quiet and pleasant – to have a sort of Philosophical Back Garden, and a cheerful holiday-keeping front one – but Alas! this can never be: for as the material Cottager knows that there are such places as france and Italy and the Andes and the Burning Mountains – so the spiritual Cottager has knowledge of the terra semi incognita of things unearthly; and cannot for his Life, keep in the check rein.[10]

But the need to mature and re-establish the health of his mind was paramount, and travel might benefit him in this. Trapped in the little house on the Strand, Keats longed for broader horizons than the dripping landscapes of Devon could provide. Brown went north every year on a walking expedition and it seems that he had now invited Keats to join him. Keats confided his plans to Haydon. 'I purpose within a Month to put my knapsack at my back and make a pedestrian tour through the North of England, and part of Scotland – to make a sort of Prologue to the Life I intend to pursue – that is to write, to study and to see all Europe at the lowest expence.' The thought of health and freedom was exhilarating. 'I will get such an accumulation of stupendous recollections that as I walk through the suburbs of London I may not see them – I will stand upon Mont Blanc and remember this coming Summer when I intend to straddle ben Lomond – with my Soul!'[11]

Meanwhile he was finishing his work on *Endymion* and was more than ever keen to despatch the poem. 'I wish it were all done,' he wrote to Reynolds, 'for I want to forget it and make my mind free for something new,' a sentiment he repeated to Haydon. The corrections were completed a few days after he had arrived in Teignmouth, and by 21 March he was writing to Taylor and Hessey to tell them he had posted the manuscript along with 'the Preface and dedication, and the title Page as I should wish it to stand'. The dedication was to Chatterton, while the title page boldly proclaimed the work a romance, 'a fine thing notwithstanding the circulating Libraries'.

The Preface was another matter. The elaborately defensive tone of the first version was extremely ill-judged, its pretentiousness only making more obvious the deep uncertainty Keats felt about publishing the work at all. As Taylor was shrewdly to observe, Keats was, for all his disclaimers, acutely sensitive to criticism from the literary world. But, in his refusal to court the public, it seemed to his publishers at least that he was doing everything to direct attention to his shortcomings. This first version would not do.[12] Taylor was already concerned that the lush sensuality of the work (especially in the second Book, which disappointed him generally) would offend the public, especially that large audience of women readers who formed so important a part of his market. By and large he had been unsuccessful in persuading Keats to tone the work down, and now he decided to tackle the question of the Preface more obliquely. Reynolds sent a letter to Teignmouth saying that the draft was considered 'affected' and that its flippancy smacked too much of Leigh Hunt.

The latter comment was particularly cutting and Keats was clearly shaken. 'Since you all agree the thing is bad,' he wrote, 'it must be so – though I am not aware there is anything like Hunt in it, (and if there is, it is my natural way, and I have something in common with Hunt).' The real clue to his feelings, however, is provided by an incidental comment in a letter to Haydon written the day before in which Keats lamented that Wordsworth had 'din'd at Kingston's'. The Deputy Comptroller of the Stamp Office was becoming a symbol of much of what Keats detested about Regency literary life or, at least, those supercilious and uncreative people whose chattering helped make it spin. As he now wrote to Reynolds, 'disquisitions on Poetry and Kingston Criticism' were anathema to him.[13]

Together, Kingston and his kind made up 'the thousand jabberers about Pictures and Books' which Keats identified with the public and branded as the 'Enemy'. He would not truckle with them for the fame that was truly in the hands of posterity alone. Indulging in literary politics would bring at best a 'Mawkish Popularity', a thing he hated. He relished the fantasy of scaring such people away in the blaze of his own merit. 'Who', he later wrote, 'would wish to be among the commonplace crowd of the little-famous – whom are each individually lost in a throng made up of themselves?' In the end, this was not pride but an absolute commitment to excellence based on humility before 'the eternal Being, the Principle of Beauty, and the Memory of great Men'. In a little rented house in Teignmouth, penned in by the rain, harassed by creative anxiety and anxiously watching over his invalid brother, Keats was achieving the awe-inspiring dedication of a Wordsworth or a Milton.

This would never leave him, and it lay behind the revised Preface to *Endymion*. Keats might agree to rein in his feelings, but he would not alter his principles. He recognised that *Endymion* was an adolescent poem, feverish and immature. He would not pretend that it was otherwise nor insult his integrity by writing the sort of Preface that would set 'a golden head upon a thing of clay'. He summed up his achievement with complete honesty:

> The first two books, and indeed the two last, I feel sensible are not of such completion as to warrant their passing the press; nor should they if I thought a year's castigation would do them any good; – it will not: the foundations are too sandy. It is just that this youngster should die away: a sad thought for me, if I had not some hope that while it is dwindling I may be plotting, and fitting myself for verses fit to live.[14]

He posted the draft to Reynolds, anxious his friends should find it 'tolerable', and then turned to his other concerns: to Tom depressed by the imprisoning rain and to a country suffering under Game Laws, Indemnity Bills and continuing repression.

He also turned to what, at the close of his epistle to Reynolds, he had called a 'new romance'. As the tale of the wrecking of the life and love of Isabella and Lorenzo by the heroine's merchant brothers, *The Pot of Basil*, as Keats always referred to the poem, reflects many of his preoccupations: the inseparability of joy from pain, thwarted passion from death and, above all, the nightmare sensation of destruction that was haunting him. Boccaccio's narrative, as starkly terrible as a ballad, was a perfect vehicle for this, and under Keats's reshaping it joins the private and personal experience of such things to the larger social vision of destruction personified by the wicked merchants.

The *Examiner* may have played its part in Keats's new concern with the havoc wrought by capitalism and unfettered laissez-faire. At just this time, on 29 March and again the following Sunday, the paper published two letters from the enlightened manufacturer Robert Owen.[15] As pleas in support of legislation to prohibit children under twelve years old from working for anything up to fifteen hours a day in the mines and factories, Owen's letters, along with Hunt's editorials, offered a vision of blind forces working to destroy the very society they enriched. Reprinted in painfully small type, Owen's letters are a description of the ruinous self-contradictions of contemporary capitalism and a terrible picture of men hastening to undermine the physical and moral health of the country in the headlong pursuit of wealth. The letters are factual and analytical, but the overwhelming impression they offer is of the country in the grip of the self-destructive madness of the Industrial Revolution, a state where 'the over-wrought exertions of our men, women, and children, under every deprivation of natural comfort, and aided by unrivalled and almost perpetually moving mechanism, will not enable us to give a bare subsistence to the wretched beings'. This was, as Owen was quick to point out, a horror unprecedented in history. The country was confronted by a novelty of alarming proportions, and many were not even aware of its dangers.

Hunt's editorials brilliantly popularised this picture of 'the graspers at profit' destroying everything that makes life bearable and distorting even themselves as their obsession makes 'their faces pale, hollow, and wrinkled with anxiety'.[16] The description recalls Keats's portrait of Isabella's brothers with their pale eyes and twisted, bitten lips. Hunt's moral outrage was genuine and eloquent. 'So completely has this country been spoiled by the appetite of money-getting,' he wrote,

> so completely has it taken leave of the real virtues and happy and natural pleasures of its ancestors, – so badly and with so many perversions even of terms themselves does avarice educate its worshippers, – so fatally do they confound industry with unceasing toil, leisure with idleness, pleasure (which is a part of virtue) with vice, an unhappy cunning with wisdom, their own false and superfluous gains with necessity and real profit, and yet at the same time the very necessity of others with superfluity, – that it is become necessary to ring the commonest and most obvious truths in their ears in order to waken them out of their feverish absurdities.

In *Isabella*, and in the most outspoken stanzas he ever wrote, Keats offered his own vision of this ravening inhumanity, allying it to the capitalists of the old regime:

> With her two brothers this fair lady dwelt,
>   Enrichèd from ancestral merchandise,
> And for them many a weary hand did swelt
>   In torched mines and noisy factories,
> And many once proud-quivered loins did melt
>   In blood from stinging whip – with hollow eyes
> Many all day in dazzling river stood,
> To take the rich-ored driftings of the flood.
>
> For them the Ceylon diver held his breath,
>   And went all naked to the hungry shark;
> For them his ears gushed blood; for them in death
>   The seal on the cold ice with piteous bark
> Lay full of darts; for them alone did seethe
>   A thousand men in troubles wide and dark:
> Half-ignorant, they turned an easy wheel,
> That set sharp racks at work to pinch and peel.

Why were they proud? Because their marble founts
   Gushed with more pride than do a wretch's tears? –
Why were they proud? Because fair orange–mounts
   Were of more soft ascent than lazar stairs? –
Why were they proud? Because red–lined accounts
   Were richer than the songs of Grecian years? –
Why were they proud? again we ask aloud,
Why in the name of Glory were they proud?[17]

Cruel men living a life sheltered from the outward signs of how their wealth is obtained, the brothers blight the world with a mania that leads to madness and death in others. Hunt had seen clearly the analogies between unchecked capitalism and insanity, the suffering inflicted both on the nation at large and on the capitalists themselves. 'They are like people in a delirium,' he wrote, 'who should toss unceasingly in their beds, and fancy the restlessness proper labour, – who should grasp the bedclothes, and hug them to their hearts as gain.'

In *Isabella*, the heroine is driven mad after her lover has been murdered for daring to seduce the merchants' sister, a woman they see as no more than a commodity who could have been profitably exchanged in the marriage market. In the end, the murderers themselves are forced to flee their society, having destroyed love, youth, beauty, hope and the goodness of nature. It was a conclusion well suited to the times. In both his editorials, Hunt showed himself well aware of the terrible threat posed by such upholders of the economic order, and his leader of 5 April concludes with a vivid picture of the society in which *Isabella* was written. 'We live, at this very moment, in awful times, – kings and emperors foolishly breaking their promises, the community well informed and exceedingly discontented, and (to say nothing of spies and other grounds of disgust) a system of finance in our own country which calculators, who have never yet been disproved, say must infallibly tumble about our ears.' The anger and anxiety aroused by the corruption of the old regime and its blind, headlong greed is perfectly reflected in Keats's reworking of Boccaccio's medieval story.

These public aspects of the poem were paralleled by more intimate concerns. This tale of love destroyed is riddled with images of disease. Before Lorenzo and Isabella declare their passion, frustrated ardour reveals itself through physical symptoms. Their consuming emotions produce 'sick longing', pale cheeks, thinness. Their repressed love is a 'malady' threatening to destroy them, and they read the signs of their distress on each other's faces. Imagined joy lives close to pain, and while joy fulfilled leads to health, to love blossoming 'like a lusty flower, in June's caress', such health does not destroy the close relation of pleasure to pain, health to sickness:

> Even bees, the little almsmen of spring-bowers,
> Know there is richest juice in poison-flowers.[18]

After the murder of Lorenzo, frustrated passion again becomes sickness. Isabella falls into a 'gradual decay', and the 'pale shadow' of her dead lover's ghost takes a perverse delight in her pallor. The frustrated energies of life are turned to their dreadful opposite. Isabella burns with 'feverous hectic flame'. Deprived of love and in her growing madness, she tries to draw life from death, comfort from Lorenzo's severed head concealed in the pot beneath the flourishing basil plant. The avarice and ancestral pride of the brothers have destroyed love and perverted the forces of life. When finally her kinsmen steal the basil pot itself, not only are they obliged to flee, but they leave their sister to pine away, bereft and consumed by fatal passion. Keats's brooding on 'fierce destruction' during these painful weeks in Devon with Tom reaches its climax in this portrayal of young life condemned to death by savage forces of perversion.

The poem was rapidly composed, but by the time the first draft was complete Keats had his suspicions about the merit of the work. 'The Compliment is paid by us to Boccace, whether we publish or no,' he wrote to Reynolds.[19] The tone of *Isabella* worried him particularly, and this was an element to which he had given a great deal of thought. In particular, he had been reacting against Hunt's attempts to prettify such romances. In an outburst to Haydon, Keats declared: 'it is a great Pity that People should by associating themselves with the finest things, spoil them. Hunt has damned Hampstead and Masks and Sonnets and italian tales.' Keats's own poem reacts against Hunt's techniques. A soft, adjectival diction is stiffened with consonants and verbs. Hunt had disparaged antithesis and repetition, Keats deliberately used them, sometimes to excess.

But, in the attempt to honour the stark, factual simplicity of Boccaccio, Keats was forced to recognise that a modern poet could not imitate the 'simple plaining of a minstrel's song'. He was obliged to dwell, as Boccaccio was not, on the horror in the story, the 'wormy circumstance' of the exhumation of Lorenzo's body especially. The contrast between such scenes and the innocence of the young lovers accounts for the poem's tone of high sentiment. It is not and could not be a medieval work. A modern consciousness obtrudes, and Keats was in time to condemn this as 'mawkish'. His reaction against *Isabella* was to be stronger than that he harboured against any of his other works.

But now further disappointment awaited him. Back in London, George was actively planning his new life. Looking into his grand-mother's inheritance with a practical rigour altogether beyond his elder brother, he discovered he was heir to between £1600 and £1700. He wrote to tell Keats about this and eventually promised, in addition to paying off his loans, to put aside £500 to make up 'some means for my brothers'. The rest he would use to finance the arduous future that the contemporary conditions of the country seemed to force on him. George outlined his plans in a letter now lost. He had resolved, perhaps under the influence of Morris Birkbeck's *Notes on a Journey in America* (a book published by Taylor and Hessey), to emigrate. His inheritance would buy him acres of virgin prairie in Illinois, and Georgiana Wylie, whose mother had given her consent to their marriage, would make him an excellent wife.

Keats's reaction was inevitably divided and ambivalent. Although younger, George had always protected him. He had restrained his outbursts at school, nursed his melancholy, endured his moods and introduced him to people of their own age. Keats was about to lose an invaluable support, but it would be selfish to stand in the way of George's freedom. Yet he knew what such a loss would mean. 'My brother George', Keats later wrote to Sarah Jeffrey, 'always stood between me and any dealings with the world – Now I find I must buffet it.' That George was being generous with his money both to Tom and Keats himself only made his feelings more complex. Keats now had a little more financial security than he had imagined and could even think of travelling widely. But the fact remained that he was obliged to stay in England to be with his sister and a brother who was probably dying. Nor was he losing George himself to some assured, safe future. The picture of the continent familiar to Keats from Robertson's *History of America* was a grim account of degraded nature and degraded people, a picture of a place where human life could only affirm a minimal existence.

The brute horrors of the verse epistle to Reynolds weighed on Keats ever more oppressively. An unanticipated weekend visit from James Rice cheered him sufficiently to stimulate the composition of a tepid sonnet on the occasion, but the markings Keats made in the translation

Engravings after Poussin's 'The Realm of Flora' and 'Apollo
Inspiring the Youthful Poet'. Such works were shown to Keats by
Leigh Hunt, and classical mythology, the figure of Apollo
especially, entered deep into Keats's poetry

Above left: John Hamilton Reynolds who, after his death in 1852, was proud to be memorialised as the 'Friend of Keats'. A miniature by Joseph Severn
Above right: Keats's 'ardent friend' Benjamin Haydon by G.M. Zorlin, 1825
Below: View of the Isle of Wight contemporary with 'Endymion'

Above left: An anonymous portrait of Benjamin Bailey who described Keats as 'the most *loveable* creature' he had ever known
Above right: 'Dear, generous, noble' James Rice in an anonymous portrait
Below left: By September 1817 Keats and Charles Dilke were 'capital friends'. An anonymous portrait of *c*. 1825
Below right: The warm and universally popular Maria Dilke in an anonymous and undated portrait

The life mask of Keats made by Haydon as a study for his friend's portrait in 'Christ's Entry into Jerusalem'

Above left: For Keats, 'Hazlitt's depth of Taste' was one of the 'three things to rejoice at in this Age'. A portrait by William Bewick, 1825

Above right: Edmund Kean as Richard III by John James Halls, 1814. Keats wrote a review of the performance and later hoped Kean would play the lead in *Otho the Great*

Below: Keats's autograph in his volume of Shakespeare

Mr. WILLIAM

SHAKESPEARES

COMEDIES,
HISTORIES, &
TRAGEDIES.

Publiſhed according to the True Originall Copies.

Charles Brown, a portrait bust of Keats's 'capital friend' by
Andrew Wilson, 1828

of an old Spanish tale Rice brought down suggest that in his despondency Keats was coming close to some of his most painful half-buried memories. It seemed that all his supports were being taken from him, and his mind went back to the first insecurities of his earliest childhood. The hero of the Spanish tale had had a whore for a mother. Pleasing her two husbands, she had confused her son about his paternity. Keats's memories of his own dead father and the rapid substitution of William Rawlings were stirred along with what he later hinted to Bailey were memories of even 'earlier Misfortunes'.

The arrival of an advance copy of *Endymion* on Friday 24 April did nothing to lift this mood. To read over the pages was to see that his great efforts only proclaimed his immaturity. The need to re-create himself was ever more pressing, but he tried to preserve his usual standards of courtesy to Taylor. He recognised that despite the circumstances he had been at fault in leaving him with 'all the trouble of Endymion'. He prepared a list of errata and felt obliged to say 'the book pleased me much – it is very free from faults'. But the undertow of the letter was that continuing uneasiness which Keats now recognised 'as an habitual sensation'.

He felt sufficiently exposed to write about these changes taking place in his personality and his hopes for a maturing understanding of them. 'I have been hovering for some time between an exquisite sense of the luxurious and a love for Philosophy,' he declared.[20] 'Were I calculated for the former I should be glad – but as I am not I shall turn all my soul to the latter.' He was still planning on walking north with Brown, but he also felt some years of retreat and study were essential. His 'cavalier days' were behind him. His present state of mind made him all the more aware of what had always been his deepest moral impulse, 'the idea of doing some good for the world'. But his inexperience was starkly obvious, and this at least was something he could hope to change. 'I know nothing I have read nothing and I mean to follow Solomon's directions of "get Wisdom – get understanding",' he told Taylor.

But, as always during this period, it was to Reynolds that Keats opened his heart and confided his plans. He wrote to his friend on 27 April promising he would soon start to learn Greek and probably Italian.[21] At some time he bought a Greek grammar, and an ideal of Homer as the blind bard inspired by nature to insight was much on his mind. A sonnet to Homer probably dates from this April, and Keats longed to 'feast' on his work with Reynolds, hoping his friend might read him passages and share the luxury of a misty understanding of the poet. But Keats also recognised the need for more rigorous thought. Although poetry was still the 'Chief' thing in literature, what he believed would be the calming influence of philosophy was also important, and he relished the idea of doing a year's preparatory reading before asking Hazlitt about 'the best metaphysical road I can take'.

For all this, Keats's uneasiness still shaded into profound gloom, and in such moments of mental blight he felt he could not write to the ailing Reynolds. The presence of Tom, unable to sleep and over-burdened with fever, deepened his distress, and only one of his brother's periodic appearances of improvement could raise Keats's spirits. Now Tom was keen to return to London, and Keats himself looked forward to sunny days on Hampstead Heath such as he and Reynolds had enjoyed the previous year. They would read his newly acquired black-letter Chaucer together.

Nonetheless, his thoughts kept returning to his present state. Again he insisted on the importance of knowledge as a balance for the mind. All learning, even medicine or the law, which Reynolds was studying and which Keats hoped to interest himself in, went to form 'a great whole'. It was a 'needful' thing, calming, broadening and able 'to ease the Burden of the Mystery' even if it could not, finally, console the heart for the experience of pain and death. Keats's quotation from *Tintern Abbey*, however, suggests the direction in which his thoughts were moving. His recent experiences had raised his respect for Wordsworth's inwardness, his 'thinking into the human heart'. The jejune dislike of three months earlier was replaced by a deepened respect. Trapped in the 'labyrinth' of his own confusion, Wordsworth's profound investigation of the human condition was a comfort if not a guide. But what about the question of Wordsworth's egotism, and how did he compare to Milton, whom Keats had been reading so extensively? An answer to such questions was essential both to his development and to the balance of his mind.

Keats tried to clarify his ideas in a letter to Reynolds of 3 May in which the spontaneous efflorescence of ideas offers an exhilarating sense of the speed and inventiveness of Keats's intellect.[22] He had never written with such a mastery of exuberance. The mental energy is vertiginous and Keats rejoices in its abundance.

I must be quaint and free of Tropes and figures – I must play my draughts as I please, and for my advantage and your erudition, crown a white with a black, or a black with a white, and move into black and white, far and near as I please – I must go from Hazlitt to Patmore, and make Wordsworth and Coleman play at leap-frog – or keep one of them down a whole half-holiday at fly the garter – 'from Gray to Gay, from Little to Shakespeare' – Also, as a long cause requires two or more sittings of the Court, so a long letter will require two or more sittings of the Breech wherefore I shall resume after dinner.

As the letter progresses, Keats's reading, his knowledge of pain and the blackest doubt and anxiety, are placed in a new and altogether more objective light by the sheer energy with which they are examined. Here is a unique intellect re-creating itself out of the depths of its own essential strength.

In the longer part of the letter, written when he had returned from dinner, Keats took up the question of Wordsworth again. Previously, he had wondered 'whether Miltons apparently less anxiety for Humanity proceeds from his seeing further or no than Wordsworth'. In other words, did the grand objectivity of renaissance epic perhaps have its basis in what now appeared a circumscribed vision? Keats did not feel quite ready to answer this yet, for describing the problem immediately posed another question. Was Wordsworth's apparently fuller heart something that inhibited him from writing in the true epic manner attained by Milton? Did works such as *The Excursion* reveal a poet who 'has in truth epic passion'?

To raise these problems, to try and evaluate the relative stature of the very different poets of the past and present, was not immediately to find a solution. Keats proceeded by way of feeling and personal experience. These suggested that Wordsworth's poetry was at least true to Keats's own experience as a contemporary man. He was himself keenly aware of 'the burden of the mystery', that unenlightened state, deprived of imaginative vision, when the weight of what Wordsworth called 'this unintelligible world' bears wearily down upon us. Indeed, in his verse epistle to Reynolds, he had gone even further and suggested that panicked state of mind when the world cannot be seen as having the essential benevolence of nature revealed in *Tintern Abbey*, that sustaining sense of the benign and the sublime 'deeply interfused' in the ocean, the air and the setting sun. For Keats, the air of Devon was 'of a deteriorating quality'. His thoughts had not taken their colour from the sunset and, seeing too far into the sea, he had glimpsed a universal anarchy. To read Wordsworth to his depths was to recognise a great and matured mind acknowledging solutions to these problems won from his own experience. Such ways of thinking chimed with Keats's own: 'We find what he says true as far as we have experienced.'

And it was this touchstone of personal experience that was all important. Keats's mistrust of sweeping theory was never more important to him than now. 'Axioms in philosophy are not axioms until they are proved upon our pulses: We read fine things but never feel them to the full until we have gone the same steps as the Author.' The proof of this was the fact that these bitter Devon weeks meant that 'now I shall relish Hamlet more than ever I have done.' Quoting Byron, he continued '"Knowledge is Sorrow"; and I go on to say that "Sorrow is Wisdom".' Then, realising that he was verging on portentousness, he let laughter supervene and carry him away from his subject in a series of riddling puns as inventive as anything in Shakespearian prose.

But the issues would not go away. 'I will return to Wordsworth.' Did Wordsworth have 'an extended vision or a circumscribed grandeur', and how did his achievement relate to Keats himself? There follows one of the best-known passages in the Letters. Taking the Christian image of heaven as a house with many mansions, Keats creates a wholly secular image of his own development:

Well – I compare human life to a large Mansion of Many Apartments, two of which I can only describe, the doors of the rest being as yet shut upon me. The first we step into we call the infant or thoughtless Chamber, in which we remain as long as we do not think – We remain there a long while, and notwithstanding the doors of the second Chamber remain open wide, showing a bright appearance, we care not to hasten to it; but at length are imperceptibly impelled by the awakening of this thinking principle – within us – we no sooner get into the second Chamber, which I will call the Chamber of Maiden-Thought, than we become intoxicated from the light and the atmosphere, we see nothing but pleasant wonders, and think of delaying there forever in delight: However among the effects of this breathing is father of is that tremendous one of sharpening one's vision into the heart and nature of Man – of convincing one's nerves that the world is full of Misery and Heartbreak, Pain, Sickness and oppression – whereby This Chamber of Maiden Thought becomes gradually darken'd and at the same time on all sides of it many doors are set open – but all dark – all leading to dark passages – We see not the ballance of good and evil. We are in a Mist.[23]

The beautiful description of the clouding of the Chamber of Maiden Thought is profoundly true of Keats's development from 'I stood tiptoe' to the verse epistle to Reynolds. The dark passages exactly suggest the 'labyrinth' in which Keats felt he was lost. And the religious imagery suggests that at heart he knew this was a spiritual problem and one that had to be borne without the help of the conventional Christianity he had rejected.

Other phrases in the passage support this. Keats's worry about being unable to see 'the ballance of good and evil' – the panic he had expressed in the verse epistle to Reynolds – borrows its vocabulary from contemporary theological debate and uses the language employed by his acquaintances. Both Bailey and Hunt regarded the existence of evil as a 'mystery', and Hunt, like many other philosophers of natural religion, was much exercised to show (to the satisfaction of his own temperament if not to the stricter requirements of logic) that the balance inclined in favour of the good. 'What evils there are', he wrote in his *Autobiography*, 'I find for the most part, relieved with many consolations.' Keats was now very far from such bland assumptions. He felt circumscribed by a darkening sense of the malignant underlying human unhappiness. What was the balance of good and evil when Tom was spitting blood?

Paradise Lost suggested that the existence of evil could be explained in a poem that was itself a magisterial account of how man by his own sin was responsible for bringing into this world 'a world of woe' and how God offered redemption through the sacrifice of his Son. But the doctrine of the atonement was something Keats had rejected and with it had gone intellectual assent to Milton's ideas. What Keats saw as a now outmoded way of thinking could be accounted for only by the historical conditions in which Milton himself lived. His Protestantism was a theology one step on from the superstitions of the Roman Catholic church and the horrors of the Inquisition. It was an improvement on these, Keats suggested, and Milton appeared content with them. But time moved on and conditions changed. This happened, Keats believed, because all people are borne along 'upon the general and gregarious advance of intellect' which had now brought modern mankind to the position where a great contemporary poet was obliged, as Milton was not, to 'think into the human heart'. As a result, Wordsworth was, of necessity, 'deeper than Milton'. He was so not because he had a finer mind but because he lived in a different time.

A truly modern poetry had to be more inward, more subjective, but that did not make it any less genuinely spiritual than Milton's work. Quite the reverse, since Keats's use of the phrase 'thinking into the human heart' was again borrowed from contemporary religious debate. Indeed, it was much used by Hunt, who declared: 'God has written his religion in the heart, for growing wisdom to read perfectly, and time to make triumphant.' The subjectivity of the modern poet was a spiritual quest, and to be a truly modern poet was to be in the vanguard of spiritual discovery. Providence, Keats declared, had decreed this by subduing 'the mightiest Minds to the service of the time being, whether it be in human Knowledge or Religion'. As Milton was of his age, so a Wordsworth or a Keats would have to be of theirs. Change was inevitable, and Keats saw it as inseparable from progress. 'There really is a grand march of intellect.' Those who were at the forefront of it were those who could see most deeply into their own hearts and souls. Such an evolution towards ever more Godlike knowledge would be the philosophy on which, in time, he would rear his own epic of modern consciousness, *Hyperion*.

In the meantime, 'we are in a Mist.' This image of uncertainty would become almost an obsession over the next few months as Keats wandered the dark passages of his intellect, but the longing for light, for resolution and for a poise of mind that could balance the inward wisdom of the moderns with the objective amplitude of the classics was the power that led him to imagine life beyond the darkening Chamber of Maiden Thought. It also inspired him to write, and this letter to Reynolds contains one of the greatest of Keats's fragments, the 'Ode to May'.

> Mother of Hermes! and still youthful Maia!
>   May I sing to thee
> As thou was hymnèd on the shores of Baiae?
>   Or may I woo thee
> In earlier Sicilian? or thy smiles
> Seek as they once were sought, in Grecian isles,
> By bards who died content in pleasant sward,
>   Leaving great verse unto a little clan?
> O, give me their old vigour, and unheard
>   Save of the quiet primrose, and the span
>   Of Heaven and few ears,
> Rounded by thee, my song should die away
>   Content as theirs,
> Rich in the simple worship of a day.

The imagined serenity of a Grecian spring radiates through this poem, which itself evokes an ideal of poetry that is at one with the health and light of circumambient nature. But there is perhaps, under the persistent interrogatives and the subtle use of tense, a suggestion that this cannot be, that the hoped-for calm magnificence is no more than a fiction created out of the very longing its achievement would still. Such drama, the dialectic of beauty and pain, would become the subject of the great completed odes of the following year.

* * *

Now, however, with Tom apparently in remission and longing to return to London, it seemed that the weeks in Teignmouth could be brought to a close. They set off, despatching a message to the Jeffrey family from Honiton, where they boarded the coach for London. But at Bridport Tom suffered a violent haemorrhage. After this, they travelled back by slow, painful stages of fifty miles a day. For three weeks Keats wrote neither poetry nor letters, being, as so often when he was anxious, 'very much engaged with his friends'. There was the expedition with Brown to plan for and precious last days to spend with George. They went to see the comedian Charles Mathews at the Lyceum and met coincidentally with Isabella Jones, who, unknown to Keats, was now, in the coterie world of literary London, being courted by Taylor.

But neither the theatre nor the chance encounter could lift Keats's deepening depression. The pressing facts of Tom's health and George's departure spoiled the precarious balance he had so recently achieved. It was natural that part of him should be 'almost stony hearted' about George's wedding, even if such feelings made him guilty. At times he wondered if he would accept Bailey's invitation to Oxford, where he might study Greek with his friend. He did not go. Instead, he confided his thoughts to Bailey in a letter written between 21 and 25 May.[24] His wretchedness, so often carefully hidden from his friends, could not be covered up. 'I am now so depressed that I have not an Idea to put to paper.' Again, 'I am in that temper that if I were under Water I would scarcely kick to come to the top.' Such moods, 'nonsense' though they might be, meant he could not even take pleasure in Bailey's glowing review of *Endymion*.

This mood did not seriously lift, despite an amusing evening with Hazlitt and others at Haydon's and an improvement in the health of Reynolds and Rice. Circumstances indeed only continued to make things worse. George was married at St Margaret's, Westminster on Tuesday 28 May, Keats signing the register in a ceremony which surely underlined the remorseless breaking up of the brothers' intimate triumvirate. The pain this caused numbed Keats into pessimism. 'I have two Brothers,' he wrote to Bailey, 'one is driven by the "burden of Society" to America the other, with an exquisite love of Life, is in a lingering State.'[25] His bitterness verged on misanthropy: 'I have suspected everybody . . . and now I am never alone without rejoicing that there is such a thing as death.' His mind ran again on disease, the suffering no fame could alleviate. 'I would reject a petrarchal corona- tion – on accou[n]t of my dying day, and because women have

Cancers.' Such moods, he recognised, were a form of egotism, but 'I am not old enough or magnanimous enough to annihilate self.' This was a damning self-indictment and it was not quite true. His own complexity and responsiveness saved Keats from the narrowed sentimentality of a mere curmudgeonly gloom and he was, besides, determined to be generous where he could.

He genuinely harboured little jealousy of Georgiana, for example. He was 'very fond of her', he confessed, and was coming to like her more and more. No doubt this came in part from the woman's own genuine tact, her imaginative sympathy with her brother-in-law's feelings. Georgiana's behaviour was such that Keats could even declare her to be 'the most disinterested woman I ever knew'. This was the highest praise, but it could not obliterate the pain or that old discomfort with women generally which emerged rather spitefully when Keats put Georgiana's natural happiness down to a want of imagination. The fate of his brothers, however, brought a terrible awareness of isolation. 'My Love for my Brothers from the early loss of our parents and even for earlier Misfortunes has grown into a[n] affection "passing the Love of Women" – I have been ill temper'd with them, I have vex'd them – but the thought of them has always stifled the impression that any woman might otherwise have made upon me.' This is a revealing sentence and shows just how protected Keats had been and how inexperienced he still was. Now his greatest protection was being stripped away and he would have to confront both his life and the immaturities in his nature without a shield.

'Life must be undergone,' but, if the thought of writing poetry was a consolation, it was one fraught with anxiety. Keats did not know that his publishers were secretly unhappy with his work. '"Endymion" does not by any means please me as I had expected,' Taylor wrote, but he was determined to reveal his disappointment only to his most immediate circle.[26] He was also resolved to do what he could to forestall what he sensed would be the hostility of the press to so obvious a pupil of Hunt's. Keats himself was well aware of this particular threat, for *Blackwood's* had just reviewed Hunt's new volume *Foliage*, which contained the two sonnets he had written months before during the laurel-crowning episode. The absurdity of that situation was not lost on the reviewer, who sneered at this parody of a 'petrarchal coronation' and Hunt's crown fixed on his head by that 'amiable but infatuated bardling, Mister John Keats'.[27] The notoriety of his erstwhile master, whom he had now left so far behind, was threatening to damage whatever hopes of reputation Keats was nurturing. 'They have', he lamented, 'smothered me in "Foliage".' Hoping to avoid a repetition of this, Taylor tried to placate Gifford of the *Quarterly Review*, but to no effect.

In the meantime, he gave George an introduction to Birkbeck in Illinois while offering Keats himself a copy of his conveniently tiny three-volume reprint of Carey's version of the *Divine Comedy*. These Keats would put in his knapsack for his northern tour, which was now about to begin despite problems with a sore throat. With Tom left in the kindly hands of Mrs Bentley, their Hampstead landlady, Keats and Brown, George and Georgiana, set out on 22 June aboard the Liverpool coach. The journey of about thirty-two hours was broken at Redbourn in Hertfordshire, where the passengers dined and Keats found time briefly to meet up with his old friend Stephens, who was now in medical practice there. Then, driving on through the showers, they reached Liverpool late in the afternoon of 23 June. They found rooms at the Crown Inn, and very early the following morning Keats and Brown slipped away. The farewells had been said the night before, and now their coach drove the two men north through the dawn air. Before them lay the long-promised sight of lakes, mountains and hills. In exposing himself to their beauty, Keats would put sickness and 'mawkishness' behind him. As he had promised weeks earlier to Haydon, 'I shall clamber through the clouds and exist.'[28]

At the Cable's Length

at the cable's length
Man feels the gentle anchor pull and gladdens in its
strength . . .

('*Lines Written in the Highlands after a Visit to Burns's
Country*')

THE COACH DROPPED Keats and Brown off in Lancaster. This was the
first time Keats himself had seen the grinding poverty of an industrial
town or heard the remorseless thrum of its machinery. Here were the
'noisy factories' only imagined in *Isabella*. This was already a different
world and, with their leather knapsacks and appearance of metropolitan
smartness, the two men looked, as a scornful passer-by declared, like
gentlemen with nothing better to do than go walking in order to make
work for themselves.

Lancaster itself was more than usually lively since Parliament had
been dissolved and a general election called. Liberals everywhere were
fired with the hope of getting 'as many *additional* and staunch advocates
of their cause in the House as possible'.[1] The *Examiner* beamed with
optimism: 'I believe the Ministers will be startled when they meet the
fresh faces next session, – fresh in every way, with youth, hope, and
public virtue.' In Lancaster the inns were loud with argument and
candidates buying votes for drink. The supper Keats and Brown ordered
took two hours to arrive, and, when they finished it, they were told the
inn was full. They had to seek private lodgings where they might get a
good night's sleep before rising the following morning at four.

They woke to the disappointment of rain and sat for three hours
reading *Samson Agonistes* before walking to Bolton-le-Sands for
breakfast. By midday the rain had cleared again, and by three o'clock
they had reached Burton-in-Kendal, where they ate at the King's

Arms, the Green Dragon being full of the military. As their landlady sighed, giving vent to the local distress: 'Ah! gentlemen, the soldiers are upon us! The Lowthers had brought 'em here to be in readiness. There'll be sad work at Appleby! There's Mr. Brougham, a great speaker in the house, I understand, comes down to oppose the Lowthers. Dear me! dear me! – at this election time to have soldiers upon us, when we ought to be making a bit of money.'[2] The contest between the great Whig lawyer Brougham, the defender of Leigh Hunt, and the sons of Lord Lowther, the Tory patron of Wordsworth, was to cast its shadow over the early days of Keats's tour. As Brown wrote, 'the turmoil of an election was a nuisance to the tranquilly disposed.'

For, like the increasing number of tourists in the area, Keats and Brown had come to glimpse the sublime in nature. At the beginning of his account of the expedition, Brown declared: 'We were not bound on a journey of discovery into "the busy haunts of men." Not that cities, their rise, progress, and increasing prosperity, or the reverse, or their prevailing interests and politics, were objects of indifference; but attention to them, and a love of the beauty and sublimity of nature are so widely distinct in character as not to be harmonised together.' The disharmony between them, the gulf between the splendours of nature and the wretchedness of the human condition, was to preoccupy Keats for much of the journey, but both he and Brown set out with ideals of the benevolent and sublime firmly in mind.

This was the convention underlying such expeditions, and guidebooks both popular and literary put an emphasis on those 'stations' where the visitor could stand and glimpse the picturesque, the historical and the sublime itself to particular advantage. Much of what Keats would see on the earlier part of his travels at least was widely familiar and attitudes to it were already enshrined in an orthodoxy of awe whose poetic spokesman was now Wordsworth. The sublime had curative and even religious powers, as the author of one of the more highbrow travel books was keen to emphasise. Standing on a bright day before a beautifully wooded valley, Hazlitt's brother-in-law Sir John Stoddart enthused as he was gradually enveloped in a thick curtain of mist, 'I was left alone, on the mountain top, far above the clouds of the vale, the sun shining full upon my head; it seemed as if I had been suddenly transported into a new state of existence, cut off from every minor association, and invisibly united with the surrounding purity and brightness.'[3] This was an ideal to which Brown gave annual consent, renting his house each summer (this year to the widowed Mrs Brawne and her family) in order to fund the experience. Keats, altogether more shrewdly aware of the bewilderment and chaos that could threaten the mind that 'peered too far' into nature, was to examine such notions with a more troubled consciousness.

For the moment, however, he was by turns genuinely exultant and amused. His curiosity was excited by all he saw. After their meal at the King's Arms, he and Brown pressed on to Endmoor through the rain. The local landlady took pity on their drenched state, despite the fact that she was in a 'squeer' because she was whitewashing her inn, and she ushered the two men into the room which served as both her parlour and her kitchen. Here, living on a pension of 1s 3d a day, sat a friendly soldier who, as Keats noted, 'had been in all the wars for the last seventeen years'.[4] A garrulous drunk occupied another corner. Staggering forward to the now bedraggled strangers, he wondered if they were pedlars selling spectacles and razors. Having been put right, the man tried to sponge a drink but, failing in this, eventually left. As Keats and Brown were to learn during the course of the evening, the man, Richard Radshaw, had fallen into alcoholic despair after the death of his wife and sons. His daughters had remained in Lancaster, his farm had fallen into decay, and now the man scratched a living as a day labourer. 'Without elevating him to the rank of a Lear in humble life, or degrading his daughters into a Regan and a Goneril, he may be commiserated, and, perhaps, they may be blamed,' Brown wrote. The story was an insight into the human misery that throughout the trip was continuously to qualify Keats's appreciation of the sublime in the worlds of nature and art.

The following morning saw Keats at his most excited. He and Brown had passed Kendal and, as they approached Bowness through the clearing mist, Lake Windermere opened before them. 'Hitherto, Keats had witnessed nothing superior to Devonshire,' Brown recorded, 'but, beautiful as that is, he was now tempted to speak of it with indifference.' At the first turn from the road, before descending to the hamlet of Bowness itself, both men came to a full stop. The lake lay before them, and Keats's 'bright eyes darted on a mountain-peak' and 'thence to a very small island, adorned with the foliage of trees, that lay beneath us, and surrounded by water of a glorious hue'. He burst out in his excitement: 'How can I believe in that? – surely it cannot be!' It was as if he had rediscovered the landscape of his own first poem and found it to be altogether grander than his imagination had conceived.

In fact, Keats's reaction to Windermere was both as exultant as Brown claimed and more complex, a combination of the sublime with a shrewd awareness of that which spoiled beauty and threatened the relief of spirits it might offer. Keats himself tried to present these two impressions simultaneously. 'There are many disfigurements to this Lake,' he wrote to Tom, 'not in the way of land or water. No: the two views we have had of it are of the most noble tenderness – they can never fade away.' The landscape was no longer the troubled and febrile vision of *The Enchanted Castle* or the submarine horror of the epistle to Reynolds, and Keats's exultation was one of the most powerful experiences of joy he had known. His views of Windermere, he declared, 'make one forget the divisions of life; age, youth, poverty and riches; and refine one's sensual vision into a sort of north star which can never cease to be open-lidded and steadfast over the wonders of the great Power'.

This image, caught in a moment of exultation, was to penetrate deeply into Keats's unconsciousness and re-emerge in one of his greatest sonnets. The hapless veering of the mind did not always have to distort nature with 'an eternal fierce destruction'. Nor was this merely the exhilaration won from a sense of holiday freedom. It was something both universal and permanent – 'there is no such thing', Keats wrote in his rapture, 'as time and space,' and such pleasure seemed able to translate itself almost effortlessly into art. 'I shall learn poetry here,' he declared. The landscape of the Lake District was powerful beyond his fretting egotism, and 'I live in the eye; and my imagination, surpassed, is at rest.'

Nonetheless, the 'disfigurements' around Lake Windermere could not be brushed aside. Tourism was destroying the very thing it had come to enjoy. 'The disfigurement I mean', Keats wrote, 'is the miasma of London.' There were fashionable, or would-be fashionable, people everywhere. Keats and Brown were to find Keswick wholly adapted 'to please a London taste', boasting a library, a museum, art exhibitions and a camera obscura. Some visitors believed nature was improved when observed through a reflecting 'Claude Glass', and such affectations were corrosive. Keats and Brown found the bragging of a young man at their hotel in Bowness particularly irksome, while the coldly polite service and over-opulent curtains of their inn seemed like an affront to the view beyond the window.

Altogether more troubling, however, was the way that politics were so forcefully making their presence felt in this beautiful location. Just a week before Keats and Brown arrived, an anonymous Tory 'Yellow Boy', in a letter to the *Westmorland Gazette*, had urged fashionable visitors to enhance their pleasure in Lake Windermere by 'laughing at the jacobinical speeches . . . concerning the politics of the nation' uttered by the locals.[5] Trouble had been brewing since February when Kendal was shaken by anti-Lowther riots and the stone-throwing and mud-slinging of Brougham's 'Blue Boys'. Soldiers, as Keats knew, were stationed at Burton-in-Kendal in case of trouble, but now through one of the waiters in their hotel he discovered that no less a figure than Wordsworth (aided by his sister Dorothy, by Thomas De Quincey and by Southey) was actively canvassing for the Lowthers' cause. His disillusion was intense. 'What think you of that,' he wrote to Tom, 'Wordsworth versus Brougham!! Sad – sad – sad – and yet the family has been his friend always. What can we say?'

He would say nothing yet, his indignation needing time to mature. When an angry Wordsworth left London in February, Keats had made excuses for him. 'I am sorry', he wrote to his brothers, 'that Wordsworth has left a bad impression wherever he visited in Town – by his egotism, Vanity and bigotry – yet he is a great Poet if not a Philosopher.' Now it was not so easy to make excuses for him. Keats may have gauged what the *Caledonian Mercury* later asserted, namely that the decided opinion in the county was that the liberal cause would prevail against the influence of the Lowthers and that 'the bets were five to one in favour of Mr Brougham.'[6] What he probably did not know, however, was that the Lowthers themselves 'considered their castle attacked, and were resolved to spare neither labour nor money to carry their effort'.[7] Their labour involved some fairly blatant vote-rigging, while among the expenses they were prepared to shoulder was the establishment, partly with Wordsworth's help, of the *Westmorland Gazette*, where the Yellow Boy's letter crudely voiced the sentiments of the right, concluding that 'those famous petty orators' in Brougham's camp 'would have been better employed behind their counters, in tanning colts, or using their looms.'

Keats was determined nonetheless to pay his respects to Wordsworth on his own ground, and the following morning he made his way with Brown to Rydal Mount. But Wordsworth 'was not at home nor was any Member of his family – I was much disappointed.' Keats left a note and set forth again. In fact, Wordsworth was by the Lowthers' side at the poll in Appleby and, as Brown recalled many years later, 'the young poet looked thoughtful at this exposure of his elder'. Even Wordsworth's deserted house seemed symbolic of his public identification with the old regime. As Keats wrote bitterly to Tom, 'Lord Wordsworth, instead of being in retirement, has himself and his house full in the thick of fashionable visitors quite convenient to be pointed at all the summer long.' What Keats did not realise was that he was writing to a brother now rapidly becoming too sickly even to care. Tuberculosis was tightening its terrible grip.

From the flea-ridden inn at Wythburn, meanwhile, Keats wrote a letter to George and Georgiana which he hoped, vainly as it turned out, would reach them at Liverpool before they set sail. Much of what he said merely recapitulated the experiences already outlined to Tom, but at the close of the letter Keats turned to 'my dear Sister George', wondering what her mood might be and what kind of poem might match it. In the end, Keats resolved on an acrostic. Such a work could be little more than album verse, but as Keats spun his lines from the letters of his sister-in-law's new married name, so a sense of familial warmth, of 'love and brotherhood', began to emerge. Georgiana's kindly, disinterested nature, along with George's evident happiness in his marriage, had impressed Keats, and the fact of his separation from his brother forced him to consider his own position in a new light. One of the great changes wrought by the walking trip would be an often painful maturing of Keats's attitude towards women and the very gradual exposure of his vulnerability to love.

Keats and Brown rose early the following morning to walk in the drizzle the eight miles to Keswick. Brown thought the town irksomely metropolitan but their walk there, past Helvellyn and round Derwentwater, included a ten-mile detour to see the falls of Lodore. This all delighted Keats, despite some disappointment with the falls themselves and the discomfort of slipping one of his legs into a squashy hole. Then, in the evening, while their supper was being prepared, the two men walked a mile and a half up the Penrith road to see the stone circle near the Vale of St John. This was another sight that was to lodge itself firmly in Keats's memory and later reappear in his poetry. 'Surrounded by a majestic panorama,' Brown wrote, 'the spot is suited to render the human mind awestruck, and, possibly, with the ignorant, superstitious.' Here, on Brown's part at least, was the conventional attitude expected of the well-read and intelligent tourist.

The two men had arranged for a guide to meet them at four the following morning so they could climb Skiddaw. The ascent was a tiring one. The air got colder and colder, and Keats comforted himself with a couple of glasses of rum and water, but it was hard when, looking up at the peak, their guide told them that they had only got half-way. They proceeded 'merrily' nonetheless, until the guide himself began shaking his head and prophesying rain as a cloud swept downwards over the mountain. By the time the climbers were three-quarters of a mile from the summit, they were enveloped in mist. Visibility was cut to less than twenty yards and it was useless to go on. Keats consoled himself with the thought that, like Brown, he 'was not much gratified by this sort of bird's-eye view' anyway and, during the jolting trot down the mountain, he took a third glass of warming rum and water.

Nature was beginning to pall. 'Scenery is fine, but human nature is finer,' Keats had written from Devon, and now, when they arrived at Ireby, his fascination with human activity again asserted itself. Brown thought Ireby 'a dull, beggarly looking place', but when they entered the neat, half-timbered dining-room of the Crown Inn, they heard 'obstreperous doings overhead' and Keats was delighted to find a children's country dancing class in full swing. This was, he wrote, quoting Burns, '"no new cotillon fresh from France." No, they kickit & jumpit with mettle extraordinary, & whiskit, & fleckit, and toe'd it, and go'd it, & twirld it, & wheel'd it, & stampt it, & sweated it, tattooing the floor like mad; The differenc[e] between our country dances & these scotch figures, is about the same as leisurely stirring a cup o' Tea & beating up a batter-pudding!'[8] This was an amusing comparison, but it sprang from a deeper consideration.

For a week now, Keats had been immersed in beautiful scenery. His imagination had soared with the sublime and he had relished the insentient beauty of nature. He had walked a hundred miles, his thighs were tired and he was soon to become a little blistered. Now the contented and delightful faces of the dancing children brought home to him what the natural world could not provide. 'I fear', he wrote, 'our continual moving from place to place, will prevent our becoming learned in village affairs; we are mere creatures of Rivers, Lakes and Mountains.' Human community, both the proximity and the otherness of other people, stirred him, and, as he looked at the row of boys and girls, noting here a beautiful face and there an 'exquisite' mouth, so he was 'extremely gratified to think, that if I had pleasures they knew nothing of, they had also some into which I could not possibly enter'. Such a contrast between the human world, moving yet far from straightforward of access, and the natural world, sublime yet often impersonal, was to deepen painfully as the trip progressed.

Now they passed on through Wigton with its ancient, red-coloured castle, to Carlisle. Here, in a few weeks' time, Bailey was due to be ordained by the bishop. Unknown to Keats, his friend was facing a crisis in his personal and professional life. Bailey's pursuit of Marianne Reynolds was foundering on her indifference, and he had apparently made a proposal that had been declined. He asked her to take more time and think her decision over, but back in Oxford Bailey was also developing his friendship with his room-mate George Glieg, for the good reason that Glieg's father was the Primate of the Scottish Episcopalian Church. Having been disappointed once over church affairs, Bailey was not going to be turned down again. He went back to London, seeing Keats's publishers while he was there, but soon he would be coming north for his ordination when, in his naivety, he would wreak appalling damage on his friend's career.

It was Bailey who had first introduced Keats to Dante, and it was perhaps now, when blisters and Brown's assurance that there was little worth seeing between Carlisle and Dumfries persuaded them to take the coach, that Keats turned to the *Inferno*. Certainly, the descent into hell, the oppressive multitude of suffering spirits, and the terrible figure of Minos impartially consigning souls to eternal torment, was much on Keats's mind as he crossed the border into Scotland. The dancing children of Ireby had made him feel 'the glory of making by any means a country happier', but now, when they neared Dumfries and the tomb of Burns, so Keats's mood began to darken. The two men approached St Michael's churchyard, and the clouds, the sky and the dour houses appeared to Keats 'anti-Grecian and anti-Charlemagnish'. Glory and loveliness, it seemed, had passed away.

Brown, now on his home territory, felt quite the reverse. The expedition to see Burns's tomb took on for him the air of a pilgrimage. 'Such memorials to great men in the intellectual world, especially over their graves, should not be neglected,' he wrote. 'They may excite emulation; they must inspire reverence and gratitude, two feelings of which man is susceptible to the improvement of his nature.' But for Keats, at this moment, such was not the case. The frigid mausoleum was 'not very much to my taste, though on a scale, large enough to show they wanted to honour him'. He was disturbed and, after dinner and 'in a strange mood, half-asleep', he composed a sonnet 'On Visiting the Tomb of Burns'.

> The town, the churchyard, and the setting sun,
>   The clouds, the trees, the rounded hills all seem,
>   Though beautiful, cold – strange – as in a dream
> I dreamèd long ago. Now new begun
> The short-lived, paly summer is but won

From winter's ague, for one hour's gleam;
    Though saphire-warm, their stars do never gleam –
All is cold Beauty; pain is never done
For who has mind to relish, Minos-wise,
    The real of Beauty, free from that dead hue
        Fickly imagination and sick pride
    Cast wan upon it! Burns! with honour due
        I have oft honoured thee. Great shadow, hide
Thy face! I sin against thy native skies.

The sense of crisis is clear even where the grammar is not. Once again, Keats suggests that the imagination projects its own discomfort on to the natural world, thereby distorting it. The dilemma faced in the epistle to Reynolds has returned. There had been moments during the last week when Keats had seemed to be free of this, when the loveliness of Windermere had been so much more powerful than his own fretting consciousness that time and space had disappeared and with them 'the divisions of life', all the contraries that make up the interplay of pleasure and pain. But in the end such happiness was at best a temporary refuge. Human nature could not be permanently calmed by the grandeur of nature. Keats was painfully aware that, 'Health and Spirits can only belong unalloyed to the selfish Man – the Man who thinks much of his fellows can never be in Spirits.' As the sonnet suggests, the pursuit of beauty as an end in itself is a denial of full humanity, and those who indulge it are, in their way, as monstrous as Dante's pitiless Minos.

Those who really know the reality of beauty recognise that it can never be truly experienced except in its relationship to suffering, the pain that is never over, 'never done'. In the horror of this recognition, beauty itself becomes drained of warmth and life. The mausoleum of a great poet, glimpsed in the setting sun, becomes coldly impotent. As the awareness of pain and the futility of escape darken the mind, so the fickle imagination corrodes the very thing that could give a temporary respite to its anguish. Even the endeavour of a great poet becomes spoiled by such thoughts. Art and those who make it cannot permanently replace the reality of human suffering. Mere aestheticism is as much a delusion as dreams of lasting peace in nature.

What Keats saw around him confirmed the reality of pain, but with that open and balanced health of mind which recognised the dangers of a merely facile pessimism, he refused to indulge what he called his 'prejudices'. He strove to remain curious and even amused. The vigour of the Scots dialect delighted him, and '*whuskey*' was 'very smart stuff'. The cageyness with which a well-dressed Scot revealed he was a deist was 'very amusing'. Even the poverty and simplicity of the people had its charm. 'Yesterday', he wrote to Tom, 'was an immense Horsefair at Dumfries, so that we met numbers of men & women on the road, but the women nearly all barefoot, with their shoes & clean stockings in hand, ready to put on & look smart in the Towns.'

It was partly from such sights as these, as they were walking towards Auchencairn and Brown was telling Keats about Scott's *Guy Mannering* and the character of Meg Merrillies, that Keats himself composed for his sister his ballad on the legendary gipsy woman. This delightful poem (enclosed in the letter along with the humorous doggerel of 'A Song about Myself') marks an important advance in Keats's poetic thinking. The element of escape and wish-fulfilment in romance is recognised and indulged as Keats inveigles the reader into a fresh and healthy outdoor world free from money and longing, a world that is spartan yet satisfying, giving and essentially heroic:

> Old Meg was brave as Margaret Queen
>   And tall as Amazon,
> An old red blanket coat she wore,
>   A chip-hat had she on.
> God rest her agèd bones somewhere –
>   She died full long agone![9]

The poem leads the reader into a world of innocence only to show that such qualities belong to an irrecoverable past. After delight, we are left firmly in the suffering of the present – that Scotland opening up before Keats where 'the horrible dominion of the Scots Kirk' seemed to expend its mortmain over all the people.

The suffering inflicted by organised religion was patent, and Keats's anticlericalism, shared by Brown, was roused. He felt that the barefooted girls in the countryside around him were so many Susannas exposed to the lascivious interest of the Presbyterian elders. These men were concerned to deny everything that gave joy and spontaneity. They also placed such an emphasis on money that the entire nation was 'formed into Phalanges of savers and gainers'. Laughing, punning and kissing were all under embargo. Spontaneity had been crushed. 'Were the fingers made to squeeze a guinea or a white hand? – Were the Lips made to hold a pen or a kiss?' Even poetry withered in such an atmosphere, and Keats's mind turned, as it was often to do in these weeks, to Burns. He thought of Burns's drunkenness and of his love-life constantly made a subject of enquiry by the church elders. Burns was, Keats decided, a man of southern temperament caught in the deadening north. The divide between the squalor of Burns's physical life and the ideal Keats held of his poetry preoccupied him increasingly, and, surveying the poverty and hypocrisy around him, he was obliged to recognise that hopes of real progress in social life were frail at best. 'The world is very young and in a very ignorant state,' he lamented. 'We live in a barbarous age.'

They were now making for Portpatrick through the rich countryside around Kircudbright, which reminded Keats of the best parts of Devon. Brown was again enthusiastic. 'As we nearer approached the town through the valley,' he wrote, 'every thing was in a most luxuriant state; the trees, the corn, the verdure, and even the hedges – nothing could surpass them.' After 'cold, solemn Dumfries', such landscape was a delight and both men began 'to like the natives much better'. As they walked along, Brown talked to everyone willing to converse and, in the intervals, noted the neatness of the people's dress and their cleanliness, despite their smoke-filled cottages. He objected, however, to the women's not wearing shoes, but 'Keats was of an opposite opinion, and expatiated on the beauty of the human foot that had grown without an unnatural restraint, and on the beautiful effect of colour when a young lass's foot was on the green grass.'

They were now well away from the usual tourist haunts. At Creetown their landlady was surprised to have visitors from the south at all. Gaelic was the tongue generally spoken, and Gaelic customs prevailed. Keats and Brown saw the inhabitants of Creetown trooping down to the saltwater river to take advantage of the high tide to wash, the women on one side of a large rock, the men on the other. From Creetown, they pressed on through the sun to Glenluce and Stranraer. This was tiring, and the welcome sound of a post-horn announced the mailcoach making for Portpatrick and the boat for Ireland. They stopped it, climbed aboard and, by the evening, having crossed in the packet, were resting at an inn at Donaghadee at the head of Belfast Lough. From here they had planned on going to see the Giant's Causeway, having been told it was only forty-eight miles distant, a round journey they thought they could manage on foot in a week. In fact, things turned out differently. Living in Ireland was as pricey as the most expensive London hotel, while 'we found these 48 Miles to be Irish ones which reach to 70 English – so having walked to Belfast one day and back to Donoghadee the next we left Ireland with a fair breeze.'

Brief though this diversion was, what Keats saw in Ireland affected him as profoundly as anything experienced during the whole of his trip. The wretchedness and hopelessness of the Irish people appalled him. The humblest Scots cottage was a palace compared to an Irish one. 'On our walk in Ireland,' he wrote, 'we had too much opportunity to see the worse than nakedness, the rags, the dirt and misery of the poor common Irish.' But while the sight of such people carting peat from a 'dreary, black, dank, flat and spongy' bog depressed him, Belfast was far worse.

For the past twenty years, the country people had flooded into the city to find work in the cotton factories, and, as Keats and Brown made their way through the dreadful accommodation in which these souls lived, they heard 'that most disgusting of all noises, worse than the Bag pipe, the laugh of a Monkey, the chatter of Women *solus* the scream of [a] Macaw – I mean the sound of the Shuttle'. Such industrial horrors were compounded by economic depression and reduced wages. A recent strike had done something to improve the latter, but the crowded and insanitary living conditions produced their own terrors. Belfast was in the grip of typhoid. Up to 7000 weavers died in three years, and nearly 300 patients were admitted each month to the fever hospital. Many others drank themselves stupid in the wretched public houses. Fleeing the city, Keats came across a sight that seemed to symbolise the entire moral and social horror crowded about him:

the Duchess of Dunghill – It is no laughing matter tho – Imagine the worst dog kennel you ever saw placed upon two poles from a mouldy fencing. In such a wretched thing sat a squalid old Woman squat like an ape half starved from a scarcity of Buiscuit in its passage from Madagascar to the cape, – with a pipe in her mouth and looking out with a round-eyed skinny lidded inanity – with a sort of horizontal idiotic movement of her head – squab and lean she sat and puff'd out the smoke while two ragged tattered Girls carried her along. What a thing would be a history of her Life and sensations.[10]

The imagination retreated baffled before such depravity. The backwardness of Scotland had troubled Keats, but in Ireland he was reduced to hopelessness. 'What a tremendous difficulty is the improvement of the condition of such people. I cannot conceive how a mind "with child" of Philant[h]ropy could gra[s]p at possibility – with me it is absolute despair.' Even a political solution seemed out of the question. The *Belfast News Letter* for 7 July, the very day Keats was in the city, carried the news that, back in Wordsworth country, the liberal Brougham had been defeated and Lord Lowther's Tory sons were returned to the House of Commons.

Keats and Brown arrived back in Scotland and walked the twenty-seven miles from Portpatrick to Ballantrae via Stranraer. They were passing through landscape of the greatest beauty and caught sight of Ailsa Rock 'seventeen miles distant, rising perpendicularly from the sea nine hundred and forty feet'. They arrived at Ballantrae in the heavy rain and quartered themselves in a dirty little inn. The sight of a wedding prompted an unsuccessful imitation of a Galloway song which Brown wanted to pass off to Dilke as genuine.[11] That night, a storm blew up, depriving both Keats and Brown of sleep. The following day they walked through the rain with the great rock still lowering in the distance and seeming to follow them like some primordial companion. The sight began to disturb Keats, since, by an optical illusion, the rock appeared to float in the misty rain, giving him 'a complete Idea of a deluge'. He was, as he wrote, 'a little alarmed', and that evening, in their hostelry at Girvan, he wrote out a sonnet expressing something of the horror he felt in the timeless and inert presence of this 'craggy ocean pyramid'.[12]

But, as always, Keats turned back to human nature. He and Brown were now approaching Ayr and Burns country. Both the loveliness of the landscape and the prospect of honouring his ideal of a great poet raised Keats's spirits. For the moment, the doubting and divided consciousness that had spoiled his reflections at Burns's tomb were put out of mind. He wrote to Tom conveying his excitement at crossing Tam O'Shanter's bridge over the Doon and of living among the sights that had inspired Burns's work. He was now very close to Burns's cottage itself, and as he wrote to Reynolds, 'one of the pleasantest means of annulling self is approaching such a shrine as the Cottage of Burns – we need not think of his misery – that is all gone – bad luck to it – I shall look upon it hereafter with unmixed pleasure as I do upon my Stratford on Avon day with Bailey.'[13] Great poetry, severed from the contingencies of suffering daily life, would, he hoped, like the landscape of the Lake District, bring him an opportunity of harvesting material for his own work. The disinterested imagination would soar, free from egotism and tragic speculation.

Keats's excitement was intense, his corresponding disappointment a mixture of comedy and deepening bitterness. The low, thatched, whitewashed building turned out to be the worst sort of tourist attraction presided over by a drunken, garrulous Scot whose accent was so thick that Keats could catch only five words in a hundred. 'There was something good in his description of Burns's melancholy the last time he saw him,' but the endless anecdotes and obligatory whisky spoiled any hope of the sublime. 'O the flummery of a birth place! Cant! Cant! Cant! It is enough to give a spirit the guts-ache.' As he confessed, 'the flat dog made me write a flat sonnet,' which Keats himself destroyed, but not before Brown had made a copy.[14] The poem was indeed a 'bad' one, but its record of failing to capture the innocence of Burns's youthful 'budded days' and Keats's own identi-fication with the latter part of the dead, drunk and cruelly suffering poet's life – the failure of ecstasy and the return to pain – repeat one of the main motifs of the journey and of Keats's major poetry itself.

And now the wretchedness of Burns, the misery of that southern temperament caught in the blighting chill of the Presbyterian north, began to haunt Keats. Burns becomes exemplary of his own worst fears. 'His Misery is a dead weight upon the nimbleness of one's quill,' he wrote. 'I tried to forget it – to drink Toddy without any Care – to write a merry Sonnet – it wont do – he talked with Bitches – he drank with Blackguards, he was miserable – We can see horribly clear in the works of such a man his whole life, as if we were God's spies.'

As in 'my occasional rhodomontade in chit-chat', sex here becomes one aspect of a wider state of human degradation and something terribly to be feared. Such a revulsion had been expressed once before, in that chaotic seedbed of Keats's mature concerns, *Endymion*. The enslavement of Glaucus to Circe in the third Book of that work is an appalled vision of destructive female sexuality triumphant. Under the sway of Circe herself, 'this arbitrary queen of sense', men are transformed into grovelling, bestial deformities forced to utter the shrieks, yells and groans of 'torture pilgrimage'. They are mere victims of 'gross, detestable, filthy' flesh.

As Keats had written to Bailey, the love of his brothers had sheltered him from a serious emotional interest in women up until now, regardless of whatever naive flirtations or brief physical experiences he may have had. Now, however, with that protection torn away, with George happily married and Reynolds engaged, Keats was obliged to reconsider his state. Marriage and his sexual prospects had previously seemed 'so blank, that I have not been unwilling to die'. Now changed circumstances were leading him to change his mind. The deadly 'blank' of unresolved sexual tension was eased by the example of others. There were models more happy than that set by his mother, and they were, like the 'Sun, Moon & stars and passages of Shakespeare' evoked in Devon, things that 'are real'. Keats could begin to project an image of his own sexual content by reason of other people's experiences. The thought calmed him. 'One of the first pleasures I look to is your happy Marriage,' he wrote to Reynolds, 'the more, since I have felt the pleasure of loving a sister in Law.' But this was at best a simplification. Circe could not be routed by sentiment.

Such thoughts preoccupied Keats as he and Brown, keeping up their '20 miles a day in general', reached Glasgow, where they felt 'under the most oppressive Stare a body could feel'. It seemed that the whole city had turned out to look at them, and Keats was accosted by a drunk. Stone-built Glasgow was impressive, but other than the cathedral, which the authorities had 'devilled' into a 'High Kirk', Keats's and Brown's real interest lay in pressing on to Loch Lomond. Since Brown was now breaking in a new pair of shoes, they made a fairly leisurely perambulation of the loch's western side, which, despite the steamboats and barouches, was 'extremely beautiful'. Moved by the scene, Keats even declared himself 'worldly enough to wish for a fleet of chivalry Barges with Trumpets and Banners just to die away before me into that blue place among the mountains'.

After the arduous crossing of Glen Croe, and mistaking a site named 'Rest and be thankful' for an inn when it was only a stone seat, Keats and Brown were obliged to walk twenty miles for their breakfast. Bathing in the loch, Keats was attacked by the gadflies that had been annoying him all through the journey. His irony and anger broke out in a doggerel poem, 'All gentle folks who owe a grudge', in which he suggested the flies go and sting not him but 'many a horried bore', among them the Tory winners of the Westmorland election. The humour suggests Keats's energy and resilience at this stage of the trip, and when they reached Inverary, while Brown felt obliged to rest, Keats went off to amuse himself at a barnstorming production of Kotzebue's *The Stranger*, a performance complete with bagpipe accompaniment.

Because of the state of Brown's feet, he and Keats spent the following morning in Inverary, and Keats himself took the opportunity of beginning a letter to Bailey.[15] He knew his friend was coming north and had promised Reynolds that he would try and meet Bailey on the proposed return leg of the journey. For the moment, however, Keats felt he must confide some of the deeper concerns he could not share with the altogether more worldly and lubricious Brown. His letter to Bailey is intimately confessional and shot through with an honest awareness of his own volatile spontaneity: 'I carry all matters to an extreme.' Nonetheless, 'I will say a few words written in a sane and sober Mind, a very scarce thing with me.'

Then he got down to the point. He apologised to Bailey for not visiting the Reynoldses in Little Britain as often as he might and, after making some excuses about the pressure of study and the state of his health, he confessed to feeling that he brought a 'Vexation' into the household. This, he was sure, stemmed from the unresolved conflicts of his sexuality. Suddenly, the long-hidden problems of his emotional life begin to emerge. 'I am certain I have not a right feeling towards Women,' Keats wrote. 'At this moment I am striving to be just to them but I cannot.' He wondered at first if his bitterness stemmed from disillusion and the contrast between the women he actually knew and the extreme idealisation he had nurtured in early adolescence. The *Endymion* world of soft bowers and nests, of sentimental and depersonalised erotic fantasy, rose again in his mind and, with this, its conflicting obverse – the resentment that women existed independently of his own imaginings. 'I do think better of Womankind than to suppose they care whether Mister John Keats five feet high likes them or not,' he wrote, but this was more an assertion than a truth. The twinge of self-pity and the rare glimpse of his resentment about his stature give Keats away. He cared very deeply, and the caring was closely connected with the fear of rejection, a fear made sharper by his own poisonous thoughts: 'I do not like to think insults in a Lady's Company,' but he did think them and he was racked with guilt.

The self-analysis proceeds with extreme honesty, and, as it does so, Keats reveals aspects of himself previously unseen: the quick conflicts of a highly sexed young man who is intensely alive in the presence of women, desiring, and yet, at the same time, borne on currents of fear and suspicion so deep that they emerge as a sudden, stabbing resentment at a carelessness, a silly cliché or the momentary unattractiveness of a familiar face. 'When I am among Women I have evil thoughts, malice spleen – I cannot speak or be silent – I am full of Suspicions and therefore listen to nothing – I am in a hurry to be gone.' In such moods, his sexuality, threatening his defences, made sex itself repulsive, a violation, the 'tooth, tusk, and venom-bag and sting' of Circe's slaves writhing in poisoned tumescence. 'You must be charitable,' he begged, 'and put all this perversity to my being disappointed since Boyhood.'

Keats could only discuss such problems with the closest of his male friends, and his sense of threat in the presence of women had its obverse in the complete ease he felt with his male intimates. 'When among Men I have no evil thoughts, no malice, no spleen – I feel free to speak or be silent – I can listen and from everyone I can learn

– my hands are in my pockets I am free from all suspicion and comfortable.' Keats was approaching a crisis and he regarded it as such. 'I must absolutely get over this,' he wrote, 'but how?' His answer was profoundly perceptive. 'The only way is to find the root of evil, and so cure it "with backward mutters of dissevering Power" – that is a difficult thing; for an obstinate Prejudice can seldom be produced but from a gordian complication of feelings, which must take time to unravel and care to keep unravelled.' He would tear his fingers fretting at this knot and find it would loosen only to become the writhing coils of the snake-woman of *Lamia*.

The walking tour with Brown had been in part taken in an attempt to come to terms with such problems. 'I should not have consented to myself these four Months tramping in the highlands but that I thought it would give me more experience, rub off more Prejudice, use [me] to more hardship, identify finer scenes, load me with grander Mountains and strengthen more my reach in Poetry, than would stopping at home among Books even though I should reach Homer.'[16] But it was not immediately obvious that his reach in poetry had been strengthened. The sonnet written in Burns's cottage was, in his view, a failure. He had not been able adequately to picture what he had described to Reynolds as his 'annulling self' as he approached one of the shrines of poetry. Now, at the end of his letter to Bailey, he added some new lines, 'Cousin-German to the Circumstance'. They were, Brown wrote later, composed with more than usual care, and they are not restricted simply to their ostensible subject. 'Lines Written in the Highlands after a Visit to Burns Country' are an epitome of much of the experience of the journey so far.

The poem begins as a kind of quasi-religious quest, a pilgrimage in search of the origins of history, myth and, above all, poetry. So all-absorbing is the last in its combination of pleasure and pain that the pilgrim, preoccupied with thoughts of the sublime, becomes severed from the world about him, abstracted in self-forgetfulness. And, with self annulled, he is at peace:

At such a time the soul's a child, in childhood is the brain;
Forgotten is the worldly heart – alone, it beats in vain.[17]

Then, very subtly, the poem begins to turn on the ambiguities of its own vocabulary. The innocence of 'child' and 'childhood' becomes merely the inexperience of 'the infant or thoughtless Chamber, in which we remain as long as we do not think'. Falsely abstracted from the complexities of his humanity, the self-annulling pilgrim is seen as a madman. Danger and insanity lurk in his ecstasy, and would threaten him permanently were it not that ecstasy itself (in Keats's consciousness at least) invariably returns to the normalcy of mankind – here the imagined, benevolent world 'of Brother's eyes, of Sister's brow'. At the end of its tether – 'at the cable's length' – the mind is saved from its own extremes. The winds of madness have blown themselves out and, for the moment at least, doubt is stilled as the poet's thoughts ride back to pictures of normal humankind.

Keats wrote the second half of this threatening and highly sophisticated account of sexual and spiritual torment on the island of Mull. He and Brown had walked for twenty miles beside Loch Awe to Ford, 'every ten steps creating a new and beautiful picture'. They had gone on to Kimelford and then trudged fifteen miles in the soaking rain to Oban. They were now deep in the West Highlands, and Keats was once again delighted by the beauty of the landscape around him. Freshwater lochs and saltwater inlets lay between mountains around which eagles glided on still wings. But, if all this lifted the spirits, the region was also foreign and hard. The local people mainly spoke Gaelic. The monotonous diet of eggs and oatcake did not agree with Keats, who fell eagerly on morsels of white bread wherever he could find them. A group of 'Whisky Men' chattering until one in the morning annoyed him, as did the inordinate charge of seven guineas for the crossing to Staffa, which they decided not to make. Keats and Brown were going to press on to Fort William instead when a guide appeared and they decided to cross with him to Kerrera and thence to Mull.

Here the going was very hard. Brown described a walk of 'thirty seven miles of jumping and flinging over great stones along no path at all, up the steep and down the steep, and wading through rivulets up to the knees, and crossing a bog, a mile long, up to the ankles'. Keats wrote to Tom about how they walked with their trousers tucked up and their stockings in their hands until about eight in the evening when they eventually arrived at a shepherd's hut. These wretched hovels, built of birch and turves, had depressed Keats earlier in the journey, but now, utterly exhausted from the first part of his wet and gruelling walk across Mull, hungry, and with little prospect of good food, he stooped through the doorway and into 'a little compartment with the rafters and turf thatch blackened with smoke – the earth floor full of Hills and Dales'. Here he finished his letter to Bailey, promising he would take greater care of his health in future. He may have been aware that he had already caught a cold.

Keats was very tired but, lounging on two chairs, he watched the vigorous Brown writing voluminous accounts of their expedition to Dilke. 'He affronts my indolence and Luxury', Keats declared, 'by pulling out of his knapsack 1st his paper – 2ndy his pens and last his ink – Now I would not care if he would change about a little – I say now, why not Bailey take out his pens first sometimes – But I might as well tell a hen to hold up her head before she drinks instead of afterwards.' The relationship between the two men was never less than cordial, but the slight irritation here perhaps suggests Keats's fatigue. That night he slept in his clothes, which were probably damp, the guide snoring beside him an arm's length away. The following morning, as they walked their six miles before breakfast, the man sang Gaelic songs for them, then, having traversed the island, and with Keats's energy and resistance now depleted, they crossed by boat to Iona.

The forlorn magic of the island affected Keats deeply, and its medieval stone ruins, round arches and windows, abbey chapel and nunnery lodged in his imagination to provide images that, like so many garnered on this expedition, would re-emerge transformed in his poetry. By St Oran's, 'we were shown a spot in the Churchyard where they say 61 kings are buried, 48 Scotch from Fergus 2nd to Macbeth, 8 Irish, 4 Norwegian and 1 french – they lie in rows compact.' They also saw 'many tombs of Highland Chieftains – their effigies in complete armour face upwards – black and moss covered'. They admired the intricate carving on one of the island's two remaining Celtic crosses, Keats noting that the Presbyterians had destroyed 300 others during the turmoil of the Reformation. Walking along the wide cobbles of 'The Street of the Dead', they came finally to the abbey with its exquisite, mournful cloisters. 'Who would expect to find the ruins of a fine Cathedral Church, of Cloisters, Colleges, Monasteries and Nunneries in so remote an Island,' Keats exclaimed.

But, if the works of man were impressive, the works of nature were more so. Securing 'at a bargain' a boat to take them to Staffa, Keats glimpsed the island from a tolerably calm sea and during a brief intermission in the weather. Fingal's Cave in particular stirred him profoundly. 'Suppose now the Giants who rebelled against Jove had taken a whole Mass of black columns and bound them together like bunches of matches and then with immense Axes had made a cavern in the body of these columns – of course the roof and the floor must be composed of the broken ends of the Columns – such is fingal's cave except that the Sea has done the work of excavations and is continually dashing there.'[18]

The epic scale of *Hyperion* is evident in these lines. 'I shall learn poetry here,' Keats had written five weeks before, but time was needed for such experiences to be assimilated. For the moment, all he could manage was the doggerel 'On Visiting Staffa'. Here, just as he had in the Lake District and at Loch Lomond, Keats was aware of the harmful effect of too many tourists and the 'taint' that so threatened the magic of the place that the *genius loci*, Milton's Lycidas, resolves to abandon the site, leaving it:

> free to stupid face,
> To cutters and to fashion boats,
> To cravats and to petticoats.[19]

The place of the heroic imagination in Regency Britain remained problematic, but Keats could not address it seriously now. 'I am sorry I am so indifferent as to write such stuff as this,' he wrote to Tom. The fact was, he was ill. The cold he had caught trudging across Mull had worsened into a sore throat that was now so painful he had to rest for a couple of days back in Oban. The rain, the exertion and the poor food were taking their toll, and, with his resistance lowered, Keats was vulnerable to more serious disease. What he did not know when he signed his latest letter to Tom was that the boy was now dangerously ill and that he himself would soon be summoned back to London to nurse him.

Nor did Keats know that Bailey, who had now arrived in Stirling to preach his maiden sermon, was innocently doing his reputation irreparable damage. While Keats was lying in Oban nursing his sore throat, Bailey was dining with Bishop Glieg. Also at the table was a fellow Oxonian, John Gibson Lockhart. Cold-blooded, small and excessively aware that his education gave him the status of a gentleman, Lockhart eked out his earnings as a young lawyer by supplying William Blackwood with the abusive and scurrilous articles the editor knew would sell his magazine. War against Hunt and Hazlitt had already been declared, and being, like Keats himself, neither Oxbridge men nor members of a recognised profession, both writers could easily be abused as socially anomalous and pretentious, mere publishers' hacks. Keats, as a fellow Cockney, was also in Lockhart's sights, and Bailey seemed an easy figure to play along for his guttersniping purposes. Anything Bailey said might be turned to bad account, and the new priest was no match for the young advocate.

Lockhart began, as was his habit, with abuse. Despite being keenly aware of the decorum expected at his patron's table, Bailey 'could hardly keep my tongue'.[20] This was just what Lockhart wanted, and he listened intently as Bailey tried to defend Keats with becoming charity. 'I said that I supposed he would be attacked in Blackwood's.' Lockhart replied 'not by *me*', which clearly but wrongly insinuated that someone else would abuse him. The letter 'Z' with which the articles against the Cockneys were always signed was sufficiently opaque to hide their authorship. Besides, Lockhart continued, the objection to Keats's work harboured by *Blackwood's* was hardly serious and 'chiefly respected the *rhyme*'. Bailey may or may not have believed this, but he had a sure instinct for where the real danger lay: in Keats's association with the liberal Hunt and in *Endymion*'s eroticism, Keats's espousal of what Bailey himself later termed 'that abominable principle of Shelley's – that *Sensual Love* is the principle of *things*'. Bailey wanted to protect Keats from what he saw as his follies and perhaps he also wanted to avoid giving the bishop the impression that he had undesirable friends.

To achieve this, Bailey painted a picture of Keats as a decent lower-middle-class schoolboy who had been apprenticed to a lowly if worthy trade and as a man who was altogether more interested in poetry than politics. Slowly, ingenuously, lethally, point by point, as his earnestness struggled with his pomposity, Bailey was giving Lockhart just what he needed. Lockhart's silent relish of copy so easily obtained can be guessed at. Perhaps it even betrayed itself, for suddenly, and with a ghastly premonition, Bailey seems to have realised what he had done. In the savage, class-ridden world of Regency England, he had portrayed Keats as one of those pretenders to aristocratic culture whose trespassing on the Elysian fields of the old regime would have to be punished. Surely, Bailey urged, a gentleman such as Lockhart would not betray a confidence, and 'I distinctly remember saying something to this effect "Now do not avail yourself of my information, which I give you in this friendly manner, to attack him in your next number of Blackwood."' Lockhart replied sardonically, '*that he certainly should not do so*'.

Laying up in Oban, Keats felt his sore throat turning ulcerous as he fell victim to tonsillitis, but he would not let this hold him back from the next stage of the tour. By 1 August, he and Brown had reached Fort William, and before them reared Ben Nevis, which was to be climbed.

Despite his sore throat, Keats had already walked the fifty-two and a half miles from Oban to Fort William, passing through forested areas, along the side of Loch Linnhe, and taking the ferry at Ballachulish. The weather had been getting poorer and, when they rose at five in the morning to begin their ascent, accompanied by a guide in a cap and tartan with his dog, they were dressed in their warmest clothes. They had a great plaid apiece. Brown wore a tartan coat and trousers (a sight, Keats said, to make his own shadow split with laughter) while Keats himself sported a warm fur hat.

The ascent and, even more, the descent of Ben Nevis was the most extreme and, in the circumstances, the most foolhardy of all Keats's adventures on the walking tour. When it was over, he wrote to Tom that he was 'heartily glad' it was done and vowed he would never ascend another British mountain again.[21] He was by then thoroughly exhausted, but the letter also recalls the energy Keats put into the climb and the freshness and variety of his observation.

'After much fag and tug and a rest and a glass of whiskey', he and Brown got to the top of the first rise, saw the peaks towering above them, and walked for a mile through a valley before beginning the next ascent. This was among shale and was far more trying than the earlier climb. In keeping with the comic realism that so adds to the truth of his letter, Keats described 'getting on among the loose stones large and small sometimes on two sometimes on three, sometimes on four legs – sometimes two and a stick, sometimes three and a stick, then four again, then two, then a jump, so that we kept on ringing changes on foot, hand, stick, jump, boggle, stumble, foot, hand, foot, (very gingerly) stick again, and then again a game at all fours'.

The going was like this for three miles. Then, as they were gaining the summit, a thick and potentially treacherous mist descended. Such mists can be very frightening to the inexperienced, but, as they cleared away, they were replaced by 'large dome curtains which kept sailing about, opening and shutting at intervals here and there and everywhere'. As a result of these, Keats's climb up Ben Nevis was not rewarded with a breathtaking panorama but with 'something perhaps finer – these cloud-veils opening with a dissolving motion and showing us the mountain region beneath as though through a loophole'.

But if there was beauty on the mountain there were also awe, fear and discomfort. There was no vegetation on the summit, not even moss on the cairn which Keats climbed up 'to be a little higher than old Ben himself'. The 1500-foot chasms, appearing like rents in the very substance of the mountain, were 'the most tremendous places'. Keats and Brown threw stones in them and shouted their names to hear their echo. But, while Brown himself was unwilling to go too close to the edge, Keats, standing in the cold wind and drinking a glass of whisky, was moved by the chasms and the mist to write a sonnet:

Read me a lesson, Muse, and speak it loud
    Upon the top of Nevis, blind in mist!
I look into the chasms, and a shroud
    Vaporous doth hide them; just so much I wist
Mankind do know of Hell. I look o'erhead,
    And there is sullen mist; even so much
Mankind can tell of Heaven. Mist is spread
    Before the earth, beneath me – even such,
Even so vague is man's sight of himself.
    Here are the craggy stones beneath my feet –
Thus much I know, that, a poor witless elf,
    I tread on them, that all my eye doth meet
Is mist and crag, not only on this height,·
    But in the world of thought and mental might.

The early expectations of the journey have here been completely reversed. There are no benevolent lessons to be learned from the sublime at all. There is no radiant contact with transporting and ennobling states of existence, no sense of unity with the universe. The mists that swirl above Keats are the clouds that darken the Chamber of Maiden Thought, and they do not allow him the assurance of a transcendental reality holding the world together. He had vowed, weeks before, that he would clamber through the clouds and exist. He had seen sights so beautiful that time, space and misery could temporarily be forgotten. But so much of the excursion with Brown had revealed to him the measure of his perplexity and doubt. He had brought with him Dante's account of the afterlife, but the reality of heaven and hell as these were now tested upon his pulses was as doubtful as the earth he could not see and the worlds of the intellect he could not penetrate. There was no revelation, no loss of self. Nor was there any bowing to conventions that were not true. All Keats found at the top of his mountain was confusion, disappointment and comedy. As he wrote to Tom, 'There is not a more fickle thing than the top of a Mountain.' To worshippers of the sublime, this was heresy.

And now Keats had to descend. This was altogether more arduous and frightening than climbing to the top. ''Twas the most vile descent – shook me all to pieces,' Keats wrote. Although he managed to compose a rather poor piece of comic bawdy on mountaineering, the fact was his health was now seriously impaired.[22] He had begun his letter to Tom saying that he felt better, but he ended professing that 'my sore throat is not quite well and I intend stopping here a few days,' resting in the dirty inn at Letterfinlay before setting off for Inverness.

When they reached the town, Brown insisted Keats see a doctor. The state of his friend's health was worrying him greatly, and the doctor confirmed his fears and persuaded Keats that an early and swift return to London by sea was essential. As Brown wrote, 'he is not well enough to go on; a violent cold and an ulcerated throat make it a matter of prudence he should go to London in the Packet; he has been unwell for some time, and the Physician is of the opinion he will not recover if he journeys on foot, thro' all weathers, and under so many privations.'[23]

To catch the boat, Keats and Brown probably followed the route north-east to Fort Augustus and thence along General Wade's road, past the spectacular Falls of Foyers, and so to Inverness. By this time it seemed expedient to take a coach through Beauly and Dingwall and thence to the port at Cromarty. Brown wrote a letter to Dilke from Inverness, informing him of the position. Then, telling his friend about how Keats's cold had been caught on Mull, he commented on his 'thin and fevered' state. This was all a cruel disappointment, for 'we have been as happy as possible together'. Unknown to Brown himself, however, the news of Keats's return was welcome to the Dilkes for Tom's health had now declined so seriously that his doctor thought Keats himself ought to be summoned to his bedside. Dilke had already reluctantly written a letter, but he and his wife feared how Keats might take such news isolated from his brother in distant Scotland. Now he was coming home.

Keats sailed from Cromarty on 8 August aboard the *George*, having first paid a brief visit with Brown to Beauly Abbey, where he managed to join his friend in a bout of doggerel rhyming.[24] The voyage took nine days. Although the passage was rough, Keats was not sea-sick and he even managed to rebuild something of his strength on the beef so welcomely provided after his recent diet of oatcake. His spirits were gradually raised and he had much to reflect on. As he wrote to George's mother-in-law, during his trip he had walked about 600 miles. 'I have got wet through day after day – eaten oat-cake, & drank Whisky, walked up to my knees in Bog, got a sore throat, gone to see Icolmkill & Staffa, met with wholesome food, just here & there as it happened; went up Ben Nevis, & – N.B. came down again.'[25]

On his arrival in the City, finding an upholstered chair to fling himself in, Keats cried out with a Shakespearian pun: 'O bottom, bottom! thou art translated!' Then, arriving in Hampstead, he went straight to the Dilkes. As Maria Dilke commented, 'John Keats arrived here last night, as brown and as shoddy as you can imagine; scarcely any shoes left, his jacket all torn at the back, a fur cap, a great plaid, and his knapsack. I cannot tell what he looked like.'[26] The Dilkes naturally invited him in and then, seeing from his light-hearted mood that he had not received their letter, they found the courage to tell him that Tom was now mortally ill.

A Giant Nerve

horrors, proportioned to a giant nerve

(*Hyperion*)

DURING HIS WALKING expedition Keats had imagined that his mind, stretched to its limit 'at the cable's length', would gently return to the familiar comfort of a brother's eyes and face. He had not envisaged that that face would be so pallid with tuberculosis and the eyes so glittering with disease. Whatever slight remission Tom had undergone at the close of June, or however well he had disguised his symptoms so that Keats himself could go to Scotland unburdened by responsibility, Tom's suffering was now all too evident. 'Tom has not been getting better since I left London,' Keats wrote to their sister, 'and for the last fortnight has been worse than ever.'

There were days of slight improvement, but it is clear that Tom was well advanced in the secondary stages of his disease.[1] His coughing would have been more frequent, his evening chills more severe. Morning sweats were to become abundant, while his wasting skin, when it flushed, would have been noticeably warmer. A hectic fever attacked both the body and the mind at this stage, and was accompanied by a quickened pulse and hurried breathing. Keats's letters show that Tom was exhausted all the time, unable easily to face the exertions of body and mind he had previously been used to. He perhaps felt pains like rheumatism in his sides and shoulders, and he would certainly have been expectorating blood. Softened tubercular matter was now passing into his bronchial tubes, and he would have experienced pains in the upper part of his chest. These areas would have moved with difficulty when he breathed and would soon start to flatten out. Meanwhile, as he coughed and the cavities in the upper lobes in his lungs became ulcerated, so the lower portion gradually became tubercular too, the progress of disease being usually from above downwards.

Keats watched with pity and hopelessness. His own health meanwhile continued to cause him trouble and expose him to the risk of contagion. His sore throat, 'a little Indisposition of my own' as he now described it to Fanny, seemed to disappear only to return. No doubt aware of what medical men believed to be the dangers of this when in the proximity of tuberculosis, Keats began dosing himself with quantities of mercury which, in their turn, caused his gums to ache and induced 'nervousness', a state of tension greater than that he was already enduring.

His own health and his duty towards Tom meant that Keats was virtually a prisoner in Well Walk, 'confined by Sawrey's mandate in the house'. The doctor was obliged to attend on both young men, while Keats himself struggled to keep his relationships alive through his correspondence. He wrote often to Fanny at her school in Walthamstow. He had brought her a few pebbles back from Iona but was afraid they were 'rather shabby'. Answering her schoolgirl letter point by point while suffering from an acute attack of toothache, Keats promised he would try and find time to buy her a flageolet if she wanted one, although he did not really advise her to start learning it. Perhaps Fanny had turned to such ideas because she was unhappy that her guardian was muttering about taking her away from school. 'I will speak to Mr Abbey on what you say concerning the school,' Keats promised.

But Abbey was raising objections to Fanny having contact with her brothers at all. Fear of Tom's illness may have played a part, although there was no general understanding of contagious disease. Concern for respectability was probably a more powerful motive. Neither Tom nor Keats had settled to what Abbey would have regarded as decent employment, and it seemed to him that Keats in particular was surrounded by bohemian acquaintances while merely squandering his inheritance. A young girl needed to be protected from such wastrels. Besides, on the one occasion when he relented, it seems that Fanny met the Dilkes and later, in all innocence, gave what was perhaps a garbled impression of what happened. At all events, the visits stopped. For weeks Keats tried to change this cruel ruling. He went to see Abbey on no less than three occasions, but all he was able to obtain was a promise for one more visit between the beginning of November and the start of Fanny's Christmas holidays.

Keats felt guilty about his sister, and even found it necessary gently to chide Fanny for telling Abbey where else she had been other than

Tom's bedside. 'I do not mean to say you did wrongly in speaking of it, for there should rightly be no objection to such things: but you know with what People we are obliged in the course of Childhood to associate; whose conduct forces us into duplicity and falsehood to them.' The most guileless of men himself, Keats counselled Fanny that he did 'not recommend duplicity but prudence with such people'. His concern was evident, and he keenly wanted to see her for himself, but 'what can I do?' he wrote. He would have liked to have been able to go and visit her in Walthamstow, 'but I am not able to leave Tom for so long a time.' Instead, he tried to write to her with what comfort he could. 'The Title of my last Book is "Endymion",' he told her, adding, 'you shall have one soon.'

But copies were already in the hands of the reviewers and, at the close of August, *Blackwood's* launched its long-awaited attack. If Keats had to some degree been prepared for an onslaught on his debt to Hunt and his liberal convictions, the detailed and very personal nastiness of the reviewer's laboriously jocular scorn was wholly unexpected. Lockhart, perhaps abetted by his fellow hack, the bullying and facetiously scatological John Wilson, had profited from every crumb of gossip Bailey had let fall, and when Bailey had said that Keats had abandoned being an apothecary for poetry, he had given the reviewers their cue. In throwing over medicine for literature, they suggested, Keats had abandoned health for insanity, a humdrum lower-middle-class usefulness for lawless trespass. This, the reviewer claimed, was all too common a mania, 'turning the heads of we know not how many farm-servants and unmarried ladies; our very footmen compose tragedies, and there is scarcely a superannuated governess in the island that does not leave a roll of lyrics behind her in her band-box.'[2] This was little more than a résumé of the abuse hurled in the first article on the Cockneys, but now its purport was concentrated by an abrasive more-in-sorrow-than-anger tone: 'To witness the disease of any human understanding, however feeble, is distressing; but the spectacle of an able mind reduced to a state of insanity is of course ten times more afflicting.' Grotesque sickness metaphors accumulated as Keats was exposed as the apothecary turned madman and the review itself moved on from the 'phrenzy' of the *Poems* to the 'calm, settled, imperturbable drivelling idiocy' of *Endymion*. Perhaps, the reviewers suggested, only the pungency of their own comments could cure Keats now.

As a disciple of Leigh Hunt, that 'most worthless and affected of all the versifiers of our time', Keats was merely a vulgarian who 'has already learned to lisp sedition' while interlarding such corrupt political views with the prurient and immature sexual imaginings of an adolescent boy. 'Johnny's affections are not entirely confined to objects purely ethereal,' Lockhart opined. Such open sexuality again worried the *British Critic*, whose issue for September satisfied itself by commenting: 'we will not disgust our readers by retailing to them the artifice of vicious refinement, by which, under the semblance of "slippery blisses, twinkling eyes, soft completion of faces, and smooth excess of hands," he would palm upon the unsuspicious and the innocent, imaginations better adapted to the stews.'[3] Keats's poetry, in other words, would corrupt its women readers, a possibility whose commercial dangers had already worried Taylor and which would, by the end of the year, develop into serious irritation.

The united Tory attack on Keats's manhood, morals and politics – the assumption that he was merely a smutty boy who did not know his place – is given such a fresh edge as the writers can manage by their own forced horror at the new social class Keats and his friends represented. The social insecurity of the time re-emerges. Metropolitan, literate, but decidedly not of the gentry or the respected professions, Keats and his like are seen as 'uneducated and flimsy striplings', mere 'city sparks' who 'are pleased to look upon yourselves as so many future Shakespeares and Miltons!' Their pretensions to understanding the classics pitifully revealed their lower-middle-class origin, and Endymion himself 'is merely a young Cockney rhymester, dreaming a fantasist's dream at the full of the moon', the creation of a poet who 'knows Homer only from Chapman'. Oxbridge and the greater public schools remain the one true (and truly masculine) access to the world of culture. 'No man, whose mind has ever been imbued with the smallest knowledge or feeling of classical poetry or classical history, could have stooped to profane and vulgarise every association in the manner which has been adopted by this "son of promise".'

A loose, nerveless rhymester and 'only a boy of pretty abilities', Keats's efforts have put him among those feeble outsiders deprived of the wherewithal 'to distinguish between the written language of Englishmen and the spoken jargon of Cockneys'. For such a corrupting figure there is only one suitable course. 'It is a better and a wiser thing to be a starved apothecary than a starved poet; so back to the shop Mr. John, back to "plasters, pills and ointment boxes," &c. But, for Heavens' sake, young Sangrado, be a little more sparing of extenuatives and soporifics in your practice than you have been in your poetry.'

The repeated references to sleep and excrement in the article suggest one source of the writers' values: Pope's *Dunciad* with its analogous attack on the mainly lower-class hacks whose offerings Pope believed so threatened the canons of an elite culture that civilisation itself eventually dies in 'a total oblivion of all Obligations, divine, civil, moral or rational'. In this context, Keats's attack on Augustan propriety and Pope in particular was especially offensive to the guardians of orthodoxy, and while the *Blackwood's* criticism might be dismissed as crudely *ad hominem*, a third critique of *Endymion* to appear that September, John Wilson Croker's unsigned, mauling article in the *Quarterly Review*, was altogether more damaging.

Croker himself was a great admirer of Augustan poetry, and the 'contempt of Pope' nursed by the Hunt circle was deeply offensive to his sense of order and propriety.[4] Croker confessed that after 'efforts almost as superhuman as the story itself appear to be', he had failed to get beyond the first Book of *Endymion*. A tone of supercilious sneering dominates his article, and, while he was clearly a party man seizing every opportunity to reinforce his position, Croker was less blinkered than the *Blackwood's* reviewers. 'It is not', he wrote, 'that the author has not powers of language, rays of fancy, and gleams of genius – he has all these; but he is unhappily a disciple of the new school of what has been sometimes called Cockney poetry; which may be defined to consist of the most incongruous ideas in the most uncouth language.'

Croker then proceeded to illustrate his point in detail. He had already established to his own satisfaction that the narrative of *Endymion* lacked logical and narrative coherence: 'our author, as we have already hinted, has no meaning.' In addition, 'there is hardly a complete couplet enclosing a complete idea in the whole book.' The form of the poem was as meandering as the meaning, while Keats's neologisms and compound epithets were equally disagreeable to Croker's sense of decorum.

> We are told that 'turtles *passion* their voices'; that 'an arbour was *nested*'; and a lady's locks '*gordian* up'; and to supply the place of nouns thus verbalised Mr. Keats, with great fecundity, spawns new ones; such as 'men-slugs and human *serpentary*'; the '*honey-feel* of bliss'; 'wives prepare *needments*' – and so forth.

Croker was too intelligent consistently to miss the point, and some of his objections are telling, but more important than this is the fact that he believed such usages debarred Keats from the elite centre of the nation's true culture. The passion of Croker's political conviction carries the cultural warfare between the new school and the old regime into the very detail of Keats's language, attempting thereby to exclude Keats himself from the canon of serious consideration in the name of a closed hereditary world of end-stopped couplets and prescriptive grammar. The challenge Keats posed is here laid bare in the most precise detail.

Keats himself remained unbowed by the thunder breaking round his head. Tom's health was an altogether more serious concern. Friends rallied to him, but Keats was still a prisoner in Well Walk. Jane Reynolds offered to visit there, but Keats gently advised her that she would be welcome only if the visit could be managed 'without agitating my Brother'. The febrile state of Tom's mind was as distressing as his bodily collapse, and Keats strove to protect him from the slightest cause of excitement. Hour after hour he watched his symptoms with the careful gaze of a brother and a doctor. When he could, he sent his friends good news. 'For the last two days Tom has been more cheerful,' he wrote to Jane Reynolds, 'you shall hear again soon how it will be.'

When such remissions occurred, Keats felt he could go out, and on 14 September he went to a reception at his publishers in Fleet Street. Taylor himself was away, but Hessey was there along with some relatives, business associates and a number of writers, including Hazlitt, who had published his *Lectures on the English Poets* with the firm that summer. Hazlitt had also been attacked in the edition of *Blackwood's* that had savaged Keats. He was so 'excessively vexed' by the personal nature of the abuse heaped on his morals and appearance that, although he did not choose to discuss the matter at the time, he had resolved to sue the magazine. Suffused with the anger of righteous indignation, Hazlitt was a frightening enemy, and Blackwood eventually agreed to settle out of court, a decision which cost him the backing of John Murray.

Hessey noticed that Keats himself seemed to be in good spirits, but as the evening wore on there was an outburst about the state of literature and the future of his own writing. He had resolved that he would write nothing more, Keats said. Perhaps the presence and conversation of Hazlitt spurred him on to develop the idea that there was nothing original to be done. Poetry was finished. Its riches were all exhausted, its beauties used up. But this outburst was the sheet lightning of anger and tension, brilliant rather than destructive. Hessey, who was perhaps used to his authors behaving in this way, was not prone to take Keats too seriously. He had invested money in him, however, and he observed Keats carefully, making a note of his conversation. Keats apparently declared with the level seriousness that was the obverse of his excitement that, instead of writing, he was now going to give himself over to a life of study. He was planning on recovering his Latin and, once again, was promising himself that he would learn Greek. He seemed, Hessey thought, 'altogether more rational than usual', then he added, 'but he is such a man of fits and starts he is not much to be depended on. Still he thinks of nothing but poetry as his being's end and aim, and some time or other he will, I doubt not, do something valuable.'[5] Others were less sanguine. Woodhouse, who was also present, believed Keats was serious about giving up poetry and he left that night for his holidays a troubled man.

Keats would later try to reassure Woodhouse that this outburst had been nothing but a flash in the pan, but it would be too simple to assume that Keats's anger was merely a response to the reviewers. He had already worked out his public stance to these men, writing first about it to Hessey in a letter which shows the increasing inwardness and dedication, the judgement of himself at the tribunal of his own intuition, which was one of the chief strengths won from these weeks of trial. There is a defensiveness about what Keats wrote, but in his very turning in on himself he was discovering the depth of his own resources, the impersonal and untainted springs of a mature art. Compared to this, he could see, in his best moments at least, that the gaucheness of his enemies was no more threatening than the gadflies that had bitten him in Scotland.

Keats was coming to feel assured, in the unforced and marvellous deepening of his art that was taking place, that he was his own surest critic. The comments of others were so much noise, kindly or more irksome according to their own convictions rather than his. 'Praise or blame has but a momentary effect on the man whose love of beauty in the abstract makes him a severe critic on his own Works,' he told Hessey.[6] 'My own domestic criticism has given me pain without comparison beyond what Blackwood or the Quarterly could possibly inflict.' The disillusioning period of proof-reading *Endymion* and subsequent weeks spent reflecting on that time show their burden here. But such moods were merely the obverse of an altogether more radiant certainty: 'When I feel I am right,' Keats declared, 'no external praise can give me such a glow as my own solitary reperception & ratification of what is fine.' The choice of the word 'reperception' is apt, conveying as it does the delighted surprise of finding that what he had written from the depths of his concentration was true to his hopes of his own achievement. The 'slip-shod Endymion', by contrast, could be safely dismissed as a rash but necessary step to this insight. Its worth for Keats lay largely in the fact that it now allowed him to write something altogether more true.

Others were concerned that this process might be impaired. Keats wrote his letter to Hessey partly to thank him for a cutting from the *Morning Chronicle* that contained two letters of warm support for *Endymion*. They reviled 'the merciless tomahawk of the Reviewers' and praised Keats's poems, claiming 'beauties of the highest order may be found in almost every page'.[7] The hapless Bailey also tried to persuade *Blackwood's* to publish a reply to this review, but he was, not surprisingly, turned down, and was again refused by Constables.

But there were others who could more ably defend Keats. As early as 7 June, an anonymous article had appeared in the *Champion* praising *Endymion* for its objectivity and lack of egotism. This, the reviewer warned, was bound to make the work unpopular. 'The secret of the success of modern poets, is their universal presence in their poems,' the writer declared, but Keats did not foist himself on the reader and point out the beauties of his own descriptions.[8] He had, rather, the abstract and dramatic quality seen in Shakespeare's early narrative *Venus and Adonis*, a quality which made *Endymion*, the reviewer believed, 'among the finest specimens of classic poetry in our language'. The author of this piece may possibly have been John Hamilton Reynolds. Certainly, the same argument was developed by Reynolds in an article first published in a Winchester newspaper and then reprinted in abbreviated form in the *Examiner*.

As a Cockney himself, Reynolds poured measured scorn on Croker as the embodiment 'of that unfeeling arrogance, and cold ignorance, which so strangely marked the minds and hearts of Government sycophants and Government writers'.[9] The patent political bias of the *Quarterly* undermined the worth of its contents, Reynolds suggested as he fought a battle which Keats, with his altogether deeper and more creative concerns, did not choose to join. Reynolds' praise, however, while Keats himself had nothing to learn from it, shows how the more intelligent of his contemporaries understood his achievement and the direction of his art. Reynolds freely admitted Keats's weaknesses and immaturities, but he was equally certain Keats had two unique and immense gifts. The first of these was 'the power of putting a spirit of life and novelty in to the Heathen Mythology'. The second was that, in the structure of his verse, and 'the sinewy quality of his thoughts, Mr. Keats greatly resembles old Chapman, the nervous translator of Homer.' The first quality put Keats in the company of Milton, the second was an abiding rebuff from the Cockneys to the

Quarterly. It was they, not the conservatives, who knew the true, creative use of their inheritance.

What Reynolds achieved in this article was the writing of the public manifesto Keats himself never cared to issue. Basing himself on the ideas of Hazlitt that had so influenced them both, Reynolds advanced the idea of Keats as the one great contemporary who, overcoming the egotism that was held so to bedevil modern poetry, would mature towards the classic objectivity and amplitude of Shakespeare and Milton. Keats would become an emperor of great provinces and not one of those little dictators of a petty state who counted the straws swept from his highways. In so doing, Keats would recast the language in the rich and complex mould of the Elizabethans and create a universal poetry out of a preoccupation with timeless myth.

Such admiration was rooted in the sincerest friendship. 'The overwhelming struggle to oppress you only shows the world that so much of endeavour cannot be directed to nothing,' Reynolds wrote. He begged Keats to publish *Isabella*, the 'simplicity and quiet pathos of which' would be 'a full answer to all the ignorant malevolence of cold lying Scotchmen and stupid Englishmen'. As for Reynolds himself, 'I give over all intention and you ought to be alone.' There was no question of a joint volume of tales any more. 'I can never write anything now – my mind is taken the other way: – But I shall set my heart on having you, high, as you ought to be.' Reynolds could recognise genius, and he had the grace to bow before it.

Some time after the party at Hessey's, and possibly the following morning, Keats called on the Reynolds household in Little Britain, perhaps with some reluctance. Bailey had reminded him that he had not visited regularly there for some time, and the truth was that Keats had begun to find the lighthearted chattering of the women of the house irksome. It was this that in part prompted the spleen and hard thoughts about women in general that he had written of to Bailey while in Scotland. Something of this tone can be caught again from Keats's description of an earlier visit when he had listened to the Reynolds girls enthusing about their mother's niece Jane Cox, who was currently staying with them after a row with her grandfather. 'At the time I called,' Keats wrote, 'Mrs. R. was in conference with her upstairs and the young Ladies were warm in her praise down stairs, calling her genteel, interesting and a thousand pretty things to which I gave no heed, not being partial to 9 days wonders. Now however, all is completely changed – they hate her.'[10]

The reason for this was immediately obvious when Jane Cox appeared. She was intensely attractive to men. 'She walks across a room in such a manner that a Man is drawn towards her with a magnetic Power,' Keats wrote. His excitement is clear from his language. As he watched her, he felt she had the fine and subtle allure of a leopardess. 'She is not a Cleopatra, but she is at least a Charmian. She has a rich eastern look; she has fine eyes and fine manners.' Some of Keats's prejudices against women evaporated in the presence of such imperious femininity. Jane Cox's social and sexual confidence put him at his ease and called forth a sense of wondering pleasure, 'a life and animation which I cannot possibly feel with anything inferior'. Such beauty roused Keats's delighted empathy: 'I am at such times too much occupied in admiring to be awkward or on a tremble. I forget myself entirely because I live in her.' Keats recognised that this was not love but an apprehension of sensual pleasure, something alluring and potentially dangerous, but wholly separate from the 'unearthly, spiritual and ethereal' which he valued in his sister-in-law. 'As a Man in the world I love the rich talk of a Charmian; as an eternal Being I love the thought of you,' he wrote in a letter to Georgiana and her husband.[11] 'I should like her to ruin me, as I should like you to save me.' Such a division of women into saints and temptresses again underlines Keats's continuing uncertainties and inexperience with women, the 'gordian complication' of his feelings.

The journal letter to George and Georgiana which Keats was now writing was the first of that great series of letters sent to America in which he discussed many of the issues that concerned him: his poetry, his politics and his relationships especially. Their basis is an intensely imagined affection nursed in solitude. Although Tom's declining health was obviously an important part of this first letter, Keats felt he could not write it in his brother's presence for fear of over-stimulating Tom's feelings. Indeed, the letter is in part an attempt to balance an omnipresent sense of death with life and love. 'Ours are ties which independent of their own Sentiment are sent us by providence to prevent the deleterious effects of one great, solitary grief,' Keats wrote. 'I have Fanny and I have you – three people whose Happiness to me is sacred – and it does not annul that selfish sorrow which I should otherwise fall into, living as I do with poor Tom who looks on me as his only comfort.'

Keats does not dwell in detail on Tom's disease nor on his own almost continuous exposure to its symptoms. Rather, through the strength of his feelings, he creates a radiance at one with the natural world. 'Your content in each other is a d ''ght to me which I cannot express,' he told George and Georgiana. 'The Moon is now shining full and brilliant – she is the same to me in Matter, what you are to me in Spirit.' Keats encircles the young couple in an affection through which they become so vivid in his mind that the letter seems like a passage of conversation. Yet this is not quite so, for, while the letter form allowed Keats to make confessions he could never have spoken, he is also able to meditate on the concerns that his deepening understanding of himself produced. These are offered as part of the letters' wider generosity of spirit and convey a profound sense of vocation which touches at times on a near mystic intensity. It is against such exaltation that Keats contrasts the equally real wretchedness of his existence: Tom 'no better but much worse', the attacks on his work which he nonetheless felt able to dismiss as 'a mere matter of the moment', and the political situation in England.

The state of the nation, the egoists of tyranny obtruding their oppressive identities on his exaltant consciousness, take up the middle part of Keats's letter, placing it firmly in the depressing late months of 1818, which were to lead to an explosion of violence during the middle of the following year. 'As for politics,' Keats declared, half doubting his conviction even as he wrote, 'they are in my opinion only sleeping because they will soon be too wide awake.' The prospect of a talentless government filled him, as it did all liberals, with dismay. For the past two years, the *Examiner* had been prophesying the imminent collapse of affairs at home, and in the months before Keats wrote his letter Hunt turned his attention to the European scene in the aftermath of Waterloo, lamenting its headlong return to reaction. 'Shallow men of the world, hypocrites, real bigots, all began unconsciously showing what they thought of these odd victories, and ostentatiously placing themselves on the side of *power* for its *own* sake, whether earthly or heavenly,' he lamented.[12]

The revival of the Inquisition in Spain roused Hunt's contempt, as did the nonsense of the Holy Alliance, whose purpose was 'to keep "the Gospel of Peace" . . . in good bristling condition with bayonets, and put down any Anti-Christian enthusiasts who should really be for freedom and peace hereafter'. While Keats sympathised with much of this, he also had his independent observations to make. Liberals like Hazlitt and Hunt himself, for example, revered Napoleon as the man who had risen by his own merits on the back of revolution to be a symbol of liberation, but Keats was far from sharing this belief, recognising that Napoleon had done immense harm by teaching 'the divine right Gentlemen' to 'organise their monstrous armies', which he saw, somewhat wildly, as threatening world peace from Russia through to the Far East. Where could he turn for reassurance?

Dilke, a follower of Godwin, believed that the progress of humanity, which seemed to have faltered in Europe, would be continued in America. Cobbett also praised a land where there were no 'long-sworded and whiskered captains, no Judges escorted from town to town by dragoons, no packed juries of obsequious tenants, no hangings and rippings up'.[13] But this was a proposition with which Keats again disagreed. He could respect figures like Franklin and Washington, but he could not admire them. The first he considered 'a philosophical Quaker full of mean and thrifty maxims the other sold the very Charger who had taken him through all his Battles'. The Americans, Keats thought, and he included Birkbeck, the originator of George's Illinois plans in this sweeping condemnation, were incapable of reaching the sublime. There was, he alleged, no inspiring imaginative force to these men, and he begged his brother carefully 'to infuse a little Spirit of another sort into the Settlement', hoping that 'thereby you may do your descendants more good than you may imagine'. Georgiana was now pregnant, and it was Keats's hope that one of their children might become the first American poet. The lullaby he improvised for them gives beautiful expression to this idea:

Child, I see thee! Child, I've found thee
Midst of all the quiet around thee!
Child, I see thee! Child, I spy thee!
And thy mother sweet is nigh thee!
Child, I know thee! Child no more,
But a Poet evermore![14]

But it was English politics that principally concerned and depressed Keats. Despite Castlereagh's assertion that 1818 had been 'the most splendid year ever known in the history of British commerce', the murmuring discontent of thousands of over-worked, over-taxed and underpaid labourers was a genuine threat.[15] Immense wealth was concentrated in the hands of an uncaring few who packed Parliament with their placemen and profited from loans made to keep despots in power abroad. From this derived what Haydon called Keats's 'fierce hatred of rank' and his contempt for a priesthood who were success-fully urging Parliament for grants to build more churches in which to

A portrait of Keats by Charles Brown made on the Isle of Wight in 1819

Above left: William Wordsworth by Richard Carruthers, 1817
Above right: An anonymous portrait of John Taylor, Keats's
enterprising and sympathetic publisher
Below: Georgiana and George Keats in later life, anonymous
silhouettes *c.* 1830

Keats by Joseph Severn, 1821

Above left: Fanny Brawne in a silhouette cut by Augustin Edouart in 1829
Above right: The ring given by Keats to Fanny Brawne and which may have been his mother's
Below: Manuscript of 'Bright Star', the sonnet which most ardently expresses Keat's infatuation with Fanny Brawne

Bright Star, would I were stedfast as thou art—
  Not in lone splendor hung aloft the night
And watching, with eternal lids apart,
  Like nature's patient, sleepless Eremite,
The moving waters at their priestlike task
  Of pure ablution round earth's human shores,
Or gazing on the new soft-fallen masque
  Of snow upon the mountains and the moors.
No — yet still stedfast, still unchangeable,
  Pillow'd upon my fair love's ripening breast,
To feel for ever its soft swell and fall,
  Awake for ever in a sweet unrest,
Still, still to hear her tender-taken breath,
  And so live ever — or else swoon to death.

Left: Front view of Wentworth Place, the house in Hampstead Keats shared with Charles Brown and the Brawne family
Right: Interior of Stansted Park Chapel which helped to inspire the gothic masterpiece *The Eve of Saint Agnes*

Above left: Manuscript of 'Ode to a Nightingale' written by Keats in the garden of Wentworth Place
Above right: Manuscript of a love letter to Fanny Brawne
Below: A contemporary cartoon of the massacre at Peterloo, an event which for Keats and many of his contemporaries personified the oppressive regime under which they lived

Above left: A self portrait by Joseph Severn who devotedly nursed the dying Keats in Rome
Above right: Keats's last lodgings, 26 Piazza di Spagna, Rome
Below: Keats's burial place, the Protestant cemetery in Rome, by Samuel Palmer

'A deadly sweat was on him.' Keats on his death bed by Joseph Severn, 28 January 1821

teach 'the doctrines of that truly excellent religion which exhorts to content and to submission to the higher powers'.[16]

Keats looked about him with despondency: 'There is of a truth nothing manly or sterling in any part of the Government.' All he could see, even among avowed reformers, was the desire to do something for the sake of 'eclat' or 'a principle of taste', or even a mere desire for public status. 'The motives of our wo[r]st Men are interest and of our best Vanity.' Government had lost what Keats believed to be its old simplicity, its integrity and direction of purpose. Greatness was now reckoned to consist not in moral stature but in the accumulation of ribbons, orders and titles. 'We breathe in a sort of Officinal Atmosphere,' he declared, and Milton and the republican heroes of the seventeenth century increasingly became exemplary of an altogether more noble integrity, a form of patriotism and politics Keats could genuinely admire. But 'we have no Milton, no Algernon Sidney.' In the nation's state of moral bankruptcy, 'there are none prepared to suffer in obscurity for their Country.'

The obverse of such political despair was a poetic euphoria never so deeply experienced by Keats before. In his enforced isolation, he could at times imagine himself free from the world he had been so painfully describing. 'My solitude', he wrote, 'is sublime.' It was the solitude of a man who knows that his work is fundamentally visionary and who, because his profound convictions do not seem to spring from a manipulated and negotiated world, appeared, when he was occasionally in society, almost as an innocent:

> Think of my Pleasure in Solitude, in comparison of my commerce with the world – there I am a child – there they do not know me, not even my most intimate acquaintance – I give in to their feelings as though I were refraining from irritating a little child – Some think me middling, others silly, others foolish – every one thinks he sees my weak side against my will, when in truth it is with my will – I am content to be thought all this because I have in my own breast so great a resource.

This inner strength was not fed by incident, often the reverse. 'When I am in a room with People if I am ever free from speculating on creations of my own brain, then not myself goes home to myself: but the identity of every one in the room begins to [*for* so] press upon me that I am in a very little time an[ni]hilated – not only among Men; it would be the same in a Nursery of children.' Such meetings as Keats had with his friends could be dismissed with the sentence that described them. 'I have been over to Dilke's this evening – there with Brown we have been talking of different and indifferent Matters – of Euclid, of metaphysics of the Bible, of Shakespeare, of the horrid System and conseque[nce]s of the fagging at great Schools.'

Nor could Keats see women as a fundamental necessity to him at this time. The beauty of Jane Cox might stimulate, might even keep him awake for a night as a phrase of Mozart's could, but 'I don't try to take the moon home with me in my pocket not [*for* nor] do I fret to leave her behind me.' In such moods, the old dislike of 'the generallity of women' reappeared (they seemed to him 'as children to whom I would rather give a Sugar Plum than my time') and even the most amiable family life was a hindrance to his true vocation, to Keats's increasingly priest-like devotion to disinterestedness, to negative capability and to what his imagination saw as truth. Familiar impulses were, in their ever greater concentration, leading him to a deepened awareness, and these last two weeks of October 1818 were a period of exhilarating inner dedication:

> The roaring of the wind is my wife and the Stars through the window pane are my Children. The mighty abstract Idea I have of Beauty in all things stifles the more the more divided and minute domestic happiness – an amiable wife and sweet Children I contemplate as a part of that Beauty. but I must have a thousand of those beautiful particles to fill up my heart. I feel more and more every day, as my imagination strengthens, that I do not live in this world alone but in a thousand worlds. – No sooner am I alone than shapes of epic greatness are stationed around me, and serve my Spirit the office of which is equivalent to a King's body guard – then 'Tragedy, with scepter'd pall, comes sweeping by.' According to my state of mind I am with Achilles shouting in the Trenches, or with Theocritus in the Vales of Sicily. Or I throw my whole being into Troilus, and repeating those lines, 'I wander, like a lost soul upon the stygian Banks staying for waftage', I melt into the air with a voluptuousness so delicate that I am content to be alone.[17]

Keats expanded on these ideas in a letter to Woodhouse, who had fretted all through his holiday about the implication of Keats's outburst at Hessey's party, eventually writing Keats himself a careful, solicitous letter. 'The wealth of poetry is unexhausted & inexhaustible,' he assured Keats, and the true poet 'need never fear that the treasury he draws on can be exhausted, nor despair of being always able to make an original selection'.[18] Woodhouse promised Keats that he believed him to be a 'bard who "preserves his vessel" in purity, independence & honour – who judges of the beautiful for himself, careless who thinks with him – who pursues his own self-appointed & self-approved course right onward', regardless of reviewers and the like.

This was an intelligent and perceptive letter, but it limped far behind the discoveries of its recipient. Keats's 'clerk-like' reply contains his definition of 'the poetical Character itself', his vision of the mind free from the constraints of personality and absorbing all experience with the heedless spontaneity denied to those 'Men of Power' who force their identity on the world.[19] 'A poet', by contrast, 'is the most unpoetical of any thing in existence; because he has no identity.' As such, his consciousness can absorb everything. 'It enjoys light and shade; it lives in gusto, be it foul or fair, high or low, rich or poor, mean or elevated.' The poetic imagination possesses above all things that Shakespearian negative capability whereby 'it has as much delight in conceiving an Iago as an Imogen.' This quality of sympathetic identification, unfettered by the constraints of a prejudging moral, political or religious outlook, is both radical and free. 'What shocks the virtuous philosopher, delights the camelion Poet. It does no harm from its relish of the dark side of the things any more than from its taste for the bright one; because they both end in speculation.'

Here was an ideal of the poet liberated from the fetters that had previously so concerned Keats. This was an awareness free from the theological specialisation of Milton or the excessive concern with self, the 'egotistical sublime', of Wordsworth. It preserved above all that openness to experience that was so fundamental to Keats and was, he came to believe, a new and revolutionary form of consciousness that would lift mankind above old and corrupting forms of repression into a newer, more Godlike awareness. Here was a means of being in the van of the grand march of intellect, and Keats would dedicate himself to it. 'I am ambitious of doing the world some good,' he told Woodhouse, and he was determined for the present at least to achieve this by devoting himself to poetry. 'The faint conceptions I have of Poems to come brings the blood frequently into my forehead – All I hope is that I may not lose all interest in human affairs.'

There was little possibility of that. The terrible accompaniment to this sky-reaching euphoria was the continuing sickness of Tom. Looking through the window of his Hampstead lodging 'with the yearning Passion I have for the beautiful, connected and made one with the ambition of my intellect', Keats might, in the exaltation of his commitment, imagine himself wedded to the wind and fathering the stars. Turning to Tom, he was obliged to stare into the crushed face of human misery. As he wrote to Dilke, 'I wish I could say Tom was any better. His identity presses on me so all day that I am obliged to go out – and although I intended to have given some time to study alone I am obliged to write, and plunge into abstract images to ease myself of his countenance, his voice and feebleness.'[20]

The new poem was his promised epic *Hyperion*. For his subject, Keats went back to the earliest episodes of Greek mythology to recount how Saturn and the Titans were overthrown by their children, the Olympian gods. According to Woodhouse, Keats intended to treat of the dethronement of each of the Titans but to concentrate particularly on the ousting of Hyperion by Apollo, his own special deity. The work is unfinished, and *Hyperion* is a heroic fragment that begins in silence and ends with a scream.

The silence is the silence of defeat and a humiliated Saturn lying prostrate amid an awesome quiet:

Along the margin-sand large foot-marks went,
No further than to where his feet had strayed,
And slept there since. Upon the sodden ground
His old right hand lay nerveless, listless, dead,
Unsceptered; and his realmless eyes were closed;
While his bowed head seemed listening to the Earth,
His ancient mother, for some comfort yet.[21]

The extraordinary advance from the verse of *Endymion* and *Isabella* is at once apparent from the solemn euphony of the vowel play in the first line. The rapidity of *Endymion* especially has been replaced by something altogether more deliberate, an attention to melodious invention which enhances the meaning. The repeated 'a' sounds, together with the subtle irregularity of the stressed syllables, perfectly conveys the pain of effort sinking to defeat. Such technical concerns had become of the greatest interest to Keats, and Bailey recorded that one of his 'favourite topics of discourse' was his theory whereby 'vowels should be so managed as not to clash with one another so as to mar the melody, – & yet that they should be interchanged, like different notes of music to prevent monotony.'[22] Keats's mature verse is a near faultless exemplification of this technique, which never, as with some of his later followers (Poe, for example, or Tennyson) descends to mere fastidiousness or aesthetic display.

The placing of the caesuras contributes greatly to the effect, particularly in the third line where the stop after the first four syllables exactly conveys the inertia of defeat while making the 'sodden ground' where Saturn is lying seem all the more oppressively physical. But it is the accumulated negatives in the description of the Titan's hand and the wonderful running over of 'Unsceptered' into the next line which so movingly conveys the absolute loss of power. By following these three syllables with his caesura, Keats shows a mastery of the pathetic sublime, which equals Milton's while being distinctly his own. In details such as these, as well as in the broader sweep of the poem, Keats wholly justifies Reynolds' claim to his mastery of myth and a language as rich and sinuous as that of the sixteenth and seventeenth centuries. It was indeed the Cockney who was remaking English poetry, giving it both a new richness and the suppleness by which it was reborn out of the greatest masters of the past.

Nor was this success simply a matter of language. Keats's use of what he himself called Miltonic 'stationing', the ability to present, as a renaissance painter or sculptor might, the exact gesture expressive of his subject's emotional state, is deeply eloquent. The years of exposure to the classic traditions of the visual arts, the prints seen at Hunt's, the models posed in Haydon's studio, all went to form this. So too did repeated exposure to the Elgin Marbles, for *Hyperion* is imbued with Keats's enthusiasm for Hellenic art. He had promised Haydon that after *Endymion* he would create something in 'a more naked and grecian Manner'. His fallen Saturn is one of many figures in the poem which shows how he succeeded.

The first two Books of *Hyperion* present the debate of the Titans wretchedly fallen to the earth, intensely present in their suffering, but utterly in confusion about the source of the unknown power that has defeated them. They thereby precipitate the drama of how and why one hierarchy gives way to another. What Keats is offering here is neither merely pleasing myth nor a purely decorative exercise in the heroic sublime. *Hyperion* is an attempt to probe the sources of social and political change by examining an idea of the natural evolution of consciousness whereby the higher and more refined states represented by Apollo and the Olympians naturally replace the less sophisticated dominion of Saturn and the Titans. The poem is, in other words, an attempt to present a fundamentally progressive account of life to a Regency society which Keats, in common with other liberals, believed was doing all it could to reverse direction and return to the closed despotism of church and state propounded by the autocrats of the *ancien régime*. Byron and Shelley would turn to Prometheus for their image of an essentially secular revolt against an oppressive and outworn political theology. Keats turned to refashion his own most deeply considered deity in order to present Apollo, the god of poetry and healing, as his answer to the new consciousness required to throw sunlight on the dark 'Officinal Atmosphere' of his time.

But if *Hyperion* is a fundamentally hopeful work, the greater part of what was written is riddled with anxiety and pity for the hapless Titans caught and defeated in the mighty process of historical change. Saturn's anguished questions echo through the work:

> Who had power
> To make me desolate? whence came the strength?
> How was it nurtured to such bursting forth,
> While Fate seemed strangled in my nervous grasp?
> But it is so; and I am smothered up,
> And buried from all godlike exercise
> Of influence benign on planets pale,
> Of admonitions to the winds and seas,
> Of peaceful sway above man's harvesting,
> And all those acts which Deity supreme
> Doth ease its heart of love in. – I am gone
> Away from my own bosom; I have left
> My strong identity, my real self,
> Somewhere between the throne and where I sit
> Here on this spot of earth.[23]

Fallen from the serene and benevolent exercise of power (there is no sin, no guilt, no moral explanation of the tragedy), Saturn becomes like one of the 'Men of Power' whose existence Keats had lamented in his letter to Bailey. Fallen from untroubled benevolence into impotence, Saturn can only crave for the forces of the ego. In defiance of his fate, he apostrophises the very things that ensure his fall and which will be wholly superseded by the new generation of gods: identity, selfhood, egotism, delight in power for its own sake.

Such outmoded states of consciousness are shown at their most violent when Saturn, accompanied by the magnificent figure of Thea, approaches the desolate circle of the fallen Titans. Enceladus' 'ponderous syllables' try to stir the Titans to revenge, to the sort of destructive but impotent vengeance that is the only direct political action this spokesman of the old regime can manage. The fear and bewilderment of an outworn hierarchy is seen here at its most crudely aggressive. There are, however, responses altogether more sophisticated, and the speech of Oceanus in the second Book conveys both an explanation and a stoic acceptance of the Titans' position. Having stared into the 'atom universe', the primordial and material world of things, Oceanus the philosopher, scientist and sage glimpses a world destined to metamorphose into ever higher and more beautiful states of being. Just as in the beginning the light of the sun fathered heaven and earth, so the earth itself from which the Titans arose will go on to produce ever more lovely and sophisticated children who, like Apollo, will aspire to ever more subtle and beautiful forms of godhead. It is a fundamental law of nature that species replaces species as more nearly perfect generations aspire to increasingly complex forms of divinity:

> Say, doth the dull soil
> Quarrel with the proud forests it hath fed,
> And feedeth still, more comely than itself?
> Can it deny the chiefdom of green groves?
> Or shall the tree be envious of the dove
> Because it cooeth, and hath snowy wings
> To wander wherewithal and find its joys?
> We are such forest-trees, and our fair boughs
> Have bred forth, not pale solitary doves,
> But eagles golden-feathered, who do tower
> Above us in their beauty, and must reign
> In right thereof. For 'tis the eternal law
> That first in beauty should be first in might.[24]

This is not merely a pretty piece of paganism. It was a profound and subtle challenge to the aristocratic and Christian hierarchy of contemporary England, that 'mammoth-brood' of increasingly outdated oppressors who would, Keats seems to imply, be supplanted by new and youthful Olympian visionaries. And it was the task of the servants of Apollo, suffering for their country, to emerge like Milton and smite with 'noble and collected indignation against Kings'. As Keats noted in his copy of *Paradise Lost*, Milton's epic was 'a mighty mental blow' against 'that feeble animal' a Stuart monarch and 'the exertion must have had or is yet to have some sequences.'[25] So too, perhaps, with *Hyperion*.

But Keats's poem, subtle and anxiety-ridden as it is, is radically liberal without being crudely propagandist, and the true dramatic focus of the first two Books lies in the figure who gives the work its name, the yet unfallen Titan, Hyperion. Here, in the agonised uncertainty of a god caught between the wholly fallen state of Saturn and the soon to be triumphant Apollo, Keats provides a profoundly original image of the paranoia of a dying breed, a dying class. The Titan's troubled mind, merging with the unprecedented horrors of historical change, projects its own fears on to the troubled world about it. Heaven becomes a place of menace, 'horrors proportioned to a giant nerve' shake the god and, in this state, his passionate outbursts reach the sublime.

> O dreams of day and night!
> O monstrous forms! O effigies of pain!
> O spectres busy in a cold, cold gloom!
> O lank-eared Phantoms of black-weeded pools!
> Why do I know ye?[26]

Urged by the thin and whispering voice of Coelus to reverse the disintegration of his divinity and place himself in the van of circumstance, Hyperion dives from heaven to his kin huddled in agony like the giant druid circle Keats had seen outside Keswick, there to urge heroic if futile struggle. The conflict of hope and despair, energy and lassitude, anxiety and resolve, is prepared for on a massive scale, and its pattern is tragic. Keats noted in his *Paradise Lost* that his exemplar Milton 'is godlike in the sublime pathetic'. The greatest of his contemporaries believed Keats equalled his stature. Shelley extolled the 'colossal grandeur' of *Hyperion*, while Byron, who had been so disparaging about the Cockney pretensions of Keats's earlier work, saw fit to compare this poem to Aeschylus.[27] But Keats himself was best aware of what he had achieved. 'I think', he wrote to George and Georgiana, 'I shall be among the English poets after my death.'

Keats's friends were concerned by the evident distress the care of Tom was placing him under, and someone, perhaps William Haslam, an acquaintance from the Mathew days who was loyally devoted to Tom, arranged for some relief nursing to be obtained. Keats was now able to leave Well Walk more often. He visited Abbey to plead with his ex-guardian for Fanny to be allowed to see her brother, dined with George's mother-in-law, and visited Hessey, in whose office he met Hazlitt, who was negotiating the advance for his next book. He also called on Hunt, a visit made difficult by the presence there of Ollier, his erstwhile publisher. On another visit into town, Keats met up by chance with Isabella Jones.

She was clearly pleased to see him again, and the couple walked through the variously shabby and respectable streets to Islington, where Isabella called on a friend. That visit paid, she then strolled back with Keats and invited him into her lodgings in Queens Square. Such unconventional freedom from a woman intrigued him, and his 'guessing' was keenly at work as she led him into her apartment, 'a very tasty sort of place', furnished with books, pictures, a piano, the obligatory Aeolian harp, and a tray of expensive drinks. Such fashionable trappings of romantic taste perhaps suggested details for the concluding passage of Keats's unfinished satire on such things, 'The Castle Builder'. This was clearly a place where Mrs Jones was used to entertaining her men friends, and Keats thought it would be 'living backwards' not to try to kiss her again now. Very gently she rebuffed him, disappointing him 'in a way which made me feel more pleasure than a simple kiss could do'. She went on to tell him how she had been to a party which George and Reynolds had also attended and then, with that delight in intrigue which was clearly spontaneous with her, she suggested they 'should be acquainted without any of our common acquaintance knowing it'. Keats was willing enough to play along. 'I have no libidinous thought about her,' he told George and Georgiana, but 'I expect to pass some pleasant hours with her now and then.' He then signed off his first journal letter on 31 October, the day of his twenty-third birthday.

But such excursions were only a light relief from his writing and his ever more harrowing duties towards Tom. By November, the boy was in the last stages of his disease. Watching the slow processes of death exhausted Keats. He told Severn 'that not only was his brother dying, but that with the ebbing tide of his life was going more and more of his own vitality'. Keats could only watch appalled and helpless as Tom sweated into the deathlike chills that afflicted him night and morning. Harassed by almost constant coughing and expectoration, with pains in his flattened chest and terribly rounded shoulders, his body wasted with his strength of mind.[28] Tom was probably too weak even to clean himself after terrible, sinking attacks of diarrhoea. The aphthous state of his mouth was the certain forerunner of his approaching dissolution, his moods became ever more hysterical, and it was probably during one of these attacks that he told Keats he was dying from frustrated love of the mysterious Amena Bellefilia. Keats later found out (although Tom himself probably never knew) that this woman was no more than a hoax invented by Wells. Keats himself, in the haunted depths of his fury, never forgave him.

'The last days of poor Tom were of the most distressing nature,' he wrote to George, 'but his last moments were not so painful and his very last was without a pang.'[29] Tom died on 1 December, barely nineteen years old, and his funeral took place a week later at the family vault in St Stephen's, Colman Street. Keats's friends immediately came to his support. For the ten days after Tom's death they ensured he was constantly distracted. 'I have been everywhere,' he wrote. He was taken to see Kean in a new play, to a bare-knuckle boxing match on the South Downs. He called on the Reynoldses and the Dilkes. He saw Haydon and Hazlitt. Only once, it seems, did his grief fall into morbidity. While he was with the Dilkes a white rabbit came into the garden. Dilke shot it, and 'Keats declared that the poor thing was his brother Tom's spirit.'[30] But in the depths of his mind he was firm. 'I will not enter into any parsonic comments on death,' he wrote to George and Georgiana, 'yet the commonest observations of the commonest people on death are as true as their proverbs. I have scarce any doubt of immortality of some nature of [*for* or] other – neither had Tom.' Such a belief was to become the foundation of the mature philosophy Keats was soon to build for himself and on which he was to base some of his greatest work.

But it was Brown above all who looked after him, his vigour and his sometimes caustic tongue for the most part fending off any temptation on Keats's part to give way to excessive grief. Something of this tartness even rubbed off on Keats himself for a while. For example, Hunt invited both Keats and Brown to a *musicale* at the Novellos. Brown evidently loathed the occasion, the tinkling of the piano and the yet more irksome tinkling of the puns. He conveyed something of his distaste to Keats, who was sickened by it too. In his second, long· journal letter to George and Georgiana he turned on Hunt, who now embodied for him everything that was petty, false and meretricious. 'In reallity,' he wrote, 'he is vain, egotistical, and disgusting in matters of taste and morals.' In his grief, Keats was tearing up the redundant vestiges of his immediate past, disposing of everything that was false and useless. With the death of Tom, his own youth had died and, with it, the attachments of his youth. Keats's hardness to what remained was the necessary reaction to the dangers of slothful sentimentality. Hunt's latest *Literary Pocket-Book*, which contained two of his own sonnets, appeared to Keats a particularly nauseating little effort, 'full of the most sickening stuff you can imagine'. In a similar vein, the Reynolds girls were 'all as usual', while even the company of Reynolds himself had begun to pall: 'I see very little of him now, as I seldom go to little Britain because the Ennui always seizes me there and John Reynolds is very dull at home.'

His own lodgings at Well Walk were also oppressive, and it was time to leave them. Once more, Brown came to his support. Early in the morning following Tom's death, Keats had gone in the numbed agony of his confusion to call on his friend. As Keats took his hand, Brown knew at once what had happened. He turned and spoke to him. "'Have nothing more to do with those lodgings – and alone too. Had you not better live with me?" Keats, after a moment, said, "I think it would be better.'"[31] By 17 December, when his old landlord staggered round with a clothes basket full of his books, Keats had moved into Wentworth Place. For the moment he was unaware that he had caught tuberculosis during the course of nursing his dying brother.

When Brown returned from Scotland, his tenants had of course vacated his house. Mrs Brawne, her eighteen-year-old daughter Fanny, her son Samuel and her youngest child Margaret were still living in Hampstead, however, having moved to Elm Cottage on Downshire Hill. From time to time they visited the Dilkes, and it was probably on one of these occasions, some time in November when Tom was so desperately ill that Keats could allow himself to go no further afield than Wentworth Place, that he first met Fanny Brawne.

Barely a handful of facts and suggestions survives to show the origin of this most poignant of love affairs. In a life so fully documented as Keats's and so rich in self-revelation, the first stages of his passion for Fanny Brawne are occluded by that secrecy with which Keats himself wished to hide his love from his friends. Not a note from this time survives from either his hand or Fanny's to tell of their awakening feelings, and, when the great series of Keats's love letters begins in the middle of the following year, Fanny emerges in the full blaze of a matured obsession, the incarnation of Beauty and the focus of a torturing desire. Because of this lack of information about her, Fanny herself is obliged to appear less as a fully rounded young woman, a person in her own right, than as the creation of her lover's desire. Fanny becomes someone snatched from day to day reality to emerge as a figure rendered all but insubstantial by the fierce lights and darkening suspicions projected on to her. The record of her reality has been largely subdued to Keats's obsession, and when we see her what we really see is him.

It is clear however that Fanny found Keats attractive from the start, a handsome, intense young man of twenty-three with glowing hair and the manners and independence of a gentleman, despite what the journals had written about his dangerous politics and keen interest in sex. His conversation showed he was intelligent, although Fanny herself did not greatly care for literary talk. There were moments too when his good spirits would suddenly sink as he became anxious and dejected about Tom. On one of these visits to the Dilkes, Keats brought Severn along with him, and Fanny, with the quick instincts of her eighteen years, started to flirt with the young painter in an attempt to rouse his friend.

It seems she in part succeeded. She was attractive in a way a score of girls of her age might be, darting about and teasing with unconscious sexual vitality, being a little rude to her mother sometimes, and very conscious of how her brown hair, cut in the latest fashion, showed off her blue eyes. Keats later told her that during the first week of knowing her he wrote her a love letter but burned it because it seemed to him the next time he saw her that she showed a dislike for him. Perhaps she over-played her hand, but it is more likely that Keats himself, harassed by impending grief, did not have the resilience for the first moves in a flirtation. Certainly, it would be some months before he was ready for love. Meanwhile, he kept noticing her, and by 16 December he felt he could write about her to his brother and sister-in-law. That he still did not know Fanny well is suggested by his getting her age wrong, and it says much about her that Keats thought she was under seventeen when she was actually eighteen and a quarter.

'Shall I give you Miss Brawn?' he wrote. Then he went on:

> She is about my height – with a fine style of countenance of the lengthen'd sort – she wants sentiment in every feature – she manages to make her hair look well – her nostrills are fine – though a little painful – he[r] mouth is bad and good – he[r] Profil is better than her full-face which is indeed not full but pale and thin without showing any bone – Her shape is very graceful and so are her movements – her Arms are good, her hands baddish – her feet tolerable – she is not seventeen – but she is ignorant – monstrous in her behaviour flying out in all directions, calling people such names – that I was forced lately to make use of the term *Minx* – this I think no[t] from any innate vice but from a penchant she has for acting stylishly.[32]

Keats's resentment of the fashionable silliness affected by the Reynolds girls has evaporated in what is clearly an intense sexual curiosity heightened and made more complex by the vivacity of the mannered flirtatiousness he otherwise found irksome. If, as he later confessed, Keats at once wrote himself down as Fanny's slave on meeting her, there was in his initial attraction to her something that ran contrary to his impulse to idealise. In the early stages of their affair at least, Fanny both delighted and exasperated him. Keats did not, Haydon wrote, 'bear the lovely little sweet arts of love with patience', and Fanny soon turned this to her advantage. 'We have a little tiff now and then – and she behaves a little better or I must have sheered off.'

But he did not. The 'Minx' could intrigue him in ways over which he had no control and which were novel to him even in their banality. As far as Fanny's literary interests were concerned, she knew French and a little German, she enjoyed comedy, paid conventional obeisance to Shakespeare, and, like virtually every other teenage girl in England, she adored Byron and Gothic novels. But her real interest was clothes. Her father, who had died of tuberculosis when she was ten, had been a cousin of Beau Brummel's, and Fanny was a skilled dressmaker who would fill scrapbooks with French fashion-plates and sketch gowns and hats in her letters. Writing to Keats's sister a few years later, she told her that any woman of sense could cut a good figure with a little practice. 'Dress, manner and carriage are just what she wants, a person must be a great beauty to look well without them, but they are certainly within the reach of any body of understanding.' Reynolds and Brown, reading the girl from such attitudes as these, might look in barely comprehending resentment as they saw their friend becoming entrammelled. They might even raise between themselves doubts about whether Fanny was worthy of the Keats they admired, but for the moment obsession lay in the future.

In the period immediately after Tom's death, Keats's heart was still with his brother and sister-in-law. Probably writing to George and Georgiana from Wentworth Place, he declared: 'the thought of you both is a passion with me but for the most part a calm one.' Keats's intensely imagined community with the young people was a vital support, and near the start of his second long journal letter Keats suggested they all read a passage of Shakespeare at ten o'clock every Sunday, thereby uniting themselves under the protecting veil of poetry.

Keats also knew he must return to his own writing. This was not just from a sense of duty. Both indolence and the sort of unrelieved socialising his friends had propelled him into inhibited the working passions of his mind. When with other people, good manners obliged him 'to smother my Spirit and look like an Idiot' rather than 'amaze' people with the full power of what he was thinking and feeling. The sublime isolation he had known during his last weeks in Well Walk was now an imperative. Without it, 'I live under an everlasting restraint – never relieved except when I am composing – so I will write away.' He had already composed 'Fancy' and the ode 'Bards of Passion and of Mirth', two 'specimens of a sort of rondeau' which pleased him as being a form freer than the sonnet. They also suggest that he was searching after the supreme formal sophistication he would achieve a few months later in the great odes.

However, in the weeks before Christmas, the pressures of daily life continued to assert themselves. Keats was, naturally enough, exhausted and in lowered spirits. He was also in lowered health. Possibly on visits to his sister in Walthamstow, travelling through the thick winter fog, his sore throat returned and would take some time to clear up. The Dilkes were urging that he go with Brown to stay with Mrs Dilke's parents-in-law at Chichester and then on to Dilke's married sister, Mrs John Snook, at Bedhampton in Hampshire. The idea was that he would be 'very much amused' by such scenes from provincial life, and Maria Dilke wrote recommending Keats as 'a very odd young man, but good-tempered and very clever indeed'.³³ But Keats himself was not enthusiastic. 'I cannot', he wrote to George and Georgiana, 'always be (how do you spell it) trapsing.' He managed to avoid meeting a popular lady novelist who had been much taken with *Endymion*, but the question of how he would pass Christmas still remained. He had invitations from both Mrs Reynolds and Mrs Brawne, and he eventually chose the latter, thereby causing a lasting dislike between the two mothers and their daughters. It seems, however, that the Christmas period marked an important advance in Keats's relationship with Fanny. Withdrawn and apart in the secrecy of their growing passion, Fanny could later confess that that Christmas was the happiest day she had ever then spent. It would be several months, however, before their love finally emerged in its most passionate declaration, and for the moment it remained hidden by winter darkness and secrecy.

Meanwhile, Keats's sore throat would not clear up and remained sufficiently painful to prevent him going down to Chichester. As he waited in London, Haydon began to pester him for money. Trouble with his eyes had prevented the painter from getting on with the *Triumphal Entry*, and, clearly believing not only that Keats had ample funds but that these would be augmented by what he would inherit from Tom, Haydon had no compunction in asking for a loan. Keats tried gently to turn him down. His own innocence in money matters is clear from his behaviour. He did not know that over £1000 and a considerable accumulation of interest still lay unclaimed in Chancery. He did, however, assume that the £700 worth of shares due to him from Tom's portion of their grandmother's inheritance represented actual cash rather than nominal capital and that this was already at his disposal. He tried tactfully explaining to Haydon how he proposed to use this money.

He was planning a withdrawn life of study and contemplation. He knew that he would never earn anything from his poetry and he disdained the idea of writing for money. He had vowed that he would compose great poetry for a fit audience though few. Could not the painter turn elsewhere? 'Believe me Haydon I have that sort of fire in my Heart that would sacrifice every thing I have to your service – I speak without any reserve – I know you would do so for me – I open my heart to you in a few words – I will do this sooner than you shall be distressed: but let me be the last stay – ask the rich lovers of art first.'[34] Haydon took this as being an assurance of the money, and Keats was obliged to write to his publishers on Christmas Eve for a loan of £20. This he gave to Haydon over dinner on 27 December. It was accepted with alacrity and Haydon immediately started negotiating with Keats for a much larger sum which in turn required Keats to make visits to the City to see Abbey. As always, such discussions caused him great stress and were, he confessed, horrors worse than Dante could have devised. With his sore throat still paining him, all Keats wanted to do was stay at home, visit the Dilkes, play with their cats, see the Brawnes and write.

The dinner with Haydon and a meeting with Isabella Jones were to be more productive than Keats could possibly have imagined. At the painter's studio he was shown the sumptuous volume of engravings by Carlo Lasino of the frescoes in the Campo Santo at Pisa. Here were images in complete contradistinction to the classical forms that had filled his imagination while working on *Hyperion*. Medieval costuming and detail replaced Grecian energy. A mysterious, hushed intensity invited his imagination into a Gothic world. In Orcagna's *Triumph of Death*, a party of horsemen with hawks and hounds is suddenly halted by three open coffins as an ancient monk points to the hideously decomposing bodies. Pleasure and pain, joy and mortality, are contrasted to tremendous effect. Here was something 'Grotesque to a curious pitch' and wholly apt to his present mood.

A visit to Isabella Jones deepened this seam of invention. She had a fashionable taste for the Gothic and a genteel knowledge of popular superstitions. Conversation seems to have turned to these, for Isabella told Keats about the notions surrounding the evening of the feast of St Agnes when, if young girls would go supperless to bed, they would receive a vision of their true love. In the lyric 'Hush, hush', Keats played with ideas of a youthful couple seizing their pleasure under the noses of their elders, but this was only a slight intimation of the exceptional narrative forming in his mind. A medieval superstition and an engraving of a medieval masterpiece were combining to help shape a narrative which would allow Keats a temporary respite from his struggles with *Hyperion*, and now, on 18 January, as he at last set off on the coach for Chichester, they would join with the Gothic beauties of that cathedral city and with thoughts of Fanny Brawne to inspire the most sumptuously dramatic of all his poems.

Particles of Light

straining at particles of light in the midst
of a great darkness

(*Keats to George and Georgiana, March 19, 1819*)

THE COACH THAT brought Keats to Chichester, speeding through the frozen landscape of a Sussex winter, stopped in the centre of the city, where Brown was waiting to greet him. Brown was staying with Dilke's parents and thoroughly enjoying himself by amusing the elderly provincial couple with his heavy-handed clowning. Everybody was aware of what Keats himself had undergone during recent months and was determined that as far as possible he should be taken out of himself in their houses and beside their warm winter fires. Brown was engaged in a mock flirtation with Miss Sarah Mullins, who had made him shave off his whiskers. Laughing at the result, they all told him he looked like a woman, and Brown duly appeared at breakfast the following morning dressed in old Mrs Dilke's hood and talking in a high-pitched voice. There were excursions to the cathedral, while a couple of evenings were spent in what Keats described as 'old Dowager card parties'.[1]

These were four or five days spent pleasantly enough, but the burden of Keats's grief for Tom remained along with fatigue from the labour of *Hyperion* and the consequent dissatisfaction with the apparent stifling of his creativity. As Keats had written to Haydon before he left London, he had been composing 'nothing to speak off – being discontented and as it were moulting'. Such depression, Keats assured the painter, was not suicidal (as it had been in his early days at Edmonton), but, by constantly pondering what he had achieved, his limitations were becoming clearer even as the way forward seemed dauntingly laborious. 'On my Soul,' Keats lamented, 'there should be some reward for that continual "agonie ennuiyeuse".' His sister's unhappiness also disturbed Keats, sometimes so much that he was obliged to lay aside whatever he was writing or the book he was studying. Visits to Abbey about Haydon's loan further wore at his nerves, and hints that he might not be entitled to Tom's money until Fanny reached her majority in nearly six years' time raised the fearful prospect of financial hardship. For the moment, Keats managed to persuade himself that this problem was just a ploy invented by the trustees.

Although his throat was no better, Keats and Brown walked the thirteen miles to Bedhampton on 23 January, where Dilke's sister and brother-in-law John Snook lived in the old mill-house. Here, Brown later recalled, Keats and Snook discussed politics and religion, while Keats also joined with Brown in composing a delightfully facetious letter to Maria Dilke. The momentary high-spirited word-play and description suggest the badinage of Wentworth Place – 'I beg leaf to withdraw all my Puns,' Keats concluded, 'they are all wash, an base uns' – along with the anticlericalism of these young and liberal households.[2] An unusual event was now to focus this. Keats and Brown were to attend a great local occasion two days after their arrival at Bedhampton for, as Brown wrote, 'to-morrow we shall go to Sanstead to see Mr. Way's Chapel consecrated by the two Big wigs of Gloucester & St. Davids.'[3]

This event was to move Keats in subtle and contradictory directions. Lewis Way was a wealthy lawyer who had given up his profession for the priesthood on inheriting his fortune, much of which he was now spending on a plan to convert the Jews. During the previous year he had persuaded the Great Powers to add a protocol to their promise of toleration signed at Aix-la-Chapelle. He had also completed the exquisite Regency Gothic chapel at Stanstead, decorating it with triple-arched windows and carvings, and organising its iconography around biblical prophecies of his favourite theme. The consecration took place on 25 January, the Feast of the Conversion of St Paul, and, probably because it was raining, Keats and Brown drove over to the ceremony, accompanied by John Snook's son, in a chaise drawn by 'a leaden horse'.

Keats was equally affected by the beauty seen in the chapel and the finely wainscotted and tapestry-hung house, as well as by the ranks of the established church at one with those grandees who had arrived in considerable numbers in their carriages. Here were the united forces of the old regime displayed at an opulent and, to Keats, an absurdly misconceived event. He found the lengthy service far from amusing. 'I begin to hate Parsons,' he wrote later and started a diatribe against what he saw as their combination of vested interest and social fawning. He hated such a suppression of true feeling and the resentment this caused among believers and unbelievers alike. The stifling of the spirit, along with the subservience to rank, was repellent. Soldiers cheated into daring by the scarlet of a uniform were 'not half so pitiable as the Parson who is led by the nose by the Bench of Bishops – and is smothered in absurdities – a poor necessary subaltern of the Church.'[4] The contrast between the beauty of the escutcheoned stained-glass windows and this congregation of the emasculated and the haughty made a profound impression, and probably by the time Brown left two days later Keats, who was staying on at Bedhampton to nurse his sore throat, was at work on a poem in which these sentiments mingled with his grief and that secret blossoming of his love for Fanny Brawne, first recognised on Christmas Day and so far hidden from his acquaintance. Writing very quickly on thin sheets of paper that Haslam had provided for letters to America, Keats turned from the problems of epic to what he regarded as no more than the minor distractions of romance. In so doing, he achieved his most nearly perfect narrative poem.

The Eve of St. Agnes begins, as it ends, in winter silence and death, in coldness, stillness and the failure of the body and spirit. The natural world barely stirs and in man the imagination is inert. Death hangs about the Gothic mansion where the action is to take place, and the first character to appear is a beadsman, a figure paid to pray for the departed, and himself poised eerily between the living and the spectral. For all this, Keats evokes him with a greater subtlety than the anger in his letter against the priesthood might suggest. The poem recognises the man's patience, his piety and dedication, but the failure of his imagination, the lack of sympathy for the 'sculptured dead' portrayed in the oratories around him, suggests a mind haunted by sin and mortality, severed from humanity and, in the end, unwanted by them. Paid to perform an office no one either cares for or truly believes in, the beadsman's lonely death at the close of the work speaks of organised religion extinguished by the forces that obsess it.

A similar subtlety pervades Keats's portrayal of the rout of aristocrats in the poem. The 'argent revelry' that bursts upon the poem amid the call of 'silver, snarling trumpets' seems, by contrast to the beadsman, marvellously alive and youthful, the very stuff of romance. As the poem proceeds, however, all their 'rich array' appears increasingly as the meretricious gloss over a society riddled with violence, mental illness and anxiety, a picture of a group racked by feuds and obsessed with family honour – 'Hyena foemen, and hot blooded lords'. This undertow of aristocratic violence and brute power was entirely in keeping with views of the Middle Ages presented by such historians as Keats's favourite William Robertson, but archaeological accuracy was not, of course, Keats's principal purpose. His concern was to evoke the allure of such motifs, to insist on the faery quality of romance, while tacitly juxtaposing such escapism to the realities of the society around him. The poem delights in artifice while simultaneously commenting on Regency England.

The plumes and tiaras sweeping through this Gothic mansion suggest the contemporary aristocracy revelling in their own new-built Gothic extravaganzas: Knowsley, for example, or Ashridge with its immense walls covered with pictures of the Allied nobility's triumph in the Revolutionary Wars. The fanatical elitism and stupendous wealth of the old regime are inevitably present here, and the tiaraed women prompt memories of Lady Londonderry so weighed down with diamonds at a ball that a servant had to follow her with a chair, or Lady Shelley entering a room 'with a sort of hoisted-up look in her figure, tight satin shoes, a fine, thick plait of hair, bloodshot eyes, parched lips, fine teeth, and an expression of conscious accomplishment in her face'.[5] Keats's 'dwarfish Hildebrand' and 'old Lord Maurice' personify an ancient and deformed order devoted to blood feuds and arbitrary power, the nightmare world of 'witch, and demon, and large coffin-worm' which, borrowed from the engravings Haydon had shown Keats, plagues them at the close of the work and allies them to the dead beadsman as church and aristocracy, the twin forces of the old regime, move deathwards in their outworn modes of consciousness.

Both forces are, of course, opposed to what Keats offers as the palpitating heart of this romance, the awakening and consummated passion of Porphyro and Madeline, the love that is so radiantly contrasted to the surrounding death from which it is snatched. Keats's handling of the St Agnes Eve superstition perfectly suggests this. In its original form this was a Christian legend which, while it allowed for intimations of sex, nonetheless preserved the value of young women in what is here the aristocratic marriage market. It was little more than an empty and virginal fantasy to be indulged amid the winter chill. In Keats's poem, when Porphyro actually enters Madeline's bedroom, such beliefs are transformed into a fully sexual encounter, glowing, rich and warm, whereby the body is satisfied even as the imagination is nourished by dreams fulfilled and an awe that touches on religious veneration. The progress is thus from fantasy to fulfilment, from constraint to liberty, and from death to life.

It is a progress fraught with peril. While Madeline can ward off the advances of those in the castle by the intensity of her virginal self-absorption, this house of death is a place where Porphyro may very well be slain. Such a bringing together of possible murder with passion is dramatic in the extreme, but it is noteworthy that the ardour of both young lovers matures towards greater fullness and frankness as the poem progresses, and for each it is the St Agnes Eve legend itself that is central to this process. When Porphyro first appears, his ambition seems to reach no further than to 'speak, kneel, touch, kiss', and it is only when Madeline's nurse, the ageing Angela, reflects on the St Agnes Eve superstition, holding the ardent lover in aching expectation, that Porphyro seems fully to realise what his entering the bedroom might mean.

Keats's handling of this situation is highly sophisticated, keeping as it does a fine balance between an ardent innocence and the passage to adult experience. Porphyro's 'stratagem', his convincing the elderly Angela that she help him enter Madeline's bedroom so that he may watch her undress while himself remaining unseen, has much about it that suggests the predatory and the voyeuristic. There is the strong suggestion that Madeline is an object for male fantasy and seduction. This element is frankly accepted, but running parallel with it is Porphyro's intense sensual and imaginative wonder, that longing for union and loss of self in which, finally, both the young people will merge. The complexity of the passage from innocence is thus acknowledged along with its richness.

That this last is something of deep and benevolently transforming power is suggested by the way in which it seems able to turn the castle of death, this place of spectral ecclesiastics and murderous aristocracy, into an image of a new and altogether truer nobility and awe. The beautiful stanza describing the window in Madeline's bedroom, for example, evokes the loveliness of the romance world of saints and kings, and literally suffuses Madeline in its light. The natural world of the moon shining on the glass joins with Porphyro's ardour to create a new life out of the old – a new life where sanctity and nobility are things of the delighted senses and the heart:

A casement high and triple-arched there was,
All garlanded with carven imag'ries
Of fruits, and flowers, and bunches of knot-grass,

> And diamonded with panes of quaint device,
> Innumerable of stains and splendid dyes,
> As are the tiger-moth's deep-damasked wings;
> And in the midst, 'mong thousand heraldries,
> And twilight saints, and dim emblazonings,
> A shielded scutcheon blushed with blood of queens and kings.[6]

The beauty of this, augmented as it is by our sharing in Porphyro's delight in the imagined feel of Madeline's 'warmed jewels' and the sound of her silk dress as it 'creeps rustling to her knees', is a technical achievement of a high order. Despite the fact that Keats was writing at a rate previously matched only in *Endymion*, there is nothing here of the often slipshod voluptuousness of that poem, and the surviving manuscript shows the pains Keats took to achieve this match between formal artistry and narrative and dramatic complexity. The original draft is thick with hatchings out and phrases scribbled in.[7] We can see the rapid change from 'A casement ach'd' to 'triple arch'd' along with the insertion and deletion of Madeline's 'white hands devout'. Difficulties with the details of the carving (including the rejection of some inappropriate 'sunny corn') are also evident. The manuscript allows us to watch Keats's progress towards 'the tiger-moth's deep-damask'd wings', and to observe his brave decision to keep the heraldic 'gules' for a later and less prominent line, while substituting for it the 'shielded scutcheon' that 'blush'd with blood of queens and kings'. All this speaks of a tremendous technical concentration, and one made all the more remarkable by the fact that Keats had barely used the Spenserian stanza employed here since his days as an apprentice in Edmonton.

Keats himself would later speak of such effects rather slightingly as 'coloring' and 'drapery', and it is true that their principal purpose is to serve his slow-built climax of richness and ardour: the undressing of Madeline, her dreaming 'wakeful swoon', Porphyro's love-gift of the banquet, and the performance of the old Provençal ballad whereby Madeline is finally awoken and undergoes the painful yet ultimately satisfying union of her dream of Porphyro with her sight of his actual, palpitating presence. Deep in the recesses of her imagination, her ideal is fused with the reality so vividly present to her.

With a rich and all-embracing delicacy, Keats manages to make this a moment in which dream and actuality are merged. The lovers' separate identities are united in a moment of imaginative penetration which both blesses and makes natural the seemingly effortless way in which their physical penetration is also suggested. And, as he does so, the world of danger in which this consummation and marriage occur impinges on the couple once again. The sleet falling on the glorious casement rouses the lovers with its menacing tattoo. Madeline and Porphyro with their 'fine Mother Radcliff names' emerge into the world of the Gothic novel and then, as they escape the castle of death, are snatched from us for ever. 'And they are gone – aye, ages long ago.'

The lovers' happiness belongs both to fiction and to the past. It is something glimpsed and taken away, something pertaining to the romance world that, for the duration of the poem, has so beguiled us by seeming like reality raised to its highest intensity. What we are left with in the end, however, is the degraded and dying consciousness of the old order: the nightmare-ridden aristocrats, the palsy-stricken Angela, and the unregarded beadsman left 'among his ashes cold'. This is a near perfect dramatic balance created by the juxtaposition of death to a dream of love which, for all its elusive nature, for all that it is snatched from us, seems, on the imaginative level at least, to resolve the 'gordian complication' of Keats's own difficulties with sexuality. He has created a joyous and ideal union of the body and the imagination. But for all its appeal, this was, for Keats himself, a solution that was radically unstable, and by September 1819, a sick and insecure man, he would be seeking in clumsy desperation to spoil the imagined harmony he had here so briefly achieved.

Although his sore throat was still no better, Keats returned to Hampstead during the first week of February, from where he wrote to his sister telling her how he meant to nurse himself until he was well again. But a letter Fanny sent to Bedhampton had caused him distress. Abbey had now not only removed Fanny from her school, thereby obliging her to live with him and his coarse-grained wife, but had placed an embargo on her receiving any letters from her brother. Keats was hurt and angry, especially as he felt himself to be the only real protector Fanny had. He confessed he had supposed all along he could do little in the matter of her schooling save trying to encourage her to keep up her music and her reading, but now he took steps to see that Abbey's embargo on his correspondence was lifted. He apparently succeeded in this, partly by means of a plain-spoken letter, and, having offered to send Fanny an edition of Goldsmith, he wrote again at the end of the month promising to fulfil her request that he correspond with her at least once a fortnight.

In the meantime, having remained indoors for ten days, Keats ventured into the City on 13 February to talk to Abbey not only about Fanny but about money as well. This and the meetings that followed were inevitably stressful occasions with Keats probably angry, volatile and confused, while Abbey was brisk but cautious. Abbey could perhaps justify removing Fanny from school by saying that what was saved on fees could be added to her dowry, but his control over the Keatses' inheritance from their grandmother had now been strengthened by the departure of his fellow trustee for Holland. Keats himself perhaps felt he had to tread carefully if he were quickly to secure his money from Tom's estate as a loan for Haydon, but Abbey quite properly referred him to Walton, the lawyer who had drawn up Mrs Jennings' original deed. It is unlikely that Keats saw Walton himself, who, at home and dying, was the one man who could explain the true terms of the deed he had drawn up for Mrs Jennings as well as informing Keats that there lay in Chancery a wholly unsuspected sum left to him by his grandfather. By the cruellest irony of circumstance, Keats was forced into a position which was both false and unsettling and from which perhaps only the absent George could ever have abstracted him. Meanwhile, Keats had to draw a further £20 from the money George had left on account in order to settle his housekeeping expenses with Brown.

But Brown himself was causing other problems for Keats, although it is not clear quite how conscious he was of doing so. Certainly, he was jealous of his friendship with the poet and was liable to pick quarrels with such male acquaintances as Woodhouse. Brown even confessed to putting bawdy verses of his own among the fair copies of Keats's poems to ward off prying female eyes. Now, however, and most suspiciously of all, he began a mock flirtation with Fanny Brawne. Whatever his motives – jealousy perhaps, or a mean desire to seize what he probably only guessed was his friend's girl – he sent Fanny a lame little valentine poem. This made a sufficient impression for her to get it by heart and, years later, she could still repeat it to her children. The verses were of the type Brown could, if asked, dismiss as merely jovial, but Keats later made it clear that he was hurt, even if he said nothing at the time.

The state of his feelings for Fanny Brawne at this stage was, nonetheless, troubling and ambivalent. The deeper understanding they reached at Christmas had in part opened the vein of intense and joyous eroticism seen in *The Eve of St. Agnes*, although Fanny herself, flying out in all directions, was certainly no Madeline, and Keats's comparison of her to Millament was altogether more apt. She continued to call on the Dilkes next door in Wentworth Place, and on these occasions she and Keats would meet for 'a chat and a tiff'. If this was a wary playing with a depth of emotion each half-recognised and half-shunned, Keats's own feelings were expressed in a way Fanny could not surely wholly appreciate. Keats had some time before his return from Bedhampton given her a copy of Hunt's *Literary Pocket-Book*, in which Hunt himself had written. While Fanny might be convinced that this was a prestigious little love-gift from a literary man, there is something unsettling in Keats giving her a work he found reprehensibly meretricious. Was this a way of equating Fanny with such feelings and so enjoying a sense both of contempt and of power over a woman who roused his desire equally with his fear? Certainly, Keats as yet felt no impulsion to offer her his latest poem. Fanny was merely given a copy of 'Hush, hush' to copy into Hunt's album.

Keats did, however, show *The Eve of St. Agnes* to Isabella Jones. He may have visited her in her 'tasty' apartment when he went to town on 13 February, a day when he also shared a bottle of claret with Woodhouse. This was a drink which, while Keats now drank only three glasses at any time, so raised his spirits that he felt it made him 'a Hermes – and gives a woman the soul and immortality of Ariadne'.[8] Perhaps under the influence of the wine, Keats began to tell Wood-house something of the personal background to his earliest poems, and it was perhaps while 'the more ethereal Part of it' was still mounting to his brain and walking round it 'like Aladdin about his own enchanted palace', that Keats made his call on Isabella. She was so pleased to see him that she offered him a pheasant, which Keats gave to the Dilkes. Later that evening, when he arrived back in Hampstead, he began a poem which was almost certainly suggested by Isabella, the unfinished *Eve of Saint Mark*.

The legend on which the poem was based concerns the belief that those who sat waiting in a church or cathedral porch on 24 April, the eve of the feast of the saint, would, in the third year of their attendance, see the ghosts of all those who were to die the following year. Exactly how Keats was planning to use this superstition cannot be ascertained, but D.G. Rossetti, who was much influenced by the work, guessed that the heroine Bertha, 'remorseful after trifling with a sick and now absent lover – might make her way to the minister-porch to learn his fate by the spell, and perhaps see his figure enter but not return'.[9] However this may be (and the suggestion has the merit of focusing on the nearness of sexuality to death which was so dominant in Keats's mind at this time), the surviving fragment shows the depth and plenitude of Keats's Gothic imagination. This was an inspiration fed not just by what Keats himself called 'the spirit of Town quietude' such as he had glimpsed in Chichester, but by the Regency Gothic of Stanstead and the medieval revivalism of Chatterton's poetry, *Aella, a Tragic Interlude* providing both the name of Keats's heroine and the manner of his imitating Middle English. One of the most powerful influences, however, was medieval manuscript illustration, and the book Bertha is shown so luxuriously enjoying is rich with these:

> The stars of Heaven, and angels' wings,
> Martyrs in a fiery blaze,
> Azure saints 'mid silver rays,
> Aaron's breastplate, and the seven
> Candlesticks John saw in Heaven,
> The wingèd Lion of Saint Mark,
> And the Covenantal Ark,
> With its many mysteries,
> Cherubim and golden mice.[10]

But such delighted sympathy with the medieval world could only be a respite from the greater problem of *Hyperion*. Although the sophisticated simplicity of *The Eve of Saint Mark* was greatly to influence a younger generation of Pre-Raphaelites, Keats himself regarded the poem as a slight achievement – too slight, in fact, to lure him away from his baffled epic. On 17 February, he abandoned the work in mid-line and spent the following days going to nine-year-old Charles Dilke's birthday tea, where he met Fanny Brawne, visiting Isabella Jones and chattering with the kindly Mr Lewis about Cobbett and the prospect for the liberals in the forthcoming Westminster elections.

He also wrote to Haydon about his discussions with Abbey over Tom's inheritance, confident that his erstwhile guardian's comments about having to wait until Fanny reached her majority were 'all a Bam'. Neither Keats nor Haydon mentioned that a slump, panic and bankruptcies had hit the City and that the worth of Tom's shares had fallen sharply. Haydon indeed was rejoicing in the bombast of his own confidence. An exhibition of work from his studio had recently enjoyed some success, and 'by Heaven', he wrote, 'I'll plunge into the bottom of the sea, where plummets have now never sounded, & never will be able to sound, with such an impetus that the Antipodes shall see my head drive through on their side of the Earth to their dismay & terror.'[11]

The Eve of Saint Mark had been abandoned, *Hyperion* could not be proceeded with. Keats was sunk in poetic silence and, with it, bitterness. He was tired and still suffering from his sore throat, and in this state of lowered resistance he withdrew into himself. 'I see very little now and very few Persons – being almost tired of Men and things,' he wrote in his third long journal letter to George and Georgiana. He was greatly worried that he had not heard from them. He was daily expecting a letter and was sure his own had got lost in transit. His feeling of being deprived of their affection added to his disillusion, and trifling things upset him. When he heard that old Mr Lewis, going into town with Mrs Brawne, had called him 'quite the little Poet', he had found the comment 'abominable' and, jealous of the immense success Byron was currently enjoying, burst out: 'You see what it is to be under six foot and not a lord.' His diatribe against parsons followed closely on this, along with fears about the economic state of the nation – 'I begin to think of a national Bankruptcy' – and concern that Richard Carlisle, another free-thinking publisher, had been arrested for issuing the deist writings of Tom Paine and others.

While the public world remained as depressing as ever, the behaviour of Keats's friends variously wore him down, saddened and disgusted him. Brown was labouring away at a ponderous tale about an old woman and the devil, while the methodical Dilke, having fretted about how he would educate his son, had at last decided to send him as a day boy to Westminster and was now planning to move from Wentworth Place and closer to his son's school. Haydon hovered irksomely in the background, pestering Keats for money. The conduct of Bailey, meanwhile, had greatly shaken him.

The widely read, enlightened scholar of the Oxford days now appeared as little more than a lubricious man in search of a good marriage. Having pursued a number of women and been turned down by Marianne Reynolds, Bailey was now engaged to Hamilton Glieg, daughter of his patron. The bishop had given his blessing to this arrangement after Bailey had retrieved his love letters from Marianne and shown them to his future father-in-law to prove that the relationship had been blameless. While Keats regarded Marianne as having behaved honourably in the matter (she had lost not just a potential husband but the £3000 that would come as Bailey's marriage settlement), he could not help pointing out rather spitefully that such apparent deception served the Reynolds family right. They had been so obsessed with Bailey's supposed merits that they had been blind to his faults.

It was for Bailey himself, however, that Keats reserved his true contempt. He wondered how an intelligent man could behave in such a callous manner. Was it lack of delicacy, principle or knowledge of polite society? Then Keats hit upon what he thought was the true explanation. Although Bailey had gone courting in Little Britain with the Bible under his arm, he was a man weakly indulgent to his own craving for sex. There was no excuse for snapping up Miss Gleig quite so quickly 'except that of a Ploughmans who wants a wife'. This harsh and rather snobbish comment probably sprang from more than just a fit of moral pique. Rice, whose opinion on such matters Keats respected, had decided to cut Bailey, but it is likely that Keats himself had heard rumours of the damage Bailey had foolishly done him at Bishop Gleig's dinner table. Keats's diatribe against the clergy and his belief that a parson 'must be either a Knave or an Ideot' may have had a personal as well as a general application. Certainly, the bitterness he felt against the reviewers now rose to the surface along with his 'despair' at the failure of *Endymion*.

Indeed, what Keats saw as the malevolent power of the magazines began to preoccupy him. He had once hoped that their obvious bias was so evident that people would cease to take notice of them. He now realised that not only did the general public enjoy the quarrels raised while being indifferent to the rights and wrongs of the issue, the magazines also had a more vicious influence. As they became increasingly powerful, they stopped people thinking for themselves and, with criticism thus suspended, they grew ever more powerful in the vacuum that resulted. Keats thought that *Blackwood's* and the *Quarterly* acted in a way comparable to the worst abuses of power and religion. 'They are like a superstition which the more it prostrates the Crowd and the longer it continues the more powerful it becomes.'[12]

Such an undermining of the real values of literacy disturbed Keats greatly and was an issue where once again he shared Hazlitt's strongly voiced opinions. Copying out a long extract from Hazlitt's 'A Letter to William Gifford Esq', Keats offered George and Georgiana an image of the country's intellectual life being progressively emasculated by the insidious grip the Tory party had over the media. Gifford himself symbolised this. 'You are the government critic,' Hazlitt wrote, 'a character nicely differing from that of a government spy – the invisible link, that connects literature with the Police.'[13] The nature of repression in Regency England is chillingly rammed home and, with it, the moral corruption that inevitably ensued. Gifford was led by 'mercenary malice' into betraying his principles. His political hack work fequired him to 'sacrifice what little honesty and prostitute what little intellect you possess to any dirty job that you are commission'd to execute'. Here was an indignation Keats felt but could not himself match for style. Personally wounded by the reviewers and aware of the more general damage they inflicted, Hazlitt's murderously sardonic tone was a great relief of spirits. 'The manner in which this is managed,' Keats wrote, 'the force and innate power with which it yeasts and works up itself – the feeling for the costume of society; is in a style of genius.'

He promised to copy out more the next day. It was getting late. The candles, he wrote, were burned down and he was writing by the poor light of a wax taper. The fire had almost died. 'I am sitting with my back to it with one foot rather askew on the rug and the other with the heel a little elevated from the carpet.' He was using an edition of *The Maid's Tragedy* as a desk (he had earlier written out 'Bards of Passion and of Mirth' inside it and had been reading the play itself since teatime) while a couple of volumes of Chaucer and a new, insignificant poem by Tom Moore lay on a table beside him. Somewhere in the room was the engraving of Shakespeare given to him in the Isle of Wight and now decorated with tassels made by Georgiana. The scene creates a touching self-portrait. The isolation and the silence are conjured up without self-pity, as are the feelings of life endured and, above all, of the quiet, industrious maintenance of civilisation in a hostile time. But for all this Keats was not inwardly confident. The hurt and the wasted effort of *Endymion* preyed on his mind. At various times he wondered if he would go to Edinburgh and renew his medical studies there. He was afraid he would not like it, yet he still occasionally felt he wanted to go. After all, 'it's not worse than writing poems, and hanging them up to be fly-blown on the Review shambles.'[14]

Throughout most of March and early April, Keats was gripped by the apathy of a long depression. His letters, which were all he was writing, are filled with references to it. 'I am mostly at Hampstead, and about nothing,' he wrote to Haydon. Such bitterness made him uneasy. 'I cannot bear a day an[ni]hilated in that manner,' he told George. 'There is a great difference between an easy and an uneasy indolence.' He confessed to his sister that he was writing nothing and barely reading anything either. The little events of such social life as he had rapidly palled. 'The only amusement is a little scandal, of however fine a shape, a laugh at a pun – and then after all we wonder how we could enjoy the scandal or laugh at the pun.'

As so often, this 'horrid Morbidity of Temperament' was clouded by a distorting bitterness. At times the world seemed populated merely by egoists. Going into an ironmongers one day, Keats felt that 'men and tin kettles are much the same in these days.' Both were loud and empty, and there was no difference between the conversation of Wordsworth and that of Leigh Hunt in this respect. 'Unpleasant human identities' and 'people who have no light and shade' prevented him from relaxing, while failing to interest him. Abbey was a particularly obnoxious example of this. Regular visits to him must have stirred Keats's concern over money, a concern underlined by the fact that Abbey himself was now actively suggesting that his erstwhile ward get a trade behind him. He seriously and repeatedly suggested Keats became a hatmaker. It was not the manifest absurdity of this that was so upsetting but Keats's belief that Abbey had a vested interest in the trade (he actually had some concern in a hatter's shop in Poultry) and was hoping to profit out of his benevolence.

Such intrusiveness was all the more galling for the oppressive and probably guilty feelings of intellectual failure inspired in Keats by his current lethargy. Near the end of February he had dined with Taylor and, since it was snowing heavily, passed two nights with him in Fleet Street. Taylor had a wide interest in philosophy, and conversation doubtless turned to this topic and to religion. Despite his anticlericalism, Keats was thinking of reading church history and, just as Taylor had praised Socrates as a great mind handed down to future generations through the writings of others, so now Keats felt he could praise the historical Christ in a similar way. It was lamentably true that what he had said had been twisted by the 'pious frauds' of churchmen, 'yet through all this I see his splendour'. This was far from being a confession of faith, but it does indicate how, in this period of confusion, Keats was searching for something in which to believe. The idea he had of philosophy seemed to answer to this, although he knew that such philosophy could be true for him only when tested on his pulses. He knew he was still confused and innocently striving. 'I am however young writing at random – straining at particles of light in the midst of a great darkness – without knowing the bearing of any one assertion of any one opinion. Yet may I not in this be free from sin?'[15]

The darkness hung thickly about him and, under its cover, Keats's melancholy merged with thoughts of death to create feelings of alluring intensity. In such moods as these, warm and velvety fantasies of annihilation swathed him deliciously. 'I will not spoil my love of gloom by writing an ode to darkness,' he told Haydon on 8 March, but some time in the next ten or eleven days Keats composed his sonnet 'Why did I laugh tonight?' The inexplicable nature of his own feelings, his aching ignorance, seems to be at one with the darkness about him. Although capable of extending his imagination to the very reaches of human happiness, such delight seems tame compared to the love of death which he evokes with rapture:

Why did I laugh? I know this being's lease
　　My fancy to its utmost blisses spreads;
Yet could I on this very midnight cease,
　　And the world's gaudy ensigns see in shreds,
Verse, Fame, and Beauty are intense indeed,
But Death intenser – Death is Life's high meed.[16]

Somewhat shamefacedly, Keats copied the sonnet out for George and Georgiana, adding: 'I am ever affraid that your anxiety for me will lead you to fear for the violence of my temperament continually smothered down: for that reason I did not intend to have sent you the following sonnet – but look over the last two pages and ask yourselves whether I have not that in me which will well bear the buffets of the world.' He would not give way to what he knew was indulgence, rather would he analyse it. The 'Agony' lying behind the poem was not suicidal despair but pain at his own philosophical ignorance. The sonnet was written 'with no thirst of any thing but knowledge'. Certainly, the work originated in pained and troubled feelings, but the actual writing of it was an intellectual exercise in craftsmanship helped, Keats had to confess, with 'a little bit of my heart'.

Such death-longing moods, at once intense and numbing, vivid yet indolent, fell like balm on his more active worries about his failure to continue with *Hyperion*. The whole project seemed an impossibility. Keats's doubts sapped his confidence and his seeming impotence preoccupied him. His letter to Haydon of 8 March shows this repeatedly. He confessed both to indolence and to 'being in a sort of cui bono temper, not exactly on the road to an epic poem'. But it was not only his own moods that were preventing composition. The tinny rattle of egocentric conversation he complained of to the painter, the forcing of effect and the lack of philosophic depth in what people said, were dangerous also in poetry. The ideal of impersonal and classic amplitude continued to haunt Keats to the degree that it seemed unattainable. He would not write for the sake of writing, nor would he write merely for money. He would either compose out of deep reflection or be dumb.

He was, in hope at least, projecting for himself the life of a mature man writing out of proven strength. For the moment, he could only see how short he fell of that ideal. 'I am three and twenty, with little knowle[d]ge and middling intellect. It is true that in the height of enthusiasm I have been cheated into some fine passages; but that is not the thing.' The writing of what Keats considered to be real poetry seemed as far away as ever. 'I know not why Poetry and I have been so distant lately,' he complained to his brother. 'I must make some advances soon or she will cut me entirely.' A month later he added more desperately now: 'I am still at a stand in versifying – I cannot do it yet with any pleasure – I mean however to look round at my resources and means – and see what I can do without poetry.'

Haydon claimed that in this period of intense apprehension Keats took to drinking heavily. 'For six weeks he was scarcely sober,' he declared and went on to tell how his friend covered his tongue with cayenne pepper 'in order to appreciate the "delicious coolness of claret in all its glory" – his own expression'.[17] Given Haydon's tendency to heroic exaggeration and that the *Autobiography* where he related this story was published over thirty years after the events it purportedly relates, this all seems unlikely. Such prolonged drunkenness would have worried Keats's friends and their correspondence would surely have hinted at it. Keats himself said that he now kept himself to three glasses a day (which suggests that he had occasionally drunk more than half a bottle at a time) and it is far from certain that he was now drinking excessively.

What is clear is that he tried to relieve his tension by lounging in bed and seeing his friends. Severn (who was hoping to exhibit a miniature of Keats he was painting) and a bookseller named Cawthorn came to Wentworth Place and, when Severn left for his studio, the remaining men went to a bad play. Keats went, again with Severn, to the British Museum, where he enjoyed looking at a gigantic sphinx with a 'most voluptuous Egyptian expression'. He was bored nonetheless, and on a visit to a new acquaintance, Bridge (or Burridge) Davenport, he fell asleep. There were also further visits to Abbey and Taylor, while on 18 March Keats got a black eye playing cricket with Brown. A leech was applied, and it is possible that Brown also gave him some laudanum. The following morning Keats woke late and in the sort of mood in which 'neither Poetry, nor Ambition, nor Love have any alertness of countenance as they pass by me: they seem rather like three figures on a greek vase – a Man and two women whom no one but myself could distinguish in their disguisement.'[18] Some time later the image of these figures on the urn was to provide the basis of the 'Ode on Indolence', but for the moment Keats's reverie was interrupted by a knock at the door. He was handed a note informing him that the kindly Haslam's father was about to die.

The reality of death obtruded on his reverie and made Keats aware how far, in his self-concern, he had fallen below his standards of disinterestedness. For others, there were sorrows springing up in 'the wide arable land of events' while he had been absorbed in his own concerns. Yet this was inevitably the case. All living creatures were by nature driven by their needs and instincts, and these in their turn circumscribed a man's vision to their own purposes: 'Very few men have ever arrived at a complete disinterestedness of Mind.'[19] Animal and human nature alike are necessarily driven by immediate and self-regarding concerns. 'I go among the Feilds and catch a glimpse of a stoat or a fieldmouse peeping out of the withered grass – the creature hath a purpose and his eyes are bright with it. I go amongst the buildings of the city and I see a Man hurrying along – to what? The Creature has a purpose and his eyes are bright with it.' The altruistic ideal of disinterestedness, so desirable in itself, was rarely achieved. Perhaps only Socrates and Jesus ever really attained it. Yet there must be 'thousands of people' who are similarly predisposed, for 'there is an ellectric fire in human nature tending to purify' with the result that 'new heroism', fresh idealism, is constantly coming into existence. 'The pity is that we must wonder at it: as we should at finding a pearl in rubbish.'

The truly disinterested and poetic mind has a profound and morally purifying empathy with all things, and although its reasonings may be erroneous it will still be 'fine'. Yet here was the rub. Poetry could delude by the power of its own enthusiasm. Inspiration is not self-critical, and so 'is not so fine a thing as philosophy – For the same reason that an eagle is not so fine a thing as a truth'. Keats was coming to see that poetry as an end in itself was insufficient and that to have real worth it must base itself on the broadest intellectual grounds of knowledge.

These various impulses of Keats's mind – the longing for knowledge and disinterestedness, the confusion and the yearning, this 'straining at particles of light in the midst of a great darkness' – are also evident in the third Book of *Hyperion*, which he had one last attempt at completing during this period before finally abandoning the work in the second half of April.

'Apollo is once more the golden theme.' The third Book of *Hyperion* offers Keats's ideal of the evolution to godhead of that altogether more developed and beautiful form of consciousness that will replace the fallen innocence of the Titans. Something of this had already been prepared for at the close of Book Two in the speech of Clymene, that virginal figure now so cruelly exiled from her erstwhile Chamber of Maiden Thought and obliged to wander the world confused by her experiences of 'this thing woe crept in among our hearts'. Feeling the intense divide between her own wretchedness and the beauty of nature, Clymene tries to make 'songs of misery' from a simple shell. She casts this aside when suddenly across the breezes comes the new lyre music of Apollo, an altogether higher form of 'blissful golden melody', wrought from the dialectic of joy and pain. Here is the artistry of the new form of consciousness that is to replace her own, and Clymene understands how irrevocably fallen the Titans are.

Keats's third Book presents the evolution of this Apollonian consciousness, but his own artistry could not always match his theme. The invocation to the muse at the start suggests the 'intensity' which goes with the Apollonian ideal – the 'intensity' Keats had found so lacking in West's *Death on a Pale Horse* – but it falls back on the merely fervid poeticism of *Endymion*. Nor is the 'stationing' of the god himself any more successful. Even Leigh Hunt carped at Keats's image of a heroic youth weeping amid the beauty of nature while his tears run down his bow. With the appearance of Mnemosyne, however, the Titan goddess memory who, as the mother of Art, knows she must give her allegiance to the new order of Olympians, Keats develops more fully his purpose of revealing Apollo as the embodiment of the new consciousness, the new poetry.

Here he was more successful. Keats's picture of the young mortal about to undergo his death and metamorphosis into divinity is shot through with the anxiety, the foreboding and the puzzlement that characterise the rest of the poem. Sublimely gifted and able with his lyre to hold the literary world in awe, Apollo's grief is a mystery to him. He needs, as Keats himself needed, the deep philosophical wisdom of the past. The process of gaining this, Apollo's absorbing the accumulated weight of human experience, is won from observing the face of the goddess of memory herself:

> I can read
> A wondrous lesson in thy silent face:
> Knowledge enormous makes a God of me.
> Names, deeds, grey legends, dire events, rebellions,
> Majesties, sovran voices, agonies,

Creations and destroyings, all at once
Pour into the wide hollows of my brain,
And deify me, as if some blithe wine
Or bright elixir peerless I had drunk,
And so become immortal.[20]

With 'fierce convulse' Apollo dies into his new life, but it is less the glory than the agony of the change that Keats focuses on. The 'death' is no simple act of triumphalism, and this Apollo is not the suave and often ruthless figure of classical myth. He is not pre-Christian but post-Christian, and herein lies the poem's quiet but radical challenge to orthodoxy. While share prices tumbled, bankruptcies multiplied and mass discontent grew daily louder, the Tory party hurried through grants to build new churches where the poor and the aggrieved might be solaced by their spiritual direction. There was much feeling against this sort of reaction, and a conspicuous evangelical, the saintly but priggish Wilberforce, became widely known as Mr Cantwell. The degree of exasperation many felt is suggested by the parting comment made to Wilberforce by the Radical Major Cartwright after Wilberforce himself expressed the wish that they would both meet again in a better world. 'I answered', Cartwright recalled, 'that I hoped we should first mend the world we were in.'[21]

Keats's knowledge of the fundamentals of orthodox Anglicanism is clear from the letter he wrote to his sister on the last day of March 1819, as she was preparing for her confirmation. His own anticlericalism remained as firm as ever, nonetheless, along with his belief that churchmen were a breed on the verge of extinction. 'Parsons will always keep up their character, but as it is said there are some animals the ancients knew which we do not, let us hope our posterity will miss the black badger with the tri-cornered hat; Who knows but some Reviewer of Buffon or Pliny may put an account of the parson in the Appendix; no one will then believe it any more than we believe in the Phoenix.'[22] Keats's own radiant Apollo suggests a new order to set against this old one: an order in which joy and pain are woven fine and suffering coexists with beauty as man evolves towards a godlike perfection.

As such, Keats's Apollo seems to go some way towards answering Haydon's objections to the myth-making of the Hunt circle, his belief that the Apollo of the Greeks was a deity only 'fit for those who live in perpetual enjoyment of immortality, without a care or a grief, or a want'. Keats's Apollo, by contrast, suffers excruciatingly to achieve divinity. He has taken on the whole burden of human history. As in the first two Books, beauty and pain are seen as inseparable. The physical and creative loveliness of Apollo achieves its full meaning only in the context of his suffering, a suffering which, by its very nature, is a higher and more evolved form of consciousness than that the Titans know. In the end, it is the consciousness not just of the god of light and poetry, but of the god of healing too. Once again, the vocation of the poet as the physician of humankind moves to the centre of Keats's work.

But *Hyperion* remains unfinished. There were many possible reasons for this. The trauma of Tom's death so strongly marked a period in Keats's life that it was virtually impossible for him to recover the energies of the time that preceded it. More subtly, the poem clearly contained within it the forces of its own deconstruction. Keats had hoped that Milton would provide him with an example of heroic objectivity which would avoid the egotism and self-consciousness of modern poetry. The impersonality of myth might also offer a means of presenting a poetic philosophy that was not centred around the poet's solipsistic self-consciousness. But this was not the case. Keats's Apollo, dying into his new life, is all too clearly a projection of the poet's own concerns, a wish-fulfilling solution to his own preoccupations. And Keats was, besides, ceasing to believe in the evolutionary perfectibility Apollo represents. Painfully through these torpid weeks, Keats was coming to see that man is made not for godhead but for suffering.

The variety of forms that suffering could take began to impinge on Keats ever more ruthlessly. He still had not heard from George and Georgiana, and his long journal letter to them aches with the worry and isolation this caused. On 3 April, he drew the last of the £500 George had left for his use, an act which not only emphasised the distance between them but hinted at the difficulties with money that would soon begin to burden Keats severely. Part of the money he now drew was needed to settle household expenses with Brown, but life at Wentworth Place was undergoing a change. Dilke, still fussily obsessed with his son's education, moved on 3 April to Westminster, and his part of the house was now occupied by Mrs Brawne and her children. No information survives to comment on this dramatic change. The silence that covers Keats's relationship with Fanny leaves a score of questions unanswered. Did the lovers themselves have any say in the matter, or was Mrs Brawne merely moving back to a house she found agreeable? Was she perhaps hoping to further her daughter's relationship with an apparently acceptable young man? As so often, Fanny's own part in events is unclear. Did she welcome the move or fear it? And did Keats himself urge its taking place or try to resist it, fearing what indeed came to be the case: that being obliged to live so close to the woman he was beginning to love would be both so stimulating and so threatening that in time it would tighten his nerves excruciatingly, tearing him with passionate idealism while bringing horribly to the surface the savagery of his ambivalence towards sexual passion?

Meanwhile, Keats had been obliged to tell Haydon that he was simply unable to lend the promised money. The painter despatched a hurt and angry letter. 'You have led me on step by step, day by day,' he wrote, 'never telling [me] the exact circumstances; you paralysed my exertions in other quarters – and now when I find it is out of your power to do what your heart led you to offer – I am plunged into all my old difficulties.'[23] The genuine affection Haydon had for Keats only made his anger the more painful and his difficulties the more depressing. Keats realised this, but in his letter of reply he stood on his dignity, saying he had not been aware of the obstacles that would be put in his way. Keats's own 'imprudence' in not trying fully to understand his financial affairs was an embarrassment to him, and he was at a loss. 'I find myself possessed of much less than I thought for and now if I had all on the table all I could do would be to take from it a moderate two years subsistence and lend you the rest; but I cannot say how soon I could become possessed of it.' His generosity is evident and he knew that in the past it had made him careless. Both he and his friends, ignorant of the second sum in Chancery, had acted as if Keats had more money than he now appeared to have. He had given out nearly £200 in small loans which he knew he had little chance of getting back and which could have been used to build up the sort of library he wanted. He was badly hurt by Haydon's reproaches. He felt he had slowly been steadying his mind and had started reading again. Now he dreaded the onset of yet another two months of 'idle fever' in which nothing might be achieved save an accumulation of nervous fatigue.

Not all of this could be told to George when Keats resumed his journal letter on 15 April. He mentioned an evening when he and Georgiana's brother dined with the Brawnes along with a party at the physician Sawrey's house where his attention was caught by an unnamed pretty girl, which shows that his emotions were not yet entirely taken up with Fanny Brawne. Although he was 'still at a stand in versifying', the company of Reynolds at the party was pleasant, and if Reynolds had now become obsessed by the law, it had not entirely overcome his interest in verse and he was about to publish his best-known work: a lethally accurate parody of Wordsworth's forthcoming *Peter Bell*. Keats promised to review this for the *Examiner*, Hunt having recently dined at Wentworth Place on what turned out to be a dull occasion. Keats was also helping Brown out with light-hearted verses for a fairy story he was writing, and when Brown himself turned to a satire on Keats and the Brawnes, he responded with a ponderously comic portrait of Brown himself written in Spenserian stanzas.

But something altogether more serious was now engaging Keats's angry attention. He had been back to his old lodgings at the Bentleys' to gather up his correspondence. As he did so, Keats came across the Amena Bellefilia letters written to Tom by Wells. He was so angry and upset by this cruel hoax that he wondered if he should tell George and Georgiana about it all. He realised that he should, any knowledge of loved ones compensating, as he believed, for the pain such knowledge might bring. Having studied the letters again, however, he was suffused with indignation. The whole plot hatched by 'that degraded Wells' was a 'cruel deception' practised on a gentle temperament. Tom had been horribly duped by a vile prank, which, Keats believed, Tom thought had led to his death. His frustrated and feverish sexuality had led to a consuming disease, and the entire tragedy had been founded on a vicious lie. Keats's anger towards Wells almost unsettled him:

> I do not think death too bad for the villain – The world would look upon it in a different light should I expose it – they would call it a frolic – so I must be wary – but I consider it my duty to be prudently revengeful. I will hang over his head like a sword by a hair. I will be opium to his vanity – if I cannot injure his interests – He is a rat and he shall have rat's bane to his vanities – I will harm him all I possibly can – I have no doubt I shall be able to do so.[24]

Meanwhile, as Keats fulminated, the whole poisonous situation – the deceit that led to Tom's sickly tubercular pallor and to his death – left an indelible stain on Keats's own psyche.

Poetry alone seemed to offer an escape from 'the dragon world' of human worry and bitterness. 'The fifth canto of Dante pleases me more and more,' he wrote to George and Georgiana. The passion of Paolo and Francesca, mingling now with his own awkward feelings for Fanny Brawne, had led Keats to the dream image he went on to describe in his letter. 'The dream was one of the most delightful enjoyments I ever had in my life – I floated about the whirling atmosphere as it is described with a beautiful figure to whose lips mine were joined at [*for as*] it seem'd for an age – and in the midst of all this cold and darkness I was warm – even flowery tree tops sprung up and we rested on them sometimes with a lightness of a cloud till the wind blew us away agáin.' The sexual delight of this is both clear and beautiful, but in the sonnet Keats wrote on it – 'A Dream, after reading Dante's Episode of Paolo and Francesca' – it is a delight environed round with hell and punishment. Joy is intimately connected to suffering and death and, as the poet identifies with Paolo himself, only the imagined world of poetry seems able to make romantic love something so passionately all-consuming that it can exist in the purity of its own obsession, untouched and untroubled in:

> that second circle of sad hell,
>   Where in the gust, the whirlwind, and the flaw
> Of rain and hail-stones, lovers need not tell
>   Their sorrows. Pale were the sweet lips I saw,
> Pale were the lips I kissed, and fair the form
> I floated with, about that melancholy storm.[25]

Here is a vision spun in defiance of the real world conflict, a vision of love and art and security that offers an all-absorbing moment beyond the cruel dialectic of joy and pain. 'I wonder', Keats wrote, 'how people exist with all their worries.' For him at least, this sonnet seemed one temporary solution. An eternity of reciprocated passion could be imagined even if it was amid hell and death.

Despite his lassitude, his hypersensitivity and his mention of feeling 'stifling' even on a cold day, it is unlikely that Keats himself was consciously aware of how closely sex and death were mingling in his own body. The tuberculosis he had caught from Tom was not yet unavoidably obvious, and while images of illness and death lurked near the surface of his subconscious, it was the events and characters of the literary world he tried to offer George and Georgiana. He wrote of his views on Wordsworth's latest poem and Reynolds' parody, along with a surprise encounter with Coleridge:

Last Sunday I took a Walk towards highgate and in the lane that winds by the side of Lord Mansfield's park I met Mr Green our Demonstrator at Guy's in conversation with Coleridge – I joined them, after enquiring by a look whether it would be agreeable – I walked with him a[t] his alderman-after-dinner pace for near two miles I suppose. In those two Miles he broached a thousand things – let me see if I can give you a list – Nightingales, Poetry – on Poetical Sensations – Metaphysics – Different genera and species of Dreams – Nightmare – a dream accompanied by a sense of touch – single and double touch – A dream related – First and second consciousness – the difference explained

between will and Volition – so m[an]y metaphysicians from a want of smoking
the second consciousness – Monsters – the Kraken – Mermaids – southey
believes in them – southeys belief too much diluted – A Ghost story – Good
morning – I heard his voice as he came towards me – I heard it as he moved
away – I had heard it all the interval – if it may be called so. He was civil enough
to ask me to call on him at Highgate Good night![26]

The passage vividly characterises the older Coleridge, his heavy
physical presence and seemingly endless flow of metaphysical speculation
which Keats evoked with just sufficient irony to suggest a mighty if self-
obsessed intelligence forever gathering up into itself the vividly incidental
as material for the most abstract reflection. What he did not realise was
how perceptively Coleridge later claimed to have observed him.[27] He
recalled Keats asking: 'Let me carry away the memory, Coleridge, of
having pressed your hand!' The older man stuck his hand out and Keats
took it. When Keats had moved on out of hearing, Coleridge turned to
Green and said: 'There is death in that hand.' Eleven years after the
incident he recalled it for John Frere. Frere asked him exactly what he
meant. Determined to scotch the idea that Keats had died from the
savagery of the reviewers (while nonetheless recognising the harm they
had done him), Coleridge focused on what he believed were the incipient
physical symptoms of Keats's decline. 'There was', he said, 'a heat and a
dampness in the hand.' Death was asserting its hold.

It expressed itself most clearly in the poem which ended this winter
period and stands before the great spring flowering of the mature odes.
On 19 April, Keats invited Taylor, Woodhouse and Reynolds to a card
party at Wentworth Place. It was during this that Reynolds persuaded
Keats to write his *Peter Bell* review for the *Examiner* and, since attacks
on Wordsworth were the order of the day, Keats might also have
shown around his sonnet 'The House of Mourning Written by Mr
Scott', in which a list of pet hates culminates in an execration of
Wordsworth's list of delights recounted in his *Composed in the Valley
near Dover, on the Day of Landing*. While the others played cards,
Woodhouse, who did not enjoy such games, sat reading *The Eve of St.
Agnes*, *The Eve of Saint Mark* and the now abandoned *Hyperion*. A storm
arose and the guests could not go home, so they stayed up till dawn.
Woodhouse took the poems he had read home to copy and the
following day, 21 April, Keats sat down to compose in his journal letter
the greatest of his ballads: 'La Belle Dame Sans Merci'.

The power of this poem lies in the way in which ancient and potent
archetypes of love and death are brought back into existence with a
subtlety which makes the questions they prompt ever more intimate

and ever more baffling. The language of the poem is of the utmost clarity yet its substance is as ambiguously alluring and as ultimately mysterious as the beautiful, destructive lady herself. Who is she and where does she come from? The purely literary answer to this question – that she comes from such sources as Spenser and from Alain Chartier's medievalisation of Celtic myth – indicates that the poem is indeed a highly literary one. But that does not explain how its effect has a wholly unselfconscious and even naive directness comparable to the texts of late medieval Border Ballads. Again, the knight, 'lone and palely loitering', owes much to the cold-humoured man of Burton's *Anatomy of Melancholy*, a copy of which Keats was reading and extensively annotating in 1819. Yet the wasteland in which the knight wanders seems to be more a projection of the poet's own desolation than the actual locations sought out by Burton's melancholy man. Nor is that desolation itself a merely personal matter. It has about it all the malevolence paradoxically associated with the beauty and love-giving of the dame herself:

> O what can ail thee, knight-at-arms,
>   Alone and palely loitering?
> The sedge has withered from the lake,
>   And no birds sing.
>
> O what can ail thee, knight-at-arms,
>   So haggard and so woe-begone?
> The squirrel's granary is full,
>   And the harvest's done.[28]

The knight wanders in a winter world which is natural yet distorted by the powerfully unnatural, and it is, of course, possible to associate the knight with Tom riddled with tuberculosis and frustrated passion, the victim of a woman who was herself an illusion:

> I see a lily on thy brow,
>   With anguish moist and fever-dew,
> And on thy cheeks a fading rose
>   Fast withereth too.[29]

Such poignancy is evidently present and, while it is not a complete explanation, it does prompt the suggestion that the power of the dame to which the knight so readily falls victim is the power given by his own hapless ability to project his erotic feelings on to her. She does not destroy consciously but knows she is the perhaps unwilling victim of the power men associate with her. She is both their eroticism and their death instinct, which, in her, are one. In her beauty and destruction, the dame, in her primordial way, is beyond the categories of innocence and guilt, an ancient creature forever alluring in her existence out of time:

> She took me to her elfin grot,
>   And there she wept and sighed full sore,
> And there I shut her wild wild eyes
>   With kisses four.
>
> And there she lulled me asleep
>   And there I dreamed – Ah! woe betide! –
> The latest dream I ever dreamt
>   On the cold hill side.
>
> I saw pale kings and princes too,
>   Pale warriors, death-pale were they all;
> They cried – 'La Belle Dame sans Merci
>   Thee hath in thrall!'[30]

Just as the relation of the poem to Tom does not explain it, so its analogies to Keats's maturing passion for Fanny Brawne are present even while the impersonality of the work denies such an application. In the end, everything we bring to 'La Belle Dame Sans Merci' fails fully to account for the subtlety of its exploration of sex and death. And, by a final paradox, Keats himself regarded the work as merely a minor achievement, an improvisation he could be ironic about even as he finished writing it down. When, later that evening, he returned to his journal letter to George and Georgiana, it was to write of matters he regarded as altogether more serious.

The Vale of Soul-Making

call the world if you Please 'The vale of Soul-making'.
(Keats to George and Georgiana, April 1819)

THE WEARY MONTHS spent 'straining after particles of light' were drawing to their crisis, and, when Keats returned to his journal letter to George and Georgiana, it was to outline some of the ideas that would soon underlie the great flowering of his mature verse. His letter, sent from a little room in Hampstead to the wilds of North America, becomes a tremendous effort to imagine human community at its most extended and warm.

Keats told George and Georgiana how he had been reading two very different books: Voltaire's *Siècle de Louis XIV*, with its account of highly sophisticated European civilisation, and Robertson's *History of America*, that grim description of savage and primordial existence he had often turned to since his brother and sister-in-law emigrated. Comparing the two works, Keats could no longer believe that human existence was an inevitable progress towards ever more perfect forms of being. The evolutionary optimism of *Hyperion* was beginning to evaporate, and the lesson to be drawn seemed harsh and clear. 'The whole appears to resolve itself into this,' Keats wrote, 'that man is originally "a poor forked creature" subject to the same mischances as the beasts of the forest, destined to hardships and disquietude of some kind or other.' Man can no more will away suffering than a rose can avoid a blighting wind. The inevitable questions posed themselves. Where in such a world lay 'the ballance of good and evil'? How was it possible to believe in a benevolent and Supreme Being who cared for his creation? Keats had long abandoned the Christian view that Jesus alone could offer salvation in a world made wretched by Adam's fall. Indeed he found the Christian explanation of suffering increasingly repellent.

'The common cognomen of this world among the misguided and the superstitious', he wrote, 'is "a vale of tears" from which we are to be redeemed by a certain arbitrary interposition of God and taken to Heaven – What a little circumscribed straightened notion!'[1] In such a view, suffering had no meaning and could be invested with no human purpose or dignity. This was wholly unacceptable to Keats. If a benevolent deity had ensured from the outset that 'the World is full of Misery and Heartbreak, Pain, Sickness and oppression' then he must have done so with a purpose that reflected his own nature. There had to be a value to suffering. Writing late into the night, Keats began to propose a solution to the problem of pain that would not affront the warm impulses of his humanity. He argued that a purpose was discoverable in the natural condition of man, a purpose that, accepting suffering, would qualify him for eternity. That purpose, he suggested, was nothing less than the creation of the soul itself. Firmly rejecting the 'vale of tears' philosophy of the Christians, Keats urged George and Georgiana to 'call the world if you Please "The vale of Soul-making". Then you will find out the use of the world.'[2]

Keats went on to suggest that the rough uses of the world would write their suffering across the heart while the intellect, sent to the heart's school, would learn to read the heart's wisdom 'for the purpose of forming the *Soul* or *Intelligence destined to possess the sense of Identity*'. The familiar notion, urged by Hunt among others, that the wisdom of God is to be heard in the beating of the heart is reasserted here, but where Keats had once believed that the intellect was at best an unreliable guide to truth and suggested that it was hard for him to see how 'a parallel of breast and heart can be drawn', now he realised this could and must be done. The heart remains sovereign but, while feeling is still seen as superior to thought, it is not in conflict with it. The heart is the teacher from which the intellect must learn. Suffering schools the mind and, under its discipline, there emerges the slowly maturing and individual soul destined for immortality. Now, turning to classical mythology for an abstraction to personify his ideas, Keats discovered the Greek goddess of the soul herself. Nine days later, he copied out for George and Georgiana his 'Ode to Psyche'.

His choice of goddess needed some explanation. Keats told George and Georgiana that Psyche was not embodied as a deity until late classical times and consequently 'was never worshipped or sacrificed to with any of the ancient fervour'. For his part, Keats was too orthodox 'to let a heathen Goddess be so neglected', and his ode would be a hymn.

Traditionally allegorised as the tale of how vagrant and mischievous love became enamoured of the soul, the assumption of Psyche and Cupid into heaven after an agonised period of search and separation in this world had clear analogies to Keats's notion of how suffering in 'the vale of Soul-making' prepares man for eternity. The 'Ode to Psyche' is thus far more than a 'pretty piece of paganism'. The necessary inwardness and subjectivity of the modern poet are its real subjects, that seeing more clearly into the 'dark Passages' forced on contemporary awareness by the 'march of intellect'. The concluding stanza explores these notions with a rich intricacy of invention:

> Yes, I will be thy priest, and build a fane
>   In some untrodden region of my mind,
> Where branchèd thoughts, new grown with pleasant pain,
> Instead of pines shall murmur in the wind:
> Far, far around shall those dark-clustered trees
>   Fledge the wild-ridged mountains steep by steep;
> And there by zephyrs, streams, and birds, and bees,
>   The moss-lain Dryads shall be lulled to sleep;
>   And in the midst of this wide quietness
>   A rosy sanctuary will I dress
> With the wreathed trellis of a working brain,
>   With buds, and bells, and stars without a name,
> With all the gardener Fancy e'er could feign,
>   Who breeding flowers, will never breed the same:
> And there shall be for thee all soft delight
>   That shadowy thought can win,
> A bright torch, and a casement ope at night,
>   To let the warm Love in![3]

At its most profound, the psyche creates the truths by which it understands the world. It creates fictions, things 'semireal', through which to apprehend what is true. Herein lies the cause of wonder and praise. In the worship of the goddess of the soul, the world of nature and the world of the mind are fused by the imagination, even as desire and the spirit meet in the union of Cupid and Psyche themselves.

Somewhat cavalierly, given his work on *The Eve* of *St. Agnes*, Keats told George and Georgiana that the 'Ode to Psyche' was the only one of his poems 'with which I have taken even moderate pains'. Such a careful exercise of his art had a calming and healthy influence, and Keats was now entering a period of intense technical preoccupation. 'I have been endeavouring to discover a better Sonnet Stanza than we have,' he told George and Georgiana. 'I do not pretend to have succeeded,' but throughout the latter part of April this experimentation continued. Such a rigorous testing of technical possibilities was clearly a preparation for the mastery of the stanza shown in the great odes, but the subjects of Keats's sonnets from this period suggest the doubts and insecurities that constantly invade that magnificent sequence.

The sonnets are works of the most conscious and deliberate artifice, yet their themes appear to challenge the entire worth of poetry itself. A sonnet on Fame argues that the pursuit of literary reputation is an aberration, a feverish sickness. The natural world does not torment and destroy its well-being in such a manner, and the contrast between quiescent nature and feverish mankind points to the all but unbridgeable divide between them. Human consciousness, as the sonnet 'To Sleep' suggests, is obsessed by darkness, and only annihilation can bring peace. Such an awareness of suffering and death again lies at the core of the odes and their exploration of the state of natural man as he turns variously to art, to nature and to the rhythms of his consciousness while painfully traversing the vale of soul-making. It is to this supreme sequence of poems, uncertain although its precise order is, that we must now turn to find not the individual man but the sudden and miraculous flowering of a major poet working with a deeply felt yet almost impersonal authority on the great themes of his life and art.

Death is literally the void at the heart of the 'Ode on a Grecian Urn', for Keats was aware that such vases were made to hold the ashes of the dead. No one urn provided the imagery for Keats's ode, and what he offers is a summing up of his own broad experience of classical art, a meditation on aesthetics and that process whereby the spirit reaches out in empathy to the accepted canons of the beautiful only to be frustrated as it inevitably returns to the world of suffering and time from which it had longed to escape. In the vale of soul-making, the elusive pleasure of art can offer only a momentary consolation – beauty and truth only temporarily coincide – yet the very richness of that moment draws on the whole tradition of western classical art, on what Keats and his contemporaries regarded as man's highest achievement.

The engravings of work by Poussin and Claude which Keats had enjoyed at Hunt's provide something of his delight in the 'stationing' of individual figures and that pleasure in processions and acts of pagan worship which had appeared in his poetry from the time of his dedicatory sonnet to his first volume. But, while Hunt made a significant contribution in these respects, Haydon too played an important role. Although the relationship between Keats and Haydon had been tested by the painter's insistent chivvying for money, May saw something of a *rapprochement* between the two men, and Keats himself had eventually lent his friend £30 from the last of George's money. Such careless generosity was soon to cause him great difficulties, although the more businesslike Brown intervened to make sure that Haydon signed a bond which made clear that this was a loan repayable after three months. Walks through the Kilburn meadows and visits to Haydon's studio were resumed, and the volumes of prints collected there, in particular engravings of classical vases, played an important part in the creation of the ode. For all his many faults, Haydon still had much to contribute to Keats's development, and his analysis of classic art throws an interesting light on the figures round Keats's urn.

'Phidias and Raphael,' the painter wrote, 'have one great decided beauty in their works: – their figures, whether in action or expression, always look as the unconscious agents of an impulsion they cannot help: you are never drawn aside from what they are doing by any appearance in them, as if they wished to make you consider how very grand they were, or how very gracefully they were moving; – they seemed impelled, irresistibly impelled, by something they cannot controul; their heads, hands, feet, and bodies, immediately put themselves into positions the best adapted to execute the intentions wanted.'[4] Here, in this pulsing and unselfconscious beauty, was that 'intensity' Keats had not been able to find in Benjamin West's *Death on a Pale Horse* but which the figures on his urn seem effortlessly to embody:

> What men or gods are these? What maidens loth?
> What mad pursuit? What struggle to escape?
> What pipes and timbrels? What wild excstacy?[5]

These figures are bodies at once spontaneous and frozen, instantaneous and out of time. In this they again correspond to Haydon's ideal. Confiding his thoughts to his diary, Haydon wrote: 'the great principal of composition in Painting is to represent the event, doing and not done . . . The moment a thing is done in Painting half the interest is gone; a power of exciting attention depends . . . upon the suspense we keep the mind in regarding the past and future.'[6] And, as in painting, so in bas-relief. It is just this state of 'suspense' – a state both of excitement and of halted time – that makes the urn the perfect fulfilment of the classical ideal in art as Keats and his contemporaries understood it:

> Fair youth, beneath the trees, thou canst not leave
>> Thy song, nor ever can those trees be bare;
>>> Bold Lover, never, never canst thou kiss,
> Though winning near the goal – yet, do not grieve:
>> She cannot fade, though thou hast not thy bliss,
>>> For ever wilt thou love, and she be fair![7]

But if the urn is the epitome of classical art, the sensibility that perceives it possesses an awareness which deconstructs the urn's promise of a life of beauty and truth beyond the reach of time. As the processional stanza suggests, the sensibility of the poet is altogether more self-conscious than the figures on the urn itself:

> Who are these coming to the sacrifice?
>> To what green altar, O mysterious priest,
> Lead'st thou that heifer lowing at the skies,
>> And all her silken flanks with garlands dressed?
> What little town by river or sea shore,
>> Or mountain-built with peaceful citadel,
>>> Is emptied of this folk, this pious morn?
> And, little town, thy streets for evermore
>> Will silent be; and not a soul to tell
>>> Why thou art desolate, can e'er return.[8]

This mysteriously moving group fails to see the pathos in its situation, fails to be aware that its existence is predicated by the little deserted town whose desolation is as enduring as the procession which has emptied it is beautiful. The burden of the observer's more fully human consciousness finds in the urn that which undoes its promise of unheeding ecstasy and, by bringing the language of this notion to its marble silence, breaks its partial spell. The urn once again becomes what it had been in the first stanza, something silent and perplexing. Briefly it is dismissed as a 'Cold Pastoral!' But this stab of disillusion is only temporary. The urn, for all it can only be fully appreciated in time, enjoys so great an antiquity, so enduring an existence, as to seem beyond the reach of time and so to abide in an eternity of beauty that is evanescently available to all men. In this lies its benevolence and the true consolation of art:

> When old age shall this generation waste,
>> Thou shalt remain, in midst of other woe

Than ours, a friend to man, to whom thou say'st,
  'Beauty is truth, truth beauty, – that is all
    Ye know on earth, and all ye need to know.'[9]

These concluding lines of the 'Ode on a Grecian Urn' are perhaps the most discussed in English literature, and the problem they present is increased by textual difficulty. When Keats republished the poem in his volume of 1820, inverted commas were placed round the phrase 'beauty is truth, truth beauty'. Such punctuation suggests that the urn's brief, gnomic comment is fully endorsed by the poet, and this in turn prompts the idea that the urn really does provide access to the eternal verities. The ode thus becomes a credo for aestheticism and art for art's sake. But such a reading distorts the subtlety of Keats's achievement and is not supported by Brown's transcript or by the form in which the poem appeared in the magazine *Annals of the Fine Arts*. Neither of these versions uses quotation marks at all so their texts imply that while the urn may offer mankind a religion of beauty and truth, the poet himself does not necessarily give this his full-hearted support.

Herein lies the pathos. The major works of the European tradition do indeed seem to offer an abiding solace. As Hazlitt had declared, such things are the mind's true home. 'The contemplation of truth and beauty is the proper object for which we were created, which calls forth the most intense desires of the soul, and of which it never tires.' The poet of the 'Ode on a Grecian Urn' felt the appeal of the first part of this proposition with all the fervour at his command, yet the very passion of his insight led him to discover that it was not a necessary or even perhaps a sufficient truth. As the philosopher of the vale of soul-making, Keats turned back from transient and ultimately deluding ecstasy to acknowledge the world of suffering and death which again underlies the 'Ode to a Nightingale'.

The spring of 1819 was forward and warm. Closing his letter to George and Georgiana, Keats told them how 'the violets are not withered before the peeping of the first rose'. He promised his sister that he would go over to Walthamstow and bring some plants for her from the Tottenham nursery. He then went on to expatiate on the delights of the season. 'O there is nothing like fine weather, and health, and Books, and a fine country, and a contented Mind and Diligent habit of reading and thinking, and an amulet against the ennui – and, please heaven, a little claret-wine cool out of the cellar a mile deep.' Brown added another to this list of pleasures. 'In the spring of 1819 a nightingale had built her nest near my house,' he recalled. 'Keats felt a tranquil and continual joy in her song; and one morning he took his chair from the breakfast-table to the grass-plot under a plum-tree, where he sat for two or three hours. When he came into the house, I perceived he had some scraps of paper in his hand.'[10] Written out on these was the draft of the 'Ode to a Nightingale'.

No single account of this great poem can explore all its richness, yet the fundamental drama of the piece, the origins of the Keatsian dialectic of suffering and joy, are clear. The heedless and unselfconscious spontaneity of the nightingale's song is the voice of nature which, by its very innocence and purity, calls forth from the poet the sumptuously fabricated syntax of desire which is the ode itself. The simplicity of nature inspires the complex consciousness of poetry, and the uses of language – language as the expression of longing and death especially – are fundamental to the work. The ode is at once the means by which the poet seeks unity with the natural world and the exploration of his irretrievably divorced and divided consciousness. Death informs every level of his perception. To be at one with the nightingale would be to experience an annihilation in ecstasy, while to recognise the fact of separation is to accept the burden of mortality in a world:

> where men sit and hear each other groan;
> Where palsy shakes a few sad, last, grey hairs,
> Where youth grows pale, and spectre-thin, and dies;
> Where but to think is to be full of sorrow
> And leaden-eyed despairs;
> Where Beauty cannot keep her lustrous eyes,
> Or new Love pine at them beyond to-morrow.[11]

In the anguish of the vale of soul-making, man longs for transcendence, escape, the annihilation of consciousness.

The delights of claret-drinking Keats described to his sister become, in the ode, an apostrophe to vibrant Mediterranean existence, a glimpse of a heedless life, of the abundance of nature, communal delight, life itself – warm, potent and yet achieving its fulfilment in an ecstasy which sheers away into welcoming darkness and oblivion. But the alcohol-induced annihilation of 'Bacchus and his pards' is eventually set aside for something altogether more rarefied. The stupefied slumber of drink is rejected for the rapture of being borne on 'the viewless wings of Poesy'. The intent now is not to relinquish consciousness in silence but to raise it to its height by the exaltation of its own medium: language.

The effect is immediate and subtle. At once the real and visible world is put aside. All that remains is night and the mysterious, paradoxically alluring potency of 'embalmed darkness' and that annihilation of the actual so that the more vital life of the imagination can flourish and language recreate the world rather than merely describe it:

> I cannot see what flowers are at my feet,
>   Nor what soft incense hangs upon the boughs,
> But, in embalmèd darkness, guess each sweet
>   Wherewith the seasonable month endows
> The grass, the thicket, and the fruit-tree wild –
>   White hawthorn, and the pastoral eglentine;
>   Fast fading violets covered up in leaves;
>   And mid-May's eldest child,
>   The coming musk-rose, full of dewy wine,
>   The murmurous haunt of flies on summer eves.[12]

This fifth stanza of the 'Ode to a Nightingale' is the most subtly ambiguous of creations. Its effect seems to deny its grammar. The poet 'cannot see' the world around him and has to 'guess' at its existence. Yet, from his very blindness and guesswork, he creates a world from words that seem so physically present that it can be smelt, heard and seen. Out of the longed-for darkness comes not nature but art, an art that appears more natural than nature herself and which, in the very intensity of its heightened perception, turns once more to death:

> Darkling I listen; and, for many a time
>   I have been half in love with easeful Death,
> Called him soft names in many a musèd rhyme,
>   To take into the air my quiet breath;
> Now more than ever seems it rich to die,
>   To cease upon the midnight with no pain,
>   While thou art pouring forth the soul abroad
>   In such an ecstacy!
>   Still wouldst thou sing, and I have ears in vain –
>   To thy high requiem become a sod.[13]

The longing for ecstatic annihilation rises to its climax only to confront, as the self once again obtrudes, the true silence of mortality and the absolute division between finite individual consciousness and the perpetual life of the non-conscious natural world:

> Thou wast not born for death, immortal Bird!
>   No hungry generations tread thee down;

The voice I hear this passing night was heard
  In ancient days by emperor and by clown:
Perhaps the self-same song that found a path
  Through the sad heart of Ruth, when, sick for home,
    She stood in tears amid the alien corn . . .[14]

These lines reveal an important shift in the poet's use of language. Words no longer create what they desire but seek instead to apostrophise the nightingale as an image of immortality, something ineluctably separate from the poet himself. No longer identified with his consciousness, the bird and its song have become objects for thought and hope to speculate on. The nightingale is now a theme to be elaborated by the poet's fancy and the delicious artifice of wishful thinking. The timeless music that solaced Ruth is also perhaps:

  The same that oft-times hath
Charmed magic casements, opening on the foam
  Of perilous seas, in faery lands forlorn.[15]

This image, at once alluring and artificial – the creation of a self-consciously literary and even attitudinising sensibility – evaporates in its aura of insubstantial pastiche. It is merely the creation of fancy, and fancy is a 'deceiving elf'. Language will assert its full power and the pains of consciousness return. As the ode moves into its last stanza, the artificial delights of the first 'forlorn' wither as the nightingale that inspired their use flies away to leave the poet 'Forlorn' in the fullest sense of the word – a man bereft, deserted and alone:

Forlorn! the very word is like a bell
  To toll me back from thee to my sole self!
Adieu! the fancy cannot cheat so well
  As she is famed to do, deceiving elf.
Adieu! adieu! thy plaintive anthem fades
  Past the near meadows, over the still stream,
    Up the hill-side; and now 'tis buried deep
      In the next valley-glades:
  Was it a vision, or a waking dream?
  Fled is that music – Do I wake or sleep?[16]

The apprehension of rapture has passed and with it that 'excellence of every Art', that state of intensity in which 'all disagreeables evaporate, from their being in close relationship with Beauty &

Truth'. The poet of negative capability has been, for the duration of the ode, 'in uncertainties, Mysteries, doubts, without any irritable reaching after fact & reason'. As he returns to his 'soul's self', however, he is obliged to ask questions about the nature of the experience he has enjoyed. 'Was it a vision, or a waking dream?' Was it insight or illusion? Where does reality lie: in the awakened state of the everyday world or in the ecstasy of the nightingale's song? The central experience of the poem is not free from doubt, and the very fact that Keats can question its worth suggests those problems about the legitimacy of all poetic experience that underlie much of the work that is to follow.

The dangers of pseudo-poetry, hinted at in the penultimate stanza of the 'Ode to a Nightingale', are altogether more explicit in the 'Ode on Melancholy'. Keats had been aware of them since his earliest adulthood when George Felton Mathew paraded his fashionably gothicised gloom. The rejected opening stanza of the 'Ode on Melancholy' is a heavy-handed attempt to ridicule such attitudes, presenting as it does the image of a headstrong youth deliberately searching out melancholy with the help of all the recognised contemporary accoutrements: bones, skulls, a fantom gibbet and the tail of a dragon.[17] Keats's point is not simply that this is a ridiculous affectation but that it is an entirely false procedure which violates and vulgarises the true nature of melancholy. This the ode seeks to explore, and the work is an attempt to write a poetry that is 'running over with . . . knowledge and experience'.

Even in its revised form, the 'Ode on Melancholy' recognises the attractions of lugubrious excess, that attitudinising of the death-wish which seeks the fatal pleasure of poisons in which to 'drown the wakeful anguish of the soul'. The true nature of melancholy is altogether more subtle, however, more fully human, and, paradoxically, more creative. Where the first stanza draws it imagery from what is lethal in nature, the opening of the second suggests that true melancholy is not something forced but is an unwilled natural phenomenon, a psychological equivalent of a spring shower which, while it shrouds the world in gloom, also has regenerative powers. The flowers that droop under the rain are nourished by it. Melancholy, death and the living and creative exist in a natural continuum and are part of the transient flux of the world. They are not to be understood apart from each other. To sunder them is to falsify the nature of existence, while fully to observe how they are related is to achieve true insight and even a measure of spiritual glory.

Having advised the sufferer from melancholy to 'glut' his sorrow on the transient beauties of the natural world, Keats goes on to discuss love melancholy, a central topic in Burton's *Anatomy of Melancholy*. Indeed, love and melancholy become identified at this point in the ode. The 'mistress' of the close of the second stanza subtly elides the beloved woman with Melancholy herself. Desire and pain, reality and abstraction, mingle, even as beauty cannot be known apart from death or delight apart from its absence. This recognition of the interchangeability and mutual dependence of opposites, Keats offers as the most refined extreme of insight:

> Ay, in the very temple of Delight
>   Veiled Melancholy has her sovran shrine,
>   Though seen of none save him whose strenuous tongue
>   Can burst Joy's grape against his palate fine;
> His soul shall taste the sadness of her might,
>   And be among her cloudy trophies hung.[18]

The 'Ode on Melancholy' suggests that the truest state of being is one that is speculative yet receptive, alert but passive. It is a poise of mind which allows the natural rhythms of the emotions to form their own insights. In this way, by surrendering to the intensities of negative capability, by accepting that beauty cannot be known save in the context of pain and death, the soul, schooled by the inevitable circumstances of the world, gradually acquires an identity and prepares itself for eternity.

The spiritual exertions of the odes are solitary endeavours. The worship of Psyche is conducted in the intense seclusion of the mind. The aesthete who views the urn is as alone as the poet who hears the nightingale. Keats's attentive listening to the rhythms of his consciousness moves between such private discovery and public statement, and relies on an intensity of the spirit which in the end is its own justification. Such a spiritual alertness placed enormous demands not only on its sources of energy but on maintaining an absolute finesse in discrimination. It also required some degree of belief in the existence of an audience capable of responding to its strenuous subtleties. The whole was a project of the utmost rigour and was easily undermined by Keats's recurring moods of lassitude and doubt. These are the subjects he addresses in the 'Ode on Indolence'.

This mood of spiritual paralysis was not new, and the 'Ode on Indolence', which is conventionally dated last in the sequence, draws directly on the entry in Keats's journal letter for 19 March. Having slept until eleven in the morning (perhaps because of whatever pain-killer Brown may have given him for the black eye he got while playing cricket) Keats wrote: 'Neither Poetry nor Ambition nor Love have any alertness of countenance as they pass by me: they seem rather like three figures on a greek vase – a Man and two women whom no one but myself could distinguish in their disguisement.' Keats frankly recognised that this was a state of laziness and 'effeminacy', a state which now, in the 'Ode on Indolence', he elaborated as a challenge to the entire project of poetry itself.

The most obvious challenge is to the excited aesthetic empathy of the 'Ode to a Grecian Urn'. Where in that poem the carved figures evoked all the poet's powers of delight only to lead him to a knowledge of how such rapture is inseparable from disillusion and suffering, here the robed forms of Love, Ambition and Poetry are merely irksome intrusions on his state of 'nothingness', his spiritual torpor. Only their third appearance provokes anything like a response, and even then the surge of recognition is immediately smothered:

> They faded, and, forsooth! I wanted wings.
>   O folly! What is love! and where is it?
> And, for that poor Ambition – it springs
>   From a man's little heart's short fever-fit.
> For Poesy! – no, she has not a joy –
>   At least for me – so sweet as drowsy noons,
>   And evenings steeped in honeyed indolence.
> O, for an age so sheltered from annoy,
>   That I may never know how change the moons,
>   Or hear the voice of busy common-sense![19]

Keats's letters from this period dwell much on indolence. 'I do not know what I did on monday – nothing – nothing – nothing – I wish this were anything extraordinary.' Again: 'I have been very idle lately, very averse to writing; both from the over-powering idea of our dead poets and from abatement of my love of fame. I hope I am a little more of a Philosopher than I was, consequently a little less of a versifying Pet-lamb.'[20] If fashionable success meant the production of the meretricious and the sentimental, Keats would abandon ambition. He would not be what, in the 'Ode on Indolence,' he called a 'pet-lamb in a sentimental farce'. But the relinquishing of ambition also meant the banishment of 'my demon Poesy', and such a relinquishing of literary endeavour appeared to be a way of shunning the pains of the vale of soul-making. The poet seems to turn his back on the spiritual exercises that are the greater odes for a purely private world of dreaming self-indulgence. The boast that he has 'visions for the night' seems to come perilously close to attitudinising, while underlying it is the wilful rejection of poetry itself and the apparent triumph of the enemies of literature: solipsism, fantasy and silence.

Between late April and May 1819 Keats wrote three or four of the supreme lyric poems in English literature, yet his doubts about the worth of poetry extended to a diffidence over even the fate of his manuscripts. Brown later recalled that after writing the 'Ode to a Nightingale' Keats went back into Wentworth Place with the drafts in his hand and began quietly to thrust them behind some books. The oddness of this gesture suggests its authenticity, and by Friday 30 April Brown had been given permission to make fair copies of any other manuscripts he could find in the house.

But Brown was now preparing to let his half of Wentworth Place to fund his summer expedition, and by the close of June Keats would have to move out. He began tidying up his books in preparation and returning those he had borrowed from his publishers. He also decided to burn some of his correspondence, and it was perhaps while looking through this that he turned up some letters from the Jeffreys. At all events, he decided to write to Sarah Jeffrey asking her, among other things, if she could recommend somewhere in Devon where he could stay cheaply to write. Keats's letter is permeated by his doubts concerning his prospects along with the uncertainty into which he had been plunged by having finally, on 12 May, received a letter from George. His brother's plans had changed and now he needed money. There was land still available in Illinois, but it was heavily wooded and could not be farmed before the exhausting business of felling and clearing was complete. Discouraged by this, George and his family had made the long journey across the Alleghenies and down the Ohio to Kentucky. Here he had finally resolved against farming and decided to go into Mississippi river trading. He needed all the capital he could raise, and Keats felt obliged to help.

The disquiet that invariably swept over Keats when money problems pressed on him returned. His vulnerability, his naivety even, were patent to him. 'I have been always till now almost as careless of the world as a fly – my troubles were all of the Imagination,' he told Sarah Jeffrey.[21] 'My Brother George always stood between me and any dealings with the world – Now I find I must buffet it.' The need to earn money was becoming of paramount importance, but what did his poetry bring in? Having heard from Haydon about the merits of the 'Ode to a Nightingale', the editor of the *Annals of the Fine Arts* began negotiations for publishing the poem in his July issue, but the amount to be earned was trifling. Keats had been forced to admit that *Hyperion* could not be finished, and while 'some grand Poem' was essential to his prospects he had, in publishing terms, achieved very little. Now it seemed that his doubts about poetry itself were draining him of the necessary confidence to write at all.

By the close of May he felt able to confirm these doubts to Sarah Jeffrey, telling her he could either sail on an East Indiaman as a medical officer or, in a last-ditch attempt to develop his art, see what he could achieve in the few remaining months he could afford to set aside for writing. 'I have the choice as it were of two Poisons (yet I ought not to call this a Poison), the one is voyaging to and from India for a few years; the other is leading a feverous life alone with Poetry.' The desperation is as evident as the embarrassment which underlies his begging Sarah Jeffrey not to let any one in Teignmouth know what a position he was in. What is clear above all, however, is the courage and resolve with which Keats tried to face the difficulties of what he knew was the only decision he could really make. Choosing energy rather than despair, he confessed: 'I would rather conquer my indolence and strain my ne[r]ves at some grand Poem – than be in a dunderheaded indiaman.'

Sarah Jeffrey wrote back telling Keats he should try staying at Bradley and tactfully suggesting the voyage he proposed would merely sap his mental energies. While Keats did not wholly agree with this, believing that to be among people who were as indifferent to him as he to them would allow him to observe human nature with 'the calmness of a Botanist', he felt she was right to discourage him all the same. Besides, on 8 June he had received an offer from the ever ailing James Rice to spend a month with him on the Isle of Wight. Despite the wear on his nerves that being shut up with an invalid would cause, Keats could not refuse. He wrote to Sarah telling her he would spend a month with Rice and then move on to Bradley.

The last of the money left by George was probably given to Rice to pay for their accommodation in Shanklin and, since he was otherwise broke, Keats hoped he would be able to call immediately on his inheritance from Tom. That meant steeling himself for a meeting with Abbey. A visit to Walthamstow 'really surprised me with super civility – how did Mrs. A manage it?', but when Keats called on his erstwhile guardian's office in the City the sheer malevolence of events shocked him into acknowledging how vulnerable he was. Abbey told Keats that his aunt, Mrs Jennings, was now threatening to file a suit in Chancery which alleged that her children had grounds for a claim on a proportion of Tom's estate. Despite this being far less serious a matter than appeared on the surface, Keats was given to understand that the expenses involved would be considerable. He also assumed, quite wrongly, that the estate would be frozen until the matter came to court, which in fact it never did. He returned to Hampstead resolved, in his desperation, to look 'for a Situation with an Apothecary'.

Brown tried to come to the rescue, taking over the organisation of Keats's affairs. While he was as unaware as anyone else of the inheritance from Keats's grandfather still accumulating interest in Chancery, it seemed to Brown that Keats could at least set about trying to reclaim the more than £200 he had lent to friends over recent years. He even offered to advance his friend money of his own on the strength of this. Haydon, he knew, owed Keats at least £30, but the painter had recently confided to his diary that his financial affairs were 'now more dreadful than ever'. Despite Keats's beseeching him to 'borrow or beg some how what you can for me', the £30 was not returned and the great, stimulating friendship between the two men began seriously to founder.

At the core of this worry over money lay the threat it posed to Keats's relationship with Fanny Brawne. Whatever the state of her feelings (and, as so often, these are hidden from us) the position Keats himself was in was both complex and intolerable. Fanny had moved with the rest of her family into the house next door to him. He could see her coming and going, watch her walking on the lawn, hear her voice and thoroughly imagine her in all her proximity. He was obliged to live almost constantly in a state of frustrated sexual alertness and this tore at his nerves. It is clear that he wanted her desperately. As he confessed: 'I am not one of the Paladins of old who liv'd upon water grass and smiles for years together.' He later made it clear to Brown that he never had sex with her, but even now it was becoming obvious to everyone that marriage was out of the question. It was brutally clear that Keats could not support a wife. He was twenty-three, deeply in love, and suffering from a torrent of frustrated sexuality that could only turn in upon itself and lacerate him. His deep uncertainty about his own sexual nature, revealed to Bailey in his letter from Mull, was returning.

The evidence for this lies not in his correspondence – the great series of letters to Fanny had not yet begun – but in the agitated annotations

Keats scribbled in the margins of his copy of the *Anatomy of Melancholy*. Burton's work was becoming a major focus of interest, and against the comment 'Love, universally taken, is defined to be *desire*', Keats wrote:

> Here is the old plague spot; the pestilence, the raw scrofula. I mean that there is nothing disgraces me in my own eyes so much as being one of a race of eyes and nose and mouth beings in a planet call'd the earth who all from Plato to Wesley have always mingled goatish winnyish lusful love with the abstract adoration of the deity. I don't understand Greek – is the love of God and the love of women express'd in the same word in Greek? I hope my little mind is wrong – if not a could – Has Plato separated these loves? Ha! I see how they endeavour to divide – But there appears to be a horrid relationship.[22]

The hatred of sexuality here claims to be as much general and universal as private and particular. Sex becomes 'disgrace', and it does so because of mankind's inherent tendency to conflate things Keats believed to be wholly opposed: the body and the soul. Nothing could be more opposite to the sensual mysticism of *Endymion*. Sexuality is no longer seen as creative. It is mere 'goatish winnyish lustful love', horrible in itself and an anathema when, at its most refined, it becomes falsely identified with the immortal and spiritual.

This is the cry of a deeply unsatisfied young man with no real experience to draw on save his own conflicting fantasies. The blissfully satiated union imagined in *The Eve of St. Agnes* is severed by the conflicts of an enforced abstinence, and behind the depths of self-disgust lies Keats's dreadful position in Wentworth Place: the isolated spasms of intense desire and the humiliating masturbations in which 'goatish winnying' could only emphasise its own futility. The situation contained the seeds of a divide in which self-abasement created an ever more remote ideal of Fanny Brawne. She would become inhumanly perfect and, whenever this image conflicted with the real teenage girl living next door to him, the divide threatened to hurl Keats down into the most anguished of psychological abysses. Now, against Burton's often virulently misogynous remarks, Keats scribbled 'good' or 'aye aye'. Soon he would take Burton's story of a young man's fatal love for a snake-woman as the subject for a poem.

Meanwhile, Keats had to face the reality of his financial position and the knowledge that, for some time at least, he would have to live apart from Fanny Brawne. He had to contemplate 'the worst that can happen', had to accept that during the time that he was away she might fall in love with someone else and might even accept a proposal. Only when he had made his name and begun to repair his fortune could Keats offer marriage. He began to pin his hopes on an idea first mooted by Brown. The two men would collaborate on a play for which Brown would supply the plot and Keats the poetry. They dreamed that Kean might star in it, and Keats had already begun to draft the opening scene when, on 27 June, he caught the coach for Portsmouth on the first stage of his journey to join Rice in the Isle of Wight.

The Face of Moneta

Then saw I a wan face,
Not pined by human sorrows, but bright-blanched
By an immortal sickness which kills not . . .

(The Fall of Hyperion)

KEATS RODE ON the outside of the coach in order to save money, but was deluged in so heavy a storm that 'I may say I went to Portsmouth by water.' As a result of these rain-soaked hours he caught a cold which, as so often, flew to his throat and contributed to the feverishness that underlay the coming strenuous weeks. The presence of the ailing Rice, tactful, considerate but constantly trying to hide his weakness under a veil of forced puns, only compounded the discomfort. Shut up in the tiny cottage they had rented, Keats and Rice 'made each other worse by acting on each other's spirits. We would grow as melancholy as need be.' The situation inevitably reminded Keats of being with Tom during his final illness, and: 'I confess I cannot bear a sick person in a House especially alone – it weighs upon me day and night.'[1]

Although the summer beauty of the island was exquisite, a vista of cottages 'covered with creepers and honeysickles with roses and eglantines peeping in at the windows', Keats felt himself 'an old Stager in the picturesque', and the need to work meant that he went out only for short walks. Even then his worries about money did not leave him. The views that had helped inspire the moon-kissed landscapes of *Endymion* took on a different hue and prompted different thoughts. It now seemed that both nature and poetry were to be harvested for cash. 'The very corn which is . . . so beautiful, as if it had only took to ripening yesterday, is for the market: So, why shod I be delicate?'[2] He would not be, and he had planned for himself a ruthless timetable of work. There was, first of all, the play to be written;

257

in addition, narratives for a new volume of poetry had to be composed and polished. During this period, Keats revised *The Eve of St. Agnes*, began a recasting of *Hyperion* and set himself to work on *Lamia*, the tale he had found in Burton's *Anatomy of Melancholy*. Other occasional pieces would also be written in these weeks of prodigious and increasingly harassed creativity.

For events conspired to distract Keats continuously, and his worries about money were made worse when, on 6 July, a letter from George was forwarded to Shanklin. George had been invited by John James Audubon to stay at his log cabin in Henderson, Kentucky, where the future bird-painter began interesting him in investing in a Mississippi steamboat. Audubon was optimistic and plausible. He showed George his apparently thriving grist and lumber mill without mentioning that it was on the point of collapse. Neither did he talk of other schemes that had failed, other debts he had incurred, but he may genuinely have not known that the steamboat he was extolling had already sunk in the Ohio river. George was nonetheless determined to realise as much money as he could. Although Keats himself found such matters more tormenting than anything imagined by Dante, he resolved to act. He wrote to Abbey, he wrote to George himself to tell him of the difficulties posed by their aunt's proposed action in Chancery, and he sent a letter to the estate's other trustee, now living in Holland, to apply for power of attorney on George's behalf.

He also pressed on with his own work. At first it had been a curious sensation to sit down and write from necessity, but Keats was determined to be diligent. By 12 July he could tell Reynolds he had completed the first Act of the play and the first Book of *Lamia*, a total of more than 800 lines. He tried to preserve his confidence in success. He told Reynolds he hoped to gain a reputation through the careful exercise of judgement in his writing, and his efforts during this period are underscored by a continuous anxiety about the nature of the public he imagined he was writing for. Much of this showed a misdirected concern over the image of the poet he was trying to project, and was to threaten, sometimes disastrously, the true nature of his genius.

The overwhelming need, however, was to produce. 'I have some confidence in my success,' he wrote to his sister and, besides, if he were to fail, there was always the possibility of returning to medicine and his 'gallipots'. Obviously he hoped this necessity would not arise, but Keats's letter to Reynolds suggests the fortitude with which he had stared at possible failure and refused to let it daunt him. 'I have spent too many thoughtful days & moralized thro' too many nights for that, and hopeless would they be indeed, if they did not by degrees make me look upon the affairs of the world with a healthy deliberation.' References to being hard at work fill the letters of these days. As he wrote to Fanny Brawne on 8 July: 'I am at the diligent use of my faculties here, I do not pass a day without scrawling some blank verse or tagging some rhymes.'[3]

The enforced distance between Keats and Fanny allowed him to express in correspondence that passion which Fanny herself complained he had been 'an age' declaring. Suddenly, after the long silence of their early courtship, Keats's obsessive love stands revealed, absolute and all-absorbing. Fanny now received some of the most profoundly felt love letters in all literature, revelations of a many-faceted and idealised passion variously radiant and tinged with threat and thoughts of death. This was a concentration hardly won. The apparent spontaneity derived from a conscious effort to achieve an honesty purged of all emotional cant and was the labour of a young man aware of how nearly the false and the ridiculous wait on the ardent and sublime. 'I am glad,' Keats wrote on 1 July, 'I had not an opportunity of sending off a Letter which I wrote for you on Tuesday night – 'twas too much like one out of Ro[u]sseau's Heloise.' With this declaration that borrowed emotion has been abandoned, the great series of Keats's love letters begins.

He thought his unaffected emotion matched by hers. 'I love you the more in that I believe that you have liked me for my own sake and for nothing else.' On both sides their love had to be imagined clean of literary pretension and the malpractices of sentiment. 'Hateful literary chitchat' was mere bad faith, as damaging to love as to poetry, and, in his confidence of what he and Fanny shared, Keats could laugh at those women of his acquaintance 'whom I really think would like to be married to a Poem and to be given away by a novel'. Only through a rigorously maintained authenticity could Keats approach the profound continuity between joy and darkness in his unconsummated passion.

For, despite their emotional frankness, these are virginal letters where, as convention demanded and perhaps the form of the emotion itself required, physical sexuality is confined to brief mentions of kissing and to imagining a state 'moistened and bedewed with Pleasure'. The focus is not on sexual union nor the specific, tough emotions of two people in love. The letters are, rather, meditations on romantic ardour and the conflicts wrought in the psyche of a still very young man by the haunting presence of a beauty so unattainable that the intensities of his own response become almost his sole subject. Fanny's individuality is all but absorbed as she becomes the embodiment of her lover's needs. 'Why may I not speak of your Beauty, since without that I should never have lov'd you. I cannot conceive any beginning of such love as I have for you but Beauty. There may be a sort of love for which, without the least sneer at it, I have the highest respect, and can admire it in others: but it has not the richness, the bloom, the full form, the enchantment of love after my own heart.'[4]

This is the projection of an inward and all but depersonalised longing. Fanny perhaps felt uncomfortable and even threatened by it, as she was no doubt right to do. To be apostrophised as the personification of Beauty was in part to be denied her existence as Fanny Brawne, and there was probably more than modesty or clever flirtatiousness behind her apparently asking Keats not to write in this way. Besides, she had already, in an earlier letter, been exposed to the altogether more unpleasant obverse of such feelings. 'I have never known any unalloy'd Happiness for many days together,' Keats told her, 'the death or sickness of some one has always spoilt my hours – and now when none such trouble oppresses me, it is you must confess very hard that another sort of pain should haunt me.'[5] Fanny, the embodiment of Beauty, becomes associated with cruelty, suffering and death. She is to be blamed for the fantasies projected on her. 'Ask yourself my love whether you are not very cruel to have so entrammelled me, so destroyed my freedom.' Only her reply, her writing 'softest words', could console him, but that consolation Keats took to his grave when he asked for her letters to be buried with him.

For she did write and: 'I took your letter last night to bed with me. In the morning I found your name on the sealing wax oblitered. I was startled at the bad omen till I recollected that it must have happened in my dreams, and they you know fall out by contraries.' In the confined space of the Shanklin cottage, constantly aware of the invalid Rice and harassed day long by financial anxiety and the strenuous, last-ditch attempt to establish himself in his vocation, night and his bedroom alone could offer Keats respite. Yet there and at such times his passion became ever more closely associated with the isolation of ecstasy and death. Love's 'proper' time might be the morning, but 'when the lonely day has closed, and the lonely, silent, unmusical Chamber is waiting to receive me as into a Sepulchre, then believe me my passion gets entirely the sway, then I would not have you see those R[h]apsodies which I once thought it impossible I should ever give way to, and which I have often laughed at in another, for fear you should [think me] either too unhappy or perhaps a little mad.'[6]

Keats observed the symptoms of his passion with something of the objectivity of a medical man. His love was like an illness, but Fanny rather than he was the physician to it. Such emotion wore him down, and he felt his nerves becoming frayed. He had been 'in so irritable a state of health these last two or three days' that he could compose for Fanny nothing more than 'an unhealthy teasing letter'. Languor and 'ardency', the symptoms of both consumption and a consuming passion, afflicted him and only she could cure them. 'What fee my sweet Physician would I not give you to do so?' He also knew his melancholy distressed her and, blaming the misfortunes of his life rather than personal weakness, he promised he would 'no more trouble either you or myself with sad Prophesies; though so far am I pleased at it as it has given me opportunity to love your disinterestedness towards me'.[7] Hazlitt's term of high praise has returned to Keats's vocabulary, yet it is telling that what Keats himself craves is not a reciprocated ardour or the expression of sexual desire, but that selfless outgoing of generosity a boy might expect from his mother. The need to be cradled runs deeply through the affair with Fanny, and one of the many images Keats projected on to her suggests a woman soothing a fretful child.

Yet even such solace contained a threat. To secure Fanny's comforting breast, Keats had to marry her. Not only could he not afford this but the idea of a settled domestic life filled him with foreboding. 'I tremble at domestic cares,' he told her, and the fear deepened in him that married life would drain his finer energies and wear him down with routine. Enlarging on a theme that must have been painful to Fanny, he wrote: 'god forbid we should what people call, *settle*.' He painted a satiric picture of what this might entail. He did not choose to 'open my Mouth at the Street door like the Lion's head at Venice to receive hateful cards Letters messages. Go out an[d] wither at tea parties; freeze at dinners; bake at dance[s] simmer at routs. No my love, trust yourself to me and I will find you nobler amusements, fortune favouring.' It was, he told her, better to be 'imprudent movables than prudent fixtures'. He proposed a wandering, vagabond life. 'We might spend a pleasant year at Berne or Zurich.'[8]

If this sometimes seemed concerning to Fanny, the letters also allowed her to see what it might mean to be married to the professional writer Keats was trying to become. His correspondence at this time is shot through with reports of alternating states of necessarily intense and even selfish application followed by lassitude and self-doubt. That Keats needed to earn money was openly accepted between them. It was clear, however, that the life of letters did not offer the safe and regular salary enjoyed by people like the Dilkes. Fanny would have to take second place in Keats's time of full inspiration even though he still wanted to see her. 'I will flit to you and back. I will stay very little while; for as I am in a train of writing now I fear to disturb it – let it have its course bad or good – in it I shall try my own strength and the public's pulse.'[9] If this was hard, such statements alternated with moods which, for a future wife, were altogether more worrying. 'I have three or four stories half done, but as I cannot write for the mere sake of the press, I am obliged to let them progress or lie still as my fancy chooses. By Christmas perhaps they may appear, but I am not yet sure they ever will.' Feverous creation offered no guarantee of a regular wage.

While his profession gave no security, the force of Keats's passion contained a threat which is clear even in the first of his letters. Jealousy lurked at the core of his love. His initial fears had some reasonable grounds. He and Fanny had arrived at a degree of understanding but there was no formal engagement. She was perfectly within her rights to go out and enjoy parties and dances without him. What frightened Keats was that she was also within her rights to receive addresses from other men. He tried to cover his fears with generosity. 'In case of the worst that can happen, I shall still love you,' he wrote, yet he felt obliged to add: 'what hatred shall I have for another.' His fears grew as July progressed: 'If you should ever feel for a Man at the first sight what I did for you, I am lost. Yet I should not quarrel with you, but hate myself if such a thing were to happen – only I should burst if the thing were not as fine a Man as you are as a Woman.'[10] He had created Fanny in his own image, invested some of his most profound longings in his creation, and consequently was frightened of what he had to acknowledge as the reality of her independence. The force of his objectless jealousy was in part a threat used to bind her to him. It was an expression both of his fervour and of his dependence. As the affair progressed, and as Keats's incipient tuberculosis became a manifest illness, so this core of jealousy would tighten with anguish and become the disfiguring motif of a hopelessly consuming love.

The affair had not reached that state when, on 22 July, Brown arrived at Shanklin, bringing with him Rice's friend the publisher John Martin, who in turn brought his sister and three of her friends. The visitors stayed in a nearby cottage, and the next few days were taken up with visits and card games. Keats was given 'no undisturb'd opportunity to write' until 25 July, when the visitors, along with Rice, eventually left. Only then could he tell Fanny how sorry he was to hear that she was slightly unwell and how he ached to be with her if only for an hour. 'You absorb me in spite of myself,' he declared, 'you alone.' His letter ended with a passionate affirmation of his feelings. 'I will imagine you Venus to-night and pray, pray, pray to your star like a He[a]then.'[11] Such imagery also underlies the supremely beautiful poem Keats probably wrote for Fanny during these days of early July:

Bright star! would I were steadfast as thou art –
    Not in lone splendour hung aloft the night
And watching, with eternal lids apart,
    Like nature's patient, sleepless Eremite,
The moving waters at their priestlike task
    Of pure ablution round earth's human shores,
Or gazing on the new soft-fallen mask
    Of snow upon the mountains and the moors –
No – yet still steadfast, still unchangeable,
    Pillowed upon my fair love's ripening breast,
To feel for ever its soft swell and fall,
    Awake for ever in a sweet unrest,
Still, still to hear her tender-taken breath,
And so live ever – or else swoon to death.

The subtlety and drama of the greatest odes are here concentrated in a sonnet. Once again, the discontinuity between man and nature and a longing for identification are Keats's subjects. The poet aspires to the fixed and ethereal beauty of the star, a beauty which, while benevolent and tender, is nonetheless solitary and, finally, non-human. The star personifies a quiet and universal fixedness, the limitations of which are implied even as the star itself is extolled. For all its steadfast loveliness, the star's is a 'lone splendour' and is something both less and greater than the lovers' union. The nature of the star's existence, 'still steadfast, still unchangeable', implies an ideal state after which the poet yearns, so bringing to his passion a hope of timeless and universal content. But the poem implies that the attainment of such a state is impossible. The heart can never be as still and tranquil as the star, for this would be to deny the interchangeability of joy and pain whereby each of these states comes to be known. For the ardent lover, there can only be ecstasy or annihilation. Desire and death are seen as inseparable, interchangeable even. As Keats wrote to Fanny: 'I have two luxuries to brood over in my walks, your Loveliness and the hour of my death. O that I should have possession of them both in the same minute.'[12]

While this passionate correspondence was taking place, the political voices of the country were rising to an ever more acrimonious pitch. A sense of impending violence hung in the air. The merciless cycles of trade had returned to their lowest point, and amid increasing bitterness, unemployment rose and widespread, wretched poverty multiplied as the purchasing power of money shrank. The nation was becoming ever more dangerously divided between the embittered and largely voteless poor and an unrepresentative ruling class who, believing that 'the present system of distress of the country arises from unavoidable circumstances', could only raise taxes and draw up plans to repress the symptoms of discontent. The new taxes on tobacco, tea, malt and British spirits fell most onerously, as the *Examiner* showed, on those least able to afford them. This, Hunt urged, was by design. The poor could not easily do without these newly taxed commodities and, because of 'Boroughmongers', because of the scandalously unrepresentative way seats were bought and sold in Parliament, 'their votes are of no consequence.'[13]

Hunt also saw that the once broadly contented members of the bourgeoisie were becoming disaffected too. The entire population was being swept up in the nation's distress. While ever larger meetings to urge reform were called to peaceful and orderly protest, and while the more extreme among the radical artisans trained in bands with their secretly forged pikes, the government increasingly believed in the necessity of armed repression by the army and gentlemen volunteers. This was something Wordsworth had long urged on his patrons and was why Keats and Brown had encountered soldiers on their walk through the Lake District. 'If the whole island was covered with a force of this kind,' Wordsworth had urged, 'the press properly curbed, the Poor Laws gradually reformed, provision made for new churches to keep pace with the population, order may yet be preserved and the people remain free and happy.'[14]

Liberal opinion was wholly opposed to this. 'The question now depending between the rich and poor, the maintenance of parliamentary corruption and the insistence upon its abolition, is simply this – Whether the most monstrous inequality is to be suffered to exist, in defiance of the law of the land, as well as the common principle of justice.' Concluding his leader of 15 August, Hunt wrote: 'For our part, we do not think force at all necessary for the settlement of the question.' The following day, when some 80,000 unarmed reformers converged on St Peter's Field, Manchester to hear Orator Hunt argue for parliamentary reform, alarmed magistrates sent in the mounted yeomanry. Eleven people were killed and many hundreds wounded. As the cavalry dismounted and wiped their swords, 'several mounds of human beings still remained where they had fallen, crushed down and smothered. Some were still groaning, and all were silent save those low sounds, and the occasional snorting and pawing of steeds.'[15]

For many, their worst fears had been confirmed in blood. The nature of a victory won after a vastly expensive war fought for two decades against the forces of European liberty was appallingly clear. Across the mainland of the continent, from Austria, through Italy to Spain, tyrants had reassumed their thrones and banded into a Holy Alliance supported by the immense burden of the British national debt, a debt serviced by a people who had no say in how their taxes were spent. Unemployment and poverty afflicted the masses, while the wealthy and autocratic protected an unjust constitution with their swords. 'Everyone', Hunt wrote, 'not actually committed with the seat-sellers in power, gave way to a burst of astonishment and indignation.' The violence and hysteria inherent in this world of corrupt and entrenched grandees also suffuses *Otho the Great*, the play with which Keats hoped to salvage his fortunes. It was also to have an important part in his plans for the future, and, in particular, his increasingly firm commitment to the liberal cause.

Nevertheless, while the vertiginous reverses of the plot of *Otho the Great*, the deceit and anarchy attendant on arbitrary power, belonged to the closed world of patrician politics, they also belonged to the degraded stage of early-nineteenth-century tragedy, and for the most part the play is confusingly sensationalistic. The ghastly fascination of the work lies less in the drama itself than in the image of Keats squandering his imagination for the sake of desperately needed money. The play is largely hack-work, and the manner in which Keats and Brown decided to compose it ensured that it could be little else.

When his guests left Shanklin, Brown was eager to set to work with Keats. As he recalled years later: 'the progress of this work was curious; for, while I sat opposite to him, he caught my description of each scene, entered into the characters to be brought forward, the events, and every thing connected with it.'[16] But richness of character and language were hardly to be achieved in this way save in isolated moments. 'Thus he went on, scene after scene, never knowing or enquiring into the scene which was to follow until four acts were completed.' Keats was diligent and hardworking nonetheless. Long hours were put into the composition of the play, and while Keats himself admitted that the work was 'Brown's child' and that he was only the 'Midwife', he recognised what he owed his friend and was spurred by the hope they might make £200 apiece. Brown after all had received £300 for *Narensky* and had at least some claim to theatrical success. Nonetheless, despite declaring it was his intention to work 'as great a revolution in modern dramatic writing as Kean has done in acting', Keats tried to preserve some measure of critical distance from what he was so laboriously producing. 'Brown and I are pretty well harnessed again to our dogcart,' he told Dilke. 'I mean the Tragedy which goes on sinkingly.' They were thinking of introducing an elephant, but Keats's suggestion 'of making the princess blow up her hair-dresser' suggests an impish defence against boredom.

Other diversions were more constructive. Seeing Keats's interest in Dante, Brown urged him to learn Italian. They also went out sketching together. Brown had a certain mechanical facility and, having already cut a silhouette of Keats while at Hampstead, he now proceeded to draw his head and shoulders in pencil. The portrait, drawn in profile with Keats's cheek resting against a sturdy, closed fist, has a vigour lacking from the vapid sentimentalisations propagated by Severn. The thick hair and sensuous mouth, along with the slightly upturned gaze, suggest both force and sensitivity. Certainly, there is little to suggest the exhausted intensity of Keats's emotions at this time.

While Brown went off to be 'a little profligate' with the local girls, Keats continued with his own work and with the play. There were only occasional breaks. 'I leave this minute a scene in our Tragedy to see you (think it not blasphemy) through the mist of Plots speeches, counterplots and counterspeeches,' he told Fanny. 'The Lover is madder than I am – I am nothing to him.'[17] The parallel was meant to be comic and to deflect Fanny's criticism of the emotions in his last letter – the comparison Keats had drawn between Fanny and Venus and the whole tenor of his erotic worship. But frustration, worry and over-work were beginning to wear Keats down. The strident voices of neighbours exasperated him. The tiny cottage was like a coffin. 'I begin to dislike the very door posts here,' he wrote, and the image was almost at once transformed to the guilt-ridden Auranthe, the beloved of the play's hero Ludolph. It was becoming vital that both Keats and Brown should have a change of scene. Besides, there was no adequate library where they could do the necessary historical research. 'This day week we shall move to Winchester,' Keats told Fanny on 5 August, and his next letter to her was posted from there twelve days later.[18]

He told her of his relief at getting away from Shanklin, of how he saw the Prince Regent's 'silent, light, and graceful yacht' as they crossed to the mainland, and how the ropes of their own vessel tangled with the mast of a little naval boat, snapping it while the men themselves remained unperturbed. But, for all that, this was a 'flint-worded Letter', full of resolute, hard determination. It seemed 'excessively unloverlike and ungallant'. Keats begged Fanny to believe the first letters he had written her. There the emotion was fresh and strong. Now he was deeply involved in the last Act of the play, stressed, uneasy and preoccupied. His financial position alarmed him. 'My cash resources are for the present stopp'd; I fear for some time. I spend no money but it increases my debts.' His heart, he told her, was like iron, while 'my Mind is heap'd to the full; stuff'd like a cricket-ball – if I strive to fill it more it would burst.' Work was as vital to his sanity as to his pocket, and it was in part a defence against Fanny. 'A few more moments' thought of you would uncrystallize and dissolve me – I must not give way to it – but turn to my writing again.'[19]

Yet when he did so she only reappeared. Keats had rejected Brown's proposals for the last Act of *Otho the Great* as over-ingenious and he was determined to frame the finale after his own ideas. His hero, the now maddened Ludolph, becomes in part at least a vehicle for Keats's own violently ambiguous feelings. At the start of the play, Ludolph's father had forbidden him to marry the poisonous Auranthe but relented when Ludolph came to his aid in war. Auranthe betrays Ludolph and, in the ecstasy of his madness, he conjures up a picture of her that bears a close resemblance to Fanny:

> wonder at her, friends, she is so fair;
> Deep blue eyes, semi-shaded in white lids,
> Finished with lashes fine for more soft shade,
> Completed by her twin-arched ebon brows;
> White temples of exactest elegance,
> Of even mould felicitous and smooth;
> Cheeks fashioned tenderly on either side,
> So perfect, so divine that our poor eyes
> Are dazzled with the sweet proportioning,
> And wonder that 'tis so – the magic chance![20]

This is the woman who has betrayed the hero and whom Ludolph himself must kill. If Auranthe is a Regency belle, beautiful but dangerous, she is also the sacrificial beast the hero must immolate on the altar of his wrath. It is in the agony of this psycho-sexual torment that Ludolph dies, the victim of a woman and of love the destroyer.

The play was finished, but Keats's ill-luck continued to dog him. Four or five days after completing the tragedy, he read in the press that Kean, the one actor who could make a success of the role of Ludolph, was setting off on an American tour and was unlikely even to consider the work before the next season. This was 'the worst news I could have had'. Keats's theatrical hopes were dashed. His financial straits were now desperate and were made the more pressing by the fact that on 23 August he had written to his publisher asking for a loan that was to be secured by Brown against receipts from their play.

The harsh and inelegant tone of this letter to Taylor reveals Keats's embarrassment and his almost total incapacity for business. 'You will perceive that I do not write to you till I am forced by necessity; that I am sorry for.'[21] After this unpropitious start, he outlined his problems: the threatened Chancery suit against Tom's estate, the failure of his friends to repay what he had lent them, and the fact that Keats himself had been obliged to borrow money from Brown who was 'not at all flush'. Having mentioned the tragedy (but not the amount he would like to borrow) Keats went on to discuss his career in a manner hardly designed to appease a publisher.

The need to earn money focused once again the difficult question of courting an audience whose taste Keats distrusted. In his anxious state, his disparaging what he knew to be a readership with a significant female element became mixed with his fear of women in general and of love in particular. 'I feel every confidence that if I choose I may be a popular writer; that I will never be; but for all that I will get a livelihood – I equally dislike the favour of the public with the love of a woman – they are both a cloying treacle to the wings of independence.' Taylor, who was ill at the time, was baffled by such passages, but the following sentence must have dismayed him: 'I shall ever consider them (People) as debtors to me for verses, not myself to them for admiration – which I can do without.'[22]

The following day Keats reiterated these points to Reynolds. 'I feel it in my power to become a popular Writer – I feel it in my strength to refuse the poisonous suffrage of a public.'[23] He was battling to preserve the integrity of his vision, and what he described to Taylor as 'the pride and egotism' of the writer's solitary life formed a protection against the intrusion of merely practical matters. Keats would not allow these to shape his development. That had to be an inward process, a long and patient observation of the rhythms of his consciousness. True poetry came from this, not from manufacturing verse tales for the marketplace. And it was because of this integrity that the buyers in the marketplace should be grateful to him rather than vice versa. The irony lay in the fact that, having squandered his energies to please the public with a play it now seemed had no chance of performance, there was an urgent need to assemble a volume of poems for the press. Less than a fortnight later, Keats completed *Lamia*.

The polish and high sophistication of this poem, its ironies, ambiguities and occasional lapses, are closely associated with Keats's ambivalent attitude towards his public and the reshaping of his ideas on romance that resulted from this. He was resolved that *Lamia* would not indulge the popular fantasies of the 'mawkish'. He would also try to avoid the 'inexperience of life, and simplicity of knowledge' shown in *Endymion*, the work the public still knew him by if they knew him at all. Finally, Keats would try to please those with a 'knowledge of the world'. He aimed at a romance that questioned the nature of romance itself and planned a work which, he hoped, would 'take hold of people in some way — give them either pleasant or unpleasant sensation. What they want is a sensation of some sort.'[24] The insecurity, the aggressive—defensive attitude to the public, is patent and conditions the whole poem.

Keats had already finished the first part of *Lamia* when Brown arrived in Shanklin. Lamia herself and the hero Lycias were happily lost to the world in magic and erotic reverie. Now, when Keats began the second part, he resolved to emphasise the way in which the illusory escapism of romance destroys itself from the inside. The conventional happy ending occurs half-way through the poem, and now, in the second Book, secret delight gives way to public humiliation and death. The implication is that romance is purchased with a lie but is destroyed at the cost of wonder and delight. Between these mutually exclusive modes of perception the hero himself dies.

Such destruction at the hands of a female has been implicit from the start. Lamia, who has once been a woman and is now a snake (the fact that we are not told the reason for this metamorphosis contributes greatly to her enigmatic being), has the magic power of fancy to send her spirit wherever she wishes, and in Corinth she has spied out the handsome Lycias. Her existence 'as a palpitating snake' becomes onerous to her and to free herself from it she strikes a deal with the love-besotted Hermes. If he will transform her back into a woman, she will give him the nymph she has protected with invisibility. Lamia's enigmatic nature is again clear. She moves easily between the worlds of gods and humans without herself being truly of either, and, though she is destructive, she is also a protector. Eventually, the deal between Lamia and Hermes is struck. The god has his nymph and disappears with her into that world of once upon a time where dreams are real and lovers never grow pale. The fictional nature of this world is clear, and the poem emphasises its artifice, its romance. Here is the life of pagan sexual revelry which Haydon had claimed was suitable only for a world that did not recognise the reality of pain. The truly human world, the boundary of which Lamia now wishes to cross, is far otherwise.

To make her transition, Lamia must metamorphose herself. By a further paradox, to do so, to recreate herself as 'a lady bright', she must spoil her exquisite serpentine beauty. Keats had previously made much of this:

> She was a gordian shape of dazzling hue,
> Vermilion-spotted, golden, green, and blue;
> Striped like a zebra, freckled like a pard,
> Eyed like a peacock, and all crimson barred;
> And full of silver moons, that, as she breathed,
> Dissolved, or brighter shone, or interwreathed
> Their lustres with the gloomier tapestries –
> So rainbow-sided, touched with miseries,
> She seemed, at once, some penanced lady elf,
> Some demon's mistress, or the demon's self.[25]

Beauty and danger coil about each other in Lamia's serpentine form while, to further the ambiguity, Keats's polished and urbane couplets, which show his close study of Dryden, are counterpointed to the mysterious and romantic figure they describe. This is no Cockney versifying but a studiously imaginative recreation of the Augustan mode Keats had once disparaged.

The orgiastic convulsions of Lamia's metamorphosis into a woman, the spoliation of her serpentine beauty, again associate female sexuality with destruction and illusion, themes emphasised once more in her seduction of her victim Lycias. For Lamia's beauty is the bait that lures an ideal young man: a victorious and happy sportsman, prompt to his religious duties and willingly disciplined by philosophical studies. But what Lamia's new beauty covers is a lie. Her enigmatic shape-shifting denies the painful knowledge won from the vale of soul-making, denies the wisdom of the odes and their belief that joy and pain are a continuum from which identity emerges. What *Lamia* offers is apparent freedom from this essentially human process. She is:

> Not one hour old, yet of sciential brain
> To unperplex bliss from its neighbour pain,
> Define their pettish limits, and estrange
> Their points of contact, and swift counterchange . . .[26]

A 'lovely graduate of Cupid's college', Lamia seduces Lycias by entangling him in the all-too-human fantasy of a life of undivided bliss, the make-believe world of romance embodied in the fantastic and illusory palace Lamia creates for herself and her lover.

Lamia's finely wrought illusions will crumble at a glance from the real world and, in particular, under the stare of Lycias' philosophy tutor, the rational and critical Apollonius. Yet it is inherent in the nature of Lycias' humanity that even in the temple of his delight – his 'purple-lined palace of sweet sin' – he needs to greet the agents of his destruction. Perpetual bliss denies the reality of mankind's emotions forever shifting from joy to pain. Even unstinting love cloys and Cupid grows restless. The spirit of the satiated lover 'frets for the noisy world', grows angry at restraint, and takes a sadistic pleasure in reviling his mistress's protests. And, we are told, Lamia 'loved the tyranny'. Bullied and subdued, she eventually agrees to Lycias' desires. She will allow him to show her to his friends. Keats's comment on this passage fittingly captures its chauvinism. 'Women love to be forced to do a thing, by a fine fellow – *such as this*.'[27] Such facile cynicism is an attempt to appeal to those readers with a 'knowledge of the world', readers of whom Keats himself, in truth, had very little knowledge.

The 'herd' of guests approach the fabulously bedecked banqueting chamber. Among them is the uninvited Apollonius, under whose fixed and philosophical stare the wine-brightened festivity collapses. The 'lashless eyelids' of the old man suggest the destructive, snakelike power of rational intelligence. The beautiful illusion reared by the serpentine Lamia plunges towards suffering and death under Apollonius' reptilian gaze:

> Do not all charms fly
> At the mere touch of cold philosophy?
> There was an awful rainbow once in heaven:
> We know her woof, her texture; she is given
> In the dull catalogue of common things.

Philosophy will clip an Angel's wings,
Conquer all mysteries by rule and line,
Empty the haunted air, and gnomèd mine –
Unweave a rainbow, as it erewhile made
The tender-personed Lamia melt into a shade.[28]

The narrative dramatises the irreconcilable conflict between two fundamental modes of being. Lamia's insubstantial palace of 'sweet sin', the seat of fantasy and delight, seems to satisfy the craving for pleasure inherent even in the well-balanced and contented young man Lycias is before he meets her. The delights Lamia offer are not a refuge from anguish but a revelation of a fatal desire for the joys of the body and the imagination. Unalloyed, these are false, yet 'truth', or the world represented by Apollonius, is chilly, limited and insufficient. It brings death as surely as Lamia herself does. There is no suggestion of moral judgement here. Lamia wreaks destruction but is not consciously wicked, while Apollonius destroys a pleasure and delight founded on a lie. The poem presents the tragedy of the irreconcilably divided nature of human consciousness whose only issue is death.

By 5 September the poem was finished. Although Keats somewhat dismissively referred to it as being only a 'short' work, it was an important contribution to the projected new volume. It seemed, too, that his financial affairs were looking up. No sooner was *Lamia* completed than Keats heard that Haslam had repaid some of the money he owed him but had sent it to the wrong address. Brown, who, in a few days' time, was to visit the Snooks at Bedhampton, had also managed to find a further £30, while it seemed that Taylor and Hessey were prepared to advance a similar amount.

But this last loan was not quite as straightforward as it appeared. Hessey had sent Keats's awkward letter, now annotated with a few points of his own, to Woodhouse. The publisher had lost money on *Endymion* and Keats's new scorn for the public did not bode well. Woodhouse tried to elucidate Keats's true state of mind. 'It is not in my opinion personal pride, but literary pride which his letter shows,' Woodhouse wrote.[29] Keats's egotism was that of the true poet conscious of the great tradition to which he belongs. It was a tradition which some had suffered grievously to maintain. Slender as his own resources were, Woodhouse was resolved to do what he could to spare Keats from this. 'Whatever People regret that they could not do for Shakespeare or Chatterton, because he did not live in their times, that I would embody into a Rational principle and, (with due regard to certain expediencies) do for Keats.' Woodhouse now sent £50 of his own money to Hessey and asked that £30 be immediately forwarded to the poet in the guise of a sum offered by the firm. The remaining £20 was to be held in reserve until Keats's real needs had been ascertained.

Here was the disinterestedness of deep friendship, but the mood of release it prompted was short-lived. Five days after receiving Woodhouse's money, and while Keats was deeply engaged on his revisions to *Hyperion*, a letter arrived from George. He had lost as much as half of his own money, probably in the Mississippi steamboat venture, and was desperate. It was now no longer a question of raising capital but of finding money for decent survival. George asked if Keats would go and see Abbey and find out what could be done.

Keats caught the night coach to London and, after a journey of twelve hours, arrived at Abbey's office at nine on the Friday morning. Abbey would not be hurried and, observing that 'he should drink tea at that hour', agreed to discuss George's affairs with Keats at seven the following Monday evening.[30] 'He realy appeared anxious about it; promised he would forward your money as quickly as possible,' Keats wrote. Meanwhile, there was the weekend to fill. On Saturday morning Keats visited his publishers. Hessey was in the office, and it fell to him to temporise with Keats's insistence they bring out a volume of all his recent poems, save *Isabella*, for Christmas. Woodhouse, who was also there, noted that Hessey told Keats 'it would not answer to do so now.' Seeing how anxious Keats was, Woodhouse invited him to a Sunday breakfast at the Temple, the only free time he had before leaving on the afternoon coach for Weymouth.

London seemed strange. Keats walked the streets as if in a foreign land. Apart from Rice and Woodhouse, nobody was in town. The Dilkes, Reynolds and Taylor were all away, Haydon was bathing for his health at Hastings. Fanny Brawne, of course, was at Wentworth Place, but Keats did not dare to visit her there. Although he had promised he would 'flit to you and back', now he knew he could not do so. Her presence would obtrude too violently on his perplexed mood. The promise of joy she radiated threatened him. 'I cannot bear the pain of being happy: 'tis out of the question.' Eventually, he found himself at Covent Garden, got in for half price, and spent the night at his publishers' office.

The following morning he went to visit Woodhouse. He had

brought his manuscripts with him and read out *Lamia* in a mumbling, chanting tone. Then the two men turned to *The Eve of St. Agnes*. Keats tried to defend the alterations he had made. He believed the wonderful original conclusion that snatches the lovers out of their vivid, present-tense reality into the world of history was wrong. He was terrified by what he thought of as his own sentimentality, and now he wanted 'to leave on the reader a sense of pettish disgust'.[31] Woodhouse demurred, but other proposed changes made him anxious. Keats's attempting to please those with a 'knowledge of the world' was threatening not only the balance of the work itself but its chances of commercial success, for Woodhouse now discovered that Keats wanted to make the sexuality of the poem explicit and had revised the stanza which suggests the lovers' union to make this clear.

While Woodhouse himself had no moral objections to this and, indeed, saw some poetic merit in what Keats had achieved, he recognised the danger. When he raised objections however, he was treated to an angry riposte. Keats told him he did not want 'ladies to read his poetry'. He wrote for men. Keats insisted that Porphyro's satisfying of his desire with Madeline had to be explicit, and went on to claim he would 'despise a man who would be such a eunuch in sentiment as to leave a maid, with that Character about her, in such a situation'.

What Keats considered to be his previous sentimentality made him cringe, and *Isabella* was particularly to be condemned in this respect. He would not consent to publishing a work that seemed to him so conspicuously 'mawkish'. Woodhouse wondered what he meant by this and tried to define Keats's use of this word. For his own part, Woodhouse had been moved by *Isabella* (as indeed the critics were to be) and he was puzzled by what he considered as Keats's wrong-headed self-depreciation. 'The feeling of mawkishness seems to me', Woodhouse wrote, 'to be that which comes upon us where any thing of great tenderness & excessive simplicity is met with when we are not in a sufficiently tender & simple frame of mind to bear it: when we experience a sort of revulsion, or resiliency (if there be such a word) from the sentiment or expression.'[32] Having satisfied himself on this point, Woodhouse then began to apply it to Keats's poem: 'I believe there is nothing in any of the most passionate parts of Isabella to excite this feeling. It may, as may Lear, leave the reader far behind: but there is none of that sugar & butter sentiment that cloys & disgusts.' But Keats was not to be won over. He felt his reputation was at stake and the image of a jeering public alarmed him. 'I shall persist in not publishing The Pot of Basil,' he wrote a few days later. 'There is too much inexperience of live [*for* life] in it . . . which might do very well after one's death – but not while one is alive.' It was essential to be more calculating. 'I intend to use more finesse with the Public.' He went on: 'it is possible to write fine things which cannot be laugh'd at in any way. Isabella is what I should call if I were a reviewer "A weak-Poem" with an amusing sober-sadness about it.' Only his most recent work seemed to solve these problems. 'There is no objection of this kind to Lamia,' Keats claimed, 'a good deal to St. Agnes Eve – only not so glaring.'[33]

After parting from Woodhouse, Keats decided to call on the Wylies, where he was invited for dinner. This was not an easy occasion. Mrs Wylie brought out a lock of her grandchild's hair, but Keats felt he could not tell her the news from George. There seemed no point in worrying her about the problems her daughter and her family might face if he were unable to raise money for them. He tried instead to get through the evening with light-hearted gossip and 'quizzing' before going back to sleep at his publishers' office. There, the following morning, Keats wrote a letter to Fanny Brawne. His anxiety and depression were patent. He did not dare to see her. To visit Hampstead would be 'venturing into a fire' and he would not risk it. 'If I were to see you to day it would destroy the half comfortable sullenness I enjoy at present in dow[n]right perplexities.' The intensity of his passion was a burden to him and his exhaustion made him cruel. 'Knowing well that my life must be passed in fatigue and trouble, I have been endeavouring to wean myself from you.' But he knew this was hopeless. 'I cannot cease to love you.' He hardly knew what he was doing. 'Am I mad or not?'

He decided to pass some of Monday morning with his sister in Walthamstow, and, when he returned, the letter to Fanny was still in his pocket. He had been unable to post it, and now, as Keats entered the City, he became aware that a tremendous crowd was gathering. Upwards of 300,000 people were thronging the streets to welcome Orator Hunt, the hero of Peterloo and those liberals horrified by the blood-letting at that otherwise peaceful protest. From Islington to Highgate, along Cheapside, Ludgate Hill and Fleet Street red banners hung from the crowded windows. The people in the streets wore red cockades on their hats. Bands played and the crowds followed Hunt in his coach drawn by six bays. A young lad of fifteen or sixteen, wounded at Peterloo, excited general pity and admiration. Here was the pathetic symbol of all the country was enduring: poverty, repression, an unrepresentative government heedless of the majority it ruled. Waves of indignation rolled through the multitude, but all were resolved to show this was a peaceable, lawful demonstration against murder and injustice. When voices rose to a tumult, a cry of 'Order' ran through the crowd and the great procession again became docile. Keats was deeply stirred. For the moment he could rise above the anxiety George's affairs had forced on him and even forget the unposted letter in his pocket. 'This is no conflict between whig and tory,' he wrote, 'but between right and wrong.'[34]

Abbey meanwhile was waiting in his office. He had resolved on an appearance of helpfulness. Something would have to be done and 'as quickly as possible'. Keats showed him George's letter. It seemed to have some effect, for Abbey was the sort of man who would 'not see the necessity of a thing till he is hit in the mouth'. He undertook to raise the money for George on Tom's estate and to hurry along the lawyers involved in the Chancery case. He managed to convince Keats 'that he was anxious to bring the Business to an issue', but hinted that dealing with legal men was a time-consuming process. Keats at once offered to stay in town and be Abbey's messenger. Abbey turned the offer down and began instead to talk of poetry and literary fame. A magazine article he had come across contained a disparaging passage on the subject from Byron's *Don Juan*. Abbey now read it aloud. Byron's 'flash poem' and his laughing at the folly of literary ambition were just to Abbey's taste, despite his dislike for Byron himself. Putting the magazine down he declared, 'the fellow says true things now & then.'[35]

Having endured this, Keats walked up Cheapside and then, remembering the still unposted letter to Fanny, turned towards the General Post Office in Lombard Street, where he found he had missed the last collection. Crossing back through Bucklersbury, he encountered Abbey once more. He had now shut up his premises and was walking to Poultry, where he had his hat-making business. Again he raised the familiar topic. 'I do believe', Keats wrote despondently, 'if I could be a hatter I might be one.' But, for the moment, all he could do was return to Winchester. It seemed that everything he had striven for lay in ruins. 'What is the end of Fame?' Byron had asked and replied that it was merely filling up so much 'uncertain paper'. Hessey had been unenthusiastic about the new volume, and Woodhouse had refused to see the merits of Keats's revisions to *The Eve of St. Agnes*. His earlier volumes had failed, and Keats's mind went back to the protest he had seen in London and the works of the radical poetaster Samuel Bamford, author of *The Weaver Boy*. In the eyes of the bigoted there was nothing to choose between them. Now Keats had almost no money and there was little chance that *Otho the Great* would lift him out of 'the mire of a bad reputation' which is 'continually rising against us'. There seemed no way out of this. 'My name with the literary fashionables is vulgar,' he told George, 'I am a weaver boy to them.'

From time to time Keats took out the manuscript of his revision of *Hyperion*, the 'abstract' poem he had been working on intermittently during recent months. What he now called *The Fall of Hyperion. A Dream* is the unfinished epic of the vale of soul-making, and is a poem which reaches into the heart of Keats's mature philosophy to reinterpret his entire career. Many of his central concerns are gathered here. Keats's constantly evolving preoccupation with mythology is once again the vehicle for coming to some spiritual understanding of the nature of suffering and the role of the poet in exploring and trying to heal this. Such concerns inevitably involved consideration of the poet's response to the political and religious controversies of the time, while, like *Sleep and Poetry* and the letter on the Chamber of Maiden Thought, *The Fall of Hyperion* concerns rites of passage and initiation into mysteries. The debate between the poet and the visionary about the place of men who take an active interest in the world, a debate first mentioned in Keats's early epistle to his brother George, is also reopened. In addition, the fragment is suffused with other Keatsian concerns. It is passionately involved with the epic tradition, particularly as embodied by Milton and Dante. It urges understanding through empathy and emphasises how the intellect must be schooled by the heart. Finally, the poem displays a refusal of the dogmatic and affirms that essentially Keatsian openness to experience which doubts even the validity of its own intuitions.

This is clear from the opening paragraph. The narrator is uncertain whether his dream is the vision of a true poet or the illusion of a fanatic. Only after his death will others be able to decide this. Thus, at the very start of the poem, Keats hands his work to future generations and their continuing cultural and spiritual debate. The idea that 'truth' is relative, that the passage of history insists that insights evolve and decay, is suggested here. So too is the notion that poetry, like religious vision, has its origins in the imagination. To a large degree, indeed, they are comparable: acts of the spirit whereby man interprets himself to himself.

In this world of evolution, the individual must grow. The narrator's progress through the opening sections is an allegory of Keats's own development away from the bowers and innocent gorging on the sweets of nature that belong to 'the realm of Flora' and *Endymion*. The poem suggests that the appetite for such things is soon sated and seems to lead naturally to something more challenging. The 'domineering potion' the narrator drinks from one of the vessels he finds at the banquet causes him to fall asleep and, when he wakes, it is to find the world transformed. He is now facing 'an old sanctuary'. He has moved from the realm of innocent pleasure and the 'Life of Sensations' to the world of history, from delight to a deepening consciousness of pain.

To the dreaming narrator, the awesome temple seems objectively to exist, to be a physical fact. The reader realises it is quite as much a creation of the dreamer's mind, an epitome of the aeons of existence in which life on earth has evolved from the sway of the Titans to the present day. The immense antiquity of the place is at one with the melancholy sense of things outgrown, in particular of superseded religious beliefs. The 'strange vessels and large draperies', the censers and 'holy jewelleries' piled on the floor, suggest objects from the pagan and Judaeo-Christian faiths which are now outgrown. Death, loss and relinquished modes of faith prompt the idea that all man's deepest beliefs are the children of time. There is no faith he has not outgrown.

This was a challenging vision, for it struck at the heart of the contemporary Tory myth and its opposition to the free-thinking of the Enlightenment and the ideals underlying the French Revolution. Current Tory thought had 'put a stop to the rapid progress of free sentiments in England', Keats wrote, 'and gave our Court hopes of turning back to the despotism of the 16 century. They have made a handle of this event [i.e. the French Revolution] in every way to undermine our freedom. They spread a horrid superstition against all in[n]ovation and improvement. The present struggle in England of the people is to destroy this superstition.'[36] On the political front, this struggle showed itself in the mass meetings that culminated in the Peterloo massacre and Hunt's triumphant entry into London. On the religious front, it showed itself in the activities and trials of Richard Carlisle, the deist bookseller and well-known radical thinker. 'He has been selling deistical pamphlets, republished Tom Payne and many other works held in superstitious horror,' Keats wrote to George. 'He even has been selling for some time immense numbers of a work call[ed] "The Deist" which comes out in weekly numbers.'

Carlisle was now bravely leading his own defence, and the *Examiner* spoke for liberal opinion when it inveighed against the Society for the Suppression of Vice which was instituting the proceedings against him.

On 8 August 1819, Hunt wrote a leader to show that such works as Carlisle was circulating were not atheistic and immoral and would not lead to the collapse of social order. 'The irreligious tracts which the Reformers are accused of recommending and circulating are not only Deistical, but devoutly so. They lay great stress not merely on the existence of a God, but on his infinite goodness and benevolence.' In this the morality they preached was far superior to that revealed by those who were proceeding against Carlisle and, throughout the summer, Hunt's anticlerical tone became ever more passionate. It was only too evident, as Paine himself had made clear, that institutionalised religion was often mere priestcraft in league with repression. Man must strive for a more authentic spiritual life.

The Fall of Hyperion is a poet's contribution to this debate. When the narrator wakes from his drugged sleep he is faced with a purgatorial trial, a test of his inmost depth of resource. The vast and cloudy form of Moneta, the last of the Titans, goddess of memory and mother of the Muses, challenges him to mount the steps to where she is ministering at an altar. The effort required is prodigious and terrifying – a dying into life which can only be undergone by the true poet rather than the idle dreamer. Moneta insists there is a complete division between these two, and both are less than those who actually serve the world of human misery. This distinction, the placing of literature below social commitment, reappears in Keats's letters of this time. 'I am convinced more and more day by day that fine writing is next to fine doing,' he told Reynolds. Yet, as he wrote to Dilke, 'I am fit for nothing but literature.' It was essential he sound the full worth of his vocation.

Moneta taunts the narrator with the idea that he might be merely one of the dreaming tribe, and his efforts to refute this are as demanding as his ascent of the marble steps. Poetry must be involved with the 'great world' rather than in retreat from it, and the true poet is seen, in the narrator's words, as a 'humanist physician to all men'. Past indulgence in fantasy must be rejected and, having confronted death and his real nature, the narrator must find the strength to contemplate the endless suffering of the world. The process is symbolised by his being able to look on the face of Moneta herself and witness her timeless knowledge of anguish:

> Then saw I a wan face,
> Not pined by human sorrows, but bright-blanched
> By an immortal sickness which kills not;
> It works a constant change, which happy death

Can put no end to; deathwards progressing
To no death was that visage; it had passed
The lily and the snow; and beyond these
I must not think now, though I saw that face –
But for her eyes I should have fled away.[37]

The supreme state of negative capability is this sympathy with suffering, and it qualifies the narrator to look on the tragedy of the Titans and know himself a poet. His is the inner resource to take on the full burden of modern consciousness whose agony is like death itself and which must be borne alone. There is no 'stay or prop', no comfortable church, no easy faith. At the head of the 'grand march of intellect', all the modern poet can rely on is his 'own weak mortality'. In the vale of soul-making, he alone is responsible for his spiritual destiny. In this, Keats speaks for those who were to follow him, poets whose commitment to the imagination and the spirit could not be sustained by the conventional social order and the conventional forms of religious belief. Through his profound subjectivity, Keats as the narrator of this poem becomes an exemplar of much that poetry itself would have to become – the heroic tradition of individual spiritual experiment. At this most profound point in his work, Keats takes on an almost allegorical status, the fulfilment of his own insight that 'a Man's life of any worth is a continual allegory.'[38] This was a quality Keats had once attributed to Shakespeare, but it is a quality that may also – and superbly – be attributed to him.

During these weeks of trial, the beauty of Winchester and the surrounding countryside were a great consolation to Keats. The demure and secretive cathedral city delighted him. The quiet streets with their black front doors and all but silent lion's-head knockers were less obtrusive than the arrangements at Shanklin. Winchester was 'a respectable, ancient, aristocratical place' comfortably locked in its past. The atmosphere was like that of Keats's own *Eve of Saint Mark*, which he now copied out for George and Georgiana. 'There is not one loom or any thing like manufacturing beyond bread and & butter in the whole City,' he wrote, and it was easy to stroll out into the countryside. Keats usually took a walk for an hour before dinner, passing the beautiful cathedral front, some tree-shaded courts, some meadows and 'a country alley of gardens' until he arrived at the venerable charity foundation of Saint Cross. After that the river and the water-meadows lay before him. He knew moments of exquisite happiness. 'I am surprized myself at the pleasure I live alone in,' he told Reynolds on 21 September. 'How beautiful the season is now – How fine the air. A temperate sharpness about it. Really, without joking, chaste weather – Dian skies – I never liked stubble fields so much as now – Aye better than the chilly gleam of the Spring. Somehow a stubble-plain looks warm – in the same way that some pictures look warm – This struck me so much on my sunday's walk that I composed upon it.' The poém was the ode 'To Autumn':

> Season of Mists and mellow fruitfulness,
>   Close bosom-friend of the maturing sun,
> Conspiring with him how to load and bless
>   With fruit the vines that round the thatch-eves run;
> To bend with apples the mossed cottage-trees,
>   And fill all fruit with ripeness to the core;
>   To swell the gourd, and plump the hazel shells
>   With a sweet kernel; to set budding more,
> And still more, later flowers for the bees,
> Until they think warm days will never cease,
>   For summer has o'er-brimmed their clammy cells.[39]

Keats's reference in his letter to the visual arts hints at one element of his inspiration, and the ode 'To Autumn' captures something of the 'opaqueness and solemnity' in the landscapes of Claude and Poussin. We are asked to contemplate Keats's images as we might an old master. As the poem progresses, a series of personified figures working in the fields and barns creates an image of Autumn as the tutelary spirit of the season. Each stanza presents a different aspect of this. In the first, natural fecundity is stressed. Although mankind has planted the vines and apple trees and probably set the hives for the bees, it is non-human richness that is dominant.

Having established this, the second stanza suggests the fruitful co-operation of man and nature. The feeling for the details of real labour is so strong that the spirit of the season never becomes detached from its specifics. The sense of philosophical observation is strengthened in this way, and the feeling of natural generosity and opiated abundance is powerful. Labour, delight and natural wealth offer the impression of man happy and at peace with the world in which he lives. But again mankind is not seen as the dominant force in this union. Nature's myriad activities, her drifting evening clouds, the 'wailful choir of gnats', the lambs and the robin whistling 'from a garden-croft' are part of the non-human world, unconscious and unaware of the pathos of the cycle of the seasons. Only mankind can ask: 'Where are the songs of spring?' For all the natural wealth amid which he lives, for all his contented labour, the conflict between joy and pain is subtly inscribed in the poem.

The very beauty of autumn is a reminder of winter coming. The 'gathering swallows' twittering in the skies are naturally a part of the season, yet their activity, along with Keats's powerful placing of them in the last line of the poem, suggest winter, change and death. The melancholy of this is for man to feel. Arising out of the beauty of the world around him, he alone is obliged to recognise that he is part of nature and yet separated from her heedless activities by the burden of his consciousness, his awareness of joy and pain. The serenity of Keats's contemplation expresses something of the wisdom learned from staring on the face of Moneta. He can look on the world of pain with a sympathy undiminished by his relative calm. This was both a philosophical position and a new state of maturity observed by many of his friends in Keats himself. 'Some think I lost that poetic ardour and fire 'tis said I once had,' he wrote to George and Georgiana, 'the fact is perhaps I have: but instead of that I hope I shall substitute a more thoughtful and quiet power.'[40]

But the autumn was drawing to its close. 'I should like a bit of fire tonight,' Keats told Woodhouse on 21 September. He had been out for a walk and there was an edge of winter in the air. His mind noted scenes which seemed to be at one with the season. 'How glorious the Blacksmiths' look now. I stood to night before one till I was verry near listing for one.' Such tranquil, melancholy enjoyment was at one with the type of poetry Keats now wanted to write and the sort of life he wanted to lead. 'I am more frequently, now, contented to read and think – but now & then haunted with ambitious thoughts. Qui[e]ter in my pulse, improved in my digestion; exerting myself against vexing speculations – scarcely content to write the best verses for the fever they leave behind. I want to compose without this fever. I hope one day I shall.'

Such tranquillity could only be temporarily known, and circumstances were now conspiring to destroy all hopes of it. Both Keats's art and his way of life had reached a crisis. Woodhouse and Reynolds were pressing him to gather his recent poetry together with a view to publishing a new volume, but, with the exception of *Lamia*, Keats's verses seemed inadequate to him, work that fell below what he now felt to be 'the true voice of feeling'. His daily life would also have to undergo a change. His financial needs and what he saw as his duty towards George and his family meant he would have to get paid work. Journalism seemed the only option, and Keats hoped Hazlitt might get him work on the *Edinburgh Review*.

This change of direction was not made without idealism. Orator Hunt's triumphal procession through London had stirred Keats deeply, and, for all that he recognised his relative naivety in political matters, he felt there was now a genuine possibility of political progress. 'All civil[is]ed countries become gradually more enlighten'd and there should be a continual change for the better,' he told George.[41] Writing to Dilke, he conveyed something of his new excitement. The recent political events had put him 'into spirits', and this was no facile optimism. 'Not withstand[ing] my aristocratic temper I cannot help being very much pleas'd with the present public proceedings,' he wrote. Now he wanted to be a part of them. It was fundamental to Keats's vocation that the poet was a physician to mankind, and 'I hope sincerely I shall be able to put a Mite of help to the Liberal side of the Question.'[42]

It was clear that Keats was facing a major change in his life and he felt the need to look back on his career. 'To night I am all in a mist,' he told Reynolds. 'I scarcely know what's what – But you knowing my unsteady & vagarish disposition, will guess that all this turmoil will be settled by tomorrow morning. It strikes me tonight that I have led a very odd sort of life for the two or three last years – Here & there – No anchor.'[43] This was true, but in such a brief space of time, and in the last year especially, Keats had undergone the most concentrated and profound development of any poet in the history of English literature.

The Death Warrant

That drop of blood is my death warrant; — I must die.

(*Keats to Brown*)

FOR ALL HIS resolution, Keats stayed on in Winchester for another two weeks. Brown had written saying he wanted to discuss *Otho the Great* with him there and Keats was fully aware of what he owed his friend in both financial and personal terms. The burden weighed on him and made him feel guilty. He accused himself of having lived a 'vicious life' for the last year and told Brown that his dependence on him would only cause more difficulties in the future. 'You will see it as a duty I owe myself to break the neck of it.' The need to take up journalism was trying nonetheless. It threatened the intense idealism with which Keats surrounded his love of literature and seemed to pander to what he most feared: the merely fashionable and insincere. He did his best to convince himself that writing for the press was a lowly business whose skills were easily acquired, and he tried to make light of his own inexperience. He boasted he would quickly learn to 'shine up an article on any thing without much knowledge of the subject, aye like an orange'.[1] But such cynicism does not quite convince. It is the defence of a man obliged to do something opposed to his true nature.

In the meantime, Keats continued his long journal letter to George and Georgiana, trying to raise his spirits by telling them light-hearted stories of a practical joke played on Brown's tenant at Wentworth Place and of a misunderstanding with a couple sharing his own Winchester lodging house. A letter from George brought more 'bad intelligence', but this was slightly offset by reading a report in the *Examiner* which suggested that rumours of Kean's American tour might after all be false. However, when Brown arrived at the end of the month, it was with the knowledge that the actor was still defying the management of Drury

Lane in their attempts to hold him to the terms of his contract. *Otho the Great* stood little chance of being produced now and it was essential Keats return to London and look for work. On 1 October, he wrote to Dilke telling him he would be back in a week's time and asking him to find him 'A Sitting Room and a bed room for myself alone'.

The carefully chosen words were intended to scotch any idea Keats might be planning to elope with Fanny Brawne. He had not seen her for three months and knew that marriage would be out of the question for years to come. The position was intolerable, and there were moments when Keats tried to make light of his true feelings. 'A Man in love I do think cuts the sorryest figure in the world,' he wrote. 'Even when I know the poor fool to be really in pain about it, I could burst out laughing in his face.' On another occasion, he copied out a long and cumbrous passage of anti-feminist polemic from Burton. But none of this prepared him for his meeting with Fanny on Sunday 10 October.

'You dazzled me – There is nothing in the world so bright and delicate.'[2] Writing from the rooms Dilke had found him at 25 College Street, Westminster, Keats poured out the ecstasy of his pain and dependence. He felt himself to be entirely at Fanny's mercy. Any slight threat to her esteem threw him into panic, and always his desire was accompanied by frustration. 'When shall we pass a day alone?' He went to call on Maria Dilke, hoping to persuade her to accompany him to Wentworth Place so that his visit should have an appearance of respectability. He saw himself as Chaucer's doomed young lover Troilus and ended his letter with an apt quotation: 'Ah hertè mine!'

Over the next few days, the extent of Keats's obsession revealed itself. After seeing Fanny, he had returned to his lodgings in turmoil. It is possible that he made some effort to find some employment among the magazine editors, but it is clear that his resolution quickly evaporated. Fanny alone preoccupied him to the extent that he could not work. The fine hopes of independence he had nursed, the sense of a new life starting with his commitment to liberal politics and the ideal of trying to shape and encourage public opinion at a time when any other form of political action was out of the question – all this collapsed under the insidious and as yet hidden symptoms of tuberculosis. Weakened and in emotional extremes, unaware that he was hopelessly bound for death, Keats surrendered to his obsession, to the image of Fanny he had created and which now tyrannised him. Ill-health and the agonising frustration of desire exhausted him.

All he could think about was seeing Fanny again – 'my love', as he wrote, 'has made me selfish.' But if she roused his ardour to its peak it seemed that, in so doing, she also threatened to destroy him. 'You have absorb'd me. I have a sensation at the present moment as though I was dissolving.'[3] He could not, as he had hoped, find happiness away from her presence, while closeness to her brought intense pain. He felt himself a martyr and struggled in vain to free himself from his suffering. 'You have ravish'd me away by a Power I cannot resist; and yet I could resist till I saw you; and ever since I have seen you I have endeavoured often "to reason against the reasons of my love".'[4] Now he would no longer try. The pain was too great.

The darker element in this passion still lingered, even if it did not show itself fully in his letters. The obverse of Keats's ardour was that deep-seated neurosis about women which revealed itself now as a fear of being irrevocably committed. While marriage was out of the question, Keats knew it was the only way in which he would ever be able to satisfy his desire, but if his mind ran constantly on the imagined pleasures of marriage, his continuing annotations to his copy of Burton show how he feared it. He marked his doubts against the reasons Burton advanced for wedlock, wrote 'aye, aye' beside his arguments against it, and underlined the comment that seemed to strike home most directly. 'The bond of marriage is adamantine; no hope of loosing it; thou art undone.'

His friends grew concerned. Dilke noted that Keats's 'whole mind & heart were in a whirl of contending passions – he saw nothing calmly and dispassionately.' Observing the serious state he was in, Mrs Brawne suggested he come to Hampstead for the weekend. Keats left his lodgings on Friday for a 'three days dream' in which he resolved on his course of action. When he returned to Westminster his mind was made up. On Tuesday 19 October, he left his lodgings and went over to see the Dilkes. Would Mrs Dilke tell Fanny he had decided to move back to Hampstead? Then he wrote to Fanny himself. He was clearly afraid of the peril he was placing himself in. 'I must impose chains upon myself. I shall be able to do nothing,' but he had, he told her, 'several things to speak to you of tomorrow morning'. These almost certainly included a formal engagement, and the next day Keats was back living in Wentworth Place. He gave Fanny a garnet ring as a symbol of their betrothal, but he was far from settled. 'My mind is in a tremble, I cannot tell what I am writing.' And underneath this turmoil, ruthless and invisible, tuberculosis was entering its active stage. 'I should like to cast the die for Love or death,' Keats had written to Fanny.[5] Now it was cast for both.

Severn was concerned about the state he found Keats in. When he had called on him earlier in Westminster, he had noted how disillusioned he was with his poetry. While Severn himself found much to be impressed by in *Hyperion*, Keats disparaged the work for the very reasons Severn praised it. The Miltonic grandeur impressed the young painter, but Keats said he did not want to write a poem 'that might have been written by John Milton, but one that was unmistakably by no other than John Keats'.[6] It seemed to Severn that the summer had 'not wrought so much good' as he had hoped, and he could see that Keats was now unwell in both body and mind. Moods of listless apathy alternated with high excitement. In order to try and lessen the torments of unsatisfied desire, Keats followed Burton's advice and left off eating meat, but for all this silent discipline he tried to maintain that generosity of spirit which had won him such firm friends. 'He never spoke of anyone but by saying something in their favour,' Severn wrote, 'and this always so agreeably and cleverly, imitating the manner to increase your favourable impression of the person he was speaking of.' Keats strove to be generous even in small things. Severn himself was working on a painting based on a scene from Spenser, and he was delighted when Keats was able to quote the relevant stanza by heart. It told of the moment when Una snatches the dagger from the Red Cross Knight who has been tempted to suicide by the horrors shown him by the giant Despair.

Brown also observed Keats closely. He saw the pain in his eyes and, mistrusting 'his assumed tranquillity of countenance', decided the best thing to do was to interest his friend in work. After months of indecision, Kean had finally bowed to the wishes of his public and started a warmly received winter season at Drury Lane. Surely their play now stood a chance. The script was gone through once more and despatched to the theatre. Keats obliged by helping with revisions, but he refused to put his name to the piece since he was worried that such slight and reprehensible fame as his poetry had might spoil its chances of success. Quite as dangerous, in fact, was Brown's ploy of hinting that the play would be offered to the rival management if a production were not put on that season. Meanwhile, Brown continued to lend Keats money on the strength of his hopes for *Otho*, and he possibly also at this time encouraged him to begin work on another historical drama, this time based on the life of King Stephen. The surviving fragments show a considerable advance over the earlier work, but, despite the efforts Keats put into research – reading Holinshed and Selden, and making an index – he was not in a suitable frame of mind to continue. 'I have been endeavouring to write lately,' he told George and Georgiana, 'but with little success.'

While Brown's intentions in these areas were well meant, other aspects of his behaviour were offensive to Keats. Brown had installed Abigail O'Donaghue, a handsome but ignorant Irish girl, as the maid at Wentworth Place. He was now sleeping with her and she would soon become pregnant. Keats could not look on this with the tolerant complacency characteristic of the men of his age. He was both jealous and disgusted. Brown was able more or less openly to do the one thing society forbade Keats in his relationship with Fanny. His bitter feelings began to enter into his love, distorting it yet further, Brown's 'indecencies' complicating his own feelings to a painful degree.

Meanwhile George's affairs still needed attention. Keats finally received power of attorney in November and made several trips to Abbey's office. Some of the stock inherited from Tom was sold, despite the bad state of the market; £100 was sent to America but did not arrive until late in the New Year. Keats also sold £100 of Tom's inheritance for his own use, money he spent to pay off some debts. Abbey meanwhile was concerned about Keats's career and suggested he find a job as a bookseller. The suggestion was rejected, possibly with some bitterness, for Keats's frustration and fatigue at times made him irritable. He even had a disagreement with Dilke, who had suggested that George would have done better to stick to his original plans and become a farmer in Illinois. As Dilke himself noted: 'the very kindness of friends was at this time felt to be oppressive to him.'[7]

Keats was continuously tired. He confessed to Severn that he had been 'very lax, unemployed, unmeridian'd, and objectless these two months', but along with this lassitude went moments of high excitement. Driven now by the wretched and unpredictable force of illness, Keats was ever more obviously the volatile young man who had once told his publisher he was going to give up poetry for good. To Taylor, he still appeared in the same light. The publisher had been considerably annoyed by what he had learned from Woodhouse about Keats's revisions to his poems. The idea that the sexuality of *The Eve of St. Agnes* should be made explicit was particularly irritating, not because Taylor was a prude but because he knew how disastrously such a proceeding would affect sales. He told Woodhouse he was out of patience with Keats and that if he persisted in his 'Folly' then he would be welcome to take his work elsewhere.[8]

Woodhouse tried to patch things up. From time to time Keats had been in the habit of visiting the artists William Hilton and Peter de Wint. They were friends of Hessey's, and the publisher had possibly thought that Hilton's dour portrait drawing of Keats would make a good frontispiece for his next volume. Keats and Hilton, along with Woodhouse, were invited to dine at the Fleet Street office, where difficulties appear to have been resolved, for *The Eve of St. Agnes* was discussed in a friendly manner. Then, two days later, Keats completely changed his mind. 'I have come to a determination not to publish any new thing I have now ready written,' he told Taylor.[9] He had another project in view. He was thinking of a work which would have the colouring of *The Eve of St. Agnes* but which would show an altogether firmer and more realistic sense of characterisation. He was toying with the life of the Elizabethan Earl of Essex as a subject, and he believed that 'two or three such Poems, if God should spare me, written in the course of the next six years, would be a famous gradus ad Parnassum altisimum. I mean they would nerve me up to the writing of a few fine Plays – my greatest ambition.' He requested some books, but the project never materialised. It seemed impossible to write at all. As he confessed to George: 'Nothing could have in all its circumstances fallen out worse for me than the last year has done, or could be more damping to my poetical talent.'

Then, in his unpredictable state, Keats began to prepare his poems for the press. At Brown's suggestion he also started a work little suited to his temperament, 'a comic faery poem in the Spenser stanza'.[10] Some confusion still surrounds this fragmentary work, *The Cap and the Bells*, also know as the *The Jealousies*. Brown variously claimed that he was privy to all the details while on another occasion claiming the work was 'written subject to future amendment and omissions: it was begun without a plan, and without any prescribed laws for the supernatural machinery.' Again, while Brown suggested that the poem was written principally for relaxation, Keats seemed to have thought of it as a commercial proposition. This was something he still badly needed. He had recently been obliged to write to Haslam for a loan of £30 and had unsuccessfully submitted a poem (possibly the 'Ode to a Grecian Urn') for a prize at the Surrey Institution. He had even extracted a small sum from Abbey. A topical literary satire might appeal to a public revelling in Byron's *Don Juan*, particularly if accompanied with notes by Reynolds, who had had a great success with his parody of Wordsworth's *Peter Bell*.

Byron and the Lake Poets were to be satirized in the poem through the figures of Elfinan and Crafticanto, just as Eban seems to refer to Hazlitt and Hum to Leigh Hunt.[11] At a more personal level, Elfinan's beloved Bertha Pearl possibly refers to the heroine of *The Eve of Saint Mark*, while Keats's use of the Spenserian stanza for satire may have been an attempt to counter his use of the form in the 'smokeable' *Eve of St.*

Agnes. Brown recorded that Keats composed the work with 'the greatest facility', on one occasion writing over one hundred lines in a morning. But the poem cannot be counted a success. Its lack of focus, the welter of Keats's anxieties and his own lack of real engagement ensured this. Satire and comic light verse were, besides, not only inimical to his fullest poetic self, but whenever he had tried such pieces before, as in 'The Castle Builder', the occasional brilliance had been quickly lost.

Keats was well aware of his difficulties with such work. 'You see I cannot get on without writing as boys do at school a few nonsense verses,' he told George. 'I begin them and before I have written six the whim has pass'd.' Keats could not solve, as Byron and Shelly in their very different ways had solved, the problem of writing poetry in a contemporary idiom. His literariness too often stood in the way, and the difficulties this posed were patent. *The Fall of Hyperion* had been given up partly because of its over-use of Miltonic inversions. Keats's pursuit of subtle euphony, so evident in *The Eve of St. Agnes* and the greater odes, was gained at the price of limiting both subject and approach. Yet even while forcing himself down the false road of *The Cap and the Bells*, his mind was running on different ways of writing. It appears that just after completing the fifty-first stanza, in which Bertha, descending to the nadir of verse, embroiders on her sampler the couplet '*Cupid I – do thee defy!*', he broke off to compose something wholly different, a fragment with no clear origin. The lines are at once detached, terrible and intimate:

> This living hand, now warm and capable
> Of earnest grasping, would, if it were cold
> And in the icy silence of the tomb,
> So haunt thy days and chill thy dreaming nights
> That thou would wish thine own heart dry of blood
> So in my veins red life might stream again,
> And thou be conscience-calmed – see here it is –
> I hold it towards you.

The winter of 1820 was cruelly cold. This posed a danger to Keats's health, and on Dr Sawrey's orders some of the money he had drawn from Tom's estate was spent on a thick coat and stout shoes, in which he went visiting. He saw Leigh Hunt, still troubled by financial worries, at his lodging in York Buildings. He went with the Dilkes to their son's speech day at Westminster School, and dined with them on Christmas

Day. Brown was also invited, and when a competition was mooted between him and Dilke as to who could write the better fairy story, Keats was appointed one of the judges along with Reynolds, Rice and Taylor. But despite this conviviality, and the pleasure of knowing that the 'Ode on a Grecian Urn' was to be published in the *Annals of the Fine Arts*, Keats's declining health mingled with frustration over his long, secret engagement to Fanny and his worry about George's finances. A letter from his brother to Mrs Wylie brought bad news. George's needs were now so pressing that he had left his child and newly pregnant wife in Louisville and taken ship from New York to England. He arrived in London at the end of the first week of January and made his way to Wentworth Place.

George stayed in England for three busy weeks. It was eighteen months since the brothers had met, but there is no certain record of how they felt towards each other now. George, certainly, had been changed by his pioneering experiences in America, by his marriage and by fatherhood. He was also extremely worried about the financial position he was in. How much he knew about the situation at Wentworth Place it is difficult to ascertain. Certainly, he was aware of his brother's fondness for Fanny Brawne and clearly he picked up something of the unease that many of Keats's friends felt about the relationship. They had gradually come to know that it was 'quite a settled thing between John Keats and Miss Brawne', but as this unknown commentator added: 'God help them. It's a bad thing for them. The mother says she cannot prevent it and her only hope is that it will go off.'[12] Someone, quite probably one of the Reynolds sisters, told George that Fanny was 'an artful, bad hearted Girl', and he himself noted that she had a tendency to be rude to her sister and mother. Perhaps she felt nervous. Clearly, she did not warm towards George. 'He is no favourite of mine and he never liked me,' she wrote, but she was nonetheless sympathetic to the difficulties he was in.

Solving these was intermingled with a hectic round of social engagements. George made a two-day visit to Haslam, who had forwarded his correspondence. There was dinner with George's in-laws, with Taylor, where Dilke was judged to have won the fairy-story competition, visits to the theatre, a dance at the Dilkes and a dinner with some old friends arranged by Keats himself. But in fact the brothers had little time to talk and Keats's own mood is best revealed by the letter he was writing through this time to Georgiana. While her husband was getting his fill of metropolitan pleasures, Keats was smitten with an increasing weariness and gloom.

Part of this may have been an effort to convince Georgiana that London was as dull as she evidently found pioneering life, but Keats's disillusion went deeper. 'Standing at Charing Cross and looking east west north and South I can see nothing but dullness,' he wrote.[13] He was bored by the 'vapidness of the routine of Society', the mechanical, repetitious talk and behaviour at Hunt's, Haydon's, the Reynoldses' and the Dilkes'. He very quickly became 'piqued' by such trivial incidents as when Abigail O'Donaghue said her father 'was very much like my Shakespeare only he had more colour than the Engraving'. There was so bad an atmosphere at Hilton and de Wint's house when Severn was wrongly disparaged for winning the Academy Gold Medal that Keats walked out. Then, to add to his depression, *Otho the Great* was returned from Covent Garden unread. Possibilities of money from a theatrical success had now wholly disappeared.

On 28 January, George left at six in the morning for Liverpool. Keats saw him off. There were promises of letters, and George took with him manuscript copies he had made of his brother's poems along with a gift of Hazlitt's *Political Essays*. But an unfortunate misunderstanding now occurred. Both brothers believed the sole asset left them was their share of Tom's part of their grandmother's trust fund. In the current low state of the stock-market this was worth only £1350 and there were, besides, debts of Tom's that still had to be paid from it. Furthermore, when Keats had finally got power of attorney, he had drawn a further £300, a third of which was for himself while the rest was equally divided between Fanny Keats and George, whose £100 was still being carried to him in the United States. No more than £1000 remained, of which a part was Fanny's.

Keats, in dire financial straits himself, now took only a third of what was his and believed he had been obliged to lend the rest to George. But George did not see the matter in this light. He reckoned that Keats had spent about £300 of the £500 he had left in England for his brothers. While George regarded this sum as a loan, Keats had thought of it as a gift that in part repaid earlier loans he had himself made to George. A few days later he discovered the money now left to him was £10 less than his debts. What George had done 'was not fair, was it?' he asked. Then he added, 'Brown, he ought not to have asked me.' Writing to Fanny Brawne, Keats tried to put a brave face on things. 'George ought not to have done this,' he repeated, 'he should have reflected that I wish to marry myself – but I suppose having a family to provide for makes a man selfish.'[14]

The cruellest irony was that each brother was entitled to some £1300 of their grandfather's money still lying in Chancery. There was no need for the desperate worry at all, yet the remorseless pressures on Keats's life meant, as Brown now discovered to his horror, that Keats was dosing himself with laudanum. When questioned about this, Keats promised he would 'never take another drop' without letting his friend know, but then, on 3 February, the full horror of his plight was suddenly revealed.

Keats was returning to Hampstead on the late-evening coach and, because of a respite in the weather, was riding cheaply on the outside without his greatcoat. The chill air bit him to the bone. Staggering from the stop in Pond Street, he burst into Wentworth Place like a man wildly drunk. Brown at once asked him if he were feverish. '"Yes, yes," he answered, "I was on the outside of the stage this bitter day till I was severely chilled, – but now I don't feel it. Fevered! – of course, a little."' Brown at once suggested he go to bed and Keats calmly complied. Brown's own account captures what ensued:

> I followed with the best immediate remedy in my power. I entered his chamber as he leapt into bed. On entering the cold sheets, before his head was on the pillow, he slightly coughed, and I heard him say, – 'That is blood from my mouth.' I went towards him; he was examining a single drop of blood upon the sheet. 'Bring me the candle, Brown; and let me see this blood.' After regarding it steadfastly, he looked up in my face, with a calmness of countenance that I can never forget, and said, – 'I know the colour of that blood; – it is arterial blood; – I cannot be deceived in that colour; – that drop of blood is my death-warrant; – I must die.'[15]

A second, much larger haemorrhage followed a few hours later. Blood from a vessel broken by his coughing rushed into Keats's lungs and he felt he was suffocating. With great self-restraint he merely mumbled to Brown, 'This is unfortunate,' but he thought he was dying and, as he later told Fanny, his mind was filled only with images of her.

The gravity of the situation was clear to all, and Keats was placed on the gruesome regimen reserved for consumptives. Mr Rodd, the surgeon of Hampstead High Street, came to bleed him and Keats was put on a near starvation diet. He complained he was greatly weakened, and he was now obliged to spend long hours either in bed or, which he much preferred, lying on the sofa in the front parlour looking out of the window. The small happenings of daily life became intensely vivid to him. He wrote copiously of these to his sister. A passing pot-boy, the delivery of the coal, gipsies and 'a fellow with a wooden clock under his arm that strikes a hundred and more', all began to fascinate him. He watched as the elderly Mr Lewis, who had been so kind to Tom, passed by. He saw an old French immigrant walking with his hands behind his back and thought his face seemed full of political schemes. Bricklayers, maiden ladies and their dogs and ivory canes were all invested with the vivid, present-tense actuality that is the life of an invalid.

But such an existence was suffused with February dreariness. The half-built houses opposite seemed as if they were dying of old age. The grass in the garden at Wentworth Place had taken on a dingy tinge and nothing seemed to be growing save for a few dismal cabbage stalks. Everything conspired to impress on Keats the reality of death, and his imagination turned to what had always given him joy – the gentle, flower-strewn world of southern England. He thought of every type of blossom he had known since infancy, and their shapes and colours were as new to him as if he had just perceived them. They spoke of innocence and content. 'The simple flowers of our spring are what I want to see again,' he told Rice.

Yet there were nightmares to accompany this lassitude. Brown, who was so carefully tending to Keats's wants, spent his free time copying heads from Hogarth prints. Now the faces from *The Rake's Progress* and *Credulity, Superstition and Fanaticism* invaded Keats's dreams and mingled with his constant, wordless meditations on death. Any idea of easing his thoughts with poetry had to be put on one side. 'I am recommended not even to read poetry, much less to write it,' he told Fanny Brawne in one of the many short, passionate letters by which he communicated with her.

For, above all, it was Fanny who obsessed him. 'The consciousness that you love me will make a pleasant prison of the house next to yours,' he wrote. With the peremptoriness of an ill man, he insisted she come and see him the day after his haemorrhage. Brown told Keats that Fanny and her family were out and Keats himself spent the afternoon looking hungrily down the street for the arrival of the stage coach. 'You must see me tonight,' he added on the back of the letter, 'and let me hear your promise to come to morrow.'[16] He was desperate that she recognise the passionate innocence of his thoughts about her, but, with the loss of her letters to him, she appears absorbed in his all-mastering dependence even as he felt annihilated by his ideas of her. 'You must believe – you shall, you will – that I can do nothing, say nothing, think nothing of you but what has its spring in the Love which has so long been my pleasure and torment.'

Yet, for all this, Keats's love was riddled with anxiety. He was tormented by the thought that Fanny might be unfaithful to him, yet how could he tie her to him? He was seriously ill, perhaps even dying, and it seemed proper that he release her from their engagement. The gravity of the situation impressed Fanny deeply and called forth her reserves of strength and affection. If she was 'a little silent' when she came to see him, she would not desert him. Yet even as he wrote to thank her Keats could not suppress his jealous fantasies. Was she Cressida and he some hapless, tormented Troilus?

Such intense emotion worried those who knew about it. Rodd had ordered that Keats be kept as tranquil as possible, since their passions could do each of the lovers harm. Keats tried to be philosophical about this. 'Our friends speak and think for the best, and if their best is not our best it is not their fault.'[17] But Brown could not disguise the fact that he disliked Fanny, and he was one among many of Keats's friends who did not approve of the relationship and probably thought her unworthy of him. He saw how his passion disturbed Keats, and he may, perhaps, have been jealous of Fanny. Besides, the presence of the visibly pregnant Abigail O'Donaghue made visits from a single, respectable girl awkward. But Fanny herself would not be put off. Keats suggested she should call only when Brown was out, and she came, bringing her dress-making with her to work at while she sat beside him. Despite her mother's anxiety about this, she also, at Keats's ardent request, wrote him a note each night so that he could sleep with it under his pillow. None of these has survived. Her passion is, once again, smothered by his.

Keats knew how such obsessions threatened his health even as they seemed to imprison Fanny. 'It is certainly better that I should see you seldom,' he confessed. Meanwhile, his jealousy wracked him with guilt. How could he complain about her going into town? Yet clearly it troubled him when he saw her set off. In addition, any slight variation of her feelings towards him agitated him terribly. The symptoms of consumption meant that Keats was particularly fretful in the evening and, falling greedily on the little notes Fanny sent him, he was quick to detect even imaginary dangers in them. 'For some reason or other your last night's note was not so treasurable as former ones. I would fain that you would call me *Love* still.' When he sent her notes himself he watched desperately from the front-parlour window until she should appear for a moment on the cold and dingy grass. She was still for him the embodiment of inexhaustible Beauty, torturing and divine. 'My sweet creature when I look back upon the pains and torments I have suffer'd for you from the day I left you to go to the isle of Wight; the ecstasies in which I have pass'd some days and the miseries in their turn, I wonder the more at the Beauty which has kept up the spell so fervently.'[18]

But much of Keats's time had to be spent in silence and alone. Inevitably his thoughts turned to his poetry and the gap between his hopes and his achievements. Worst of all, it seemed to him that his love for Fanny Brawne was destroying him as a poet. His fear was perhaps justified. Although Keats had been forbidden to write, the impulse could not be denied. Yet what he produced now was sadly inadequate. Ravaged by illness and obsession, and wracked by jealousy, the handful of his last works make sorry reading. The sonnet 'I cry your mercy' uses the language of the weakest sections of *Endymion*, suffusing this with a strained sensuality and a near hysterical belief in the essential fickleness of women. In 'What can I do to drive away', Keats wants to 'kill' his love in order to be free to write, but his state of mind had betrayed his art, and the ode 'To Fanny' is the embarrassing, bullying outburst of a sick man. Keats's deity Apollo was no longer the god of light, healing and poetry, but the terrible bringer of pestilence.

Everything appeared as failure and disappointment. Neither the *Poems* nor *Endymion* had secured his reputation. Twice he had tried to write his epic on Hyperion and on both occasions he had been forced to abandon the work. So many of his manuscripts contained work he had grown out of and which embarrassed him: the mawkish *Isabella*, the problem-ridden *Eve of St. Agnes*. *Lamia* still satisfied him, but Keats seems to have been unaware of the true grandeur of the achievement in the odes. There were febrile moments of rekindled interest, even hours when Keats considered new work. But a gift from the author of Barry Cornwall's *A Sicilian Story* showed that he had been anticipated even in versifying the tale of Isabella. Taylor urged him to prepare his own work for the press, but the quick changes of mood forced on Keats by his illness caused terrible tension. During his fevered nights, when thoughts of Fanny Brawne were not beating in his head, he was obliged to survey what he could only perceive as a wrecked career, a life of promise denied. He could confess these thoughts only to Fanny, and he did so with heart-rending poignancy: '"If I should die" said I to myself, "I have left no immortal work behind me – nothing to make my friends proud of my memory – but I have lov'd the principle of beauty in all things, and if I had had time I would have made myself remember'd."'[19]

Then, on the evening of Monday 6 March Keats suffered violent palpitations of the heart. While he took to his bed, a despondent and worried Brown sent for Rodd and it was probably he who suggested calling in a specialist. The man, Dr Robert Bree, was an authority on asthma. Looking at the prostrate young man, Bree formed the belief that Keats's illness was psychosomatic in origin. Here was an instance of 'mental impression operating upon the body, and inducing morbid motions'. Keats, Bree believed, was suffering from nervous asthma and even his consumptive symptoms were the product of anxiety.

The false diagnosis brought everyone relief. Brown, who had despaired of Keats ever revising his poems, now wrote to Taylor saying 'there is no pulmonary affection, no organic defect whatever, – the disease is on his *mind*.'[20] Bree clearly thought Keats was the victim of his poetic ambition and even humorously suggested he would have done better to have studied mathematics. More usefully, he took Keats off his consumptive's starvation diet and recommended meat and light wine, helping Keats thereby to regain his strength. Bree also prescribed sedatives to calm the palpitations and ease the pain in Keats's chest. Two months of peace were purchased in this way, two months which allowed Keats to prepare one of the supreme volumes of nineteenth-century English poetry.

Day by day, Keats seemed to be recovering his strength. Brown noticed he was putting on weight, and Keats himself felt he was getting better since he could now look at Brown's copies of Hogarth without his mind being plagued by 'a psalm-singing nightmare'. His chest seemed less congested and he found he could do without the medicine he had been taking to lower his pulse. He was even planning on taking a May Day walk with Fanny, and, as a sign of his strengthened spirits, he asked her to return the manuscripts of his poems so he could set about revisions. His love became touched with a radiance he had never known so keenly. The misery of the past, the suffering of 'the most discontented and restless mind ever put in a body too small for it', seemed to have disappeared. His letters touch a sublime happiness. 'You are always new. The last of your kisses was ever the sweetest; the last smile the brightest; the last movement the gracefullest.'[21] Each sight of her was like a first falling in love. Lying beside her and seeing her new black dress that he liked so much, he knew that she loved him.

And now persistent thrush song from the garden seemed like a sound of spring and Keats could laugh in his radiance and crack a lover's joke. 'There's the Thrush again – I can't afford it – he'll run me up a pretty Bill for Music.' He felt like a man escaped into ecstasy. 'How horrid was the chance of slipping into the ground instead of into your arms.'

He wanted to run round to see her in her new dress, but he knew this was too dangerous. 'I fear I am too prudent for a dying kind of Lover,' he confessed, but he believed hope and love would heal him.[22] 'God bless you my sweet Love! Illness is a long lane, but I see you at the end of it, and shall mend my pace as well as possible.'

By the closing weeks of March, Keats even felt he was able to go out, despite an ominous recurrence of his palpitations. He dined with Taylor and then, on 25 March, he walked the four or five miles into town for the climax of something that seemed to have run through his entire adult life. Haydon's enormous *Triumphal Entry* was at last complete and its exhibition was to be one of the events of the season. Haydon had hired the Egyptian Hall in Piccadilly and Keats was to attend the private view. He found Piccadilly crowded with carriages and the assembled mass of rank, beauty and fashion so dear to Haydon's heart. Despite his private reservations about the central figure of Christ, which over the years had come more and more to look like Haydon himself, the picture was reckoned a success, and Haydon was delighted to see Keats and Hazlitt together in a corner of the Hall 'really rejoicing'.[23]

But there was reason for anxiety all the same. Brown was now planning to rent his half of Wentworth Place and to do so earlier than usual since he needed extra money to cover the expenses arising from the birth of his child. Keats would have to move out before the second week of May. While the problem preyed on his mind, help came from an unexpected quarter. Leigh Hunt had decided to save money by moving to cheaper lodgings in Kentish Town, which he described as 'a sort of compromise between London and our beloved Hampstead'. Stirred to unwonted efficiency, Hunt arranged for Keats to move into 2 Weslyan Place near by. Keats would be paying far less than he did for Wentworth Place. He would be close to Hunt himself, only a mile from Fanny, and near enough to town for the easy despatch of the proofs of his new volume. When Keats moved in to his new lodgings on 4 May, Brown, keenly aware of his responsibilities to his friend, paid Keats's expenses as well as the first week's rent; in addition to waiving Keats's debts for the moment, he also borrowed a further £50 so that the poet should have money to see him through the summer. Then Brown set off for Scotland, Keats accompanying him as far as Gravesend.

Alone in his new lodgings, Keats's thoughts returned obsessively to Fanny Brawne. 'I wish you could know the Tenderness with which I continually brood over your different aspects of countenance, action and dress,' he told her.[24] For Keats, Fanny's existence was almost wholly in his mind, and the intensity of his imaginings, fevered by his worsening disease, began to poison his thoughts. The brief rapture of the past weeks was over, and Keats once again became adept at inventing his own wretchedness. 'You have no conception', he told Fanny, 'of the quantity of miserable feeling that passes through me in a day.' The slightest rumour became magnified by distorting jealousy, and towards the end of May, when Keats was visiting the Dilkes, something was said that threw him into a paroxysm of emotion. It seems that Fanny had gone unchaperoned to one of Mrs Dilke's parties. This she was perfectly entitled to do, her hostess being a young married woman, but the thought of his fiancée enjoying company other than his was unbearable. Keats's friends had noted earlier that 'he don't like anyone to look at her or speak to her,' but now he was pitifully unable to control such occasions and felt he could bind Fanny to him only through the savagery of his letters.

'I wish you to see how unhappy I am for love of you.'[25] He had been 'haunted with a sweet vision' of her dress, and the contrast between this and the thought of Fanny flirting at a party was harrowing. It showed she had a life of her own, was independent of his imagination. Clouding the exquisite precision of his memories was the hungry panic of not possessing her entirely. He did not always know what she was doing, where she was, who she was with. 'How have you pass'd this month? Who have you smil'd with?' He felt a need to bludgeon her into submission. 'Do not think of anything but me. Do not live as if I was not existing.' Only if she matched his own obsession could he be confident of her love. His mind ran to the lurid and the cruel. 'You must be mine to die on the rack if I want you.' No sentence more terribly illustrates the collapse of Keats's love from health into disease.

The world could only contaminate the ideal of Fanny that Keats had built. 'If you could really what is call'd enjoy yourself at Party – if you can smile in people's faces, and wish them to admire you *now*, you never have nor ever will love me.' He loathed the idea of their friends gossiping about them. That Fanny had very mildly flirted with Brown, probably as she had with Severn in order to rouse Keats himself, led to a wholesale condemnation of his friend. 'Though I know his love and friendship for me, though at this moment I should be without pence if it were not for his assistance, I will never see or speak to him until we are both old men, if we are to be.' Keats felt the deepest core of his self was being trivialised by Fanny's behaviour, and he desperately wanted to remove her from temptation. 'If we love we must not live as other men and women do – I cannot brook the wolfsbane of fashion and foppery and tattle.' He was riven with guilt at such feelings, but: 'for God's sake save me – or tell me my passion is of too awful a nature for you.' His anguish had reached its climax. Keats signed the letter with his initials and then added a postscript: 'No – my sweet Fanny – I am wrong. I do not want you to be unhappy – and yet I do, I must while there is so sweet a Beauty – my loveliest darling! Good bye! I Kiss you – O the torments!'

He knew Fanny might 'call this madness' and it is clear that she answered his letters with spirit. Later, she gave a generous but level-headed account of him. 'That his sensibility was most acute, is true, and his passions were very strong, but not violent, if by that term violence of temper is implied.' She recognised nonetheless how dangerous his moods were to him. 'His anger seemed rather to turn on himself than others, and in moments of great irritation, it was only by a sort of savage despondency that he sometimes grieved and wounded his friends.'[26] The self-torment of Keats's obsession is clear, and he would soon begin to identify the consuming nature of his passion with his disease.

Amid this welter of misery, while Keats was exhausted and terribly alone, the proofs of his poems began to arrive. He could look at them only with listless indifference. He corrected the occasional slip such as Woodhouse's accidentally substituting 'cold' for 'chill' in the first line of *The Eve of St. Agnes*, but he seems to have blandly accepted Woodhouse's objections to his own revisions. Indeed, it was Wood-house who was responsible for most of the editorial work. Conscientious and deeply committed to his friend, he was ideally suited to the task. He was above all constantly alert to any sign of the technical slackness that had so preoccupied the reviewers of *Endymion*, and Keats allowed him to amend the punctuation as he pleased. This was a particularly important matter with *Lamia*, which Keats wished to be placed first in the book. A romance in couplets, the work threatened, if technical looseness were found, to bring down the wrath levelled previously by the critics. If *Lamia* were damned, the rest of the volume might go unread. Fortunately, Woodhouse also noticed (as nobody else had) that Keats had given the wrong scansion to many of the Greek names in the poem. Such an error would, if exposed, have damned him forever as a Cockney, and Keats was persuaded to make the small alterations necessary to correct his mistakes.

But, for all this detailed care, the choice of poems for the volume, along with the works it excludes, is curious. None of Keats's sonnets from this period is printed, nor did he choose to publish 'La Belle Dame Sans Merci', allowing it instead to appear in an ineffectively revised form in Hunt's new magazine, the *Indicator*. While the three romances, *Lamia*, *Isabella* and *The Eve of St. Agnes*, head the volume, making clear that Keats wished to be known principally as writer of narrative, the middle section of the book is a curious mixture of Keats's strongest mature writing with some of his weakest, and it sends a confused signal about his aims and purposes. The 'Nightingale', 'Urn' and 'Psyche' odes are followed by the frankly trivial lines to 'Fancy' and these are succeeded by three further pieces variously limp, nostalgic and lightweight: the ode 'Bards of Passion and of Mirth', the 'Lines on the Mermaid Tavern' and 'Robin Hood'. To find that these are then followed by 'To Autumn' comes with a jolt. Yet this apparent confusion seems to reflect a divide in contemporary taste, for the weaker poems were very popular in some quarters. A writer on the *Edectic Review* admired the 'pleasing and spirited numbers' of 'Fancy' while disparaging the admittedly dubiously punctuated conclusion of the 'Ode on a Grecian Urn' with the impertinent comment: 'that is, all that Mr Keats knows or cares to know. But till he knows much more than this he will never write verses fit to live.'[27]

The concluding work in the volume is the first *Hyperion*. Keats had asked for it not to be included. It was unfinished, its evolutionary optimism ran contrary to all he was now experiencing, and it was above all a symbol to him of his shattered hopes. Nonetheless, Keats allowed himself once again to be overruled. It was probably Woodhouse who wrote the publisher's note explaining the work's inclusion: 'If any apology be thought necessary for the appearance of the unfinished poem of *Hyperion*, the publishers beg to state that they alone are responsible as it was printed at their particular request, and contrary to the wish of the author.' In time, Keats came to find this offensive, and in a copy presented to a Hampstead acquaintance he crossed the whole note out, scribbling beside it: 'This is none of my doing – I was ill at the time.' The last sentence, which probably represents Woodhouse's opinion, reads: 'The poem was intended to have been of equal length with *Endymion*, but the reception given to that work discouraged the author from proceeding.' This was both incorrect and undiplomatic, and it annoyed Keats intensely. In the same volume in which he scratched out the note, he added bitterly: 'This is a lie.'[28]

As publication neared, Keats prepared himself for hostile criticism. 'My book', he wrote to Brown, 'is coming out with very low hopes though not spirits on my part.' His bitterness against the reviewers became intense, and what Hunt called Keats's 'critical malignity' led him to accuse *Blackwood's* of contributing to his illness. Reynolds told Bailey, 'that poor Keats attributed his approaching end to the poisonous pen of Lockhart,' and Hunt confirmed this notion to Severn and probably to Shelley also. From this pain and confusion sprang the legend of a young genius killed before his time by a hostile and unfeeling world. It was untrue, but it was potent. The belief underlies Shelley's sublime elegy *Adonais* and, as the century developed, so the lurid image came to play an important part in the mythology of the Pre-Raphaelites.

Taylor, however, was boundlessly confident of the quality of the book he was publishing. 'I am sure of this,' he wrote, 'that for poetic Genius there is not his equal living, & I would compare him against any one with either Milton or Shakespeare for Beauties.'[29] By and large the reviewers justified this assertion. The book came out in the last week of June and the following month the plaudits began. The *Literary Gazette* printed selections, as did the *Chronicle* and the *Monthly Review*. Lamb was warm in his praise, and the *Sun* saw *Hyperion* as 'the greatest effort of Mr Keats's genius'. Finally, in August, the prestigious *Edinburgh Review* published an article in praise of both *Endymion* and the new volume from no less a pen than that of Jeffrey, the magazine's editor.

'My book has had a good success among literary people,' Keats wrote in August, 'and, I believe has a moderate sale.' But by this time his health had so drastically deteriorated that he was all but indifferent to success.

On 22 June, he had received a worrying letter from his sister about the Abbeys. Walking out to catch the City coach, Keats felt his mouth fill with blood. He could no longer harbour doubts about his condition. The theory of psychosomatic asthma could not be sustained. Realising at once how important it was that he should not be on his own, Keats went round to the Hunts'. He told them nothing but, with intense self-restraint, quietly joined in the conversation. Shelley's friend Maria Gisbourne was there, tea was served, and Hunt's talk turned, inevitably, to music. Mrs Gisbourne mentioned how the Italian singer Farinelli 'had the art of taking breath imperceptibly, while he continued to hold one single note, alternately swelling and diminishing the power of his voice like waves'. Speaking so quietly that the rest of the company could barely hear him, Keats observed that such a technique must surely be painful for the audience, 'as when a diver descends into the hidden depths of the sea you feel an apprehension lest he may never rise again.'[30] The casual imaginative grace of the remark reveals a profound moral strength.

That strength was now to be tested to the hilt. When Keats got back to his lodgings, he suffered another violent haemorrhage. The situation was appalling and was made worse by Keats's medical knowledge and his experience of nursing Tom. Now it was essential that others nurse him. He was moved into Hunt's lodgings at 13 Mortimer Terrace, where he was attended by George Darling. Exhausted, wretched and with his nerves torn by the noise and confusion that invariably accompanied the Hunt household with its ill-disciplined children, Keats endured the fearful regimen of heavy blood-letting that fell to his lot as a diagnosed consumptive. His mind, bitter and darkened, waited for each new symptom to appear, each flush or chill. By July, Darling had concluded that the only hope lay in Keats's wintering abroad. 'He is advised – nay ordered – to Italy,' Reynolds wrote, 'but in such a state it is a hopeless doom.'

Sensing the gravity of the situation, Fanny Brawne wrote to Keats asking him to retrieve a precious token of their love from his previous lodgings. This was the volume of Dante's *Inferno* in which she had copied out 'Bright Star' and he had inscribed his sonnet on his dream inspired by Dante. Keats gave a copy of this last work to Hunt so that he could print it in the *Indicator* under the pseudonym 'Caviare', the same soubriquet Keats had used when 'La Belle Dame Sans Merci' was published there. The reference to Hamlet's phrase 'caviare to the general' implied that both works were only for an elite, the adepts of sophisticated literary insight, but it also suggests Keats's close identification with Shakespeare's prince and his casting of Fanny Brawne as Ophelia. 'Hamlet's heart was full of such Misery as mine is when he said to Ophelia "Go to a Nunnery, go, go!"' The prince's death-wish became his own. 'I should like to give up the matter at once – I should like to die. I am sickened at the brute world which you are smiling with.'[31]

Fanny was still moving in their old circles, and Keats's jealousy was poisoning his friendships. The old days at Wentworth Place would have to be brought to a bitter end. 'I will indulge myself by never seeing any more Dilke or Brown or any of their Friends.'[32] If Keats went out at all, it was to mix with people he had previously disparaged. Horace Smith, whose smart dinner-party conversation had once seemed so brittle, probably heard from Hunt of Keats's state of health and sent his coach over to bring him to his new house in Fulham. The familiar circle arrived and a crate of 'quite undeniable Chateau Margaux' was broached. Smith pointed his daughter's attention to where an exhausted Keats was sitting. 'Do you see that man?' he asked. 'That's a poet.'[33]

All through these weeks, the thought of being obliged to winter abroad tortured Keats. 'I feel it almost impossible to go to Italy,' he wrote to Fanny Brawne, 'the fact is I cannot leave you.' Yet everyone rallied to his support. A letter even arrived from Shelley suggesting Keats sail at once for Leghorn and stay as the Shelleys' guest at Pisa.[34] A rereading of *Endymion* had convinced Shelley of Keats's genius, and the Gisbournes would soon be bringing him a copy of the *Lamia* volume. When Keats replied, delicately prevaricating over Shelley's offer, he turned the subject to poetry.[35] Shelley had offered some friendly criticism of Keats's early style, finding it overloaded with 'system & mannerism'. Keats in his turn felt the need to comment on the poetry of *The Cenci*, suggesting Shelley should write in a more concentrated way 'and "load every rift" of your subject with ore'. He was well aware of the irony of such advice coming from the author of *Endymion*, whose mind when he wrote that poem had been, as Keats declared: 'like a pack of scattered cards'. Then, in this exchange of courteous professional concern, Keats gently disparaged the new volume of his own that he was sending to Shelley, confessing it 'would never have been publish'd but from a hope of gain'. It was this book, folded back in his jacket pocket, that helped identify Shelley when his drowned body was found off the Italian coast.

From time to time, Keats made painful trips to Hampstead. This was in part to say farewell, and the memories stirred in him were at times more than he could bear. He was seen 'sitting and sobbing' by the antiquary William Hone, while Hunt, who went with Keats on another occasion, recalled that, as they neared Well Walk, Keats, exhausted and overcome with emotion, sat down on a bench, turned to Hunt and, with his eyes swimming with tears, confessed he was 'dying of a broken heart'. The breakdown in Keats's reserve amazed Hunt, yet the short distance from Well Walk to Wentworth Place contained many of his most intense associations. Here he had come to live with George and Tom when, finally abandoning medicine, he had resolved on a life as a poet. From Well Walk he had set out to meet Hunt, Haydon, the Reynoldses and the Dilkes. Here too he had nursed Tom and, to deflect his mind from that agony, had composed the first version of *Hyperion*. When Tom died, it was to Brown, down the hill at Wentworth Place, that Keats had turned. It was that house which was the shrine of his passion for Fanny Brawne. Here, when the most serious crisis threatened, was his real home.

That crisis was now sparked by an incident at once trivial and typical of the Hunt household. Two days before Shelley's letter arrived, a note came from Fanny Brawne. The ever-harassed Mrs Hunt told a servant girl to deliver it to Keats, but the girl herself, resentful and on the point of leaving, did nothing about it. It was nine days later that Hunt's son Thornton was found with the note and by then the seal was broken. For several hours Keats broke down in an agony of tears. Then, in bewildered bitterness, and despite Hunt's entreaties, tired and ill, he dragged his way towards Hampstead resolved never again to be exposed to such treatment. How long the journey took is not known. He told his sister he had been resolved to take up his old lodgings in Well Walk, but that evening, and with the last reserves of his energy, Keats managed to get himself as far as the door of Wentworth Place. Because he had nowhere else to go, Mrs Brawne took him in.

Yet, even as he enjoyed what he later called his happiest home, Keats knew he must leave it. Although the idea of a voyage to Italy tore at his nerves, preparations had to be made. He wrote to Taylor asking him to find out what it would cost and how much he would need for a year's residence. But the effort of writing the letter was not only mentally painful: 'every line I write encreases the tightness in the Chest.'[36]

Taylor himself was generous and efficient. He had found out that Rome was the best place for Keats to go and that there was an excellent English doctor there – James Clark. Taylor also made the necessary financial arrangements. The success of Keats's latest volume encouraged him to buy the copyright of *Endymion* for £100 and to pay the same for the earlier *Poems* and the *Lamia* volume. After deducting the advances already paid, this left Keats with a surplus of £30, and Taylor agreed that a further £150 should be put aside to his credit. Taylor also believed that George would soon repay the £200 he thought he owed Keats. For his own part, Keats wrote to Taylor a 'scrap of Paper' which he clearly considered to be his will. 'All my estate real and personal consists in the hopes of the sale of books published or unpublish'd. Now I wish *Brown* and you to be the first paid Creditors – the rest is in nubibus – but in case it should shower pay my Taylor the few pounds I owe him.'[37]

With these arrangements agreed, Taylor went to visit Keats in Hampstead. The dying man's fear of the journey was evident. Again and again he likened it to a soldier marching against a fort. But it was clear that other obsessions were also troubling him. The earlier ruin of his reputation was preying on his mind, and at one point he burst out: 'Taylor, if I die, you must ruin Lockhart.'[38] He wanted his revenge on the periodical reviewers while, in his anxiety and depression, he had come to believe that his latest book was a failure. This he put down to the sensational effect of George IV's attempt to divorce his queen by a parliamentary 'trial'. In his illness, it seemed to Keats that the repressive, aristocratic society he resented was once again conspiring against him.

The seriousness of Keats's condition was now clear to everyone. Haydon, with characteristic tactlessness, was pestering him with requests for the return of a book (actually an edition of Chapman's Homer) which Keats had lost. When he came to call on him, Haydon found the poet 'to be going out of the world with a contempt for this and no hopes of the other'. He tried to urge Christian consolation on his friend, but Keats's only response was to say that if he did not get better he would cut his throat. The Christianity he had so firmly rejected offered him nothing, and he would not surrender to what he considered a false belief. Yet his spiritual state was far from tranquil. Throughout the period of his most splendid productivity, Keats had sustained himself with a belief in the immortality of the soul and the idea that suffering would prepare him for an afterlife in which he would live with those closest to him in a bliss of perfect understanding. This life, the vale of soul-making, was a preparation for the next. Now he was beginning to be assailed by doubts. 'I long to believe in immortality,' he wrote to Fanny, 'I shall never be able to bid you an entire farewell.'[39] Once, he had been able to take the immortality of the soul 'for granted'. Now, faced with the prospect of death from a painful and humiliating disease, Keats was beginning to lose his earlier easy confidence and, with it, the belief by which he had been able to dignify human suffering.

Thoughts of Fanny Brawne mingled constantly with these doubts. Keats wrote a letter to Brown in which he tried to express this and in which he referred to something Brown himself called 'the secret'.[40] Precisely what this was is uncertain since Brown cautiously edited the letter. Yet it is clear that Keats himself was trying to associate his love of Fanny Brawne with the growing certainty of his death. Unaware of the scientific causes of consumption and consenting to the popular thought of the day, Keats began to see his febrile state as something caused by his passion. At the very core of love itself lurked death, and Keats could believe that frustrated desire was literally killing him. Now, even if Fanny were to give herself to him, it was too late. 'My dear Brown, I should have had her when I was in health, and I should have remained well.'[41]

All he could do was to try and find a companion to go with him on his last journey. Brown was the obvious choice, but he was away in Scotland and, although he hurried back earlier than was his habit, he arrived too late. For haste was now of the essence. At the end of August, Keats had another severe haemorrhage. He was ordered to avoid every sort of fatigue, all forms of stress, yet Fanny attended him every day and, in his weakness, they began to draw up new plans. They told each other, perhaps half knowing that this could never be, that when he got better, when he returned from Rome, they would marry and live together as man and wife in Wentworth Place. Meanwhile, she sat beside him sewing a silk lining into his travelling cap and cooling her hands by holding a large, white cornelian egg.

But the question of a companion for the journey still had not been settled. Haslam, who had been deputed by Taylor to solve this problem, eventually called on Severn. Light and slight though he was, Severn seemed to be the most reasonable choice. He was unmarried and, as an artist, would surely want to go to Rome. Besides, as the winner of the Royal Academy Gold Medal, he was well placed to submit a picture for their travelling scholarship. He would be able to continue his studies in Rome for a further three years. Haslam put the case forthrightly: 'As nothing can save Keats but going to Italy, why should *you* not go with him, for otherwise he must go alone, and we shall never hear anything of him if he dies. Will you go?'[42] Severn at once agreed. It would take him three or four days to prepare himself, and he resolved to start at once. He collected £25 owed him by a sitter for a miniature and called on Sir Thomas Lawrence to get an introduction to the Italian sculptor Canova.

Meanwhile Keats himself had to make his farewells. In these infinitely precious and painful last moments together, he and Fanny exchanged locks of hair. She gave him a diary, a penknife and the travelling cap she had lined. She also presented him, most intimately of all, with the marble egg she had used to cool her hands. When, in his fever, Keats grasped it, he would be grasping something of her. Then, when he had gone and the carriage was out of sight, Fanny picked up the copy of *The Literary Pocket Book* he had given her and wrote in it, sparsely and poignantly, 'Mr Keats left Hampstead.'

This Posthumous Life

How long is this posthumous life of mine to last?

(Keats to his doctor)

On 17 SEPTEMBER, a carriage took Keats from his publisher's office to Tower Dock. Taylor, Haslam and Woodhouse were waiting there to see him aboard the *Maria Crowther*, an uncomfortable little brigantine of 127 tons. Severn arrived later and in a state of considerable agitation. Not only had he failed to get his passport, but his father, a violent and unstable man, had stood in the doorway as his son was trying to pass and knocked him to the ground. Now, as Severn looked round the ship, his heart sank at seeing the 'little Cabin with 6 beds and at first sight every inconvenience'. The cabin itself was divided by a screen, and while Keats, Severn and the master, Thomas Walsh, had bunks on one side, two women were to occupy the other half. One of them, the difficult and unfeeling lady's companion Mrs Pidgeon, had already arrived and she served the company tea. Later, as the ship made its way to Gravesend, they all dined. Keats, it was noticed, was telling jokes, but when his friends had disembarked he went to bed, the sea breezes having made him tired. What he did not yet know, although he was later to lament the cruel irony of the situation, was that Charles Brown was even then aboard a smack from Dundee and had passed within hailing distance.

The following morning, anchored off Gravesend, where they dropped the river pilot and were cleared by customs, Keats asked Severn to land and go to the town for medical supplies. These included a bottle of laudanum. By six o'clock, Severn's passport had arrived and then, two hours later, the final passenger joined the ship. Severn himself described Miss Cotterell as 'very agreeable and lady like', but as she came aboard, looking hesitatingly first at Keats and then at Severn, and asking which of them was the dying man, so she displayed that insensitivity which Keats himself was to find increasingly irksome. Miss Cotterell insisted that her own state of health was better than Keats's (something unusual in invalids, who, as Severn noted, tend to believe they are actually worse off than those around them), but her sickly presence, 'the flushings in her face, all her bad symptoms', preyed mercilessly on Keats's nerves. Mrs Pidgeon, for her part, not only appeared indifferent to her companion's state of health but seemed to dislike the company she was in as well as the surroundings.

Bad weather was to make this tension worse. The following morning a storm blew up, driving the *Maria Crowther* past Margate to Dover. Each of the passengers was sea-sick and would take nothing more than a cup of tea for the rest of the day. Keats himself tried to remain cheerful, making jokes and puns, but it is clear that much of the burden of looking after the two invalids fell on Severn, who was increasingly harassed by the demands made on him. For instance, when the portholes were opened Keats would be taken with so violent a cough that he sometimes spat blood; when they were closed, Miss Cotterell would faint, often remaining insensible for five or six hours at a time. Mrs Pidgeon showed not the slightest concern, and it was Keats, lying on his bunk and dispensing advice 'like an Escalapius of old in baso-relievo', who advised Severn on how to reduce the period of Miss Cotterell's attacks.

By the afternoon of 20 September, the *Maria Crowther*, now off Brighton, was being tossed by mountainous waves. The cabin flooded as water poured in through the skylight, and the passengers' trunks were thrown about alarmingly. Severn, staggering from his berth, 'fell down from my weakness and the rolling of the ship', but even when, at dusk, the vessel sprang a leak, 'Keats was very calm.' The master eventually decided that, given the state of the wind and tide, he would have to stop tacking and allow his ship to retrace its course. By dawn, and after a terrible night, they were twenty miles back off Dungeness, where for the next two days they were becalmed. Severn could now see how much the voyage had taken out of Keats and began to wonder if they ought to return to London. However, they were now sailing gently back in the direction of Brighton, and by 28 September had reached Portsmouth.

Here Walsh decided they would remain for twenty-four hours while he refitted and revictualled the ship. The opportunity of getting to dry land was eagerly taken, and Keats and Severn set off to see the Snooks at their mill-house seven miles away. Here Keats had written the greater part of *The Eve of St. Agnes*, and, while his surprised hosts were delighted to see him, they also had news for him. Because his half of Wentworth Place was still let out for the summer, Brown had come to stay with the Dilkes in Chichester and was now a mere ten miles away. Severn probably hoped that they would meet up and that Brown would persuade Keats to return to London. But, as his letter of 30 September shows, Keats had resolved against this. For all the cheerfulness he had tried to show towards Severn and the others, his mind was wholly preoccupied with inescapable personal tragedy. From the medical point of view, a return to London was pointless. Keats could not 'leave my lungs or stomach behind', and in his darkest moods he was without 'one heartening hope of my recovery'.

But something equally harrowing was also tearing at him. Keats had come to believe that his fatal illness had its origin in his unsatisfied love for Fanny Brawne. The woman whom he adored was the cause of his death. Keats's medical training, along with his memories of Tom dying, as they both believed, of hapless love for the imaginary Amena Bellefilia, seemed to confirm this. The forces of his love that should have gone out to the world had been turned back in upon themselves, and Keats's life, he believed, was being destroyed by its own intensity. The tragedy seemed ineluctable. 'The very thing I want to live most for will be a great occasion of my death. I cannot help it. Who can help it? Were I in health it would make me ill, and how can I bear it in my state?'[2]

Keats believed Fanny was physically destroying him, yet every thought of her was infinitely precious and the delicate intensity of his memories only increased his pain. 'I eternally see her figure eternally vanishing. Some of the phrases she was in the habit of using during my last nursing at Wentworth place ring in my ears.' In his wretchedness, Keats brooded over the idea of death. 'I wish for death every day and night to deliver me from these pains, and then I wish death away, for death would destroy even those pains which are better than nothing,' he told Brown. 'Land and sea, weakness and decline are great separators, but death is the great divorcer for ever. When the pang of this thought has passed through my mind, I may say the bitterness of death is passed.' He had not until now known the depths of pain to be endured in the vale of soul-making, and, in his distress, he began to think of an afterlife as a release from suffering, something which his previous philosophy had condemned. Pain was leading him to question the ideas that had sustained his greatest work. 'Is there another Life?' he asked Brown. 'Shall I awake and find all this a dream? There must be we cannot be created for this sort of suffering.'

By now the *Maria Crowther* was slowly making its way along the Dorset coast, and from time to time Walsh allowed his fretful passengers to disembark. Once they got off at Studland Bay and then either at Lulworth or nearby Holworth. A delighted Severn watched as Keats seemed momentarily to regain something of his old relish of life. Looking about him, he showed the painter 'the splendid caverns and grottos with a poet's pride, as tho' they had been his birthright'. With a freshening wind promising to take them speedily down the Channel and out to the open sea, the two men returned to the *Maria Crowther*. Here, when they were back on board, Keats took out the copy of Shakespeare's *A Lover's Complaint* he had once shared with Reynolds. Severn believed (or later came to imagine) that it was on this occasion that Keats composed the sonnet 'Bright Star!', writing it out on a blank page opposite the opening of the printed work. But the evidence for this is flimsy, and it seems more likely that Keats, with insistent memories of Fanny Brawne beating in his head, simply turned to the poem to brood over its vision of a love that longs for fulfilment either in a caressed sleep or in death.

The events of the next three weeks were ruinously to undermine Keats's health and to show him with certainty that all he could expect was the slow, painful and humiliating death he had watched hour by hour as Tom had died. But the circumstances were to make his own death worse. Severn, for all he was to rise to the dreadful challenge posed to him, was not a member of Keats's family or even a particularly intimate friend. Keats was bound on a journey to a country he did not know, whose sights he would for most of his little remaining time be too weak to enjoy, and where, for all the benevolence of the climate and his doctors' hopes of recovery, he knew he would almost certainly die. Even now the strains of the voyage – the cramped conditions, the constant heaving of the ship, Miss Cotterell's variously flushed and pallid face, Mrs Pidgeon's indifference and Severn's sea-sickness – conspired to weaken him.

Keats's mind, at its lowest ebb, returned again and again to the bottle of laudanum he had persuaded Severn to buy at Gravesend. Why should he endure the long agonies of a natural death when he could so easily put an end to his suffering? He broached the matter with his companion, but Severn, as a firmly convinced Christian, was horrified. To kill oneself was an act of despair, an unforgivable sin against the Holy Ghost. The burden of the spiritual problems Severn would have to bear became apparent to him. He argued with Keats about the issue of suicide and, for the moment, was able to convince his friend to endure rather than kill himself.

The misery and boredom were relieved by slight but trying incidents. The storms had subsided, and the passengers were no longer in physical danger. Keats tried to beguile his time by reading the first two cantos of Byron's recently published *Don Juan*. But the poem, and the description of the shipwreck especially, sickened him. The work seemed merely brutal and clumsily callous. In the end, Keats threw the book aside in disgust. *Don Juan*, he later declared, was in its way as depraved as the crew on the *Maria Crowther*, who sang bawdy songs in the hearing of the women passengers. Then, in the Bay of Biscay, they were ordered to heave to by a Portuguese man-of-war whose captain believed the English boat might be carrying liberal revolutionaries to Spain. The oppressive politics of continental Europe added their weight of wretchedness to Keats's thoughts, but from time to time the beauty of the distant coastlines temporarily relieved his gloom. Severn, who in the days of Keats's health had watched him pass into an almost mystic rapture as the wind roved through the corn in the fields around Hampstead, now watched him lie entranced in a reclining chair 'with a look of serene abstraction in his face' as the North African coast stretched before them and they passed the 'vast topaz' that was the Rock of Gibraltar. For the moment, Severn thought he could see changes for the better in Keats, but this hope was short-lived. The physical signs of disease all too quickly became apparent. Blood started to erupt from his stomach and with this came alarming night sweats.

By dawn on 21 October they had reached Naples.[3] Severn was thrilled by the beauty and animation of what he saw: the Bay, the ships, the bustle of colourfully dressed people and the city itself rising around the foothills of Vesuvius, which was emitting 'writhing columns of smoke, golden at their sunlit fringes'. Keats, to whom the Bay of Naples was a part of the mythology of the antique world, a place where life had been lived in the pursuit of the beautiful, could now only stare at all he saw 'with so sad a look in his eyes, with, moreover, sometimes, a starved, haunting expression' that bewildered Severn. The two men were not close enough to confess their deepest secrets to each other, and Severn could only conclude as he looked at Keats that 'so excruciating was the grief that was eating away his life that he would speak of it to no one.' Then, in the midst of their first impressions, blunt and irksome daily life asserted itself. Neither the consumptives not their companions were allowed to land. The Neapolitan authorities had heard of a small outbreak of typhus in London and the crew and passengers of the *Maria Crowther* would have to stay in quarantine for ten days, packed in close to the hundreds of other ships in the harbour.

A dreadful time ensued. The passengers and crew, already 'ill-temper'd and weary', were now forced to endure the monotony of their cramped conditions while the sun shone down and, for the two invalids, the distressing pattern of their symptoms took its regular daily toll. Each was aware of the other's chills and hectic fevers, the quickened breathing and the expectoration of blood. Keats was also terribly troubled in his stomach, and the 'imprudence' of Miss Cotterell – the mirror of his own symptoms that she constantly presented and her lack of tact – were suffocating. 'I shall feel a load off me when the Lady vanishes out of my sight,' he confessed. He tried to improve the situation through the charm of his conversation and the gaiety of his puns. He talked of 'the classic Scenes he knew so well', and, for all that such talk must have stirred memories of his abandoned poetic career, he tried to summon up for the others images of 'that old antique world where the Greek gallies and Tyrhenian sloops brought northward strange tales of what was happening in Hellas and the mysterious East'. Despite the realisation that his own hopes were over, and with a tact that amounted to moral fortitude, Keats tried to give the others at least 'an inspiration from these lovely scenes'. And, when this palled, he tried humour, summoning up, as he later wrote, 'more puns, in a sort of desperation, in one week than in any year of my life'.

But the truth was that this was merely a surface effort of will. Keats's physical weakness had sapped his curiosity and was divorcing him from all that could feed his mind. 'O what an account I could give you of the Bay of Naples if I could once more feel myself a Citizen of this world – I feel a Spirit in my Brain would lay it forth pleasantly – O what a misery it is to have an intellect in splints!'[4] Then something happened to make life yet more uncomfortable. A Lieutenant Sullivan, part of the British squadron riding at anchor outside the Bay, perhaps spotting the flag on the *Maria Crowther*, had himself rowed over by ten ratings. As soon as Sullivan himself and six of his men came aboard, the eagle-eyed Neapolitan officials descended. The Englishmen had broken the quarantine regulations and would now have to stay on the ship, worsening its already cramped conditions.

Keats continued his efforts to be entertaining, especially towards the embarrassed but cheerful Sullivan, and later to Miss Cotterell's brother, who also came aboard. But his true feelings were revealed in his letters. He wrote first of all to Mrs Brawne, yet there are sentences in the letter which show that it was meant for Fanny, to whom Keats did not dare to write in person. He told of his and Severn's trying time in quarantine, of the presence of Miss Cotterell, and added how 'at this moment I am suffering from indigestion very much'. Then he began to confess. 'I dare not fix my Mind upon Fanny, I have not dared to think of her. The only comfort I have had that way has been in thinking for hours together of having the knife she gave me put in a silver case – the hair in a Locket – and the Pocket Book in a gold net – show her this. I dare say no more.' He tried to write of other things, of friends, the scene before him, members of the Brawne family. He signed off and then, cramped at the bottom of the page, he wrote: 'Good bye Fanny! God bless you.' These were the last words he would ever send her.

But she continued to prey on his mind, and on 1 November, when he had finally been released from quarantine, he wrote a further letter to Brown.[5] The fresher air, 'cold – wet and foggy' although it was, seemed to revive his spirits after the horrors of his ten-day incarceration on the *Maria Crowther*. Now he tried to write Brown 'a short calm letter', but, even as he promised this, the obsessions that Keats had tried to silence welled up inside him and flowed over. He had, he confessed, a desperate need to 'relieve the load of WRETCHEDNESS' pressing on him. He was convinced he would never see Fanny again and this idea, along with the acute and absolute frustration of his love, he felt was killing him. The force of his passion was fatal, and all he could long for was that he might be buried near to where she lived.

Memories tortured him. He recalled the anguished stay with the Hunts and how, when he had been there, his eyes had been continually fixed on Hampstead. A letter in Fanny's handwriting, even the sight of her name or the sound of it being pronounced, he knew would be unbearable to him. The gifts she had given, hidden away in his luggage, had a terrible power. 'Every thing I have in my trunks that reminds me of her goes through me like a spear. The silk lining she put in my travelling cap scalds my head.'[6] He could bear to die, but he could not endure the thought of leaving her, and he felt with terrible certainty that if he had 'any chance of recovery, this passion would kill me'. Would Brown write him a letter at Rome and put a simple cross on it if Fanny was well. He was wholly sincere when he said he could not endure seeing her name written out. His own letter does not mention it.

He then turned to thoughts of his family, asking Brown to write a short note to his sister, still so unhappily with the Abbeys in Walthamstow, and then he turned to George, whose financial problems, unknown to Keats himself, were getting worse. It seemed to Keats that nothing fortunate had ever happened to any of the brothers, and he confessed that 'despair is forced upon me as a habit'. Wretchedness was inescapable. 'Oh, Brown, I have coals of fire in my breast. It surprised me that the human heart is capable of containing and bearing so much misery. Was I born for this end?' Although he did not say so, this was the day after his twenty-fifth birthday, but he could only stare at a brief, terrible future of mental and bodily suffering. The anguish cries from the page. 'O God! God! God!'

Yet he would be brave. 'I will endeavour to bear my miseries patiently,' and he did so for long enough to convince Severn that he had become calm. Keats even made an Italian pun and tried to lose his sense of self in the nine volumes of *Clarissa Harlowe* Severn had brought with him. They went to a performance at the San Carlo theatre together, but, when Keats learned that the soldiers placed on either side of the proscenium arch were not a part of the production but real Bourbon troops posted there in case of trouble, he was disgusted. He did not wish to be 'buried' in a place and among a people so politically abased, and he urged on Severn how pressing was his need to get to Rome.

By 7 November, visas from the British Legation and the papal Consul General had been obtained, while Miss Cotterell's brother threw a farewell dinner party at which Keats made a special effort to be entertaining. Now, having hired a *vettura* or small carriage, Keats and Severn set off for Rome. The journey of 140 miles was made slowly over rough roads and the two men were obliged to stay at poor inns and eat execrable food. Keats, Severn noted, had 'become very listless, and seldom seemed even relatively happy'. How much he knew of his friend's mental anguish is unclear, yet its signs were beginning to weigh on him. In Naples, Severn had had to leave the room to hide his tears, and later Keats began to unburden himself to at least some degree. He told Severn 'much – very much – and I don't know wether it was more painful for me or himself'. There can be little doubt that Keats mentioned Fanny Brawne, and 'the seriousness & the solemnness of his passion', but now, as the little carriage heaved its way towards Rome, all Severn felt he could do was walk beside it and pick for Keats armfuls of the wild flowers he loved so much.

They crossed the Campagna, where they were intrigued to see a cardinal and his liveried attendants shooting birds, and eventually they entered Rome by the Lateran Gate. Dr Clark was writing a letter to a friend when they pulled up outside his door and he hurried down to greet them. At Keats's request he had found them rooms across the Piazza di Spagna from his own in the house nestling at the side of the broad and beautiful Spanish Steps. The rooms were on the second floor and communicated with those of their landlady, Anna Angeletti, a smart Venetian in her early forties with a taste for the arts. The rooms were carpeted and decorated with festoons of painted roses and had been particularly recommended as suitable for two friends. At nearly £5 per month a head they were also expensive, and Keats and Severn were the only visitors in the house who did not have their own servants. The situation was pleasing all the same. Artists' models and flower-sellers lounged on the Spanish Steps by day, while at night the sound of the water from the Bernini fountain rose refreshingly into Keats's room.

For a while, Keats's spirits seemed to improve. Dr Clark observed his patient carefully but was at first unable to form a diagnosis. In the absence of a scientific test for tuberculosis, he had to rely purely on such symptoms as presented themselves. Keats's mental stress was evident, but his bodily frame was not that conventionally associated with consumption nor did he appear to exhibit the frailty and lassitude so typical of those in the last stages of the disease. Clark thought the chief part of his patient's illness was seated in his stomach and he began to attribute much of this to Keats's intense mental exertions. These Clark had some familiarity with, for not only had they formed an obvious subject of his consultation, but Clark himself, a refined and educated man, possessed copies of both *Endymion* and the 1820 poems, as well as having read Jeffrey's favourable article on Keats's work in the *Edinburgh Review*. It seemed important above all to put Keats's mind at rest. Clark forbade him to go sight-seeing since he feared both the exertion and the excitement this would rouse, but he encouraged Keats to take walks around the neighbourhood, to window-shop in the Corso, or to stroll around the Pincian Hill behind the Spanish Steps.

This last was a favourite area for promenading, and within a few days Keats had met up with a fellow English consumptive, the strikingly handsome Lieutenant Isaac Marmaduke Elton of the Royal Engineers. Since Clark thought it would help his stomach, he encouraged Keats to hire a horse at the high cost of £6 a month, and together Keats and Elton would ride round the pathways or visit the Villa Borghese, where Canova's newly executed marble portrait of a semi-nude Pauline Buonaparte was exhibited. This was a work Keats found offensive, his illness perhaps heightening the sexual unease he felt in the presence of such photographic sensuality. Certainly, when he and Elton saw the

Princess taking her exercise on the Pincian Hill and Keats realised she was staring at Elton with interest, he tried to avoid her in future.

Clark was rapidly impressed by Keats and he put himself out to provide what help he could. A week after Keats's arrival, he wrote to an agent of Taylor and Hessey's saying he wished he were rich enough to support the poet himself, declaring: 'he's too noble an animal to be allowed to sink without some sacrifice being made to save him.'[7] Clark was less certain of Severn's qualities and did not think him 'best suited for his companion, but I suppose poor fellow he had no choice.' He recognised nonetheless what Severn could do and willingly lent him Haydn scores so that he could play them to Keats on a rented piano. Keats was beguiled by the spontaneity of the musical invention, and the pleasure this brought seemed to justify the cost of renting the piano from Signora Angeletti at 28 shillings a month. Clark's kindness also stretched to introducing Severn to various members of the English artistic community in Rome, and Keats himself was soon encouraging his friend to start making preliminary sketches for a historical painting.

On occasions, Keats was strong enough to deal with the little domestic problems that arose. The food sent up at some expense from the Signora's trattoria, for instance, was disgusting. One day when the porter came in with his basket and began to lay the plates out on the table, Keats, 'smiling roguishly', opened the window which looked out over the front of the house and emptied one dish after another into the street below. Indicating that the porter should take the basket away, he turned to Severn and said that now they would get a decent dinner. In less than half an hour an excellent one came, and the Signora had the tact not to charge them for the food so unceremoniously rejected.

There were even moments when Keats apparently toyed with the idea of writing again. On board the *Maria Crowther* he had read out the Sabrina passages from *Comus* and Severn noted that Keats's new poem was to be about this goddess of the River Severn herself. But the pun was perhaps made as much in friendship as with serious literary purpose, for Keats was aware that the intensity of effort needed for composition was beyond him now. This was something he could confide only to Brown. Writing to him on the last day of November 1820, Keats confessed that merely composing a letter was 'the most difficult thing in the world'.[8] Opening a book often threatened him unbearably, for the agitation it produced went straight to his stomach. He had tried to continue his study of Italian, but a couplet of Alfieri's – 'Unhappy me! No solace remains for me but weeping, and weeping is a crime' – reduced him to tears.

Original composition was out of the question and even the thought of it was 'enough to kill me'. Keats had lost his health and his love, and now he was certain he would have to abandon poetry if there was to be any hope of prolonging his life. These ideas merged in one poignant sentence: 'I have been well, healthy, alert, &c., walking with her and now – the knowledge of contrast, feeling for light and shade, all that information (primitive sense) necessary for a poem are great enemies to the recovery of the stomach.'[9]

This last letter to Brown – the last letter, probably, that Keats ever wrote – was an act of grace and courage. The previous hopelessness has been reined in, and a stoicism that does not in any way deny a quivering despair gives the words a calm, tragic assurance. 'I have an habitual feeling of my real life having passed,' Keats wrote, 'and that I am leading a posthumous existence.' He would not write of how things might have been, rather he concentrated on what they were. To have missed Brown at Gravesend and again in Sussex seemed to personify the tragedy that had always hung over his life. 'There was my star predominant!' He tried to give the best news of himself he could, telling Brown that Dr Clark was attentive and had informed him that while his stomach was 'very bad' there was little wrong with his lungs. Thoughts of George's problems returned and, with them, the idea of a family in which 'we shall all die young'. His mind turned to Reynolds, to Severn, to Haslam and lastly to his sister, 'who walks about my imagination like a ghost – she's so like Tom.' Finally comes the valediction and Keats's turning to face his own death. It is done with the deepest feeling and a courtesy that touches the sublime. 'I can scarcely bid you good bye even in a letter,' he told Brown. 'I always made an awkward bow.'[10]

On 10 December, just after Severn had returned from posting a letter, Keats had another violent haemorrhage, expectorating two cupfuls of blood. The final and terrible stage of his illness had begun. Clark was called and, applying one of the few known remedies, drained him of a further eight ounces of blood. Keats himself was greatly alarmed that the blood should be so black and thick. Throughout, his medical knowledge increased his certainty of approaching horror, and he knew that other more dreadful and equally useless treatments would soon follow. When Clark had done, he lay back on the bed with a haunted look Severn would never forget.

But the full horror was hidden by ignorance. Undetected by his doctors, the tubercles in Keats's lungs had, weeks earlier, formed into caseous masses and started to break down. Large suppurating cavities were left behind, and now the visible symptoms of consumption would take their remorseless course: ever more intense and helpless coughing, rapid weight loss, violently fluctuating temperatures, debilitating diarrhoea, devastating night sweats and, worsening the agony of these, a frightening violence of emotion that threatened to undermine the very basis of Keats's sanity. Even now, when Clark had gone, he struggled from his bed saying this day would be his last. While he raved in his terror, Severn, remembering the conversation they had had on board the *Maria Crowther*, began to remove everything with which Keats might commit suicide: knives, razors, anything with a sharp edge and, of course, the bottle of laudanum.

Twenty-four hours later a second violent haemorrhage occurred and, once again, Clark was summoned to bleed his patient. There were to be five haemorrhages in nine days. But it was not simply Keats's lungs that were affected, nor were the haemorrhages his worst symptoms. The tuberculosis had moved down into his stomach, which could now barely digest anything. All through every night and for the greater part of each day he was tortured by hunger. This was made worse by Clark's decision to put him on a starvation diet of a little bread, milk and a morsel or two of fish. He raved constantly that he would die of hunger, and an anguished Severn, torn between pity and Clark's fearful warning that anything above the prescribed amount of food would kill him, eventually let Keats have a little more than his allowance.

The burden that fell on Severn was increasingly desperate and he rose to meet it with a fortitude that might not readily have been expected of him. By day he sat at Keats's bed reading to him and at night he talked and humoured him in his wanderings. For eight nights Keats did not sleep and only when exhaustion overcame him at four in the morning could Severn write with his terrible news to Brown. Even as he did so he prayed that Keats would not wake, for the idea that the letter would increase his anxiety greatly alarmed Severn. Meanwhile other problems began to accumulate. 'These wretched Romans', Severn confessed to Brown, 'have no Idea of comfort – here am I obliged to wash up – cook – & read to Keats all day – added to this I have had no letter yet from my family – this is a damp to me for I never knew how dear they were to me.'[11]

That he was now doing the cooking suggests that meals were no longer being sent up from the trattoria. The reason for this was almost certainly a financial crisis. For a while, their banker, Torlonia, would let them have no money. The cause of this confusion was partly of the bank's making. They had given the young men a generous rate of exchange and advised that the charges could be kept low by making one large withdrawal and then redepositing this with them in Roman scudi. Severn at once drew £120 on Taylor and Hessey's letter of credit. When news of this reached London there was consternation.

The firm had assumed that only small sums would be withdrawn and they were expecting that money from George would soon arrive for Keats. In their alarm, they wrote to Torlonia ordering him to stop all further payments. This he did. The frantic Severn, who to his eternal credit managed to hide all suggestion of this from Keats, turned to Clark. Would he advance them some money of his own? Would he write himself to Taylor and Hessey? Clark complied and, in the slow course of time, not only were payments resumed but Taylor began to raise a subscription for Keats. Five friends contributed £10 a piece and Taylor's friend, the wealthy Earl Fitzwilliam, contributed another £50, but this substantial sum would not arrive in time. Severn meanwhile was obliged to light the fires (something he found difficult to do), make the beds, sweep the rooms, cook and run to Keats every time he called him. For three weeks, he barely left his side.

But by the close of December Signora Angeletti's suspicions were aroused. She had a foreign consumptive in the house. The Roman law on contagious diseases was strict and firmly enforced. The police had to be informed (which they were), and after the visitor's death everything in his room had to be burned. The problem was that the bed-ridden Keats desperately wanted to move into the second and larger room of the apartment. Clark thought this was a good idea, but in this second room were the piano, some of Severn's painting materials and the best of the furniture. The combined value of these amounted to at least £150. If Keats were to be moved, it would have to be without the Signora knowing.

Severn was frightened and alone in a foreign city with a dying man so sensitive that not the faintest suspicion of worry must approach him. He decided there was only one thing to do. As quietly as he could, he began moving all the furniture in the larger room across the door that connected with the Signora's apartment and then made up a bed on the sofa. When he had done this, he went into see Keats and, telling him that a servant had come to rearrange the room while Severn himself had been out, he very gently picked his dying friend up and carried his frail body through to the new bed. He wondered if Keats half suspected what had happened, but Keats himself asked no questions.

He had more dreadful things on his mind. By the middle of January he was so ill that Clark was obliged to cut yet further the diet he had placed him on. Keats was reduced to a morsel of bread and a single anchovy a day. For all this, he was still haemorrhaging and was now thrown into the blackest despair. His mind returned to thoughts of the bottle of laudanum. He tried to put his case as calmly as possible to an appalled Severn. He told him that since his death was certain he wished only to save him from the long misery of watching it. Besides, Severn himself would be stranded in Rome without resources and would probably spoil the prospects of building a career. "'I am keeping you from your painting," he said, "and as I am sure to die, why not let me die now?'"

Severn's faith would not permit so humane an argument, but throughout this and the next day Keats grew increasingly distraught. He begged Severn to understand that he had long ago foreseen the dismal, comfortless nights leading to death, the wasting of his body, the abject helplessness. He was determined to escape these, and when Severn stood firm Keats turned against his friend. He told him he would willingly have died three months since, only Severn had argued him out of suicide on board the *Maria Crowther*. Now, because he was insisting that Keats remain alive still, there was no name, no treatment, no punishment adequate for a man who willed a friend to suffer in this way. Eventually a hurt and harassed Severn left the apartment. Desperately needing someone to talk to, he crossed the Piazza di Spagna to see Clark and confided all that was happening. Clark came over to their lodgings and quietly removed the bottle of laudanum. Keats grew silent and resigned, but when Clark called again he looked at him with his glittering, sunken eyes and quietly asked: 'How long is this posthumous life of mine to last?'

Such moments of lucid and terrible pathos were interspersed with bouts of hysteria and a depression made worse not simply by the churning agony in Keats's stomach but by the fact that his decomposing lungs were day by day limiting the amount of oxygen that reached his brain, thereby occluding his mind with despair. At times he became convinced that someone in London had poisoned him. The balance of his mind was being overthrown and sometimes this showed itself in the most pathetic ways. Twice Severn tried to make him some coffee and twice Keats merely dashed it aside. Severn tried a third time and Keats, deeply moved, told him 'that he was sure my endurance of his "savageness" arose from my long prayers on his behalf and my patient devotion to him'.

Keats saw the power of his friend's faith, but he could not share it. He had spent his life searching for a belief he could substitute for conventional Christianity, and with his theory of life as the vale of soul-making he believed he had found an answer to the problem of pain. Now, dying in humiliating agony, that sane and sustaining insight had collapsed. He told Severn he thought 'a malignant being must have power over us over whom the Almighty has little or no control.' Suffering had no purpose. It did not prepare the soul for an afterlife. Suffering such as he was enduring was merely part of the gratuitous cruelty of a brutal world.

The constant presence of Severn, supported and made strong by a faith Keats could not accept, only deepened his spiritual agony. There were moments when he could no longer keep this to himself. '"Severn," he said to me one day, "I now understand how you can bear all this – 'tis your Christian faith: and here am I with desperation in death that would disgrace the commonest fellow! How I should like it if it were possible to get me some of Jeremy Taylor's works for you to read to me, and I should gain consolation, for I have always been a great admirer of this devout author."'[12] Severn could not find a copy. Days passed and, as Keats's despair deepened, Severn turned yet again to Clark. Aware that Keats's state of mind was as dangerous to him as his physical disease, Clark scoured Rome and eventually came up with a copy of *Holy Living* and *Holy Dying*. Severn read to Keats every day and his kindly voice, along with Taylor's beautifully cadenced English, brought moments of calmness and relief. But Keats's spiritual horror was not assuaged and it began to play so terribly on Severn's nerves that he started earnestly to wish that Keats would soon die. He wrote to Haslam describing a scene that was probably played out many times.[13] 'He says in words that tear my very heart strings – "Miserable wretch I am – this last cheap comfort – which every rogue and fool have – is deny'd me in my last moments – why is this – O! I have serv'd every one with my utmost good – yet why is this – I cannot understand this" – and then his chattering teeth.'

This last, terrible detail conveys the agony of these long final nights of Keats's life. Severn sat with him exhausted as Keats lay 'desiring his death with dreadful earnestness'. Diarrhoea repeatedly gripped him and, as his face wasted away, so Keats's hazel eyes seemed to become ever larger and to shine with an unearthly brightness. Only occasionally did he sleep, and once when he did so, at three in the morning of 28 January, Severn made a sketch of him. The face is in repose but the deeply shaded eyes and the bedraggled hair speak of dreadful suffering, a suffering which Severn's note confirms – 'a deadly sweat was on him.' Severn made the drawing to keep himself awake, for Keats would frequently need him during the night. To make sure they always had light, Severn connected up a row of candles by a thread which ensured that another candle was lit even as the previous one guttered out. Seeing this, Keats cried: 'Severn! Severn! Here's a little fairy lamplighter actually lit up a second candle.'

But such moments of fancy were rare. When Severn told Keats of an early rose in bloom, he looked aside to weep. Returning spring could show him only the pathos of his approaching death. When a letter from Brown arrived, another note from Fanny Brawne fell out of it and the sight of her handwriting tore the last vestiges of Keats's resistance to shreds. He asked first that the letter be put in his coffin, then he changed his mind. Even in death, it seemed, his passion might destroy his peace. But by 14 February he had changed his mind yet again. On that day he asked Severn to go and visit the cemetery where those not of the Catholic faith were buried. This was just outside the Aurelian Wall, under the pyramid of Caius Cestius. Severn returned with a description of the flocks of sheep and goats that were grazing there and told how the violets and daisies were beginning to appear amid the grass. The image of the daisies growing over his corpse began to haunt Keats. He requested that he be buried with Fanny Brawne's letters, a lock of her hair and a purse made by his sister.

And with this came a calmness and a resolution that surprised and gladdened Severn. As Keats's life entered its last days, the profound and selfless humanity that had underlain his greatest poetry seemed to return. That absolute ability to lose his identity in other things and other people, that empathy which lay at the heart of all he had achieved, showed itself again as Keats gave himself over more and more to thoughts of the ordeal Severn would have to face. 'Did you ever see anyone die?' Severn confessed he had not. 'Well then I pity you.'[14]

Keats fell asleep and, when he woke, wept to find himself alive. He had promised Severn that his last moments would not be long and warned him against inhaling his dying breath. On 21 February, Severn 'thought he was going'. An English nurse who had been hired for these last days was also present, but it was to Severn that Keats directed his thoughts. Around four in the afternoon of Friday 23 February, he turned to his exhausted friend. 'Severn – I – lift me up – I am dying – I shall die easy – don't be frightened – be firm, and thank God it has come.' Severn lifted him up. The phlegm was boiling in Keats's throat and continued to do so more and more violently until an hour before midnight when, still held in Severn's arms, he sank to death so quietly that he seemed merely to fall asleep.

The funeral was held very early on Monday morning, the procession making its way to the Protestant Cemetery before daybreak, as the law required. First went a carriage with Keats's coffin, the gifts that were to be buried with him and his letters from Fanny Brawne. Clark, Severn and a handful of the English artistic community followed on behind. The Reverend Mr Wolff read the funeral service and by nine o'clock the proceedings were over. Casts had been made of Keats's face and of a hand and a foot. (When later Clark performed the autopsy and discovered that Keats's lungs were entirely destroyed, he wondered how he could have lived so long.) Now, as the mourners prepared to leave, Clark turned to the grave-digger and asked him to put turves of daisies on the grave. 'This', he said, 'would be poor Keats's wish – could he know it.'[15]

Then, back in the Piazza di Spagna, officials moved in to fumigate the apartment. The walls were scraped, some of the furniture was burned, but when the landlady tried to present the over-wrought Severn with a bill for the broken crockery she showed him lying on a table, Severn gave vent to his feelings by smashing it to smithereens with his stick. At other times, he would try to calm his nerves by visiting the grave. Sometimes he went by night to soothe his grief, and once he found a young shepherd asleep there in the moonlight – Endymion at a poet's grave.

Severn himself took charge of the gravestone. The emblem, which he had once said was Keats's idea and then claimed was his own, represented a Greek lyre with half its strings broken or untied. The problem of the inscription bothered him, however, but when Brown arrived in Italy in 1822 he insisted on the following form of words: 'This Grave contains all that was Mortal, of a YOUNG ENGLISH POET Who on his Death Bed, in the Bitterness of his Heart at the Malicious Power of his Enemies, Desired these Words to be engraven on his Tomb Stone.' There then followed the stark and poignant epigraph, the only words by which Keats himself wished to be remembered: 'Here lies one whose name was writ in water.'

Afterword

THE NEWS OF Keats's death took three weeks to reach England. Of all his friends, Fanny Brawne was best able to face it. While Brown in his grief turned on George because of the financial problems that had arisen between the brothers, and Taylor, having raised a fund to pay Keats's debts, consoled himself with his Christian faith, Fanny faced the inevitable with dignified stoicism. Only now does she begin to emerge more fully as a woman in her own right. 'I believe he must soon die,' she had told her mother. 'When you hear of his death, tell me immediately. I am not a fool!'

In fact, it fell to Brown to tell her and he was impressed by her reaction. Fanny's grief was evident and sincere. She grew thin-faced and her hair lost its lustre. She pored over Keats's letters and went for long, lonely walks across the Heath. She dressed herself in widow's weeds and continued to wear them for several years. Her inherent kindness and her sincerity also emerge in the series of letters she now began to write to Keats's sister, and it was to her that she confessed how she had not got over Keats's death and suspected she never would. It was to be over a decade before Fanny finally found a husband, a Sephardic Jew twelve years her junior called Louis Lindo. She lived with him abroad for many years before finally returning to England to die in 1865.

The two remaining members of Keats's family lived abroad. After his early financial troubles, George became one of the more prosperous citizens of Louisville, a director of the Bank of Kentucky and a member of several boards concerned with public works both literary and charitable. The family disease, perhaps brought on by over-work, finally killed him in 1841. Fanny, meanwhile, had married a young Spanish liberal, Valentine Llanos, and she spent the rest of her long life with him in his native country. Mean-minded to the last, Abbey tried to detain her legacy from Mrs Jennings, and Fanny obtained possession of it only when Dilke and Rice sued him on her behalf. After that, her

327

affairs in England were managed (with little credit to their competence) by Rice and Reynolds.

Rice himself eventually died of the illness that had so long afflicted him, while Reynolds, a broken-down and deeply unhappy man, drifted into a life of minor legal appointments and heavy drinking. He died in 1852, a man whose promise had never been fulfilled. His headstone, proudly calling him 'The Friend of Keats', proclaims his greatest service to literature and memorialises what was probably the deepest experience of his life. Another friend from the early Hampstead days also came to grief. In 1846, driven to despair, Haydon slashed his throat with a razor, leaving the world not, as he had hoped, with a wealth of great pictures, but with a diary and an autobiography of the greatest vigour. Meanwhile, the third of Keats's early Hampstead friends, Leigh Hunt, lived on as a minor literary figure satirised by Dickens and pressed by eager members of a younger generation for anecdotes about the great figures he had known. His reminiscences, published in 1828, helped fix the image of Keats as a young genius destroyed by a cruel world, a myth already propagated by Shelley in *Adonais*.

In the following year, 1829, Galignani brought out the first collected edition of Keats's poems and, partly as a response to this, Brown wrote to Fanny Brawne asking permission to publish some more of Keats's work along with a letter that referred to her. Fanny had been upset by the 'weakness of character' suggested by Hunt's book, and now she asked Brown if the writings that remained would rescue Keats from this. In fact, these writings were not published, while, facing the opposition of Taylor, Woodhouse, Reynolds, George Keats and Dilke, Brown's projected biography of the poet also foundered.

Brown's manuscript was finally passed on to Richard Monkton Milnes, who, in 1848, issued his *Life, Letters, and Literary Remains, of John Keats*. Inaccurate despite the access he had had to Keats's manuscripts (many of them secured by Woodhouse) and the memories of the poet's friends, this book in its various editions remained the standard life of Keats for many years. By the time of its publication, Keats's genius was starting to be fully appreciated and the long, infinitely rewarding study of his life and work had begun. The young man who died believing his creative endeavour had been a failure left an inexhaustible inheritance, and one in which each generation sees a reflection of its own needs and its own desires.

Notes

Formed by Circumstances

Sources: Walter Jackson Bate, *John Keats*; Charles Brown, 'Life of Keats'; J.C.D. Clark, *English Society 1688–1832*; Charles and Mary Cowden Clarke, *Recollections of Writers*; *Examiner*; Robert Gittings, *John Keats* and *The Keats Inheritance*; Donald C. Goellnicht, *The Poet–Physician: Keats and Medical Science*; Hyder H. Rollins (ed.), *The Keats Circle* and *Letters*; John Barnard (ed.), *John Keats: The Complete Poems*.

1. For the political background to the *Examiner*, see Ann Blainey, *Immortal Boy: A Portrait of Leigh Hunt* and George D. Stout, *The Political History of Leigh Hunt's 'Examiner'*.
2. William Hazlitt, 'What is the People?', *Collected Works*, VII, p. 273.
3. For Charles Cowden Clarke's memories of Keats's boyhood used throughout this chapter, see 'Recollections of John Keats', in Charles and Mary Cowden Clarke, *Recollections of Writers*, pp. 120–57.
4. Charles Brown, 'Life of John Keats', in *Keats Circle*, II, p. 55.
5. Clarke, 'Recollections of John Keats', p. 126.
6. See Keats, 'Epistle to Charles Cowden Clarke', 11. 120–26.
7. George Keats to Charles Dilke, 12 May 1828, *Keats Circle*, I, p. 314.
8. These recollections of Keats's mother are from Richard Abbey's conversation as transmitted by John Taylor to Richard Woodhouse; see *Keats Circle*, I, pp. 302–9.
9. George Keats, loc. cit., p. 314.
10. For details of this folklore, see Arthur Bryant, *The Age of Elegance*, p. 318.
11. See Robert Gittings, *John Keats*, p. 17.
12. Quoted, ibid., p. 11.
13. The intricacies of the Keats inheritance are unravelled in Robert Gittings, *The Keats Inheritance*.
14. Keats to Fanny Keats, 28 August 1819, *Letters*, II, p. 149.
15. Quoted in Gittings, *John Keats*, p. 26.
16. Keats to Fanny Keats, 13 March 1819, *Letters*, II, p. 46.
17. 'A Song About Myself', l. 68.
18. See Gittings, *John Keats*, p. 24.
19. Clarke, 'Recollections of John Keats', p. 123
20. George Keats to Charles Dilke, 7 May 1830 in *Keats Circle*, I, p. 325.
21. For Rylands' teaching methods, see James Culross, *The Three*

Rylands, and John Collect Rylands, *An Address to the Ingenious Youth of Great Britain*.

22. Charles Cowden Clarke, quoted in Gittings, *John Keats*, p. 11.
23. Ibid, p. 25.
24. Rylands, *An Address to the Ingenious Youth of Great Britain*.
25. For details of the medical profession in Keats's time, see 'Biography' in Donald C. Goellnicht, *The Poet–Physician: Keats and Medical Science*, pp. 12–47.
26. Clarke, 'Recollections of John Keats', p. 125.
27. For the details of Keats's reading, see 'Epistle to Charles Cowden Clarke', 11. 21–67.
28. For the social history of reading at this period, see Richard Altick, *The English Common Reader*.
29. Smith, *Theory of Moral Sentiments*, quoted in J.C.D. Clark, *English Society 1688–1832*, p. 106.
30. Charles Brown, op. cit., p. 55.
31. Keats to Benjamin Bailey, 18 July 1818, *Letters*, I, p. 341.
32. 'Epistle to Charles Cowden Clarke', l. 34.
33. Clarke, *Recollections of Writers*, p. 16.
34. Clarke, 'Recollections of John Keats', p. 124.
35. For Hunt and the Prince Regent, see Stout, *The Political History of Leigh Hunt's 'Examiner'*, pp. 21–6.
36. Ibid.
37. Leigh Hunt, *Examiner*, 1 May 1814, p. 273.
38. From Woodhouse's transcript of Keats's poems in the Morgan Library, quoted in John Barnard (ed.), *John Keats: The Complete Poems*, p. 558.
39. Clarke, 'Recollections of John Keats', p. 127.

Apollo's Apprentice

Sources: Walter Jackson Bate, *John Keats*; Charles Brown, 'Life of John Keats'; Charles and Mary Cowden Clarke, *Recollections of Writers*; Robert Gittings, *John Keats*; Donald C. Goellnicht, *The Poet–Physician: Keats and Medical Science*; Benjamin Haydon, *Diary*; Leigh Hunt, *Lord Byron and Some of his Contemporaries*; Hyder H. Rollins (ed.), *The Keats Circle* and *Letters*; John Barnard (ed.), *John Keats: The Complete Poems*.

1. 'Ode to Hope', l. 1.
2. 'Ode to Apollo', 11. 42–7.
3. Keats in a letter to Benjamin Haydon, quoted in Robert Gittings, *John Keats*, p. 43.
4. George Keats to Charles Dilke, 20 April 1825, *Keats Circle*, I, pp. 284–5.
5. Keats to Benjamin Bailey, 22 July 1818, *Letters*, p. 342.
6. Benjamin Haydon, *Diary*, II, p. 107.
7. George Keats to Charles Dilke, *Keats Circle*, I, pp. 284–5.
8. G.F. Mathew to Richard Monkton Milnes, 3 February 1887, *Keats*

Circle, II, p. 185.

9. Ibid.

10. 'Woman! when I behold thee flippant, vain', 11. 29–32.

11. 'O Solitude', 11. 1–8.

12. For details of Keats's course at Guy's Hospital, see Donald C. Goellnicht, *The Poet–Physician: Keats and Medical Science*, pp. 28–34.

13. Charles Brown, 'Life of John Keats', in *Keats Circle*, I, p. 41.

14. Astley Cooper, *Principles and Practice of Surgery*, p. I, quoted in Goellnicht, op. cit., p. 28.

15. William Osler, quoted in Robert Gittings, 'John Keats: Poet and Physician', *Journal of the American Medical Association*, 224 (1973), p. 52.

16. The following quotations are from Leigh Hunt, *The Feast of the Poets*.

17. Mathew's poem is printed in John Middleton Murry, *Studies in Keats*, pp. 1–2.

18. Quoted in Gittings, *John Keats*, p. 108.

19. Ibid, p. 46.

20. For Stephens' account of Keats at this period, see Walter Jackson Bate, *John Keats*, pp. 49–50.

21. Leigh Hunt in *Lord Byron and Some of his Contemporaries*, p. 249.

22. 'To my Brother George', 11. 19–22.

23. Keats to Charles Cowden Clarke, 9 October 1816, *Letters*, I, p. 113.

24. For Charles Cowden Clarke's account of this memorable evening, see 'Recollections of John Keats', in Charles and Mary Cowden Clarke, *Recollections of Writers*.

25. Hunt, *Lord Byron and Some of his Contemporaries*, p. 248.

Great Spirits

Sources: Richard Altick, *The Cowden Clarkes*; Walter Jackson Bate, *John Keats*; Charles Brown, 'Life of Keats'; Kenneth Neill Cameron, *Shelley: The Golden Years*; Eric George, *The Life and Death of Benjamin Robert Haydon*; Leigh Hunt, *Indicator* and *Lord Byron and Some of his Contemporaries*; Ian Jack, *Keats and the Mirror of Art*; Leonidas M. Jones, *The Life of John Hamilton Reynolds* and *Letters of John Hamilton Reynolds*; Stanley Jones, *Hazlitt: A Life*; Hyder H. Rollins (ed.), *The Keats Circle* and *Letters*; John Barnard (ed.), *John Keats: The Complete Poems*.

1. Details from Charles Cowden Clarke, 'Recollections of John Keats', in Charles and Mary Cowden Clarke, *Recollections of Writers*, p. 125.

2. For Hunt's 'doctrine of cheer?', see Ann Blainey, *Immortal Boy: A Portrait of Leigh Hunt*, pp. 49 and 73–90.

3. Haydon on Hunt, quoted in ibid., p. 82.

4. Leigh Hunt, *Lord Byron and Some of his Contemporaries*, p. 247.

5. A recollection of Charles Brown's; see *Keats Circle*, II, p. 56.

6. Quoted in Robert Gittings, *John Keats*, p. 85.

7. For Benjamin Haydon, see Eric George, *The Life and Death of Benjamin Robert Haydon*.

8. For Haydon at this period, see Walter Jackson Bate, *John Keats*, pp. 97–101.

9. Quoted in ibid., pp. 94–5.

10. Quoted in George, op. cit., p. 153.

11. Leigh Hunt, *Indicator*, I, p. 399, quoted in Ian Jack, *Keats and the Mirror of Art*, pp. 7–8.

12. For Hazlitt, Keats and the visual arts, see Jack, op. cit., pp. 58–75.

13. 'I stood tip-toe', 11. 47–52.

14. Bejamin Haydon, *Diary*, 5 November 1816, II, p. 138.

15. For John Hamilton Reynolds, see Leonidas M. Jones, *The Life of John Hamilton Reynolds*.

16. For Reynolds' views on Shakespeare, see ibid., pp. 81–4.

17. Ibid.

18. Reynolds to Keats, 14 October 1818, in Leonidas M. Jones (ed.), *The Letters of John Hamilton Reynolds*, p. 13.

19. 'Keen, fitful gusts are whispering here and there'.

20. See Robert Gittings, *The Keats Inheritance*, passim.

21. 'To my Brothers', 1. 5.

22. Keats to Charles Cowden Clarke, 31 October 1816, *Letters*, I, p. 115.

23. For Hazlitt and the *Triumphal Entry*, see Bate, *op. cit.*, p. 111.

24. Quoted in Stanley Jones, *Hazlitt: A Life*, p. 264.

25. William Wordsworth, *The Excursion*, IV, 1. 843.

26. John Taylor's account of the interview is reprinted in *Keats Circle*, I, pp. 307–8.

27. For Charles Cowden Clarke's account of Keats's socialising, see 'Recollections of John Keats', pp. 120–57.

28. Details of the Reynolds family at this period from Jones, *The Life of John Hamilton Reynolds*, pp. 97–150.

29. For biographical details of Shelley at this period, see Kenneth Neill Cameron, *Shelley: The Golden Years*, pp. 1–64.

30. Haydon, *Diary*, II, p. 80.

31. For Hunt's views on religion, see Robert M. Ryan, 'Leigh Hunt and his Circle', in *Keats: The Religious Sense*, pp. 71–113.

32. *Examiner*, 6 September 1818, p. 563.

33. Leigh Hunt, *The Religion of the Heart*, p. 56, quoted in Ryan, op. cit., p. 76.

34. Haydon, *Diary*, II, pp. 67–9.

35. Leigh Hunt, *Foliage*, pp. 25–6, quoted in Ryan, op. cit., p. 263.

36. *Sleep and Poetry*, 11. 138–49.

37. For an exposition of this argument, see Robert M. Ryan, 'The Politics of Greek Religion', in Hermione de Almeida (ed.), *Critical Essays on John Keats*, pp. 261–78.

38. Clarke, 'Recollections of John Keats', p. 138.

39. 'To Apollo', 11. 7–12.

40. Clarke, ibid., p. [140]

41. John Taylor's account of the interview in *Keats Circle*, I, pp. 307–8.

42. Benjamin Haydon to Keats, March 1817, *Letters*, I, pp. 124–5.

43. For Hunt, the Novellos and music, see Richard Altick, 'Some

Evening Music', *The Cowden Clarkes*, pp. 29–41.
44. Letter from Hunt to Charles Cowden Clarke, quoted in Gittings, *John Keats*, p. 125.
45. Quoted in Gittings, ibid., p. 126.
46. John Taylor to his father, ibid.

A Test of Invention

Sources: *Endymion*; John Barnard, *John Keats*; Walter Jackson Bate, *John Keats*; *Champion*; *Examiner*; Robert Gittings, *John Keats*; Stanley Jones, *Hazlitt: A Life*; Hyder H. Rollins (ed.), *The Keats Circle* and *Letters*; John Barnard (ed.), *John Keats: The Complete Poems*; Theodore Redpath, *The Young Romantics and Critical Opinion 1807–1824*; Robert M. Ryan, *Keats: The Religious Sense*.

1. Keats to John Hamilton Reynolds, 17–18 April 1817, *Letters*, I, p. 133.
2. 'On the Sea', 11. 9–14.
3. Stephens' account is quoted from B.W. Richardson, *The Asclepiad*, p. 148, in Robert Gittings, *John Keats*, pp. 121–2.
4. *Endymion*, I, 11. 13–18.
5. Keats to John Hamilton Reynolds, 17–18 April 1817, *Letters*, I, p. 132.
6. 'Hymn to Pan', *Endymion*, I, 11. 293–306.
7. Keats to Leigh Hunt, 10 May 1817, *Letters*, I, p. 138.
8. Benjamin Haydon to Keats, 8(?) May 1817, ibid., p. 135.
9. Ibid.
10. Keats to Leigh Hunt, 10 May 1817, ibid., p. 137.
11. Quoted in Stanley Jones, *Hazlitt: A Life*, p. 271.
12. Henry Brougham, quoted in ibid., p. 272.
13. The Olliers to George Keats, quoted in Gittings, *John Keats*, p. 132.
14. Keats to Taylor and Hessey, 16 May 1817, *Letters*, I, p. 147.
15. For Keats's transcription, see letter to Benjamin Bailey, 8 October 1817, ibid., I, pp. 169–70.
16. William Godwin, *The Pantheon*, p. 7, quoted in John Barnard, *John Keats*, p. 39.
17. William Hazlitt, *Collected Works*, X, p. 8.
18. *Endymion*, I, 11. 691–6.
19. Endymion's speech, Book I, 11. 769–989.
20. Keats to Benjamin Bailey, 22 November 1817, *Letters*, I, p. 184.
21. Gittings' assumption in *John Keats* of a consummated love between Keats and Mrs Jones does not seem well established.
22. Mathew's review is reprinted in part in J. Middleton Murry, *Studies in Keats*, pp. 6–10.
23. *Endymion*, II, 11. 756–61.
24. Severn's account is reprinted in Walter Jackson Bate, *John Keats*, pp. 194–5.
25. Keats to John Taylor, 27 February 1818, *Letters*, I, pp. 238–9.

26. Woodhouse's description of Keats's methods of composition are reproduced in Bate, op. cit., p. 234.
27. *Champion*, 20 July 1817, p. 230.
28. Bailey to Richard Monkton Milnes, 7 May 1849, *Keats Circle*, II, pp. 267–8.
29. Leigh Hunt, *Examiner*.
30. *Endymion*, III, 11. 52–71.
31. Bailey's account is given in Bate, op. cit., pp. 206–7.
32. Benjamin Bailey, *A Discourse Inscribed to the Memory of the Princess Charlotte Augusta*, quoted in Robert M. Ryan, *Keats: The Religious Sense*, p. 117.
33. Quoted in Bate, op. cit., p. 267.
34. Keats to George and Tom Keats, 13, 19 January 1818, *Letters*, I, p. 205.
35. Keats to Haydon *Letters*, I, p. 168
36. 'Ode to Sorrow', *Endymion*, IV, 11. 173–81.
37. *Blackwood's*, 'On the Cockney School of Poetry', October 1817, p. 39.
38. Keats to Benjamin Bailey, 22 November 1817, *Letters*, I, p. 186.
39. This and the following three stanzas make up the lyric 'In drear-nighted December'.

Uncertainties, Mysteries, Doubts

Sources: Walter Jackson Bate, *John Keats*; Charles Brown 'Life of Keats'; Charles and Mary Cowden Clarke, *Recollections of Writers*; William Hazlitt, *Complete Works*; Hyder H. Rollins (ed.), *The Keats Circle* and *Letters*; John Barnard (ed.), *John Keats: The Complete Poems*; Robert M. Ryan, *Keats: The Religious Sense*.

1. For Keats's meeting with Wordsworth, see *Keats Circle*, II, pp. 143–5.
2. For Wordsworth's life at this period, see Stephen Gill, *William Wordsworth: A Life*, pp. 288–344.
3. Charles Cowden Clarke, 'Recollections of John Keats', in Charles and Mary Cowden Clarke, *Recollections of Writers*.
4. For Keats's account of the meeting of the club, see letter to George and Tom Keats of 5 January 1818, *Letters*, I, pp. 200–01.
5. For Keats's account of his dinner with Horace Smith et al., see ibid., pp. 192–3.
6. Charles Brown, 'Life of Keats', in *Keats Circle*, II, p. 57.
7. Keats's review of Kean's acting is reprinted from the *Champion*, 21 December 1817, in John Barnard (ed.), *Complete Poems*, pp. 529–31.
8. Hazlitt's review, from *Complete Works*, XVIII, p. 138.
9. For Keats's view of West's picture, see letter to George and Tom Keats, 21, 27 December 1817, *Letters*, I, p. 192.
10. For negative capability, see ibid., p. 193.
11. For Butler's influence on Keats and Bailey, see Robert Gittings, *John*

Keats, pp. 231–2, and Robert M. Ryan, *Keats: The Religious Sense*, pp. 132–6.

12. For the spider image, see Keats to John Hamilton Reynolds, 19 February 1818, *Letters*, I, pp. 231–3.

13. Haydon's account of the 'immortal dinner' may be found in Gittings, *John Keats*, pp. 177–9.

14. Keats to George and Tom Keats, 5 January 1818, *Letters*, I, pp. 200–01.

15. Charles Cowden Clarke, quoted in Gittings, *John Keats*, p. 266.

16. Keats to George and Tom Keats, 5 January 1818, ibid., p. 196.

17. Keats's revised version of the Preface to *Endymion* is reprinted in Barnard (ed.), *Complete Poems*, p. 505.

18. Keats to J.A. Hessey, 8 October 1818, *Letters*, I, p. 374.

19. 'On Seeing a Lock of Milton's Hair. Ode', 11. 23–32.

20. Keats to Benjamin Haydon, 23 January 1818, *Letters*, I, p. 207.

21. For Hazlitt's lectures, see Stanley Jones, *Hazlitt: A Life*, pp. 280–85.

22. William Hazlitt, 'On Shakespeare and Milton', *Lectures on the English Poets*, in *Collected Works*, V, p. 47.

23. Ibid., p. 53.

24. Mary Russell Mitford, quoted in Jones, op. cit., p. 285.

25. Hazlitt, 'On Shakespeare and Milton', p. 47.

26. 'God of the Meridian', 11. 17–25.

27. Keats to John Taylor, 27 February 1818, *Letters*, I, pp. 238–9.

28. Keats to Reynolds, 3 February 1818, *Letters*, I, pp. 223–5.

29. This letter is reproduced in ibid., pp. 231–3.

30. Keats to John Taylor, 30 January 1818, ibid., pp. 218–19.

31. Hazlitt, *Collected Works*, V, p. 82.

Getting Wisdom

Sources: Sir James Clark, *A Treatise on Pulmonary Consumption*; Hermione de Almeida, *Romantic Medicine and John Keats*; *Examiner*; Hyder H. Rollins (ed.), *The Keats Circle and Letters*; John Barnard (ed.), *John Keats: The Complete Poems*.

1. This account of the symptoms of tuberculosis is derived from Sir James Clark's *Treatise on Pulmonary Consumption*. Clark was Keats's doctor in Rome.

2. For a detailed account of this important topic, see Hermione de Almeida, *Romantic Medicine and John Keats*, pp. 203–15 especially.

3. Keats to Benjamin Bailey, 13 March 1818, *Letters*, I, p. 241.

4. Keats to John Hamilton Reynolds, 14 March 1818, ibid., p. 245.

5. Keats to Benjamin Bailey, 13 March 1818, ibid., p. 242.

6. George Keats to the Jeffrey girls, March 1818, *Keats Circle*, I, pp. 15–16.

7. George Keats to Keats, 18 March 1818, *Letters*, I, p. 247.

8.◊ Keats to Benjamin Bailey, 13 March 1818, ibid., p. 242.

9. 'Epistle to John Hamilton Reynolds', 11. 92–105.

10. Keats to James Rice, 24 March 1818, *Letters*, I, pp. 254–5.

11. Keats to Benjamin Haydon, 8 April 1818, *ibid.*, p. 264.
12. This first version is printed in John Barnard (ed.), *Complete Poems*, pp. 506–7.
13. Keats to John Hamilton Reynolds, 9 April 1818, *Letters*, I, p. 268.
14. The Preface is reprinted in Barnard, op. cit, p. 505.
15. *Examiner*, 29 March 1818, pp. 194–6, and 5 April 1818, pp. 210–12.
16. Ibid., 5 April 1818, p. 209.
17. *Isabella*, 11. 105–28.
18. Ibid., 11. 103–4.
19. Keats to John Hamilton Reynolds, 27 April 1818, *Letters*, I, p. 274.
20. Keats to John Taylor, 24 April 1818, *ibid.*, I, p. 271.
21. Keats to John Hamilton Reynolds, 27 April 1818, ibid., pp. 273–5.
22. Keats to John Hamilton Reynolds, 3 May 1818. This important letter from which this and the ensuing quotations are taken is reprinted in *Letters*, I, pp. 275–83.
23. Ibid., pp. 280–81.
24. Reprinted in ibid., I, pp. 286–8.
25. Ibid, p. 293.
26. John Taylor to his brother James in Robert Gittings, *John Keats*, p. 216.
27. *Blackwood's*, 'Leter from Z to Leigh Hunt', May 1818, p. 197.
28. Keats to Benjamin Haydon, 8 April 1818, *Letters*, I, p. 264.

At the Cable's Length

Sources: *Examiner*; Robert Gittings, *John Keats*; Hyder H. Rollins (ed.), *The Keats Circle* and *Letters*; John Barnard (ed.), *John Keats: The Complete Poems*; Carol Cyros Walker, *Walking North with Keats*.

1. *Examiner*, 14 June 1818, p. 367.
2. Quoted from Charles Brown's account of the walking tour, *Walks in the North*, reprinted in Carol Cyros Walker, *Walking North with Keats*, pp. 223–41.
3. Quoted from Stoddart's *Remarks on Local Scenery and Manners of Scotland during the Years 1799 and 1800*, 2 vols, 1801, in Walker, ibid., p. 20.
4. Keats to Tom Keats, 25–27 June 1818, *Letters*, I, pp. 298–9.
5. Quoted in Walker, op. cit., pp. 12–13.
6. Quoted in ibid., p. 13.
7. Ibid.
8. Keats to Tom Keats, 29 June, 1, 2, July 1818, *Letters*, I, p. 307.
9. 'Old Meg she was a gypsy', 11. 25–30.
10. Keats to Tom Keats, 3, 5, 7, 9 July 1818, *Letters*, I, pp. 321–2.
11. 'Ah! ken ye what I met the day'.
12. 'To Ailsa Rock'.
13. Keats to John Hamilton Reynolds, 11, 13 July 1818, *Letters*, I, p. 323.
14. 'This mortal body of a thousand days'.
15. Keats to Benjamin Bailey, 12, 22 July 1818, *Letters*, I, pp. 340–45.

16. Ibid., p 342.
17. 'Lines Written in the Highlands after a Visit to Burns's Country', 11. 23–4.
18. Keats to Tom Keats, 23, 26 July 1818, *Letters*, I, p. 348–51.
19. 'On Visiting Staffa', 11. 50–52.
20. For Bailey's account of this interview, see *Keats Circle*, I, pp. 35–35, 247–47, II, 286–8.
21. Keats to Tom Keats, 3, 6 August 1818, *Letters*, I, p. 352.
22. The poem is 'Upon my life, Sir Nevis, I am piqued'.
23. Brown to Henry Snook, quoted in Walker, op. cit., pp. 214–17.
24. 'Stanzas on some Skulls in Beauly Abbey, near Inverness'.
25. Quoted in Robert Gittings, *John Keats*, p. 231.
26. Quoted, ibid., pp. 230–1.

A Giant Nerve

Sources: Sir James Clark, *A Treatise on Pulmonary Consumption*; *Examiner*; Robert Gittings, *John Keats*; Hyder H. Rollins (ed.), *The Keats Circle* and *Letters*; John Barnard (ed.), *John Keats: The Complete Poems*; Theodore Redpath, *The Young Romantics and Critical Opinion 1807–1824*.

1. The description of Tom's symptoms is derived from Sir James Clark's *Treatise on Pulmonary Consumption*.
2. The *Blackwood's* review is reprinted in Theodore Redpath, *The Young Romantics and Critical Opinion 1807–1824*, pp. 467–72.
3. *British Critic*, quoted in John Barnard, *John Keats*, p. 47.
4. Croker's review is reprinted in Redpath, op. cit., pp. 472–6.
5. Hessey's comment is reprinted in Robert Gittings, *John Keats*, p. 236.
6. Keats to James Hessey, 8 October 1818, *Letters*, I, pp. 373–4.
7. *Morning Chronicle*, 3 October 1818.
8. *Champion* review is reprinted in Redpath, op. cit., pp. 465–7.
9. Reynolds' review is reprinted in ibid., pp. 477–81.
10. From Keat's journal letter to George and Georgiana Keats, 14, 16, 21, 24, 31 October 1818, *Letters*, I, pp. 394–5.
11. Ibid., p. 396.
12. *Examiner*.
13. William Cobbett, quoted in Sir Arthur Bryant, *The Age of Elegance*, p. 381.
14. ''Tis ''the witching time of night''', 11. 27–32.
15. Quoted in Sir Arthur Bryant, ibid., p. 403.
16. Arthur Young, quoted in ibid., pp. 403–4.
17. Keats's journal letter to George and Georgiana Keats, 14, 16, 21, 24, 31 October 1818, *Letters*, I, pp. 403–4.
18. Richard Woodhouse to Keats, 21 October 1818, ibid., I, p. 380.
19. Keats to Richard Woodhouse, 27 October 1818, ibid., I, pp. 386–8.
20. Keats to Charles Dilke, 20, 21 September 1818, ibid., I, p. 369.
21. *Hyperion*, Book I, 11. 15–21.
22. For Bailey's account of these ideas, see *Keats Circle*, II, pp. 277–8.

23. *Hyperion*, Book I, 11. 102–16.
24. Ibid., Book II, 11. 217–29.
25. Keats's notes on *Paradise Lost* are reproduced in John Barnard (ed.), *Complete Poems*, pp. 515–26.
26. *Hyperion*, Book I, 11. 227–30.
27. Quoted in Walter Jackson Bate, *John Keats*, p. 409.
28. Details from Sir James Clark's *Treatise*.
29. Keats's journal letter to George and Georgiana Keats, 16–18, 22, 29(?), 31 December 1818, 2–4 January 1819, *Letters*, II, p. 4.
30. This possibly dubious anecdote is recorded in Gittings, *John Keats*, p. 265n.
31. See Bate, *John Keats*, pp. 386–7.
32. Keats's journal letter to George and Georgiana Keats, 16–18, 22, 29(?), 31 December 1818, 2–4 January 1819, *Letters*, II, p. 13.
33. Quoted in Gittings, *John Keats*, p. 272.
34. Keats to Benjamin Haydon, 22 December 1818, *Letters*, I, p. 415.

Particles of Light

Sources: Walter Jackson Bate, *John Keats*; William Hazlitt, *Complete Works*; Hyder H. Rollins (ed.), *The Keats Circle* and *Letters*; John Barnard (ed.), *John Keats: The Complete Poems*; M.R. Ridley, *Keats's Craftsmanship*.

1. Quoted in Robert Gittings, *John Keats*, p. 406.
2. Keats and Charles Brown to the Dilkes, 24 January 1819, *Letters*, II, p. 36.
3. Ibid., p. 35.
4. Keats's journal letter to George and Georgiana Keats, 14, 19 February, 3(?), 13, 17, 19 March, 15, 16, 21, 30 April, 3 May 1819, *Letters*, II, p. 63.
5. Quoted in Sir Arthur Bryant, *The Age of Elegance*, p. 343.
6. *The Eve of St. Agnes*, 11. 208–16.
7. These textual matters are copiously discussed in M.R. Ridley, *Keats's Craftsmanship*, pp. 112–90.
8. Keats's journal letter to George and Georgiana Keats, 14, 19 February, 3(?), 13, 17, 19 March, 15, 16, 21, 30 April, 3 May 1819, *Letters*, II, p. 64.
9. Cited in John Barnard (ed.), *Complete Poems*, p. 653.
10. *The Eve of Saint Mark*, 11. 30–38.
11. Benjamin Haydon to Keats, 20 February 1819, *Letters*, II, p. 41.
12. Keats's journal letter to George and Georgiana Keats, 14, 19 February, 3(?), 12, 13, 17, 19 March, 15, 16, 21, 30 April, 3 May 1819, *Letters*, II, p. 65.
13. William Hazlitt, quoted in Keats's journal letter, ibid., p. 72.
14. Ibid., p. 70.
15. Quoted in Gittings, *John Keats*, p. 483.
16. 'Why did I laugh tonight?', 11. 9–14.
17. From Benjamin Haydon's *Autobiography*, quoted in Walter Jackson

Bate, *John Keats*, p. 463.

18. Keats's journal letter to George and Georgiana Keats, 14, 19 February, 3(?), 13, 17, 19 March, 15, 16, 21, 30 April, 3 May 1819, *Letters*, II, p. 79.
19. Ibid.
20. *Hyperion*, Book III, 11. 111–20.
21. Quoted in Bryant, op. cit., p. 405.
22. Keats's journal letter to George and Georgiana Keats, 14, 19 February, 3(?), 13, 17, 19 March, 15, 16, 21, 30 April, 3 May 1819, *Letters*, II, p. 70.
23. Benjamin Haydon to Keats, 12 April 1819, ibid., II, p. 53.
24. Keats's journal letter to George and Georgiana Keats, 14, 19 February, 3(?), 13, 17, 19 March, 15, 16, 21, 30 April, 3 May 1819, *Letters*, II, pp. 90–91.
25. 'A Dream, after reading Dante's Episode of Paolo and Francesca', 11. 9–14.
26. Keats's journal letter to George and Georgiana Keats, 14, 19 February, 3(?), 13, 17, 19 March, 15, 16, 21, 30 April, 3 May 1819, *Letters*, II, pp. 88–9.
27. See Bate, *John Keats*, p. 468.
28. 'La Belle Dame Sans Merci', 11. 1–8.
29. Ibid., 11. 9–12.
30. Ibid., 11. 29–40.

The Vale of Soul-Making

Sources: Walter Jackson Bate, *John Keats*; *Examiner*; Hyder H. Rollins (ed.), *The Keats Circle* and *Letters*; John Barnard (ed.), *John Keats: The Complete Poems*.

1. For the 'vale of Soul-making' passage, see Keats's journal letter to George and Georgiana Keats, 14, 19 February, 3(?), 13, 17, 19 March, 15, 16, 21, 30 April, 3 May 1819, *Letters*, II, pp. 101–4.
2. Ibid., p. 102.
3. 'Ode to Psyche', 11. 50–67.
4. Benjamin Haydon, 'On the Cartoon of the Sacrifice at Lystra', *Examiner*, 9 May 1819, p. 300.
5. 'Ode on a Grecian Urn', 11. 8–10.
6. Benjamin Haydon, *Diary*, ii, pp. 215–16.
7. 'Ode on a Grecian Urn', 11. 15–20.
8. Ibid., 11. 31–40.
9. Ibid., 11. 46–50.
10. Quoted in Walter Jackson Bate, *John Keats*, p. 501.
11. 'Ode to a Nightingale', 11. 24–30.
12. Ibid., 11. 41–50.
13. Ibid., 11. 51–60.
14. Ibid., 11. 61–7.
15. Ibid., 11. 68–70.

16. Ibid., 11 71–80.
17. The rejected stanza is reprinted in John Barnard (ed.), *Complete Poems*, pp. 682–3.
18. 'Ode on Melancholy', 11. 25–30.
19. 'Ode on Indolence', 11. 31–40.
20. Keats to Sarah Jeffrey, 9 June 1819, *Letters*, II, p. 116.
21. Keats to Sarah Jeffrey, 31 May 1819, ibid., p. 113.
22. Quoted in John Barnard, *John Keats*, p. 70.

The Face of Moneta

Sources: *Examiner*; Hyder H. Rollins (ed.), *The Keats Circle* and *Letters*; John Barnard (ed.), *John Keats: The Complete Poems*.

1. Keats to Charles Dilke, 31 July 1819, *Letters*, II, p. 134.
2. Keats to John Hamilton Reynolds, 11 July 1819, ibid., p. 129.
3. Keats to Fanny Brawne, 8 July 1819, ibid., p. 127.
4. Ibid., p. 127.
5. Keats to Fanny Brawne, 1. July 1819, ibid., p. 123.
6. Ibid., p. 122.
7. Keats to Fanny Brawne, 15(?) July 1819, ibid., p. 129.
8. Keats to Fanny Brawne, 5 June 1819, ibid., p. 138.
9. Ibid., p. 137.
10. Keats to Fanny Brawne, 27 July 1819, ibid., p. 132.
11. Ibid., p. 133.
12. Ibid.
13. *Examiner*, 20 June 1819, p. 385.
14. Quoted in Sir Arthur Bryant, *The Age of Elegance*, pp. 409–10.
15. Ibid., p. 411.
16. Quoted in Walter Jackson Bate, *John Keats*, p. 564.
17. Keats to Fanny Brawne, 5, 6 August 1819, *Letters*, II, p. 137.
18. Ibid., p. 137.
19. Keats to Fanny Brawne, 16 August 1819, ibid., p. 142.
20. *Otho the Great*, Act V, scene v, 11. 60–69.
21. Keats to John Taylor, 23 August 1819, *Letters*, II, p. 143.
22. Ibid., p. 144.
23. Keats to John Hamilton Reynolds, 24 August 1819, ibid., p. 146.
24. Keats's journal letter to George and Georgiana Keats, 17–18, 20–21, 24–25, 27 September 1819, ibid., p. 189.
25. *Lamia*, Part I, 11. 47–56.
26. Ibid., 11. 191–4.
27. Quoted in John Barnard, *John Keats*, p. 126.
28. *Lamia*, Part II, 11. 229–38.
29. Richard Woodhouse to John Taylor, 31 August 1819, *Letters*, II, p. 150.
30. Keats's journal letter to George and Georgiana Keats, 17–18, 20–21, 24–25, 27 September 1819, ibid., pp. 184–5.
31. For a discussion of these matters, see Barnard, *John Keats*, pp. 72–5.

32. Quoted in ibid., p. 73.
33. Keats to Richard Woodhouse, 21–22 September 1819, *Letters*, II, p. 174.
34. Keats's journal letter to George and Georgiana Keats, 17–18, 20–21, 24–25, 27 September 1819, ibid., p. 194.
35. Ibid., p. 192.
36. For Keats's political views at this time, see ibid., pp. 192–4.
37. *The Fall of Hyperion*, Canto I, 11. 256–64.
38. Quoted in Robert Gittings, *John Keats*, p. 430.
39. 'To Autumn', 11. 1–11.
40. Keats's journal letter to George and Georgiana Keats, 17–18, 20–21, 24–25, 27 September 1819, *Letters*, II, p. 209.
41. Ibid., p. 193.
42. Keats to Charles Dilke, 22 September 1819, ibid., p. 180.
43. Keats to John Hamilton Reynolds, 21 September 1819, ibid., p. 167.

The Death Warrant

Sources: Walter Jackson Bate, *John Keats*; Robert Gittings, *John Keats*; Hyder H. Rollins (ed.), *The Keats Circle* and *Letters*; John Barnard (ed.), *John Keats: The Complete Poems*.

1. Keats to Charles Dilke, 22 September 1819, *Letters*, II, p. 179.
2. Keats to Fanny Brawne, 11 October 1819, ibid., p. 222.
3. Keats to Fanny Brawne, 13 October 1819, ibid., p. 223.
4. Keats to Fanny Brawne, 19 October 1819, ibid., p. 224.
5. Quoted in Robert Gittings, *John Keats*, p. 612.
6. For Severn's account of Keats in Westminster, see Walter Jackson Bate, *John Keats*, pp. 612–15.
7. Quoted in Gittings, *John Keats*, p. 365.
8. Ibid., p. 366.
9. Keats to John Taylor, 17 November 1819, *Letters*, II, p. 234.
10. Charles Brown, *Keats Circle*, II, p. 72.
11. The identifications are made in Gittings' discussion of the poem in his *John Keats*, pp. 368–73.
12. Quoted in ibid., pp. 524–5.
13. Keats to Georgiana Keats, 13, 15, 17, 28 January 1820, *Letters*, II, p. 244.
14. For Keats's reactions, see Gittings, *John Keats*, p. 379.
15. Brown's account reprinted in *Keats Circle*, II, pp. 73–4.
16. Keats to Fanny Brawne, 4(?) February 1820, *Letters*, II, p. 251.
17. Keats to Fanny Brawne, February(?) 1820, ibid., p. 258.
18. Ibid., p. 263.
19. Ibid.
20. Charles Brown to John Taylor, 10 March 1820, ibid., p. 275.
21. Keats to Fanny Brawne, March(?) 1820, ibid., pp. 275.
22. Ibid., pp. 281–2.
23. See Walter Jackson Bate, *John Keats*, p. 643.

24. Keats to Fanny Brawne, June(?) 1820, *Letters*, II, pp. 292.
25. Keats to Fanny Brawne, May(?) 1820, ibid., p. 290.
26. Quoted in Gittings, *John Keats*, p. 361.
27. See John Barnard, *John Keats*, p. 99.
28. See Gittings, *John Keats*, p. 583.
29. Quoted in ibid., p. 401.
30. Quoted in Bate, *John Keats*, p. 648.
31. Keats to Fanny Brawne, August(?) 1820, *Letters*, II, p. 312.
32. Ibid., p. 313.
33. See Gittings, *John Keats*, p. 404.
34. Percy Bysshe Shelley to Keats, 27 July 1820, *Letters*, II, pp. 310–11.
35. Keats to P.B. Shelley, ibid., pp. 322–3.
36. Keats to John Taylor, 13 August 1820, ibid., p. 315.
37. Keats to John Taylor, 14 September 1829, ibid., p. 319.
38. Quoted in Gittings, *John Keats*, p. 406.
39. Keats to Fanny Brawne, June(?) 1820, *Letters*, II, p. 293.
40. See Gittings, *John Keats*, p. 406.
41. Keats to Charles Brown, 1 November 1820, *Letters*, II, p. 351.
42. Quoted in Bate, *John Keats*, p. 656.

This Posthumous Life

Sources: Walter Jackson Bate, *John Keats*; Robert Gittings, *John Keats*; Hyder H. Rollins (ed.), *The Keats Circle* and *Letters*; John Barnard (ed.), *John Keats: The Complete Poems*.

1. For Joseph Severn's account of the voyage, see Robert Gittings, *John Keats*, pp. 411–16.
2. Keats to Charles Brown, 30 September 1820, *Letters*, II, p. 345.
3. For Keats in Naples, see Gittings, *John Keats*, pp. 417–18.
4. Keats to Mrs Brawne, 24(?) October 1820, *Letters*, II, p. 350.
5. Keats to Charles Brown, 1 November 1820, ibid., pp. 351–2.
6. Ibid., p. 351.
7. Letter of James Clarke to an unknown correspondent, 27 November 1820, ibid., p. 358.
8. Keats to Charles Brown, 30 November 1820, ibid., p. 359.
9. Ibid., p. 360.
10. Ibid.
11. Joseph Severn to Charles Brown, 14, 17 December 1820, ibid., p. 363.
12. Quoted in Robert M. Ryan, *Keats: The Religious Sense*, p. 215.
13. Joseph Severn to William Haslam, 15 January 1821, *Letters*, II, p. 368.
14. See Walter Jackson Bate, *John Keats*, p. 695.
15. Ibid., p. 696.

Bibliography

Texts

The Poems of John Keats, ed. Miriam Allott, Longman, 2nd edn, 1972
John Keats: The Complete Poems, ed. John Barnard, Penguin Book, 2nd edn, 1976
The Poems of John Keats, ed. Jack Stillinger, Harvard Univ. Press, 1978
The Letters of John Keats 1814–21, ed. Hyder H. Rollins, 2 vols, Harvard Univ. Press, 1958
The Keats Circle: Letters and Papers 1816–1878, ed. Hyder H. Rollins, 2 vols, Harvard Univ. Press, 1948

Biography, Criticism and Background

Abrams, M.H., *Natural Supernaturalism: Tradition and Revolution in Romantic Literature*, Norton, 1971
Adami, Marie, *Fanny Keats*, John Murray, 1937,
de Almeida, Hermione, *Romantic Medicine and John Keats*, Oxford Univ. Press, 1991
————, (ed.), *Critical Essays on John Keats*, G.K. Hall, 1990
Altick, Richard, *The Cowden Clarkes*, Oxford Univ. Press, 1948
————, *The English Common Reader*, Chicago Univ. Press, 1957
Barnard, John, *John Keats*, Cambridge Univ. Press, 1987
Bate, Walter Jackson, *John Keats*, Harvard Univ. Press, 1979
Bayley, John, *Keats and Reality*, British Academy Lecture, 1962
Birkenhead, Sheila, *Against Oblivion: The Life of Joseph Severn*, Cassell Co., 1943
Blainey, Ann, *Immortal Boy: A Portrait of Leigh Hunt*, Croom Helm, 1985
Brooks, Cleanth, 'History without Footnotes: An Account of Keats's Urn', in *The Well Wrought Urn*, Harcourt, Brace and World, 1947
Bryant, Sir Arthur, *The Age of Elegance 1812–1822*, Collins, ed. 1950
Bush, Douglas, 'Keats and his Ideas', in M. H. Abrams, (ed). *English Romantic Poets: Modern Essays in Criticism*, Oxford Univ. Press, 1960
Butler, Marilyn, 'The War of the Intellectuals: From Wordsworth to Keats', in *Romantics, Rebels and Reactionaries: English Literature and its Background 1760–1830*, Oxford Univ. Press, 1981
Cameron, H.C., *Mr Guy's Hospital 1726–1948*, Longmans, Green, 1954

Cameron, Kenneth Neill, *Shelley: The Golden Years*, Harvard Univ. Press, 1974.

Chilcott, Tim, *A Publisher and his Circle: The Life and Work of John Taylor*, Routledge and K. Paul, 1972

Clark, J.C.D., *English Society 1688–1832: Ideology, Social Structure and Political Practice during the Ancien Régime*, Oxford Univ. Press, 1985

Clark, Sir James, *A Treatise on Pulmonary Consumption*, 1837

Clarke, Charles and Mary Cowden, *Recollections of Writers*, 1878

Culross, James, *The Three Rylands*, 1897

Dickstein, Morris, *Keats and his Poetry: A Study in Development*, Univ. of Chicago Press, 1971

Evert, Walter, *Aesthetic and Myth in the Poetry of Keats*, Princeton Univ. Press, 1965

Finney, Claude Lee, *The Evolution of Keats's Poetry*, 2 vols, Russell, 1936

George, Eric, *The Life and Death of Benjamin Robert Haydon, Historical Painter 1786–1846*, 2nd edn, Oxford: Clarendon Press, 1967

Gill, Stephen, *William Wordsworth: A Life*, Oxford: Clarendon Press, 1989

Gittings, Robert, *The Keats Inheritance*, Heinemann, 1964

————, *John Keats*, Heinemann, 1968

Goellnicht, Donald C., *The Poet–Physician: Keats and Medical Science*, Univ. of Pittsburgh Press, 1984

Hazlitt, William, *Collected Works*, 12 vols, 1902

Hunt, Leigh, *The Examiner*, 1815–21

————, *Indicator*, 1819

————, *The Feast of the Poets*, 1819

————, *Poetical Works*, 3 vols, 1819

————, *Lord Byron and Some of his Contemporaries*, 1828

Jack, Ian, *Keats and the Mirror of Art*, Oxford: Clarendon Press, 1967

Jones, Leonidas M., *The Life of John Hamilton Reynolds*, Univ. Press of New England, 1984

Jones, Stanley, *Hazlitt: A Life*, Oxford: Clarendon Press, 1991

Levinson, Marjorie, *Keats's Life of Allegory: The Origins of a Style*, Oxford: Blackwell, 1988

Muir, Kenneth, (ed.), *John Keats: A Reassessment*, Univ. of Liverpool Press, 1959

Murry, J. Middleton, *Studies in Keats*, Oxford Univ. Press, 1930.

Redpath, Theodore, *The Young Romantics and Critical Opinion 1807–1824*, Harrap, 1973

Reynolds, John Hamilton, in *The Letters of John Hamilton Reynolds*, Leonidas, M. Jones, ed.

Ricks, Christopher, *Keats and Embarrassment*, Oxford: Clarendon Press, 1974

Ridley, M.R., *Keats's Craftsmanship: A Study in Poetic Development*, Oxford: Clarendon Press, 1933

Ryan, Robert M., *Keats: The Religious Sense*, Princeton Univ. Press, 1976

————, 'The Politics of Greek Religion', in Hermione de Almeida (ed.), *Critical Essays on John Keats*, 1990

Bibliography

Rylands, John Collett, *An Address to the Ingenious Youth of Great Britain*, 1792

Sharp, Ronald A., *Keats, Scepticism, and the Religion of Beauty*, Univ. of Georgia Press, 1979

Sperry, Stuart, *Keats the Poet*, Princeton Univ. Press, 1973

Spurgeon, Caroline, *Keats's Shakespeare: A Descriptive Study*, Oxford: Clarendon Press, 1966

Stillinger, Jack, *The Hoodwinking of Madeline and Other Essays on Keats's Poems*, Univ. of Illinois Press, 1971

Stout, George D., *The Political History of Leigh Hunt's 'Examiner', together with an Account of the Book*, Washington Univ. Press, 1949

Vendler, Helen, *The Odes of John Keats*, Harvard, Bettznap Press, 1983

Walker Carol Cyros, *Walking North with Keats*, Yale Univ. Press, 1992

Woodring, Carl, *Politics in English Romantic Poetry*, Harvard Univ. Press, 1970

Index